INFORMATION SYSTEM DEVELOPMENT PROCESS

AF708519

IFIP Transactions A: Computer Science and Technology

International Federation for Information Processing

Technical Committees:

Software: Theory and Practice (TC2)
Education (TC3)
System Modelling and Optimization (TC7)
Information Systems (TC8)
Relationship between Computers and Society (TC9)
Computer Systems Technology (TC10)
Security and Protection in Information Processing Systems (TC11)
Artificial Intelligence (TC12)
Human-Computer Interaction (TC13)
Foundations of Computer Science (SG14)

IFIP Transactions Editorial Policy Board

The IFIP Transactions Editorial Policy Board is responsible for the overall scientific quality of the IFIP Transactions through a stringent review and selection process.

Chairman
G.J. Morris, UK
Members
D. Khakhar, Sweden
Lee Poh Aun, Malaysia
M. Tienari, Finland
P.C. Poole (TC2)
P. Bollerslev (TC3)
M. Tomljanovich (TC5)
O. Spaniol (TC6)
P. Thoft-Christensen (TC7)
G.B. Davis (TC8)
K. Brunnstein (TC9)
E. Hörbst (TC10)
W.J. Caelli (TC11)
R. Meersman (TC12)
B. Shackel (TC13)
J. Gruska (SG14)

IFIP Transactions Abstracted/Indexed in:
INSPEC Information Services
Index to Scientific & Technical Proceedings®
CompuMath Citation Index®, Research Alert™, and SciSearch®

A-30

INFORMATION SYSTEM DEVELOPMENT PROCESS

Proceedings of the IFIP WG8.1 Working Conference on Information System Development Process, Como, Italy, 1-3 September, 1993

Edited by

N. PRAKASH
Division of Computer Engineering
Delhi Institute of Technology
Delhi, India

C. ROLLAND
Université de Paris I
Paris, France

B. PERNICI
University of Udine
Udine, Italy

1993

NORTH-HOLLAND
AMSTERDAM • LONDON • NEW YORK • TOKYO

ELSEVIER SCIENCE PUBLISHERS B.V.
Sara Burgerhartstraat 25
P.O. Box 211, 1000 AE Amsterdam, The Netherlands

Library of Congress Cataloging-in-Publication Data

IFIP WG8.1 Working Conference on Information System Development Process (1993 : Como, Italy)
Information system development process : proceedings of the IFIP WG8.1 Working Conference on Information Development Process, Como, Italy, 1-3 September, 1993 / edited by N. Prakash, C. Rolland, B. Pernici.
p. cm. -- (IFIP transactions. A, Computer science and technology ; A-30)
Includes bibliographical references and index.
ISBN 0-444-81594-5
1. System design--Congresses. 2. Information storage and retrieval systems--Congresses. I. Prakash, N. (Naveen) II. Rolland, Colette. III. Pernici, Barbara. IV. Series.
QA76.9.S88I3515 1993
005.1--dc20 93-11376
CIP

Keywords are chosen from the ACM Computing Reviews Classification System, ©1991, with permission.
Details of the full classification system are available from
ACM, 11 West 42nd St., New York, NY 10036, USA.

ISBN: 0 444 81594 5
ISSN: 0926-5473

© 1993 IFIP. All rights reserved.
No part of this publication may be reproduced, stored in a retrieval system or transmitted in any form or by any means, electronic, mechanical, photocopying, recording or otherwise, without the prior written permission of the publisher, Elsevier Science Publishers B.V., Copyright & Permissions Department, P.O. Box 521, 1000 AM Amsterdam, The Netherlands.

Special regulations for readers in the U.S.A. - This publication has been registered with the Copyright Clearance Center Inc. (CCC), Salem, Massachusetts. Information can be obtained from the CCC about conditions under which photocopies of parts of this publication may be made in the U.S.A. All other copyright questions, including photocopying outside of the U.S.A., should be referred to the publisher, Elsevier Science Publishers B.V., unless otherwise specified.

No responsibility is assumed by the publisher or by IFIP for any injury and/or damage to persons or property as a matter of products liability, negligence or otherwise, or from any use or operation of any methods, products, instructions or ideas contained in the material herein.

pp. 3-20, 247-264, 285-308, 325-336: Copyright not transferred

This book is printed on acid-free paper.

Printed in The Netherlands

PREFACE

The traditional view of an information system is that it is a slice of real world history. This has led to high emphasis on the development of conceptual models using which requirements specifications can be expressed. However, the route to such an expression, or the process of development, has not received any great attention. Indeed it is only recently that attention has been shifting to this aspect of the information system problem. Questions have been raised about the adequacy or otherwise of the prevalent view of the life-cycle, the assumption that development proceeds from scratch, the approach to reuse and reverse engineering and so on.

Potentially, a study of the development process can give us great benefits.
First, it can help us to understand what a realistic development process is and how it proceeds from an initial specification to its acceptable representation. Second, the nature of guidance that can be provided by the next generation of CASE tools can be substantially improved. It can be expected that these tools shall cease to be mere drafting aids and consistency checking programs. Instead, they shall provide a procreative environment of which the development engineer shall be a part. This tool/user symbiosis shall have a beneficial impact on both the productivity of the developer and on the quality of the product.

In view of this, there is great need to pool together all experience on the development process. The IFIP WG 8.1 has reacted to this in two ways
- it has set up a task group on method engineering
- it has held this conference on the development process which has tried to bring together researchers and practitioners in such diverse areas as AI, Software Engineering, Decision Support, and Information Systems.

We hope that these proceedings of the conference shall contribute to a greater understanding of the information system development process.

Naveen Prakash
Colette Rolland
Barbara Pernici

PROGRAM COMMITTEE

F. Van Assche, Belgium
F. Bodart, Belgium
B. Boehm, USA
S. Brinkkemper, The Netherlands
J.A. Bubenko, Sweden
M. Chen, USA
P. Creasy, Australia
A. Finkelstein, UK
A. Flory, France
M. Franckson, France
C. Ghezzi, Italy
B. Hendersen-Sellers, Australia
J. Iivari, Finland
M. Jarke, Germany
L.W. Johnson, USA
T. Katayama, Japan
M. Leonard, Switzerland
I.G. Macdonald, UK
B. Moulin, Canada
J. Mylopoulos, Canada
A. Olive, Spain
B. Pernici, Italy
C. Potts, USA
N. Prakash, India
C. Rolland, France
W. Schaefer, Germany
A. Solvberg, Norway
A. Sutcliffe, UK
T. Tomiyama, Japan
R.J. Welke, USA

LIST OF REFEREES

M. Ayache
C. Francalanci
C. Cauvet
M.G. Fugini
P. W. P. J. Grefen
G. Grosz
F. Harmsen
M. Jeusfeld
S. M.M. Joosten
G. Junkermann
Th. Moineau
K. Pohl
S. Sachweh
C. Souveyet
R. L.W. van de Weg
C. van Slooten
W. Song
R. Stevens
E. Teniente
X. Wu

TABLE OF CONTENTS

1.

INTRODUCTION

Information System Development Process (A-30)
N. Prakash, C. Rolland and B. Pernici (Editors)
Elsevier Science Publishers B.V. (North–Holland)
1993 IFIP.

Vision Driven System Engineering[§]

Matthias Jarke and Klaus Pohl

Informatik V, RWTH Aachen, Ahornstr. 55, 5100 Aachen, Germany
email: {jarke, pohl}@informatik.rwth-aachen.de

Abstract. Clearly defining, maintaining, and exploiting the system vision is a central prerequisite for successful system engineering. We address the question how the visions are concretized and maintained in information systems evolution. Visions are broken down into goals according to constraints imposed by context, and traded off against other goals or habits which exist in this context. Context information is organized according to four "worlds" and the context breakdown is viewed under a three-dimensional space of cognitive understanding, social agreement, and technical representation. Different uses and the evolution of goals in the system engineering process are supported by a quality and improvement oriented process model which distinguishes between product, control and improvement activities. Working with this model can be supported by a knowledge-based repository structure that is compatible with the IRDS standard.

Keyword Codes: D.2.1; D.4.1; H.4.0
Keyword: Requirement/Specification; Process Management; Information System Application

1. INTRODUCTION

The context in which software systems operate is increasingly recognized as a major determinant of system development and evolution. This is recognized in current CASE terminology by shifting the emphasis from *software* engineering to *system* engineering.

This trend has manifested itself in a number of concrete research activities. First, recent work in requirements engineering has emphasized the need for modeling the *system environment*, leading to activities such as enterprise modeling and composite systems modeling. Second, there has been a strong emphasis on measuring and improving *quality aspects* from the viewpoint of both software product and software process. Last not least, *change management* is no longer considered as a system-internal problem of version and configuration management but studied in its organizational context.

However, modeling the context independent of the actual project goals is an expensive and often poorly rewarded exercise. Practice in large system engineering efforts has shown that the clear definition and long-term perseverance of a *project vision* is important for getting and keeping a project going; nobody will sink money in a project for which the vision is unclear. A classical example of a successful vision is John F. Kennedy´s "send a man to

---

§ This work was supported in part by ESPRIT Basic Research Project 6353 (NATURE) and in part by the Ministry of Science and Research of Nordrhein-Westfalen.

the moon before the end of the decade". Counter examples abound among large ESPRIT projects where vision holders were too weak compared to the context.

It therefore seems that a careful balancing of vision and context management is a key to successful system engineering. Without vision, the best understanding of context remains passive. Without understanding and managing context, any vision is bound to fail due to naiveté. This implies two main questions:

- *where do the goals come from* — establishing the vision in context through a requirements engineering process
- *how are the goals used* — maintaining and evolving the vision and derived requirements through quality-oriented process management.

Sections 2 and 3 of this paper present a coherent set of models for these two closely interrelated tasks. These models — derived from earlier work by ourselves and various cooperation partners — are first and foremost intended to give structure to an evolutionary process that comprises both requirements engineering and the ongoing development and maintenance activities resulting from it. They can be used for analysing actual processes with the goal of understanding what is going on, or — at the meta level — for defining processes with the goal of controlling and improving them.

One of the difficulties we always face during such exercises is the data volume generated. Therefore, the models have been designed also with a second reading in mind. They can serve as the meta schema of a *repository* in which process observation and definition data are collected, and which is active in the sense that it can control the enacting of process definitions, maybe even enact some of them automatically. Section 4 of this paper therefore summarizes some technical considerations in the design of such a system. This gives an answer of sorts to the question: *how are the goals managed?*

2. WHERE DO THE GOALS COME FROM ?

Within the world in which the vision has to be realized, many habits exist. Some are based on formally stated goals, policies, or competing visions. Others are just regularly observable phenomena for which no structure or reasons are known a priori.

The task of the first phase of system engineering (requirements engineering) is therefore twofold. First, relevant habits must be analysed and the goals, policies and visions behind them must be made explicit. This is essentially a goal-directed abstraction process of existing practice (Dardenne et al. 1992). Second, new visions must be established in this context, i.e., their consequences are propagated into the existing context. Conflicts among the different viewpoints must be detected and resolved (Finkelstein et al. 1990). During this process, the vision often shifts. Many large projects appoint a "vision holder" to make sure that it does not get totally lost in the constraints of current practice.

Since context is complex and changing, some structure is needed by which context information can be organized. To bring vision and context together, nonfunctional goals, their trade-offs and implications for requirements change must be explicitly considered. To support the abstraction task, concrete and abstract, informal and formal requirements information must be related to each other.

Many requirements engineering methods emphasize one of these aspects at the expense of the other. Top-down decomposition methods such as Structured Analysis (McMenamin and Palmer 1984) do not say how context influences decomposition, whereas bottom-up approaches (ethnographics is an extreme example) have failed to provide guidance how analysis can be focused on the vision (Goguen 1993). The need for supporting both aspects simultaneously becomes more important as we are now in a situation where systems have become pervasive in the real world. Many such systems must evolve in multiple contexts and diverse configurations. Buzzwords such as composite systems (Fickas 1987) or Intelligent and Cooperative Information Systems (Brodie and Ceri 1992) accentuate this observation.

Our framework structures requirements engineering in two steps. First, it identifies four different "worlds" which impact evolution of the system and should be considered as a basis for analysing the "habits" in any requirements project (section 2.1). Second, it identifies a space of three dimensions in which the internal status and progress of the requirements process can be described (section 2.2).

2.1. How Can the Goals be Structured ?

What parts of the world are relevant and how are they related to the development process? This is in general quite unpredictable but requirements engineering simplifies the problem in various ways. First, it concentrates on identifying recurrent patterns (abstraction process) and tends to ignore spurious events. Second, certain habits can be predicted through a basic theory about the object of the requirements engineering process: the information system.

The theory we are going to follow is very simple (Jarke 1990, cf. figure 1). It sees an information system in analogy to "a telescope through which a user community observes a domain of interest" more efficiently than without the informaton system. The domain of interest may or may not overlap with the user community itself, it may or may not be changeable by the user community. But it makes sense to distinguish, from a cognitive as well as a social viewpoint, between the *usage world*, the *subject domain world*, and the *system* itself, and to describe their interrelationships. A fourth world, the *development environment*, has the basic task of assisting the vision holder in realizing the vision in the context of the other worlds (but also considering its internal development context of people, methods, experiences, and tools).

There are several advantages of organizing context information according to the four worlds. Each world is associated with certain *groups of stakeholders* who should be considered in requirements decision making. The model makes the social prediction that different areas of expertise, different languages, and different interests exist and need to be integrated. Moreover, it predicts certain *role-bound nonfunctional goals* which can be associated with the relationships between the worlds; dealing with such standard viewpoint resolution and negotiation tasks becomes a natural target for requirements engineering methods and tools. Finally, we can expect that representatives in each of the worlds will have implicit or explicit *models about their own as well as the other worlds* which leads to further social, cognitive, and technical problems.

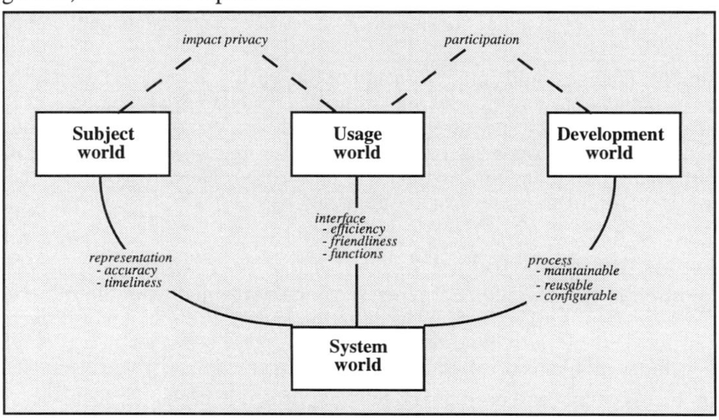

Figure 1. The "worlds" of information systems modeling.

Let us elaborate these general observations for each of the four worlds.

Subject World. The subject world is the domain which the system is intended to maintain information about. Stakeholders are directly the objects being represented, or people who have stakes in these objects but are not system users. Relationships to the usage world are often governed by legal concerns such as privacy or copyright. Relationships to the development world are difficult to establish and often very political -- quite frequently, subjects know nothing about the degree to which they are administered by systems. The relationship between system and subject world can be described by quality-of-information factors such as accuracy or timeliness. From a representational perspective, the subject world is the most general one: significant support can be offered only by domain specialization.

Usage World. The usage world comprises as stakeholders both the direct or indirect users, and the owners of the system. An organizational structure often describes their relationship, thus defining the (observed or intended) role of the information system in the work practice of the organization. The relationships between users and owners can vary widely but if both differ substantially, it is likely that the interests of the users are represented from an organizational perspective. With respect to the development world, the goal of participative design has often been cited. With respect to the system, quality-of-interaction factors such as response time, user-friendliness, and rich functionality are of interest as well as business goals such as reduced transaction costs, increased worker/organization effective–ness, worker (de-)qualification, and the like. From the representational perspective, business modeling as well as research in human-computer interaction are relevant for the usage world.

System World. The system world is often represented by technical gurus, or simply by the observed fact that the system is very hard to change, both due to its internal complexity and due to its established relationships to user and developer communities. Representation–wise, it is probably the best understood subworld with many available specification languages. It contains a representation (function-oriented, data-oriented, object-oriented, ...) of the subject world, maybe also of its users, together with some mapping of these conceptual specifications to the design and implementation levels. The latter pose their own technological requirements. A system often exists in many different versions. It may be part of several different usage environments (in fact, it may be the main communications medium between these environments), and it may have lost much of its initial structure by changes that happened before the present “vision” came about.

Development World. All of this must be considered in the fourth world, the development world. It must ensure an adequate observation (cognitive aspect), participation (socio-organizational aspect), and representation (technical aspect) of itself and of the other worlds, and it must proceed under consideration of resource constraints and competing role-bound and individual goals.

The vision for change could come from any of the worlds. It could be driven by changing technology in the system world (moving from files to databases), changes in the subject domain (protests by privacy pressure groups, new theories about the subject domain), or long-term development concerns (improved maintainability, change of development responsibility from computer professionals to end users). Most frequently, visions come from the usage world, from users or their organizations.

2.2. How are the Goals Gained ?

Only a portion of the development process can be explained from the role expectations resulting from the four-worlds model. The situation and progress of a requirements process is equally influenced by individual differences and social behavior in a problem-solving team. This includes problems of cognition and social interaction as well as technical issues.

These problems cannot and need not be fully explicated in each individual case. However, their “essence” (McMenamin and Palmer 1984) with respect to the requirements process, their influence on the basic inputs and outputs of requirements engineering, should be captured. Briefly, the requirements engineering process starts with an opaque understanding of the problem, many different and conflicting viewpoints, and and informal representation. Ideally, it should end with full agreement on a well-understood requirements specification represented precisely enough to be transformable into a correct implementation. In other words, to be successful, the RE process has to make progress along three dimensions: the specification, the agreement and the representation dimension (Pohl 1993).

Specification Dimension. The specification dimension deals with the degree of requirements understanding at a given time. At the beginning of the RE process, only the vision is clearly defined. The specification of the system and its environment are more or less opaque. Focusing on this dimension, the aim of requirements engineering is to transform the vision into a complete specification through an iterative process of definition and validation. Standards and guidelines describe how the final requirements specification should look like (e.g., IEEE 830, British Standard 6719, ESA PSS-05-0). Empirical studies have shown that problems in achieving this aim include (Curtis et al. 1988, Goguen 1993):

- incomplete domain knowledge, poor and hazy system goals
- premature search reduction on a small set of sub-optimal solutions
- inadequate articulation of requirements

Agreement Dimension. The agreement dimension deals with the degree of agreement reached on a specification. Each person involved in the RE process has a personal view of integrating vision and habits, or may even have different visions. Few requirements may be initially shared among the team. It is important to recognize that the integration of different views at the representation level (e.g., integrating formally represented views into a comprehensive view) and the agreement on the integrated view among the people involved in the process are two separate things. A detected conflict or misunderstanding must be resolved through communication among people. A process of negotiation — comprising bargaining as well as mutual learning — and coordinated subgroup actvities may lead towards a setting of better understood personal views that are perceived to have at least sufficient commonality to start building a system. The process of gaining a common view is of course affected by the social and psychological aspects of requirements engineering. Its problems are often categorized according to three different levels (Ellis et al. 1991):

- communication, the technical ability to exchange messages
- interoperability, the technical and social ability of mutual understanding
- cooperation on a common task.

Representation Dimension. This dimension copes with the different representations used for expressing knowledge about the requirements process and its products. First, both abstract requirements specifications and concrete examples and scenarios are needed in requirements engineering. Second, the representation should enable the description of states and transitions within the considered worlds, as well as perceived intentions behind them. Third and most obviously, three categories of representation are distinguished with respect to formal semantics: informal (e.g., natural languages, graphics), semi-formal (e.g., SA / ER diagrams) and formal specification and knowledge representation languages (e.g., VDM (Jones 1990), Z [(Spivey 1989), ERAE (Hagelstein 1988), Telos (Mylopoulos et al. 1990)).

Due to the unique advantages of each category, people prefer different representations in different situations. Recent surveys confirm that people use informal representation at the beginning of the requirements engineering process, then move to semi-formal graphics, at the end also to formal representations (Lubars et al. 1993). Ideally, the final specification should be transformable to executable code. The different representations used must be kept consistent and the transformation between them must be supported and recorded.The representation dimension is orthogonal to the specification dimension. A vague imagination of the system can be expressed using natural language, but also using a formal representation language. Conversely, precise ideas can be represented using natural language (law makers try to do so).

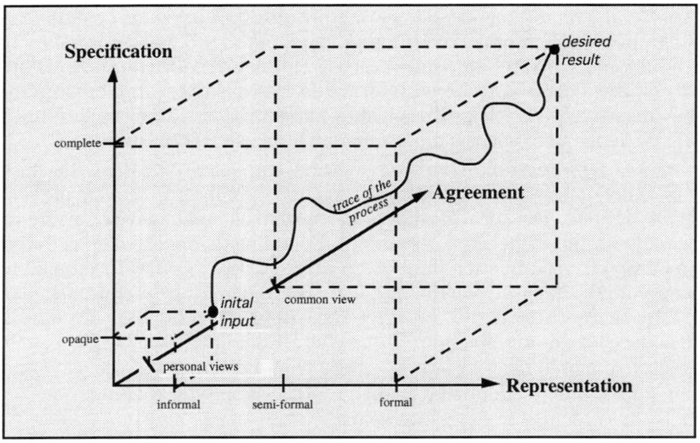

Figure 2. The three dimensions of requirements engineering.

The trace of the requirements engineering process is a curve within the three dimensions (cf. figure 2). The traditional requirements capture process would start somewhere near the origin of the framework with different personal views, little system understanding and a completely informal representation; it should end with agreement on a well-understood and formally described specification. Movement may sometimes seem erratic because the outside context of the four worlds changes.

3. HOW ARE THE GOALS USED ?

Quality orientation is one of the important aspects in product development. According to the TQM philosophy (Oakland 1989) the production process must assure that the product fullfills the customer requirements (the stated visions and goals); that quality is produced in the first place, rather than introduced through testing and rework (cf. Jarke and Pohl 1992). Therefore adequate production methods must be chosen, taking the goals under consideration. Quality control activities must check if the product satisfies the expectations. Hence, the choice of the control methods also depends on the goals. Achieving this requires that the production process is guided by a process model. This model itself must be quality oriented — the choice among alternatives must consider quality aspects. The task of system engineering involves, after transforming the vision into a requirements specification, to serve in the design and implementation tasks as a framework for the operationalization of the necessary changes in the real world. Of course, the goals change during these phases since new goals may be detected, or existing goals may be refined.

But, as the philosophy of TQM (Oakland 1989, Deming 1986) points out, quality-orientation is not enough. Continous improvement of process quality (which will automatically lead to better product quality) supported by selective process control is necessary. These process controls deliver raw data from which teamwork can derive concrete proposals for process improvement. Management commitment has to ensure that the results are actually instituted and not lost through bureaucratic hurdles.

The modeling framework we are going to propose in the sequel is not dependent on any particular formalism, although it does impose certain minimal requirements on formalisms in which it could be computer-supported. Briefly, such requirements include the need for representing multiple meta levels of typing, genericity hierarchies, complex descriptions, and some kind of logic for representing aspects such as policies, laws, or dependency structures. In our practical experiments, we are using the deductive object-oriented database language Telos (Mylopoulos et al. 1990) and its implementation ConceptBase (Jarke 1992). But most aspects of the model can be implemented in any object-oriented database environment. Since one of the syntax variants of Telos is a typed and directed graph, the graphics we use for the models can be understood as direct representations of a formal Telos knowledge base with a logical semantics (Jeusfeld 1992).

The basic concepts of our process model — situation, decision and actions — are adapted from the ALECSI model (section 3.1). Going further, we destinguish three different kinds of actions to emphasize their role with respect to goals: product, control and improvement actions, covering also the important role of teamwork in organizing and performing these actions (section 3.2).

3.1. The Basic Process Structure: Situated Decisions and Actions

Our model follows a *decision-oriented paradigm.* (Potts 1989, Jarke 1993). This gives the ability to more deeply integrate the semantics attached to the evolutionary aspects of the design. The notion of decision in the design process allows a better understanding of the designer's intention facilitating, in turn, better reuse of its results.

Even the decision-based approaches offer only limited hints when and how to decide on what. Following observations by Suchman (1987) and in the ALECSI project (Grosz and Rolland 1990), our model therefore makes the notion of situation (in which to decide) explicit and relates it to the broader question of context handling. The model associates the situation the system engineer faces to the decisions he can take to solve the local problem and to the actions to be performed to apply the decision (cf. figure 3).

A situation could be defined by itself (i.e., a subjective expressed perception of the user), by a view on a restricted set of object states (expressed using a constraint) and by a set of possible actions which could be applied in a particular situation of the defined kind. For predefined situation types, a ranking between the actions can be defined. Preconditions defined for each action make sure that it can only be applied within a given set of situations. The performance of the action can be controlled by the action constraint; e.g., assuring that changes are made to all relevant parts of the products. Postconditions test if, after executing an action, the state of the process (the actual situation) changes in a given manner. New situations are reached through actions, external events, or changing perceptions.

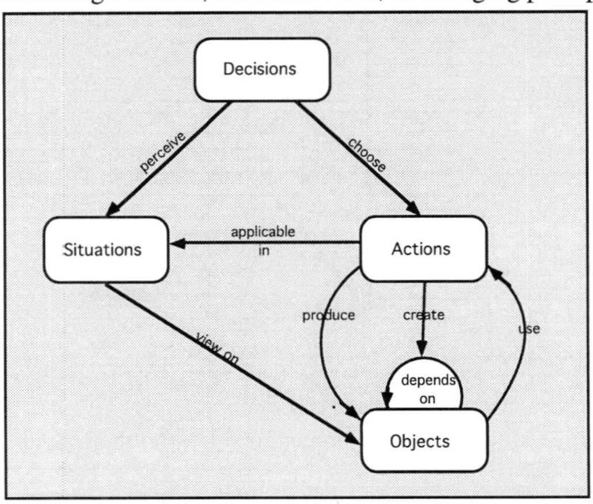

Figure 3. A process model based on situated decisions.

3.2. Goal-Oriented Differentiation of Action Types

By refining the interrelated lattices of product, situation, decision, and action types, we can model system engineering activities at macro and micro levels of detail. The decision context is structured by positioning the known situations and methods within the four worlds and the three dimensions discussed in section 2. However, we have no means yet to represent how the vision of the system can drive the process. The approach described below is intended to be carried through the full development cycle, justifying each design and implementation step by the quality goals it is intended to support. Thus, the whole process becomes effectively traceable to the interplay between vision and context.

A quality and improvement oriented process model must at least support three different kinds of actions:

- *product* process actions, which change product objects. They produce intermediate and final products and can be performed according to special product situations such as "baseline requirements model approved". Action examples of this kind are "edit source file", or "compile or map requirements into design".
- *control actions*, which control the produced quality of the product. They may be applied in special process situations, e.g., "intermediate product completed". Examples of such actions are measurements, reviews or audits.
- *improvement actions*, which change the process definition according to results of control actions, experience or general new insights; they therefore correspond to Madhavji´s meta level changes.

The term "action" refers to something that actually happens at the object level. In a process definition, we describe the kinds of product, control, and improvement actions by corresponding *product methods*, *control methods*, and *improvement methods.*

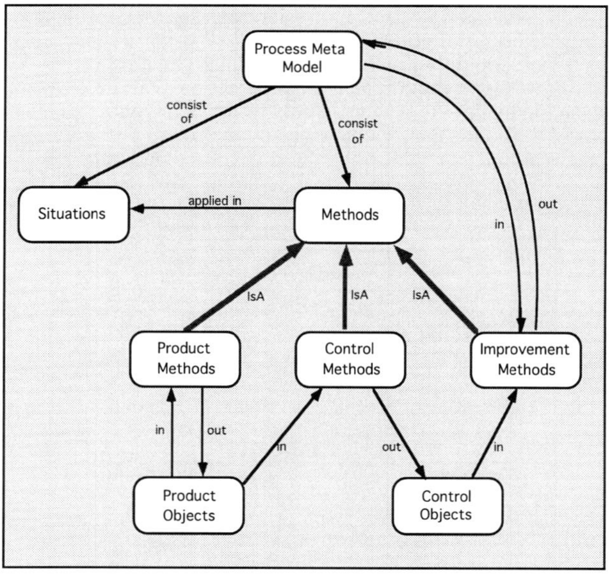

Figure 4. Three kinds of generic process actions and their input/output objects.

While all of these subtypes are basically "just actions", a careful analysis of their interrelationships and of the different situations in which they apply substantially increase the level of support offered. Formally, the three action types are gained by specializing the class *Methods*, as shown in figure 4. As part of defining the semantics of each kind of action, the objects used as input for the specialized actions as well as the output produced by them are specializations of the class *Object.* Similarly, the situations in which particular actions can be applied are defined by specializing the class *Situation* (not shown in figure 4).

Product Actions. Product actions change the state of the product objects. Methods for them are the ones normally considered by process modelling. For example, the software process is often divided in lifecycle phases such as requirements engineering, design in the large, design in the small, implementation and maintenance. Each of them is then modelled at a finer level of granularity. At the lowest level of abstraction, individual tool-supported actions are defined, e.g., for the situation "requirements model approved" the product method "map requirements to designs" is defined.

Executing a product action has several effects. First, it obviously changes the product. This change, and therefore the new state the product is in after the action is executed, does not only depend on the action used but also on the product states before the action. To make the process traceable, the dependencies between the different object states must be recorded.

The product produced by a product action serves as an input for the control actions. However, the usual product process models contain little in the way of facilitating this relationship. Few of them include quality goals (nonfunctional requirements) directly in their framework of guiding process execution.

To produce quality in the first place, selection among applicable product methods must be based on the goals. It has to be defined when a certain method should be chosen, and which goals it is supposed to satisfy. But the relationship between goals and production method must not only be made explict during the process definition task, they must also be recorded. For example, if a goal changes, the affected production methods have to be localized and corresponding changes must be made.

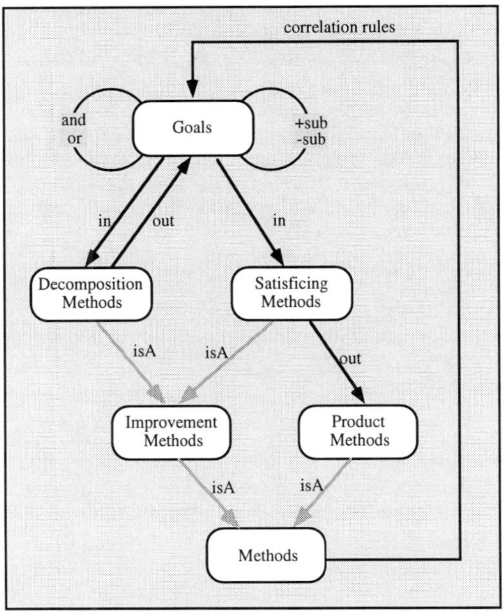

Figure 5. Metamodel for quality-driven design process.

Figure 5 is our semantic network re-interpretation of a model proposed in a search-tree formalism by Mylopoulos et al. (1992). It distinguishes three kinds of goals, and three kinds of methods which create these goals as well as links between them:

- *Decomposition methods* offer one possible scheme of subgoals that have to be achieved to achieve the overall goal.
- *Satisficing methods* describe options how to achieve these goals.
- *Argumentation methods* define the relationships between subgoals and methods — e.g., two methods exclude each other and that there are arguments for both of them.

In figure 5, the latter part of the model is omitted since we use a different approach to argumentation (cf. section 3.3). Links can be of type *and/or* (e.g., a conjunction of subgoals must be satisfied to satisfy a goal) or of type *+/-* (e.g., a method contributes positively or negatively to a goal). Correlation rules state unintended side-effects where the application of some method to achieve one goal also influences other goals. The approach is qualitative in the sense that only positive and negative influences are recorded; trade-offs in conflict situations have to be made by humans. We are currently developing a method for selection of reusable process components under multiple quantitatively expressed quality criteria.

Control Actions. The definition of product action offers the technology to ensure that the production process can be defined. This definition is the basis for applying control actions which verify or validate intermediate products or the process execution itself. The result of a control action is recorded in a control object. The control object therefore contains information about the execution of the process; for instance, if a desired quality feature was produced in the first place. This information is essential for process improvement.

There exist different kinds of control actions within the software development process. In early stages such as requirements engineering, reviews, audits or walkthroughs are used. This is based on the fact that automatic control of product quality (the requirements engineering document) is nearly impossible. With growing formalization, some (but never all!) of the control activities can be automated. Many automated control actions during the implementation phase use *metrics* to obtain indirect software quality information. Which particular metrics is used depends on the quality goals which have to be reached.

The Goals-Question-Metric (GQM) model of TAME (Oivo and Basili 1992), shown in our reconstruction in figure 6, nicely complements figure 5. TAME relates the notions of goal and method to each other through the intermediate construct of questions that *need* to be answered in order to evaluate the contribution of a process execution towards a goal, and that *can* be partially answered by specific metrics. Thus, while the model of figure 5 describes the *planned* relationships between goals and methods through a goal-based product process model, the one in figure 6 measures the *actually achieved* relationships between the application of a given method and various goals (including but not only those it was originally designed to satisfy). This provides feedback on the quality of process definitions.

The activity of recording the process execution forms the basis for a second important class of control actions. The execution of the process might not follow the defined process model, due to decisions made by human developers or due to failure to follow the process rules by either humans or tools.

The fact that a process was not executed as defined is an important observation. By analysing the reasons, new insights for process improvement may be gained. But this is only possible if the process knowledge was recorded in a suitable way. So for this kind of control action, the differences between the defined process and the actually exectuted process must be made visible, together with rationales for these aberrations.

Another use of recorded process knowledge could also lead to process improvement. If, after the product is finished, the user observes that a certain quality goal was not achieved, changes to the product must be made. During the change, control actions must make sure that all actions which lead to the missing quality are localized, tracing back the process history to the action where the production of quality failed for the first time. The decision which lead to the execution of this action must then be revised. In retrospect, this makes the actual process execution to a certain degree undefined (we have changed the process definition post-mortem). The difference between the (new) defined process and the execution could serve as the basis for process improvement. Assuring that maintenance activities (which are product actions) change the process execution and assuring that the violation of the process definition leads to a control object and builds the basis for process improvement.

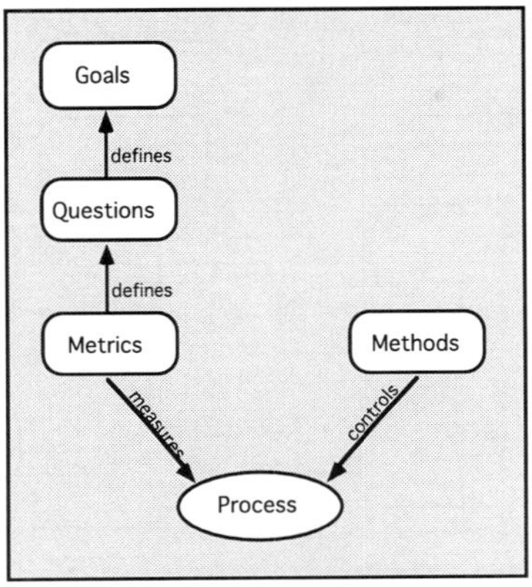

Figure 6. Process control according to the TAME meta model.

Summarizing both recording the difference between process execution and process definition (in the first place and due to changes afterwards) and the normal control activities applied on products (reviews, metrics, audits etc.) lead to control objects which serve as input for the improvement actions. Combined with the definitional facility of figure 5, the TAME framework of figure 6 could work in all three cases, provided that the notion of Goals in the figure also includes process goals.

Improvement Actions. "Improvement" is meant here similar to "change management" (Madhavji 1992), but with the added demand of explicitly considering quality factors in defining and recording the process definition change.

In contrast to product and control actions which deal with product and process objects at the execution level, improvement actions affect the definition of the process itself. Applying an improvement action either leads to an improved process model, or to a decison that no improvement is necessary. Since the latter could affect later decisions, it must also be recorded. The situation on which an improvement action is based does not only comprise the current process definition and control object information but also existing goals, policies, laws and resources. These are represented as special objects within the process model.

Our model distinguishes three possible kinds of improvement situations (fig. 7).

If *lack of quality* of an (intermediate) product was recognized by a control action, there exist control objects which characterize the improvement situation.

Where a *violation of the defined process* was recognized, not the missing quality of the product is the motivation for process improvement, but the unexpected performance of the process made to gain better quality in the first place.

In contrast to the first and second improvement situation which are recognized by performing the production process, the third kind of improvement situation is raised by *changes in the environment:* changes of goals, policies etc. For instance, changing a policy must lead to improvement actions by which the new policy is integrated into the corresponding process model. Since the goals are represented within the process models, changes made to them (which are modelled as improvement actions) constitute improvement situations which assure that the process models can be adapted to these changes.

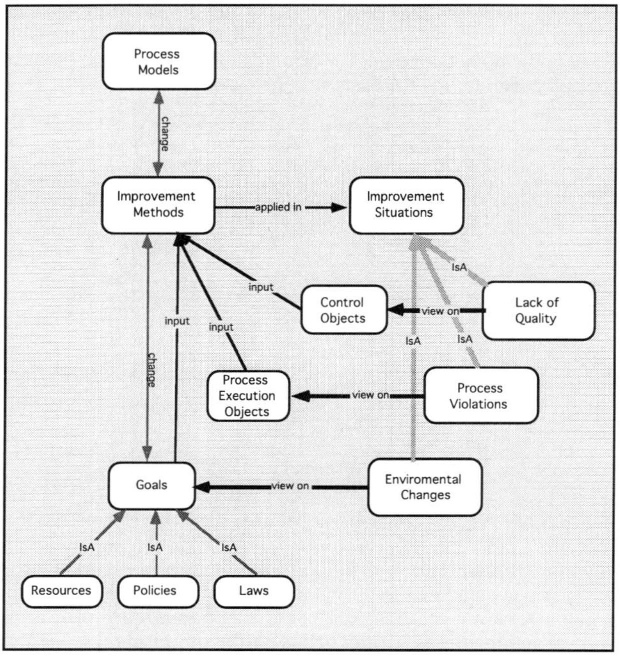

Figure 7. Improvement Methods with different improvement situations.

Improvement actions can have a different *scope with respect to organizational or product genericity* (cf. section 4.2). There are actions that affect the whole organization, but also for special product processes or even special project processes.

The different kinds of situations, the different kinds of improvement actions, and the improvement at different genericity levels make it necessary to differentiate between product process model and improvement process model. Specifically, to define the improvement process, it is necessary to investigate suitable metalevel operators that offer structure to process improvement and thus facilitate quality-oriented change management: has improvement been actually accomplished (repeatability)? how does a general improvement strategy look like (defineability)? how to manage change of improvement strategies (manageability)?.

The Integrated Model. Figure 8 shows how the three different kinds of methods for defining product, control and improvement actions are related to each other through the explicit management of quality goals.

Product processes are defined and executed using goal-oriented meta operators such as goal decomposition and satisficing. Experiences with these process definitions are captured through goal-driven control methods in the spirit of TAME. Improvement is carried out in a structured manner, again under explicit consideration of goals and with the use of structured meta operators; moreover, we recall that, similar to PRISM (Madhavji 1992), this model operates at multiple interacting levels of a genericity hierarchy of products and organizational units. Further semantics is provided to our model through the corresponding specialization of their associated situations, input and output objects, including the goals themselves.

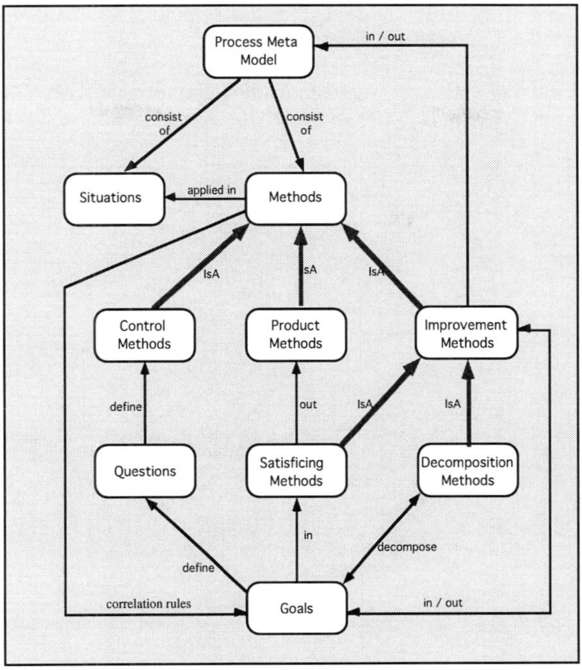

Figure 8. The integrated meta process model.

Teamwork Aspects. According to the TQM philosophy (Oakland 1989, Deming 1986), there is no process improvement without teamwork. Each person involved in a project must have the chance to understand the process definition, execution and evolution. Recording process knowledge could serve as a basis for later understanding of process execution and evolution. Teamwork is also the central means of acquiring knowledge about the quality requirements needed for our model.

We do not see process execution as an automatic transition from one state to the next one, but as a cooperation between agents. Taking a speech-act perspective (Winograd and Flores 1986), our model organizes this cooperation in conversation structures which lead to decisions that define and select actions. Since conversations may deal with knowledge not contained in the project-specific process definition (e.g., a person is ill), it is not possible to fully predict a process execution. While the process definition may propose a ranking between the actions, the decision which of them is actually applied is the responsibility of the agents executing the process. As a result of the conversation, a decision could be made which chooses another action than the one with the highest a priori ranking. Even a decision for an action which was undefined for the given situation is conceivable.

The performance of an action may require special skills. Thus, decisions depend not only on the current process state but also on the availability of suitable agents. The conversation about the action to be performed in a given situation must therefore consider the skills needed for each action and the availability of suitably skilled agents. Structured conversations do not only play a role when executing process definitions but also when deciding on improvement actions. For structuring these conversations, we use Rittel´s Issue-based Information System model which has gained wide acceptance through its use for structuring the early phases of design deliberations in the gIBIS hypertext system (Conklin and Begeman 1988) and its more formal derivatives (Ramesh and Dhar 1992).

Figure 9 shows the integration of such conversation structures with our meta process model to achieve the required team-oriented quality and improvement oriented process meta model, extending the CAD^0 model used in the DAIDA project (Jarke and Rose 1992).

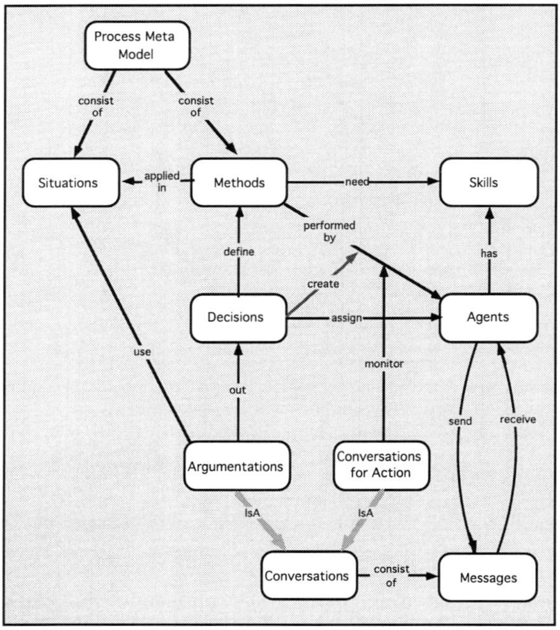

Figure 9. The meta process model including teamwork aspects.

4. HOW ARE THE GOALS MANAGED ?

The framework of goal acquisition and goal exploitation proposed in the previous sections implies a massive amount of recorded process information, even of process definitions, when used to evaluate actual projects or general process models. Abstraction mechanisms and database technology are required to deal with this flood effectively.

In this section, we present a technical solution based on the repository technology standard IRDS (section 4.1) and two different abstraction hierarchies (section 4.2). Using this approach and our implementation of Telos, ConceptBase (Jarke 1992), we have implemented a prototypical system for supporting the usage of the information gained during system engineering and are using it in several major case studies.

4.1. Extending the Repository Standard IRDS

A repository is the central information system around which design environments are layered. We start from the four-level repository classification hierarchy defined in the Information Resource Dictionary Standard IRDS (1988). Level $n+1$ formally constitutes a type system for level n. The lowest level, the *production data* layer, consists of actual databases and maybe software execution traces. The *data* layer describes and relates data and procedure schemata developed for each subsystem application. The *schema* layer represents, in a uniform framework, the individual data and application languages in which subsystems are defined — the schema of the repository. Finally, the uniform descriptive formalism used to define the schemata is defined in the fourth level, the *schema description* layer.

The first observation to be made when addressing quality improvement through repository technology is that all layers become process oriented rather than just product oriented. Figure 10 shows how, consequently, a process oriented repository hierarchy would look like.

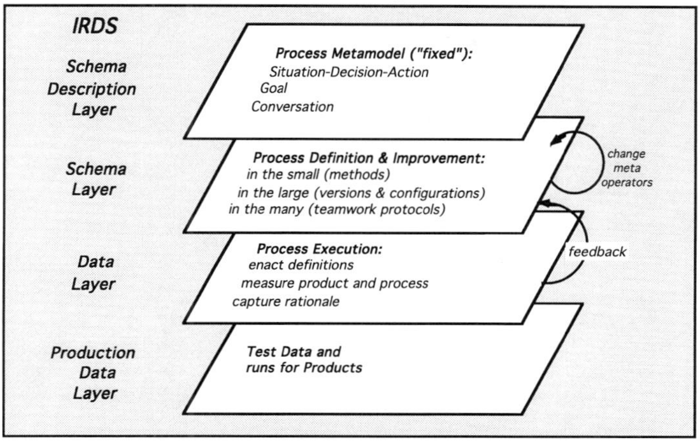

Figure 10. Repositories for process definition and evolution.

The *lowest* level contains application data and product execution traces which are interpreted as tests of product quality which can be used for feedback of process execution.

The *second* layer records process executions, e.g. capturing the rationale of design decisions for future reuse. If a formal process definition exists, recording its execution is a basis for measurement of product and process, checking correct enacting, and feedback concerning the quality of the process definition.

The *third* level contains process definitions according to various viewpoints. We distinguish development in the small (content oriented methods for specific individual tasks), in the large (version and configuration management from object and task viewpoints), and in the many (team cooperation in the preparation, execution, and evaluation of processes).

The meta model at the *fourth* level provides the basic ontological structure according to which processes are defined. The model of section 3 forms our meta model.

These different levels of modelling enable us to interrelate process definitions, their specialization, their execution and execution data, and therefore gives the needed structure for the concepts of process improvement and change management as dicussed in section 3.

4.2 Classification vs. Genericity Hierarchies

Many researchers recognize the need of distinguishing different levels of abstraction when modeling processes (e.g., Perry 1990, Madhavji 1991, Basili & Rombach 1988). However, they usually focus on one dimension of abstraction only. This mixes two concerns:

- the *classification* hierarchy as in IRDS, where each level constitutes a type system (as in programming languages) for the level below;
- the *genericity* hierarchy that deals with different modeling scopes such as organizational dimension (e.g., individual, group, department, organization, inter-

organizational, governmental, international) or product dimension (e.g., general software, information systems, knowledge-based information systems, ...).

Each level within the genericity hierarchy constitutes a specialization of a level above and therefore usually has to respect its rules, but can change those rules through some feedback formalism. The need of tailoring project independent models to project-specific models is widely accepted since (Osterweil 1987). They are the ones actually used during the project.

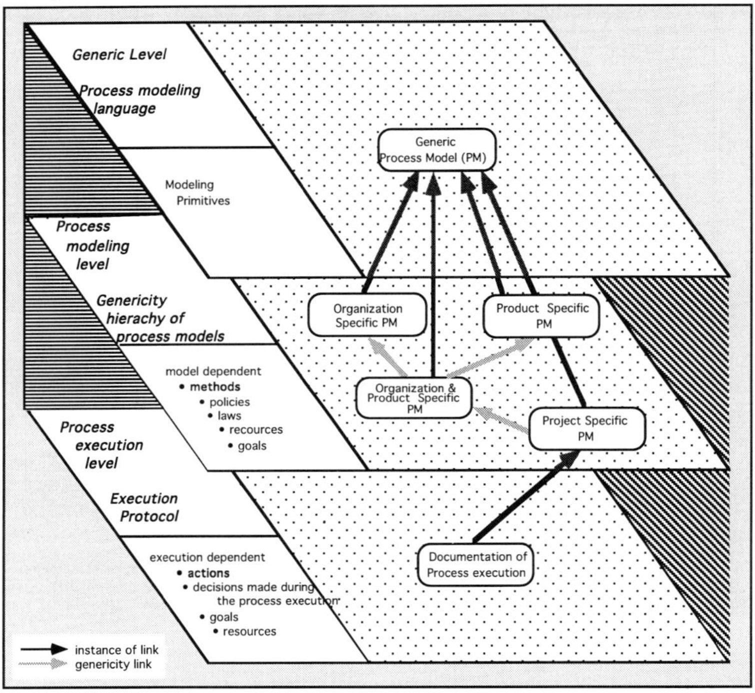

Figure 11. Classification and genericity hierarchies in process repositories.

The distinction between two abstraction hierarchies (classification and genericity) gives a richer picture of the problem-solving strategies that can be adopted in case of process breakdowns. For example, an organization may decide to use ISO 9000 as a policy. It therefore defines overall standard quality assurance methods at the organization-specific process definition level. In addition, product-specific quality assurance methods are defined. If a process model for a special product is built within an organization, both, the organization-specific and the product-specific quality assurance methods must be considered. But also additional methods could be defined for the product and organization specific process model. Further specializiation within the genericity hierarchy (e.g., for building a department model, group model or project model etc.) can be made.

In an object-oriented modeling formalism, the genericity hierarchy at the execution level need not be explicitly recorded but is automatically available through inheritance. We have *one* process execution which is indirectly an instance of each level in the genericity hierarchy to which it is attached. The different levels are views which define the process execution at their level of abstraction. Assume that there are four kinds of process models within the genericity hierarchy as shown in figure 11. Should it turn out (e.g., through failed process executions) that certain standard methods selected by the project model are infeasible, there are several choices of navigating within the space of process models to correct this:

- revise the process execution within the project process definition (e.g., choose an alternative method that satisfies the same goals).
- delegate the problem upwards to the people defining the project model, to have it solved by someone else within the organization & product specific definition.
- change the execution of the project model within the existing organization & process specific model.
- ask for changes of the organization & product specific model definition (here: the set of standard methods).

5. CONCLUSIONS

We first presented a framework for structuring the information gained during system engineering. Based on the concepts of "situation, decision and action", we then proposed a process model, whose definition and evolution is based on the goals to be reached. Finally we have shown, how the management of this information could be technically supported.

First empirical experience in analysing existing processes and formally defining some informally understood engineering methods shows, that software developers and users find it helpful to classify their knowledge according to the presented structure of

- the four worlds (development, usage, subject and system world),
- the three dimensions (agreement, representation and specification),
- the three different action types (control, improvement and product action)
- the three different improvement situations.

More work is needed, and done in the NATURE project, on elaborating detailed models within each of these four aspects. The question of how to map the goals down to production and control methods could by now only be answered for special kinds of goals, and our system experiments show that effective representation and visualization of the massive amounts of generated information is still an open issue, when we do not want to lose sight of the vision in the details.

Acknowledgments. Thanks are due to our partners in ESPRIT project NATURE, especially to the teams of Colette Rolland concerning the basic situation-decision-action model, of Janis Bubenko and Alastair Sutcliffe concerning domain and business modeling aspects, of John Mylopoulos concerning design with nonfunctional requirements, and of Yannis Vassiliou concerning Telos aspects. Also to the partners in BMFT project WibQus for providing excellent feedback on the practicability of many issues presented here.

REFERENCES

Basili, V. R. and Rombach, H. D. "The TAME Project: Towards Improvement-Oriented Software Environments" *IEEE Transactions on Software Engineering*, Volume 14, No. 6, 1988, pp. 758-773.

Brodie M.L. and Ceri S. "On Intelligent and Cooperative Information Systems: A Workshop Summary" *Intelligent & Cooperative Information Systems*, 1(2), June, 1992, 249-289.

Conklin, J. and Begeman, M. L. "gIBIS: A Hypertext Tool for Exploratory Policy Discussion" *ACM Transactions on Office Information Systems* Volume 6, No. 4, 1988, pp. 303 -331.

Curtis, B.; Krasner, H. and Iscoe, N. "Field Study of the Software Design Process for Large Systems" *Communications of the ACM*, 33 (11), 1988, 1268-1287.

Dardenne, A.; Fickas, S. and van Lamsweerde, A. "Goal-directed Concept Acquisition in Requirements Elicitation" *Proc. 6th IEEE Workshop System Specification and Design*, Como, Italy, 14-21.

Deming, W. E. *Out of the Crisis*. Massachusetts Institute of Technology, Center for Advanced Engineering Study, Cambridge, Massachusetts, 1986

Ellis, C.; Gibbs, S.; Rein G. "Groupware - Some Issues and Experiences" *Communications of the ACM* 34(1), 1991, 39-58.

Fickas S. "Automating analysis: An example" *Proc. 4th Intl.Workshop on Software Specification and Design*, Washington DC, 1987, 58-67.

Finkelstein A.; Kramer J. and Goedicke M. "Viewpoint-Oriented Software Development" P*roc. Conf Le Génie Logiciel et ses Applications,* Toulouse, 1990, 337-351.

Goguen J.A. "Social Issues in Requirements Engineering" *Proc. Int. Symposium on Requirements Engineering,* San Diego, Jan. 4-6, 1993, p. 194-195.

Grosz, G. and Rolland, C. "Using Artificial Intelligence Techniques to Formalize the Information System Design Process" *Proc. Intl. Conf. Databases and Expert Systems Applications*, 1990, 374-380.

Hagelstein, J. "Declarative Approach to Information Systems Requirements" *Knowledge Base Systems* 1(4), 1988, p. 211-220

IEEE *Software Engineering Standards.* Institute of Electrical and Electronics Engineers, Inc., 1987.

IRDS *Integrated Resource Dictionary Standard*, 1988, ANSI X3.138 und ISO WG3

Jarke, M. "DAIDA: Conceptual Modeling and Knowledge-based Support of Information Systems Development Processes" In *Technique et Science Informatiques*, Volume 9, No. 2, 1990, pp. 122-133.

Jarke, M. (ed.) *ConceptBase V. 3.1 User manual*, Technical Report, RWTH-Aachen, Germany, 1992.

Jarke, M. (ed.) *Database Application Engineering with DAIDA.* Springer Verlag, 1993.

Jarke, M and Pohl, K. "Information Systems Quality and Quality Information Systems" In *Proc. IFIP WG 8.2 Working Conf. Impact of Computer Supported Technologies on Information Systems Development*, Minneapolis, Minnesota, USA, 14-17 June, 1992, 345 -375.

Jarke, M. and Rose, T. "Specification Management with CAD^{O}" In Loucopoulos, P., Zicari, R. (eds.): *Conceptual Modeling, Databases, and CASE,* Chichester, UK: John Wiley, 1992.

Jeusfeld, M. A. "Änderungskontrolle in Deduktiven Objektbanken" DISKI Volume 17, Bad Honnef, Germany: INFIX Publ., 1992, (Diss. Univ. Passau, in German)

Jones, C.B. *Systematic Software Development Using VDM*, 2nd edition, Prentice Hall, 1990

Lubars, M.; Potts, C. and Richter C. "A Review on the State of the Practice in Requirements Modelling" *Proc. Int. Symposium on Requirements Engineering*, San Diego, Jan. 4-6, 1993, 2-14.

Madhavji, N. H. "The Process Cycle" In *IEE Software Engineering J.*, Volume 6, No. 5, 1991, pp. 234-242

Madhavji, N. H. "Environment Evolution: The Prism Model of Changes" *IEEE Transactions on Software Engineering*, Volume 18, No. 5, May, 1992, pp. 380-392.

McMenamin S.M. and Palmer J.F. *Essential System Analysis.* Yourdon Press, Englewood Cliffs, NJ, 1984.

Mylopoulos, J.; Borgida, A.; Jarke, M. and Koubarakis, M.; "Telos: Representing Knowledge About Information Systems" In *Transactions on Information Systems*, Volume 8, No. 4, 1990, pp. 325-362.

Mylopoulos, J.; Chung, L. and Nixon, B. "Representing and Using Non-Functional Requirements: A Process-Oriented Approach" *IEEE Trans. Software Engineering,* Volume 18, No. 6, 1992, pp. 483-497.

Oakland, J.S. "Total Quality Management" In *Proceedings 2nd Inernational Conference on Total Quality Management,* Oxford: Cotswold Press Ltd, 1989, pp. 3-17.

Oivo, M and Basili, V. R. "Representing Software Engineering Models: The TAME Goal Oriented Approach" *IEEE Transactions on Software Engineering,* Volume 18, No. 10, 1992.

Osterweil, L. "Software Processes are Software too" In *Procceedings 9th International Conference on Software Engineering*, Monterey, Ca, 1987, pp. 2-13.

Perry, D. E. "Policy and Product Directed Process Instantiation" In: *Proceedings of the 6th Int. Software Process Workshop*, Hokkaido, Japan, October, 1990.

Pohl, K. "The Three Dimensions of Requirements Engineering" *Proc. CAiSE Conf.,* Paris, June 8-11, 1993

Potts, C. "A Generic Model for Representing Design Methods" *Proc. 11th Intl. Conf. Software Engineering,*Pittsburgh, 1989.

Ramesh, B. and Dhar, V. "Process-Knowledge Based Group Support in Requirements Engineering" *IEEE Transactions on Software Engineering,* Volume 18, No. 6, 1992, 498-510.

Spivey, J.M. *The Z Notation*, Prentice Hall, 1989.

Suchman, L. A. *Plans and Situated Actions.* Cambridge Universiy Press, 1987

Winograd, T. and Flores F. *Understanding Computers and Cognitio*n, Ablex, Norwood, NJ, 1986.

2.

PROCESS/PRODUCT MODELING I

Information System Development Process (A-30)
N. Prakash, C. Rolland and B. Pernici (Editors)
Elsevier Science Publishers B.V. (North–Holland)

© 1993 IFIP. All rights reserved.

Customization and Evolution of Process Models in EPOS

Reidar Conradi and Maria Letizia Jaccheri

Div. of Computer Systems and Telematics, Norwegian Institute of Technology (NTH), N-7034 Trondheim, Norway.
Email: conradi@idt.unit.no.

Abstract

EPOS is a kernel software engineering environment, offering integrated software configuration and process management. The EPOS process modeling (PM) support system runs on top of the versioned *EPOSDB*, operating in client-server mode. EPOSDB offers cooperating subdatabases/workspaces for each subproject.

The originality of the EPOS approach to PM flexibility lies in a common, reflexive, object-oriented data model to describe persistent and versioned products, activities, tools, organizational contexts, and their meta-processes. A process model or schema is a set of data types for such entities and their relationships. A *PM Manager* is capable of defining and changing process models. A Planner will instantiate them into software processes. Work is going on to use roles and access rights to better control process change, and to support the full process model life-cycle by a "CASE tool" for PM.

Keyword Codes: D.2.0, D.2.2, D.2.6
Keywords: Software Engineering, Tools and Techniques, Programming Environments

1 Introduction

We need to model and manage not only the product space, but also the process aspects of software engineering. Software process modeling (PM) and its support has gotten increased attention in the last 15 years [1] [2] [3] [4]. Many PM formalisms, techniques and prototypes have been developed (Section 2.3), but with little market penetration yet.

Software process modeling and management share technology developed for organizational modeling, groupware, project management, work flow systems, configuration management, cooperating and distributed systems. This raises many interesting architectural questions: How can we develop core technologies for PM, that are sufficient powerful and yet flexible, and that also build upon standard technologies?

One of the classical conflicts is the need for overall control and planning, versus individual freedom and creativity. Ideally, the PM system should serves as an intelligent and cooperative assistant in the daily work of project workers at any level. Since most PM system are intended to serve in a hybrid machine-human environment, called *human-oriented* systems [5], flexibility through customization and evolution is a crucial property. This implies that classic programming language technologies, like strict type-checking and compiled systems, are partly unsuited. As for knowledge-based systems, many PM systems have been built on interpretative and reflexive systems.

The paper will first present some PM concepts and a meta-process framework. Then follows a list of demands and some existing technologies for process model flexibility, later called *variability*. We also characterize some existing PM systems wrt. to such variability. Thereafter follows a presentation of the EPOS support for PM variability. A short conclusion is also given, with indications of further work.

2 Background

There is no commonly agreed concepts and terminology for software PM [6] [5] [7]. We will therefore summarize some key concepts below.

2.1 General PM Definitions

A software *process model* provides a common, often *typed* description of a class of software artifacts: activities and their related products, application tools, and organization. The latter includes human roles. A process model thus resembles a database schema, and consists of related submodels (subschemas) to describe the above artifacts.

We can identify the following phases of PM meta-processes, that must be supported by methods and PM tools:

PM1. Provide PM Environment: e.g. PM tools.
PM2. Elicit/design/analyze a generic model.
PM3. Compile/customize a specific model.
PM4. Plan and instantiate process(es).
PM5. Execute and monitor these processes.

Naturally, there will be corresponding *representations* of software process models at PM2 and PM3, and similar for software processes at PM4 and PM5.

The structuring and modularization facilities of a process model will influence its possibilities and mechanisms for variability. And in PM systems with dynamic binding, the phase distinction between design of a generic/specific model and its instantiation and execution is blurred. That is, definition, customization and evolution of process models is an incremental and never-ending meta-process.

In the next subsection, we will present a taxonomy for the variability needed in software process models, and some of the available techniques. This taxonomy will be used to characterize and evaluate some existing PM systems.

2.2 Characteristics of Software Process Model Variability

We can identify the following variability issues in software process models:

1. **Categories of variability**:

    - *Customization* according to project context ("variants").
    - *Evolution*: corrections and improvements ("revisions").

    We can also mention *Refinement* linked to specialization and life-cycle phases, as a special case of evolution.

2. **Methodologies and principles to guide changes**.
    We need meta-level rules for what is allowed to change, why, when, and by whom? This may include consistency rules and impact analysis, and use of views and roles.

3. **What can be changed?**, or what is the axes of variability and their process "parameters"?

    - *Meta-model*: e.g. policies for model changes.
    - *Model- or type-level*: submodel for activities, products, tools, organizations.
    - *Instance-level*: product instances (versions, structure), activity instances (flow patterns, deadlines), tool instances (file version, command line switches), ...
    - *Environment*: tool architecture, operating system.

    And how many of the changes can be *anticipated* (and thus "parameterizable"), and how many are *ad-hoc* ("raw" versioning)?

4. **Reasons for change**
    For software products, [8] indicates the following distribution of updates (not costs): perfective (51%), adaptive (25%), corrective (21%), preventive and others (4%). For processes or process models we do not know the distribution, but at least adaptive changes will be important.

5. **Frequency of change**: Is it every minute, day or year – and for which PM artifacts? Clearly the need for change differs for different organizations and their users.

6. **Mechanisms** to support model or process variability:

    - A *flexible architecture* to substitute system parts, cf. reconfigurable distributed systems.
    - *Dynamic binding*: cf. Lisp, Smalltalk, and Prolog (cf. reflection below).
    - *Restricting access rights*: Modularization, interfaces, scoping.
    - *Reflection* with explicit types and meta-types, so that we can reason upon, manipulate, and dynamically interpret a model.

- *Variable types* = model or schema:
  - versioned types (*between* transactions): what are the consequences for the instances; must we reformat them or temporarily passivate activities?
  - subtyping (*within* a transaction)
  - views (cf. versioned types)
  - generic/parameterized types
  - instance-level delegation
  - ad-hoc or embedded mechanisms.

2.3 Related Work on PM Variability

During the study and comparisons of the different approaches to PM variability management, we concentrate on two aspects. First, which are the *process variables* in each systems, i.e. which aspects of the process models each system enables to instrument or change. Second, we concentrate on which technical aspects each system uses to manage evolution. Obviously, the process activity formalism – Task Net, Rule Based / Triggers, or Process Programming – strongly influences the approach to evolution management. It is also straight-forward that a system must exhibit some kind of reflection [9] to inspect and change its state.

In **MARVEL** [10] a process model is specified by a *rule set* denoting the activity part, a *project type set* denoting the product part, and *tool envelopes* denote the tools. All these may be loaded (meta-process PM3) into the kernel to obtain a Specific Process Model. The concept of instantiation and execution (meta-processes PM4 and PM5) coincide. Process evolution is supported by imposing a set of *constraints* that define the legal evolution steps. An evolution step is a change either to the definition of a single class or a single rule. Neither enactable process models nor executing software processes are explicitly represented. This implies that they cannot be inspected, recorded, or modified.

In **MELMAC**, generic process models are expressed as refinable FUNSOFT nets. A FUNSOFT net mainly consists of a hierarchical Petri net where each transition may be marked with a *modification point* denoting that the transition may be refined before executing it. An instantiated process model is given by a FUNSOFT net whose transitions are linked to tools and where an initial marking is defined. The system does not exhibits reflection, because FUNSOFT net definitions are not explicitly represented nor updatable by the system. Thus FUNSOFT net enables refinement or specialization, but not evolution by corrections.

[11] has recently proposed to extend Petri Nets with reflection to manage process evolution in the **SPADE** system.

APPL/A [12] extends Ada with persistent relations, triggers, predicates, and transaction statements. A process model corresponds to an APPL/A program that is statically compiled into an executable program (an enactable process model) and then executed. Neither APPL/A programs, nor their executables may be manipulated and changed on the fly. However, relations are explicitly stored in the underlying storage management and together with triggers and transactions mechanisms are useful to manage product changes.

IPSE 2.5 [13] enables to express process models in terms of *Roles* and *Interactions* that are described by object-oriented classes. Executing roles may be evolved by introducing new classes of roles and interactions (StartRole), creating new role instances, modifying the behavior of existing roles (BehaveAs), and changing the network topology of the interacting instances. The IPSE PML is highly reflexive: definition, customization, instantiation, execution, monitoring and evolution of a given process model are supported and well documented.

HFSP [14] demonstrates a successful and formal attempt to apply reflection techniques to process modeling. A set of meta-operations enable inspection and manipulation of the state of enaction, that is explicitly represented. However, no explicit representation, nor manipulation of process model definitions is allowed. The meta-operations give support for software processes execution and monitoring, but do not help in the meta-processes PM2-PM3.

The **Darwin** [15] environment is based on the concepts of *law*, that provides rules under which both the product and the model itself operate and *evolve*. A Law Governed System consists of a set of objects interacting by message exchange, a law regulating the exchange of messages, and a mechanism enforcing the law. The law may be tailored for distinct projects and may be evolved in the context of one context. The advantage is the possibility to introduce global dynamic constraints, regulating the interaction and evolution of an object-oriented system. There is no explicitly representation of executable software processes, whose models are given in a totally declarative way.

Process WEAVER [16] from Cap Gemini Innovation allows dynamic reconfiguration of enacted processes. A task network is here modeled as a set of inter-linked Petri nets. The links between the nets are expressed in terms of actions, which are attached to the net transitions. These links can be dynamically restructured. New models written in C++ can be dynamically constructed and later linked into the enacted model.

3 EPOS Survey: SPELL and Subdatabases

3.1 EPOS Summary

EPOS is a multi-user, kernel software engineering environment. The PM support is based upon a software engineering database, EPOSDB, as shown in Figure 1. EPOSDB offers a structurally object-oriented data model ("OO Entity-Relationship" with entities as objects). EPOSDB implements a *Change Oriented Versioning* model (COV) [17], being largely independent of the data model. COV enables uniform versioning of entities and relationships, and their types[2]. An EPOSDB type corresponds to a *class* in the OMG terminology, and has an extent.

EPOSDB is a client-server database with nested and cooperative transactions against checked-out workspaces containing files. A transaction is executed on the current database *version*, i.e. the *visible* subdatabase. The transaction has a scope (*ambition*) to indicate into *which* other versions a local change should be propagated (made visible) after commit.

[2] NB: from a representation point of view, see Section 4.5 on change semantics.

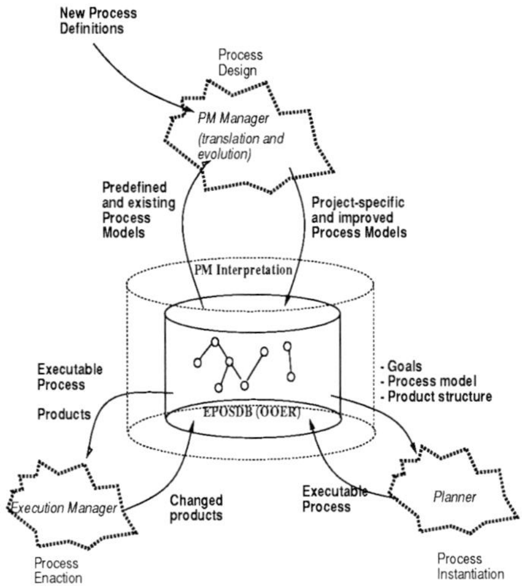

Figure 1: EPOS Architecture

A transaction is associated to a project description, see Section 3.3.

The **SPELL** [18] process specification language extends the DDL and DML of the underlying EPOSDB with user-accessible types and meta-types (reflection), type-level attributes with declarable inheritance rules, type- and instance-level procedures and triggers, and concurrency (tasking).

A task type expresses an activation rule (Section 3.2). Activities (tasks) are connected in a typed task network, where products act as actual parameters between "horizontally" connected tasks, which also can be "vertically" composed. The horizontal task network resembles a Petri-net, where transition nodes are connected with places. Task execution is performed by the EPOS Execution Manager (meta-process PM5), Incremental instantiation of tasks in a network is done by the EPOS Planner [19] (meta-process PM4), interacting closely with the Execution Manager.

The EPOS *PM Manager* incorporates a SPELL Translator/Editor to manage the set of types, and their customization and evolution (meta-processes PM2 and PM3). The SPELL Interpreter implements the binding and invocation of procedures and triggers, and provides an interface to the EPOSDB and the operating system. It also gives access to and interprets type-level attributes.

The *type representation* in EPOSDB consists of one (possibly subtyped) `TypeDescr` object per declared type, as well as a meta-type[3]. There are also inter-type relationships, like `is_a` for subtyping and those representing certain type-level attributes (FORMALS and DECOMPOSITION, see next subsection).

See Section 3.3 for a scenario on subprojects.

[3]Technically, the type- and meta-type are stored together as two sections in one `TypeDescr` object.

The EPOSDB is implemented in C on C-ISAM, and the surrounding EPOS-PM system is implemented in SWI-Prolog using XPC graphics.

3.2 SPELL: A Process Specification Language

We will not explain the SPELL syntax and semantics formally here, see e.g. [20]. Note, that types have both an *instance-level* part and a *type-level* (meta-type) part, as for class definitions in Smalltalk. Below, we will present the system-defined `TaskEntity` subtype (Figure 2) of the root type `Entity`. In addition, there is a `DataEntity` subtype for passive products, not described here.

The set of procedures and triggers in a type is potentially dynamic, and with dynamic binding as in Smalltalk. Most of the type-level procedures and -attributes guide and instrument the PM Manager, Execution Manager, and Planner. Many procedures concern creation, update and deletion of types, as well as creation and evolution of instances. The instance-level procedure `i_convert` can be used to refine the type of an instance, and procedures `start`, `stop`, and `restart` to control task execution. The procedure parameters `SelfO` and `SelfT` have the normal semantics of `self`.

The type-level task attributes serve as shared *process parameters*, and can be redefined by subtyping. Most of them are described below.

PRE_STATIC, PRE_DYNAMIC, POST_STATIC, and POST_DYNAMIC are formulas in first-order predicate logic. *Static* conditions are evaluated by the Planner for task instantiation, and *dynamic* ones by the Execution Manager at execution time.

CODE defines the actions performed when the task is executed, i.e. each time its dynamic PRE-condition is `true`. The CODE is written in an appropriate *sequential* language, p.t. Prolog. It often contains a tool script, in which case the task type serve as a *tool envelope*.

DECOMPOSITION constrains the task types of *decomposed* subtasks of a given task. A task subtype may either describe an atomic task, performed by a single tool EXECUTOR (see below), or a composite one (DECOMPOSITION is non-empty). DECOMPOSITION it is mainly used by the Planner.

FORMALS is a task (tool) *signature* to constrain the product types of *actual* in/out-parameters of a given task. `$` means a list, and `(r)` and `(rw)` indicate read/write access. FORMALS is again mainly used by the Planner.

EXECUTOR refers to the logical name of the tool that should execute the task, and corresponds to a "soft" type-instance relationship.

ROLE refers to the role or responsibility description of a generic human actor, e.g. a `Software Developer`. This description will be bound dynamically to certain persons or teams, and thus defines access rights (Section 5.2).

3.3 Projects and Their Subdatabases: A small Scenario

A project instance is a special task, associated to each database transaction. Its subtasks will defaultly be executed in this transaction, which has its own PM Manager.

A subproject (child transaction) will "inherit" or start with the subdatabase of the superproject (parent transaction). It can incrementally customize or evolve this sub-

```
ENTITY_TYPE TaskEntity:Entity {
  INSTANCE_LEVEL
    ATTRIBUTES
      Exec-state: ... = ...; % For task impl.
      Taskstate: String := 'Created'; % Similarly.
    PROCEDURES.
      i_delete(SelfO:OID) = ...;
      i_convert(SelfO:OID, NewT:TID) = ...;
      start(SelfO:OID) = ...;% Used by Exec.Mgr.
      restart(SelfO:OID) = ...;% Similarly.
      stop(SelfO:OID) = ...;% Similarly.
    TRIGGERS
      ON-PROC = start   WHEN = BEFORE
      COND = ...   ACTION = ...;
  TYPE_LEVEL
    ATTRIBUTES
      PRE_STATIC (Inher=append)
        Pred = true
      PRE_DYNAMIC (Inher=append)
        Pred = true
      CODE (Inher=concat)
        Prog = ... INNER ...
      POST_STATIC (Inher=append)
        Pred = true
      POST_DYNAMIC (Inher=append)
        Pred = true
      FORMALS (Inher=redef)
        String = 'in:$DataEntity (r) - >
                  out:$DataEntity (rw)'
      DECOMPOSITION (Inher=redef)
        String = 'REPERTOIRE(TaskEntity)'
      EXECUTOR (Inher=redef)
        String = 'ToolName ...'
      ROLE (Inher=redef)
        String = 'RoleName ...'
    PROCEDURES % See under PM Manager.
      model_check(SelfT:TID) = ... % Consist. check.
      t_create(SelfT:TID, NewT:TID,
              <Defined properties>)= ...;
      % Called by SPELL translator in PM Manager.
      t_delete(SelfT:TID)= ...; % See PM Manager.
      t_change(...)= ...; % Same parms as t_create.
      i_create(SelfT:TID, ...= ...; % Special NEW.
      subgoals(...)=...;%Subtyped, used by Planner.
  } % TaskEntity-type
```

Figure 2: The TaskEntity type

database, by redefining global types, extra subtyping, or other additions and extensions.

Thus, several parallel subprojects can co-exist and have customized process models, perhaps initially "borrowed" from a common superproject. This means that the *same*, shared products can be governed by *several* customized or versioned process models (views), belonging to different subprojects. See also [21] on cooperating transactions.

We start up a (sub)project in four steps:

First, we instantiate a `Project` instance and link it to the superproject, and initialize some key values.

Second, we bind the actual subdatabase version, being a subset of the parent's. We must here set up coordination protocols for the interaction with possibly overlapping and cooperating transactions: e.g. tight (automatic propagation), loose (manual propagation), or delayed-upon-commit. These protocols are interpreted by pre-defined tasks.

Third, we should possibly adjust and customize the process model through the PM Manager, by changing or augmenting some activity or product types, or even their meta-types. The PM Manager contains procedures to help the Project-Manager (or Process-Designer) for such customization and to perform consistency checks. Consistency checks are based on the invariants described in Section 4.1.

Fourth, the external workspace of files etc. is checked out.

Then the activities (tasks) of the project can start, involving updates of products, generation of more activities including new subprojects, and possibly modifications of the process model. During the transaction, possible updates on *any* piece of shared data, including types, may propagate from other transactions (if the coordination protocols allow this), and they must be treated (e.g. merged).

Upon project termination, workspace files must be checked in, the local subdatabase committed, and possible remaining update conflicts resolved.

4 Process Models, Consistency and Variability

4.1 Process Models and Consistency

An EPOS process model consists of four submodels for, respectively, the activity, product, tool, and organizational aspects of the process. A process model or schema is then a *configuration(!)* of several submodels, each controlling their software process instances.

Such a PM configuration is *consistent* if a set of type-invariants holds. These are expressed as an instrumentable `Invariants` attribute (Prolog script) in the PM Manager, and are for instance:

- A type name must be *unique* over all versions.
- A type must have *one* super-type (single inheritance).
- Correct *topological* definition order: all supertypes or entity types occurring in relation types must exist before defining the given type.
- The type and all supertypes of an instance must be *visible* in the actual database version.

- Likewise for the visibility of the related entities of a relationship.

  NB: all the above constraints are imposed by the data model.

- For task types: The "in-FORMALS" parameters of a task type must be non-empty, and partially match the "out-FORMALS" of another task type.

- Likewise, the task types mentioned in the DECOMPOSITION must exist.

- Generally the instances of a type must conform to the type specification, e.g. concerning attribute layout. See Section 4.5 on further constraints for task instances.

Possible checks could be run on:

- The set of types accessed from a given type, i.e. *subschema analysis* as in MARVEL?

- The structure of possible trigger chains, with simulations?

Each type may redefine a `model_check` procedure, which the PM Manager will execute after type changes.

4.2 Mechanisms for PM Structuring and Variability

We repeat the described machinery for PM variability: EPOS provides a versioned database for all PM artifacts including types, long "design" transactions, and a data model with fully object-oriented subtyping. Process model fragments are types, with reflexive meta-types. Type-level attributes serve as process parameters, and type-level procedures (meta-rules) drive and instrument the EPOS PM tools. There are no formal sub-schema or sub-model mechanism, other than COV to hide the invisible parts of a model.

We can regard PM variability *within* a project as a special case of schema evolution in object-oriented databases [22].

All in all, there are three axes of structuring and variability in EPOS process models:

— *Vertical* structuring by subtyping and
  other project specialization;
  i.e. the activity rule base is *hierarchic*.

— *Horizontal* evolution inside projects and
  versioning between projects.

— *Combined* vertical/horizontal, e.g. by
  dynamic binding semantics.

4.3 The PM Manager

The purpose of the PM Manager is to enable the process designer/user to define, customize and evolve models (types) in a uniform way, and to selectively convert the respective instances.

The PM Manager is implemented as a meta-task, mainly with type-level inputs/outputs and executing type-level procedures. As mentioned, a part of the PM Manager is a textual *SPELL Translator*. There is also a graphical *SPELL Editor* to browse types and modify parts of an existing type definition. We can either make a new *subtype* (leaf level) or *overwrite an old type* (at any level). Depending upon the scope of the transaction's subdatabase, these changes may end up as distinct, new *type versions*.

The current schema (set of all types) is only available by an unparse of all `TypeDescrs` in the local subdatabase.

4.4 Building New Process Models

A process model is always built by reusing existing types, at least the pre-defined ones, as indicated above.

Creating a new subtype is trivial from a technical point of view: the `t_create` type-procedure in the intended supertype, or the one in `TaskEntity`, will be called by the PM Manager. This will also perform the consistency checks mentioned above. The interface of this procedure is:

```
t_create(+SelfT,         -NewT,
         ?InstAttrs,     ?TypeAttrs,
         ?InstProcs,     ?TypeProcs,
         ?InstTriggers, ?TypeTriggers,
         -Status)

  Legend: +: mandatory input  parameter
          ?: optional  input  parameter
          -: mandatory output parameter
```

Further, along with a type we also define the knowledge of how to create a subtype of itself. It is realistic to foresee that the first time we create a type, we do not want to bother with how to reuse it. We do not then redefine the `t_create` type-level procedure, but let it be inherited from its supertype. Only when a type has been used and found useful, type-level procedures telling how to change and reuse the type may be added.

Then, building a new model resembles changing an existing model. Such building implies a long creative work, during which the model is still incomplete and may be inconsistent (see also Section 5.3). On the other hand, we should try to change models, that have proven to be consistent and useful, but these may have existing and perhaps active instances – see below.

4.5 Changing Existing Process Models

We distinguish between an actual *type-change* and a proposed *type-change request*. The feasibility of a requested type-change has to be evaluated against its possible *impact* on the whole PM configuration. This resembles classical configuration management problems, where changes to a part of a software system have to be propagated to other parts.

A type-change may affect:

- The instances of the modified type, or its subtypes. See below for further details.
- The subtypes of the modified type.

- The types otherwise related, like entity-types occurring in relation type or those connected by FORMALS/DECOMPOSITION.

Thus, when a type-change request is issued, the PM Manager checks that for each of the possibly affected (type-)instances, that the requested change does not violate the consistency constraints. If ok, the PM Manager performs the requested change. Otherwise, it notifies the change requester about the possibly impacted objects, and gives some hints about how to reestablish consistency after a contemplated change.

If the impact is too big, a new *subtype* might be defined, so that only a *subset* of the extent of the old type will be affected. Here we can use the `i_convert` procedure to refine the type of an existing instance into a new subtype, thereby possibly adding and initializing new attributes.

The interface of procedure `t_change` is similar to that of `t_create`. This procedure may potentially modify all properties of the actual type, except names and domains of instance-level attributes and except the original supertype. Thus, we distinguish between *hard* and *soft* type-changes.

The *hard* ones imply changes in instance-level attributes or in the subtype structure. Such changes are generally disallowed, see however [23] [24] and Section 4.7.

The *soft* type-changes are the PM-specific ones, as they modify the behavioral part of a type. The procedures `start`, `restart`, and `stop` may be used on tasks during a soft type-change, if the task state allows it (`initiated`, `waiting`, `active`, or `terminated` – see below).

For task types we can further distinguish between the following soft type-changes:

- Changed CODE:
  This assumes that no task instance is currently executing it, i.e. the affected tasks are all passive.

- Changed dynamic PRE- or POST-CONDITIONs:
  This can be done as soon as no task instance is no longer evaluating these.

  Both these two kinds of changes impact the Execution Manager.

- Changed FORMALS, DECOMPOSITION or static PRE- and POST-CONDITIONs:
  This may force the Planner to reexamine all the nodes in the task network to check the constraints, and possibly rebuild parts of the network (if feasible).

- Changed procedure or trigger: This also assumes that no task is executing this procedure/trigger just now.

All these cases are covered by the `Invariants` of the PM Manager.

Note, that type-changes often will affect subtypes through inheritance, and some locking must be observed, see [25] on ORION. However, due to quasi-concurrent task execution and disciplined inter-transaction propagation, this can be solved in EPOS PM [26]. Type-level triggers may e.g. assist such propagation.

As mentioned, structural reshuffles of the type hierarchy are *not* legal, but the issue is being pursued by us and by colleagues elsewhere.

Lastly, *deleting* a type by `t_delete` is much more delicate. A subtype can only be deleted, if there are no instances of it, and if it is not referred to from other types (subtypes etc.), cf. Section 4.1.

The next two subsections deals with variability in process *instances*, not process models, but we will focus on type-related changes.

4.6 Instantiating Software Processes

Software process instances are represented by task/product networks. The tasks are incrementally and automatically[4] instantiated by the Planner, cf. Grapple [27]. Many PM systems based on task networks rely on manual instantiation here.

The type-level procedure `i_create` is defined in root type `Entity` to generate arbitrary instances. The `TaskEntity` type re-defines it with extra in/out-parameters, in order to satisfy the FORMALS constraint.

4.7 Updating Process Instances

The process state is constantly evolving due to normal process execution. Some process changes may affect individual task instances, e.g. tool switches or busy/lazy recompilation policy of a specific programming module.

However, if the product topology is changed, the associated task network may have to be reconstructed. This may also happen if the FORMALS constraint of a task has changed. In both cases the EPOS Planner can perform almost automatic restructuring of the task network.

As mentioned before, instance-level updates (reformatting) may be needed to incorporate *hard* type-changes, cf. the effect of schema evolution in DBMSes. Therefore, dynamic techniques like *delegation* may prove advantageous. Indeed, our *soft* type-changes fall partly in the delegation category.

5 Proposals for Control of PM Changes

5.1 Why do Process Models and Processes Change?

When execution feedback signals that a process, or part of it, has given wrong or unsatisfactory results, the process or its model must often be corrected. Changes in the surrounding organization or operating environment may also lead to adaptation (customization) of the process model.

Further, better understanding of the process often leads to improvement of the process model, a meta-process called *learning*. *Automatic* learning, i.e. how to abstract new process models from modified task instances and networks, is a challenging problem that we have addressed, but not yet solved. At least we will need proper feedbacks and monitoring facilities, often missing in PM systems, but implementable in EPOS.

[4] Manual instantiation is also allowed.

5.2 Access Rights and Methodology for Change

Technically we are using the same *mechanisms for changes* in models, as for changes in products and activities; namely modification and subtyping combined with versioning, plus dynamic binding. In addition, we need to structure the *meta-process* for process change, and to associate developers/maintainers of the process model with proper access rights.

For the meta-process, we rely on the EPOS reflexive facilities. For access rights, the ROLE type-attribute in task types can be connected either to (static) scope/interface specifications in SPELL, and/or to dynamic database protection facilities. The latter includes classic locking and access rights, and how to control these (meta-level again!). There is a rich database literature on all this, e.g. coupling access rights to views expressed as queries, but the current EPOSDB provides only simple locking.

We will sketch how such protection can be achieved in an extended EPOSDB: Any property in a SPELL type could be declared with an extra set of *access specifications*: an `Access-right`: [`Read, Write, Execute, None, Visible`], and a `User-category`: [`Private, subtype-Protected, Friend, Public`]. These type specifications could be versioned, according to which view (or version) we want to see in a transaction. It is easy for the SPELL interface to interpret such specifications.

In addition, we need to connect the above `user-categories` and `access-rights` to dynamic or versioned access-right lists in a `role` object. This object will be indicated by the ROLE of the current subproject. The `role` object, will again be related to a person or team. Typical roles are Process-Designer, Process-Manager, and Process-User. Only privileged "meta-tasks" (with sufficient access rights!) in the superprojects may change such information.

On top of all this apparatus, a methodology for PM change must be developed and tested. We have none now, but see [28] [13].

5.3 A CASE Tool for PM models?

The life-cycle of process models brings up the idea of a *CASE tool for PM*, as a generalization of our PM Manager. This could be an integrated PM tool kit to support model acquisition, analysis, design, verification, simulation, refinement, transformation, evolution and customization, possibly at different levels of abstraction.

Further, many of the proposed formalisms for process modeling, specially for activity modeling, are very cryptic, and with poor structuring facilities to facilitate model libraries or reuse. It will be a challenge to develop more high-level formalisms, that support semi-automatic translation and powerful yet controlled variability.

6 Conclusions and Further Work

EPOS offers a common model for versioning and object-oriented modeling of process artifacts, both at the instance- and type-level, i.e. reflection. The use of reflection to manage PM evolution is not new [14], but we exploit an integrated, object-oriented architecture for managing type-changes. It also appears, that many of our mechanisms, originally aimed at the PM field, can be applied to schema evolution in the database field.

Future work will concentrate on further controlling and guiding change in process models, developing a minimal CASE tool for PM models, and getting more experience with practical applications.

Acknowledgements

Many thanks go to the participants of the 2nd European Workshop on Software Process Technology, 7–8 Sept. 1992 in Trondheim for clarifying discussions, and to the members of the EPOS team at NTH. A special thank goes to M. Letizia Jaccheri at Politecnico di Torino, an ex-EPOS team member.

References

[1] M. M. Lehman, "Process Models, Process Programming, Programming Support," in *Proc. of the 9th Int'l ACM-SIGSOFT/IEEE-CS Conference on Software Engineering, Monterey, CA*, pp. 14–16, Mar. 1987. (Response to an ICSE'9 Keynote Address by Leon Osterweil).

[2] D. E. Perry, ed., *Proc. 5th Int'l Software Process Workshop – ISPW'5*, (Kennebunkport, Maine, USA), IEEE Computer Society Press, Oct. 1989.

[3] W. S. Humphrey, *Managing The Software Process.* SEI Series in Software Engineering, 493 pages, Addison Wesley, 1989.

[4] J.-C. Derniame, ed., *Proc. from EWSPT'92, Sept. 7–8 1992, Trondheim, Norway*, Springer Verlag LNCS 635, Sept. 1992.

[5] R. Conradi, C. Fernström, A. Fuggetta, and R. Snowdon, "Towards a Reference Framework for Process Concepts," in *J.-C. Derniame (ed.): Proc. from EWSPT'92, Sept. 7–8, Trondheim, Norway, Springer Verlag LNCS 635*, pp. 3–17, Sept. 1992.

[6] P. H. Feiler and W. Humphrey, "Software Process Development and Enactment: Concepts and Definitions," Jan. 1992. 12 pages (Second version).

[7] J. Lonchamp, "A structured conceptual and terminological framework for software process engineering," in *Leon Osterweil (ed.): Proc. from 2nd Int'l Conference on Software Process (ICSP'2), March 1993, Berlin. IEEE Press (forthcoming, 15 p.)*, 1993.

[8] R. S. Pressman, *Software Engineering – A Practioner's Approach (2nd Ed.).* McGraw Hill International Editions, ISBN 0-07-100232-4, 1987.

[9] P. Maes and D. Nardi, eds., *Meta-Level Architectures and Reflection.* North Holland, 1988.

[10] N. S. Barghouti and G. E. Kaiser, "Scaling up Rule-Based Software Development Environments," in *Proc. of the 3rd European Software Engineering Conference, ESEC'91, Milan, Italy*, Oct. 1991.

[11] S. Bandinelli and A. Fuggetta, "Computational Reflection in Software Process Modeling: the SLANG Approach," tech. rep., CEFRIEL–Politecnico di Milano, Sept. 1992. (Submitted to ICSE'15).

[12] S. M. S. Jr., D. Heimbigner, and L. Osterweil, "Language Constructs for Managing Change in Process-Centered Environments," in *Proc. of the 4th ACM SIGSOFT Symposium on Software Development Environments, Irvine, California. In ACM SIGPLAN Notices, Dec. 1990*, pp. 206–217, Dec. 1990.

[13] R. Snowdon, "An example of process change," in *J.-C. Derniame (ed.): Proc. from EWSPT'92, Sept. 7–8, Trondheim, Norway, Springer Verlag LNCS 635*, pp. 178–195, Sept. 1992.

[14] T. Katayama, "A Hierarchical and Functional Software Process Description and its Enaction," in *Proc. of the 11th Int'l ACM-SIGSOFT/IEEE-CS Conference on Software Engineering, Pittsburgh, PA*, pp. 343–352, 1989.

[15] N. Minsky, "Law-Governed Systems," *Software Engineering Journal*, vol. 6, pp. 285–302, Sept. 1991.

[16] C. Fernström, "Process WEAVER: Adding Process Support to UNIX," in *Leon Osterweil (ed.): Proc. from 2nd Int'l Conference on Software Process (ICSP'2), March 1993, Berlin. IEEE Press (forthcoming)*, 1993.

[17] A. Lie, R. Conradi, T. M. Didriksen, E.-A. Karlsson, S. O. Hallsteinsen, and P. Holager, "Change Oriented Versioning in a Software Engineering Database," in *Walter F. Tichy (Ed.): Proc. of the 2nd International Workshop on Software Configuration Management, Princeton, USA, 25-27 Oct. 1989, 178 p. In ACM SIGSOFT Software Engineering Notes, 14 (7)*, pp. 56–65, Nov. 1989.

[18] R. Conradi, M. L. Jaccheri, C. Mazzi, A. Aarsten, and M. N. Nguyen, "Design, use, and implementation of SPELL, a language for software process modeling and evolution," in *J.-C. Derniame (ed.): Proc. from EWSPT'92, Sept. 7–8, Trondheim, Norway, Springer Verlag LNCS 635*, pp. 167–177, Sept. 1992.

[19] C. Liu, "An Expert System for Program and System Development," in *Proc. AVIGNON'91, Avignon, France, May 27–31, 1991, Volume 3*, pp. 97–110, 1991.

[20] C. Mazzi, "SPELL: The Revised EPOS Process Model Language," Nov. 1992. EPOS TR 171 175 pp.

[21] R. Conradi and C. C. Malm, "Cooperating Transactions and Workspaces in EPOS: Design and Preliminary Implementation," in *Proc. of CAiSE'91, the 3rd International Conference on Advanced Information Systems, Trondheim, Norway, 13–15 May 1991* (R. Andersen, J. A. B. jr., and A. S. lvberg, eds.), pp. 375–392, LNCS 498, Springer Verlag, 578 p., 1991. Also as DCST TR 47/90, EPOS TR 119.

[22] A. H. Skarra and S. B. Zdonik, "The management of changing types in an object-oriented database," in *Proc. of the ACM SIGPLAN Conference on Object-Oriented Programming Systems, Languages and Applications (OOPSLA'86)*, (Portland, OR, USA), pp. 483–491, 1986. In ACM SIGPLAN Notices 21(11), Nov. 1986.

[23] E. Odberg, "A framework for managing schema versioning in object oriented databases," in *Proc. from DEXA'92, Sept. 2–4, Valencia, Spain. 12 p.*, 1992.

[24] S. E. Bratsberg, "Unified class evolution by object-oriented views," in *G. Pernul and A. M. Tjoa (editors), Proc. 11th Int'l Conf. on the Entity-Relationship Approach, 7–9 October 1992, Karlsruhe, Germany, Springer Verlag LNCS 645 (17 p.)*, Oct. 1992.

[25] J. Banerjee *et al.*, "Semantics and implementation of schema evolution in object-oriented databases," in *ACM SIGMOD'87*, pp. 311–322, May 1987.

[26] M. L. Jaccheri, "Customization and evolution of process model support." 135 p. (draft PhD thesis), Feb. 1992.

[27] K. E. Huff, *Plan-Based Intelligent Assistance: An Approach to Supporting the Software Development Process.* PhD thesis, University of Massachusetts, Sept. 1989.

[28] P. J. Kawalek, "The process modelling cookbook: Orientation, description and experience," in *J.-C. Derniame (ed.): Proc. from EWSPT'92, Sept. 7–8, Trondheim, Norway, Springer Verlag LNCS 635*, pp. 227–229, Sept. 1992.

Information System Development Process (A-30)
N. Prakash, C. Rolland and B. Pernici (Editors)
Elsevier Science Publishers B.V. (North-Holland)

© 1993 IFIP. All rights reserved.

The Evolutionary Object Model (EOM)

M. Moreno, C. Souveyet

Centre de Recherche en Informatique, Université Paris I - Sorbonne
17 rue de Tolbiac, 75013 Paris, France

Keywords Codes : H.1.1; H.3.2; I.2.4
Keywords : Systems and Information Theory, Information Storage, Knowlegde Representation

Abstract

The aim of the F3 Esprit III project is to define a methodology that integrates into a coherent whole a selection of adequate techniques, all aiming at improving requirements acquisition and validation. The contribution of the University of PARIS1 in this project is to define a tracing mechanism of the RE process in order to be able to explain the history of any component of the RE specification. This communication presents our product meta model called the Evolutionary Object Model (EOM) and corresponding tracing model which is able to keep track of the product evolution. This evolution is described with a decision-oriented modeling process approach.

1. INTRODUCTION

The research presented in this communication is conducted as part of the F3 European Esprit III project n°6612. The objective of this project is to define a methodology that integrates into a coherent whole a selection of adequate techniques, all aiming at improving requirements acquisition and validation. This methodology will be supported by a Requirement Engineering (RE) workbench, i.e. a working environment supporting these techniques, as well as general facilities for managing the RE process and reuse of earlier works.

The contribution of the University of PARIS1 in the F3 project is to define a tracing model for the RE process in order to be able to explain the history of any component or part of the RE specification. A RE methodology is used by engineers in order to produce a specification of the solution to develop. This specification is also called the *product*. The route travelled to reach it is called its *development process*. The tracing mechanism is based on the description of a product which is able to remember its development process history.

This has led to study the models (actually meta-models) dealing with the product and the process definitions.

The *product models,* such as found in [Olle88], define only the different components resulting from a process and don't provide the description of the process itself. In addition, they don't care about the successive versions of a product achieved during its development process. According to our objectives they don't allow to keep track of the product evolution.

Considering the development *process models,* they determine a way of expressing how to reach the final and satisfactory version of a product under development. In these models, three categories appear (figure 1) : activity-oriented models, product-oriented models and decision-oriented models.

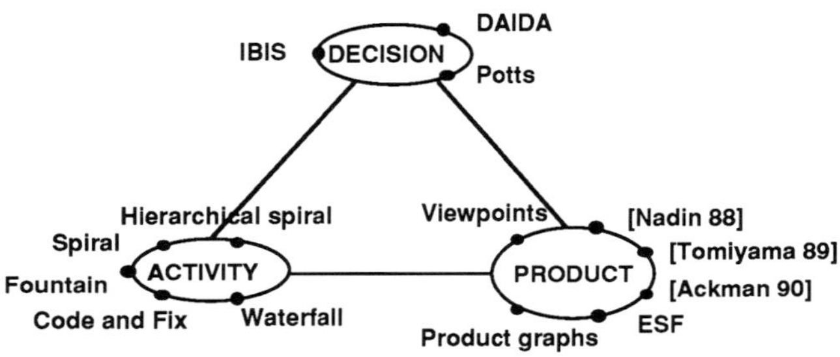

Figure 1 : Classes of Process Development meta-models

The activity-centered category includes well-known process models such as [Boehm88] [Lehman87] defining the development process by finding and executing a plan of actions leading to the solution without mentioning a particular connection to the resulting product.

The product-oriented process models such as [Tomiyama89] represent the development process through the evolution of the product. Their advantage is to put the product definition in the foreground and push the process definition in the background. But, the process is defined as an organized set of transformation activities which do not allow the capturing of the semantic attached to them.

The purpose of the more recent approach gathering process models such as [Potts89], [Jarke90] is to emphasize the decisional aspect of the process. The successive transformations of the product are consequences of decisions. Such models are semantically more powerful than the previous ones because they explain not only how the process proceeds but also why transformations happen. But they don't focus on the product definition as it is done in the previous category.

We have chosen to define a product meta model called the Evolutionary Object Model (EOM) which is able to keep track of the product evolution. This evolution is described in terms of a decision-oriented process model.

The EOM emphasizes a strong coupling between the product and the process. Finally, each transformation is viewed as an atomic step in the process and recorded into the product description.
This communication introduces the modeling evolution of product objects in the EOM and the underlying process model in section 2. The F3 trace model is detailed in section 3.

2. MODELING EVOLUTION OF PRODUCT OBJECTS

The Evolutionary Object Model is an object-oriented model of the product. Its characteristic is to regard the product as a network of evolutionary objects.
The history of each object is encapsulated in its memory. The underlying process model defines how the history of each object is told and recorded.
This section is composed of three sub-sections : the first one defines the different levels of abstraction in EO modeling, the second one gives an intuitive introduction to what may evolve in an object, the third one explains succintly how evolutions will be described.

2.1. Levels of abstraction in EO modeling

In EO modeling we have defined three levels of abstraction (figure 2) :
at level 1, a particular product is described ; at level 2, the product model of a given methodology is defined ; at level 3, the EOM is defined.

The purpose of EOM is to define the EO Type which is independent of any model. The justification of the EO Type is that the description of an EO evolution is the same for all the EOs of any product. This description explains what may evolve in an object (sub-section 2.2) and how the evolutions are obtained (sub-section 2.3).

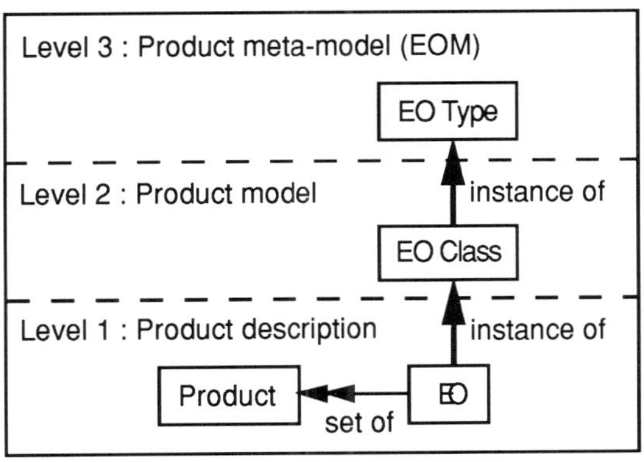

Figure 2 : Levels of abstraction in EO modeling

The instanciation of the EO Type is made for a given methodology in order to define its product model. So, this product model contains the model of evolution of any EO.
In fact, the image in the product of an EO, at a given point in time, is related to a particular instance of concept or constraint of the methodology involved. And the definition of *what may evolve* for each one can't be the same.
For instance, the definition of an entity-type *client* , in a E/R schema, may evolve by adding attributes or roles. But the definition of a role may not evolve in the same way because, instead of attributes, a role may only have cardinalities.
Consequently, the product model is defined by a collection of EO Classes. An EO Class is an instance of EO Type and is referring to a concept or constraint of the methodology for which this product model is elaborated.
Each EO Class encapsulates the shared and specific definition of the allowed evolutions of their instances (the EOs themselves).

For instance, the product model defined by instanciation of the EOM, for a methodology using the E/R model, may contain the following EO Classes : the EO Class *entity-type* referring the entity-type concept, the EO Class *attribute-type* referring the attribute-type concept, the EO Class *relationship-type* referring the relationship-type concept, the EO Class *role-type* referring the role-type concept, and so on.

The instanciation of a product model, describing an application domain knowlegde, defines a specific product. This product is then only composed of instances of EO Classes. For instance, in an E/R product describing the client concept in an ordering system, the entity-type *client* and the entity-type *product* will be two particular EOs obtained by instanciation of the same EO Class *entity-type*. Thus, the product can be viewed as composed of a set of objects. In fact, the detailed section 3 will show that the product is rather defined as a network of evolutionary objects. But before, it is necessary to introduce the evolutionary dimension of an object.

2.2. What may evolve in an Object

Considered alone, the evolution of an object is not significant because the information carried by the object is very poor. Fortunately, an object is always involved in a meaningful semantic structure. For instance, in an E/R product, an attribute *client_number* is involved in the semantic structure of the entity-type *client*. As a matter of fact, if the definition of this attribute changes (its domain for example) then the definition of the entity-type *client* changes too. In a same way we may also :
- attach attributes (*client_name* , *client_address*),
- define roles (*has_ordered*),
- define sub-types (*company* , *individual*), to the entity-type *client*..
Each of these components may contribuate to the evolution of the definition of the object entity-type *client* .

If we generalize now for any object the definition of what may evolve, we may determine three clearly distinct categories :
- the *inner part* defines the intrisic components (called properties) of an object. For instance, the properties *name* and *card_min* belong respectively to the inner definitions of entity-type and cardinality_constraint. As these properties may not be considered as evolutionary objects themselves, there are generally very few properties in the inner definition of an object. More often, there is only a property *name* ;
- the *spatial part* defines the semantic structure of an object. Such as mentioned at the beginning of this sub-section, this definition integrates the objects carrying a part of the domain knowlegde covered by it. For instance the attribute *client_number* is part of the spatial definition of the entity-type *client* and they are both evolutionary objects. In fact, in almost all methodologies, several models are used to get a complete product. Each one supplying with its partial view a part of the IS conceptual specification which is scatted in different schemas. For instance, the *client* concept may have in an E/R schema a view of its static structure and in a state-transition diagram a view of its dynamic structure. All the EOs involved in both structures are belonging to the spatial definition of the entity-type *client* ;
- the *temporal part* defines the object mutations. It explains what is the new form of the inner and spatial definitions of an evolutionary object after its description has changed.

The representation changes or mutations are of two types :
- the first one is the consequence of refinement decisions. For instance the decision to objectify a relationship *order* creates an entity-type *order* which is put down in the temporal definition of the relationship ;
- the second one is the consequence of a temporal process which defines development steps in the product building. For instance, if two steps namely conceptual and logical are defined in a product development, respectively supported by the E/R and relational models, the temporal definition of the entity-type *order* will contain the reference to the table *order* . We may observe with this example that the complete temporal definition of an object is recursively defined by the complete temporal definition of its object components. Because the temporal definition of the relationship *order* is completed by the temporal definition of the entity-type *order* which is pointing to its second and last mutation : table *order* . This observation can be applied to the whole object definition.

As mentioned in the previous sub-section, each EO Class has its own definition-type referring to a concept of a model. To describe it, a possible way is to draw a semantic network with three link types : a *property link* from a concept (lexical node) to a property (non lexical node), a *spatial link* between two concepts, a *temporal link* between two concepts.

For instance, let us consider a part of the semantic network describing the definition-type of the EO Class entity-type (figure 3). In this network, *entity-type_name, table_name, attribute_name* are properties and *entity-type, table , key constraint* are concepts.

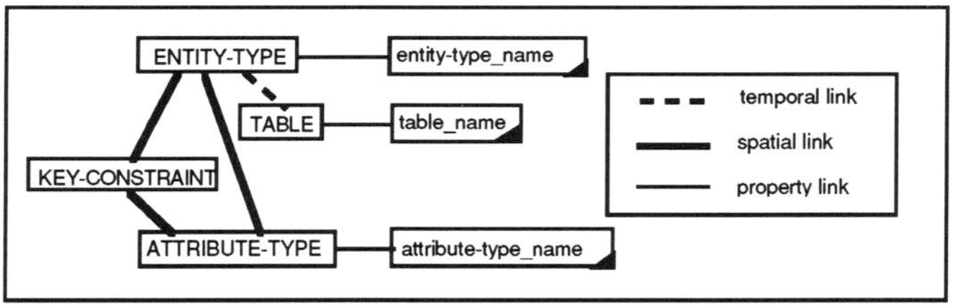

Figure 3 : Partial definition-type of EO Class entity-type

For instance, if we consider the example of figure 4, the entity-type *client,* has an inner definition described by property links, a spatial definition described by spatial links and a temporal definition described by temporal links.

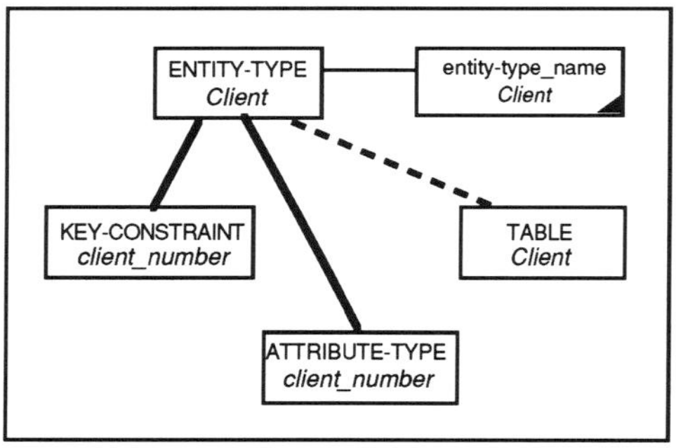

Figure 4 : Definition of the EO entity-type Client

The evolution of an EO is defined by the history of its three-dimentional definition which are the inner, the spatial and the temporal ones. The purpose of the next sub-section is to explain how this history is told.

2.3. How evolutions are performed

The history of the definition of an EO can be told and performed in many ways. As mentioned in sub-section 2.1, an object evolves when an action modifies a component of its definition. In order to capture the semantic of actions, we have chosen to describe this temporal process by a decisional approach.

A decisional approach allows to acquire the design choices made by a requirement engineer. We also describe explicitly the notion of situation in which the requirement engineer make his decision. A detailed example is provided in section 3.

The four basic concepts of our process model are shown in figure 5 :

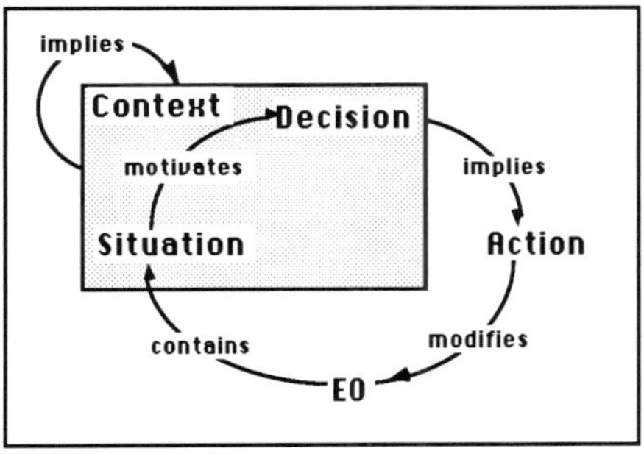

Figure 5: F3 Process model basic development loop

- *situation* to explain the decision context,
- *decision* to represent choices done by requirement engineer,
- *context* to improve the semantics attached to a decision. It is an aggregate of situation and decision,
- *action* to perform the object definition evolution.

The conclusion of this section is that the product is defined as a network of Evolutionary Objects which encapsulate their historical definition, according to three dimensions (inner, spatial and temporal), in terms of the mutational process model.

3. F3 TRACING MODEL

The tracing model proposed in the F3 Esprit Project is a product model deduced from the EO definition. The description proposed in figure 7, defines a common way to record the history of EO. We propose an unique EO generic class in order to describe a common recording structure and associated mecanisms. According to figure 2, this class is defined at level 2 as a generalization of all the EO Classes of the F3 methodology.

The F3 tracing model is sumarized in figure 7. It is composed of one concept, the EO Type, which allows an historical recording of EO definitions. As shown in figure 7 an EO has two parts :

- the first part tells the history of its definition (grey boxes). This explains what have been the successive definitions of objects (each successive definition is called a version) ;
- the second part describes the mutation process explaining the successive product definitions (dotted boxes). Each mutation describes how an object has evolved from one definition to another.

In other words, the second part describes the mutations, whereas the first one describes the results of these mutations.

The presentation of this model will be illustrated through an E/R approach. The schema, in figure 6, shows an E/R product composed of a set of 8 EOs. It will be the support of our example as starting point of a short scenario showing how the history of EOs definition is traced.

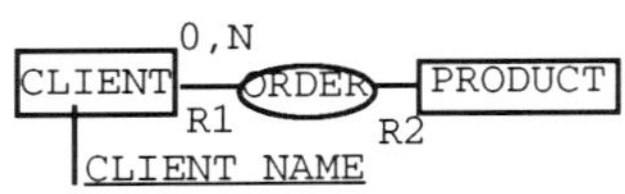


```
EO1 : entity_type client
EO2 : entity_type product
EO3 : role r1
EO4 : role r2
EO5 : relationship-type order
EO6 : cardinality_constraint (0,N)
EO7 : attribute_type client_name
EO8 : key constraint
```

Figure 6 : an example of E/R product.

The two parts of the EO Type are now detailed in turn.

3.1. Historical aspects of the EO type

According to what has been introduced in section 2, the definition of an object consists of viewing it through three perspectives : the inner, the spatial, the temporal perspectives.

The *inner definition* of an EO is composed of the properties allowing its characterization. The entity-type *client* (EO1) and the entity-type *product* (EO2) they have both a property *entity-type_name* which are respectively valued as *client* and *product* for EO1 and EO2.

The *cardinality_constraint* (EO6), on the *role r1* (EO3), is defined by a couple of values (0,N). Its inner definition includes two properties *card_min* and *card_max* with their respective values 0 and N.

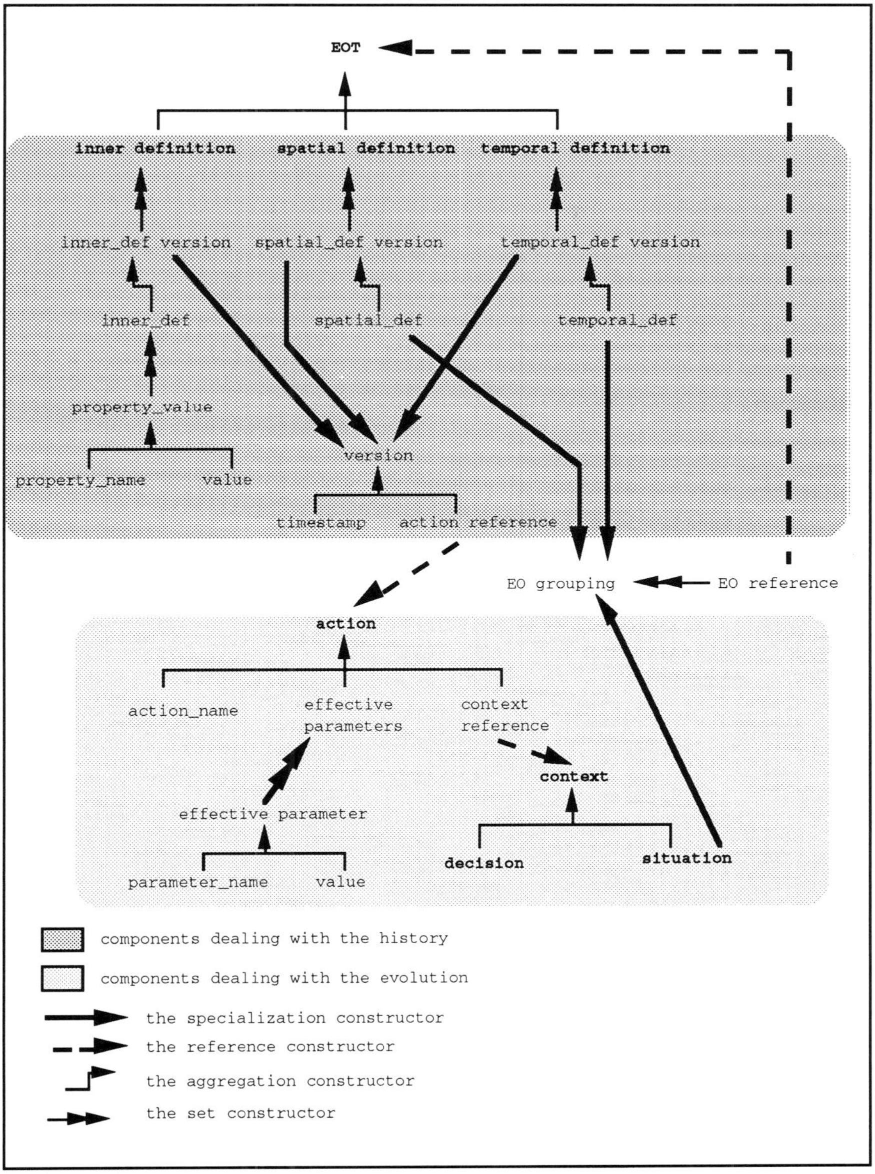

Figure 7 : F3 trace model

These aspects are represented in figure 7 by the *inner_def* component which is defined as a set of properties. Each *property* has to record the *property_name* and the *value* associated to it.

The *spatial definition* of an EO considers the set of EOs which are part of its environment. For instance, the *entity-type client* (EO1) includes, in its spatial definition, references to the *attribute-type client_name* (EO7), to its *key_constraint* (EO8) and to the *role r1* (EO3) with its *cardinality_constraint* (EO6).
Constraints have also a spatial definition. The *cardinality_constraint* (EO6) and the *key constraint* (EO8) have into their spatial definition respectively the { the *role r1* (EO3) } and { the *entity-type client* (EO1) and the *attribute-type client_name* (EO7)}.
This aspect is modeled in figure 7 by the *spatial_def* component. This component is regarded as an *EO grouping* (specialization link). Any EO grouping is defined as a set of *EO references*.

The *temporal definition* of an EO is used to express into which EOs of another model it has mutated.

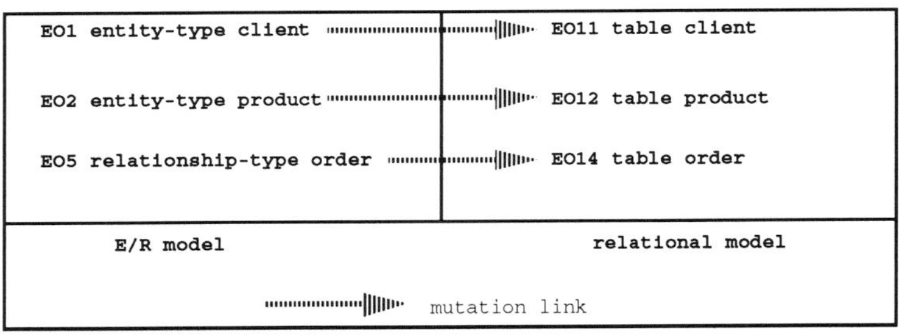

Figure 8 : Mutation examples.

For instance, the *entity-type client* (EO1) can be mutated into the *relational table client* (EO11) as shown in figure 8. In this case, the *relational table client* (EO11) is mentioned into the temporal definition of the *entity-type client* (EO1). Similarly, the *entity-type product* (EO2) and the *relationship-type order* (EO5) have in their temporal definition a reference to respectively the *relational tables product* (EO12) and *order* (EO14).

Recording it requires a structuration similar to the spatial definition. Thus, the *temporal_def* component in figure 7 is also a set of EO references (EO grouping).

These three definitions will change during the development process. Thus the EO has to keep track of the successive versions.

As an illustration, consider the EO *entity-type client* which has been named in a previous version *customer*. Thus, the inner_definition will include two versions at t1 and t11 as illustrated in figure 9.

Similarly the *cardinality constraint* (EO6) has been created with the values (0,N) but has been refined as shown in figure 9. Its inner definition has recorded the two versions defined at t7 and t18.

```
EO1 :
 inner definition : <t1, {entity-type_name = "customer"} >
                    <t11, {entity-type_name = "client"}  >

 spatial definition : <t1, {}                              >
                      <t4, { EO3 }                         >
                      <t9, { EO3, EO7 }                    >
                      <t10,{ EO3, EO7, EO8 }               >
```

```
EO6 :
 inner definition : <t7, {cardmin=0, cardmax=N}  >
                    <t18, {cardmin=1, cardmax=N} >

 spatial definition : <t7, { EO3 }               >
```

Figure 9 : The inner definition and spatial definition of EO1 and EO6.

The spatial definition of an EO can also change during the development process. For instance, the EO *entity-type client* has been created at time t1 without attribute, and then the *role r1* created at time t3 has been related to the entity-type at time t4. EO1 has been completed by a first attribute named *client_name* at time t9. Its *key constraint* has been added at time t10. The entity_type EO records in its spatial definition these four versions as presented in figure 9.
The *cardinality_constraint* has been created with its relation to the *role r1* at time t7. This implies that the spatial definition of the *cardinality constraint* (EO6) has to keep track of only one version at t7 (figure 9).

The temporal definition of an EO expresses how it has mutated. A mutation of an EO results of its inner and spatial definition transformations.
For instance, the designer has tranformed the *relationship-type order* (EO5) into the *relational attribute-type order* (EO13) at time t28 and then has decided it would be better to transform it as a *relational table order* (EO14) (time t29). Consequently the temporal definition of this EO is composed of three versions as shown in figure 10.

Figure 10 shows also that the *entity-types client* (EO1) and *product* (EO2) have been mutated into a relational table (resp. EO11 and EO12) respectively at time t26 and time t27. Thus, they have two temporal definition versions (figure 10).

```
EO1 :
  temporal definition :  <t1, {}           >
                         <t26, { EO11 } >

EO2 :
  temporal definition : <t2, {}           >
                        <t27, { EO12 }  >

EO5 :
  temporal definition : <t5, {}           >
                        <t28, { EO13 }  >
                        <t29, { EO14 }  >
```

Figure 10 : the temporal definition of EO1, EO2 and EO5

The temporal definition of an EO is used to regard mutations of objects from conceptual specification to implemented code. Whereas changing the inner and spatial definitions reflect an improvement of a specification.

As showned the three main components of the EO type definition are its *inner definition*, its *spatial definition* and its *temporal definition.*

They have the purpose to historize the successive versions of object definitions. The inner definition, the spatial definition and the temporal definition components are thus structured as a set of versions which are in turn defined respectively by the *inner_def version*, the *spatial_def version* and the *temporal_def version* components.
These three kinds of version are considered as specializations of a generic component called *version.* The component "Version" provides the generic information which characterises a version, whereas the inner_def version (resp. the spatial_def version and the temporal_def version) adds the specific information modeled by the component inner_def (respectively the spatial_def and the temporal_def component).

The relationship between the historical knowledge and the evolutionary knowledge is made through the component version. The generic information attached to any version is :
- the *timestamp* representing the date of the change,
- the *reference to the action* which causes the transformation of the change.
The *action* component explains how the evolution is performed.

Let us consider the EO1 definition shown in figure 11. Each version includes a reference to the action which explains it creation. For instance, the action a1 representing the creation of the entity-type customer done at t1 time implies that:
- the first inner_definition is composed of the value "customer" of the entity-type name property ;
- the first version of the spatial and the temporal definitions is empty.

Then, renaming the entity-type client done by action a11 at t11 time is referred into its second version. Relying the attribute *client_name* (EO7) to the *entity-type customer* (EO1) is the purpose of the action a9 which causes the modification of the spatial definition of EO1 and EO7. The a10 (creation of the key_constraint) and a4 (linking the *role r1* to the *entity-type customer)* actions have as consequences to relate to the entity-type client respectively the *key-constraint* (EO8) and the *role r1* (EO3). But, they also imply to add the reference to EO1 into the spatial definition of respectively the *key-constraint* (EO8) and the *role r1* (EO3). The mutation of the *entity-type client* (EO1) into the *relational table client* (EO11) is realized by the action a26 which is mentioned into the last temporal version of EO1.

```
EO1 :
 inner definition : <t1, {entity-type_name = "customer"},a1   >
                    <t11, {entity-type_name = "client"}, a11 >

 spatial definition : <t1, {}, a1                             >
                      <t4, { EO3 }, a4                        >
                      <t9, { EO3, EO7 }  ,a9                  >
                      <t10, { EO3, EO7, EO8 } , a10           >


 temporal definition : <t1, {} , a1                           >
                       <t26, { EO11 } , a26                   >
```

Figure 11 : The EO1 definition.

In order to explain more completely the action, we have added components which are introduced and illustrated in the next section.

3.2. The evolutionary components of the EO Type definition

In order to have a more powerful explanation of the development process encapsulated into the product objects, we introduce the *context* component additionally to the *action* component.

According to our process modeling approach introduced in section 2.3, an action results of a *decision* on a *situation*.
We call *context* the couple <*situation, decision*> which explains when and why an action has been performed.

The situation allows to explain the part of the product used by the analyst to take a particular decision. A decision expresses the RE choice made by the analyst during the RE process.

For instance, figure 12 shows that the analyst has defined the *role r1* played by the *entity-type client* without cardinality_constraint and at time t7. In this case *entity-type client* is the situation considered by the analyst to take the *define_cardinality* decision. The consequence of this decision is a7 action creating the *cardinality_constraint* (EO6) linked to the *role r1* (EO3). The consequences (figure 13) of the action a7 is to create a new object E06 but also to include it into the spatial definition of the *role r1* (EO3) and into the *entity_type customer* (EO1) (see figure 12).

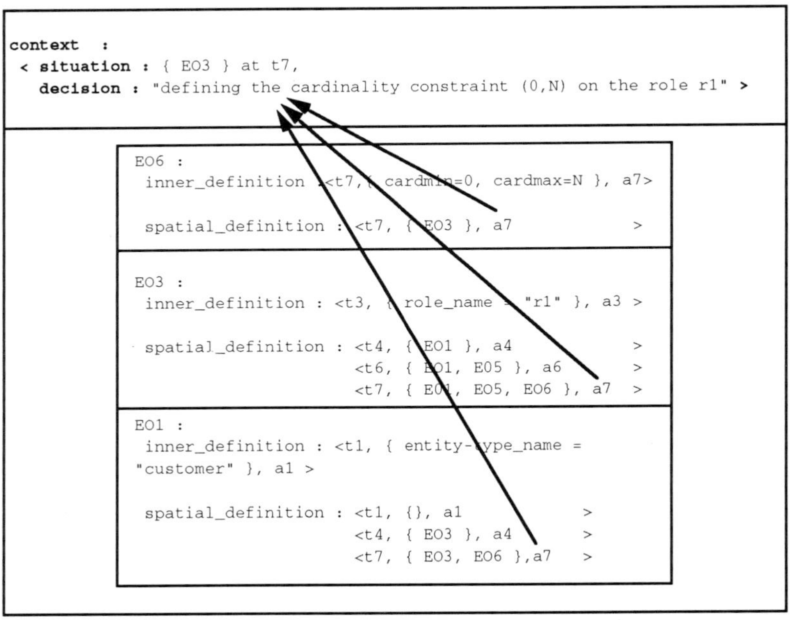

Figure 12 : Consequences of a context to the definition of EOs.

The context in figure 7 is structured as an aggregate of the situation and the decision. The situation is a set of EO references at a particular time on which the analyst takes a decision. The action is regarded as a call of procedure which modifies the product objects. The informations attached to an action are its *name*, its *effective parameters* used in the procedure call, and the *reference to the context* which has triggered it. An effective parameter is represented by the value associated to a parameter defined by its name.

Let us conclude this section by an example of entity-type history.

3.3. Example of an entity-type evolution

The evolution of the *entity-type customer* showned in figure 13 is expressed in terms of decisions taken by the analyst and leading to the modification of either its inner, or spatial or temporal definitions.
For instance, the decision "the entity-type customer plays the role r1" at t4 is a decision which modifies the spatial definition of the entity-type customer.
But, the decision "creation of a role r1" at t3 is encapsulated into the role r1 and is also part of the evolution of the entity-type as the role r1 belongs to spatial definition of the entity-type.

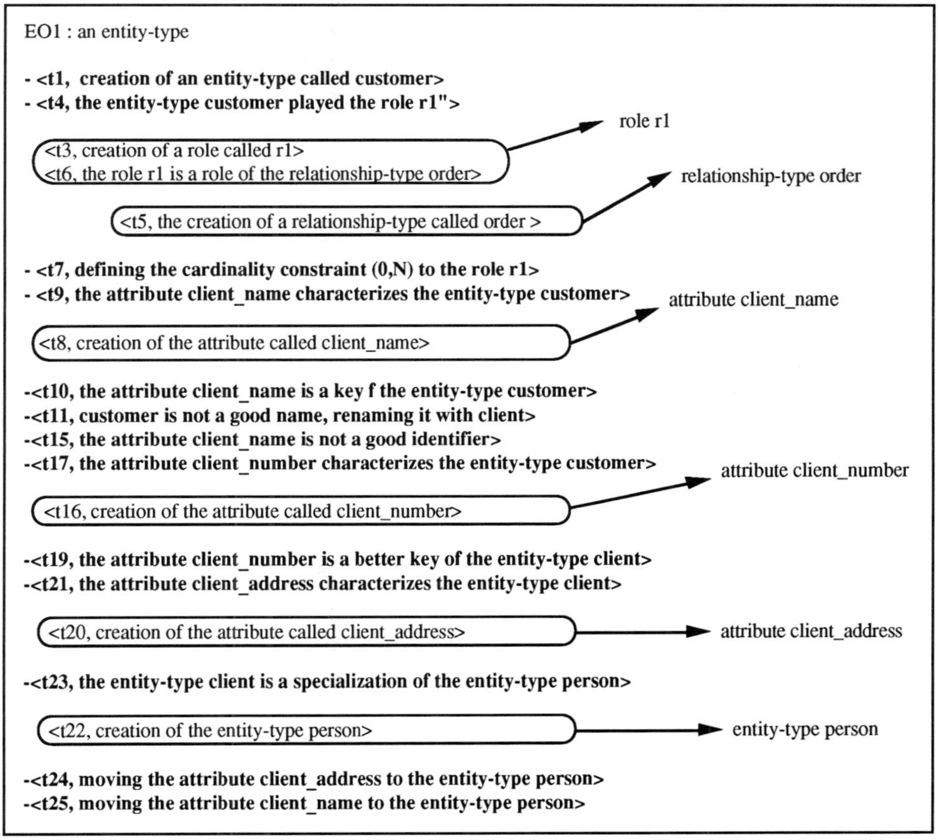

Figure 13 : The evolution of the entity-type customer.

In the same way, the creation of a relationship-type order at t5 is a part of the evolution of the relationship-type but also appears in the evolution of the role r1 because the relationship-type is included into the spatial definition of the role r1. Finally, for the same reason it belongs to the customer history.

At t1, the entity-type has been created, and at t4, its spatial definition is extended to include the role r1.
The role r1 has been created at time t3 and has included at t4 the entity-type customer into its spatial definition. At t6 the relationship-type order has been added to its spatial definition.
The relationship-type in turn has in its history the decision of its creation at t5.

At t7, a cardinality constraint has been defined simultaneously to creation and inclusion in the spatial definition of the entity-type customer and role r1.
At t9, the attribute client-name is related to the entity-type.
At t10, this attribute is defined as key of the entity-type. This results in the creation of a key constraint and extension of the spatial definition of the entity-type as well as the one of the attribute.

At t11, the entity-type has been renamed *client*. This is recorded in its inner definition.
Decisions at t15, t17 and t19 represent refinement decisions leading to a more detailed entity-type description. As consequences the key-constraint is dropped, and *client_number* is defined as a key of *client* .
The decision taken at time t21 introduces the attribute *client_address* into the entity-type client.
Finally, the decisions taken at t23, t24 and t25 show that the analyst has considered that the attributes *client_name* and *client_address* are properties which characterize a person and can be inherited by the *client* entity-type.

4. CONCLUSION

The work presented in this communication is part of the F3 Esprit III project n°6612 aiming at improving requirements acquisition and validation. Our contribution is to define a tracing model for the RE process in order to be able to explain the history of any component of the RE specification. A RE methodology is used by engineers in order to produce, in a *development process* , a specification (or *product*) of the solution to develop. The tracing mechanism is based on the description of a product which is able to remember its development process history.

Section 2 has introduced the two main ideas of the Evolutionary Object Model which are : the definition of the product object and its encapsulated history. This object-oriented model describes a product meta model which is independent from any methodology.

Its characteristic is to regard the product as a network of evolutionary objects. The history of each object is encapsulated in its memory and integrates the one of its environment. The underlying decision-oriented process model defines how the history of each object is told and recorded.

The underlying tracing model is detailed in section 3. It allows an historical recording of EO definition for the F3 methodology. The F3 tracing model is composed of one concept, the EO Type which has two parts : the first one describes the mutations, the second one describes the results of these mutations. A mutation is described as a RE decision applied by an action. Finally, the situation on which a decision has been taken is also recorded.

REFERENCES

[Akman90] : Akman V., ten Hagen P.J.W., Tomiyama T.; *A fundamental and theoretical Framework for an intelligent CAD System*; Computer Aided Development, Vol 22, n° 6, 1990.
[Ben-Arieh88] : Ben-Arieh D.; *Product and process Development in Intelligent CAD Workstations;* Intelligent CAD Systems II, Springer Verlag, 1988.
[Benington56] : Benington H.D.; *Production of Large Computer Programs;* Proc. Int Conf Software Engineering, n° 9, IEEE CS, 1987
[Boehm88] : Boehm B.W.; *A spiral model of software development and enhancement;* Computer Vol 21, 1988.
[Dowson87] : Dowson M.; *Iteration in the Software Process, Review of the 3rd International Software Process Workshop;* Proc. 9th Int Conf Software Engineering, p 36, 1987.
[Fillmore68] : Fillmore C.J., *The CASE for CASE,* in Universals in linguistics theory ; Holt, Rinehart and Winston, Inc., Bach E./Harms R.T. (pub), 1968.
[Finkelstein90] : Finkelstein A., Kramer J., Goedicke M.; *ViewPoint Oriented Software Development;* Proc. Conf "Le Génie Logiciel et ses Applications", Toulouse, p 337-351, 1990.
[Henderson-Sellers90] : Henderson-Sellers B., Edwards J.M.; *The Object-oriented Systems Life-Cycle;* Comm. ACM, 09/1990.
[Humphrey89] : Humphrey W.S., Kellner M.I.; *Software Process Modelling: Principles of Entity Process Models;* Proc. 11th Int. Conf. Software Engineering, 1989.
[Iivari90] : Iivari J.; *Hierarchical spiral model for information system and software development. Part 1: theoritical background;* Information and software technology, Vol 32, n° 6, 1990. and *Hierarchical spiral model for information system and software development. Part 2: development process;* Information and software technology, Vol 32, n° 7, 1990.
[Jähninchen85] : Jähninchen; *Towards an alternative model for software development;* Proc. 2nd Software Process Workshop, p 66, 1985.
[Jarke90] : Jarke M., Jeusfeld M., Rose T.; *A Software Process Data Model for Knowledge Engineering in Information Systems;* Information Systems Vol 15, n° 1, 1990.
[Lehman84] : Lehman M. M.; *A Further Model of Coherent Programming Processes;* Proceedings of 1st International Software Process Workshop, IEEE, p 27; 1984.
[Lehman87] : Lehman M. M.; *Process Models, Process Programs, Programming Support;* Proc. 9th International Conference on Software Engineering, pp 14-16, 1987.
[McCracken82] : McCracken D.D. , Jackson M.A.; *Life-Cycle Concept Considered Harmful;* Software Engineering Notes, ACM, p 29, 04/1982
[Nadin88] : Nadin M., Novak M.; *Interactive Diagrams for Development Genetics, Impleting Intelligent Processus;* Intelligent CAD Systems II, Springer Verlag, 1988.
[Olle88] : William Olle T., Hagelstein J., Macdonald I.G., Rolland C., Sol H.G., Van Assche F.J.M., Verrijn-Stuart A.A.; *Information Systems Methodologies,* Addison-Wesley Pub., 1988.

[Osterweil87] : Osterweil L.; *Software Processes are software too;* Int. Conference on Software Engineering, pp 2-13, 1987.

[Potts88] : Potts C., Bruns G.; *Recording the Reasons for Development Decisions;* Proceed. 10th Int. Conf. on Software Engineering, 1988.

[Potts89] : Potts C.; *A Generic Model for Representing Development Methods;* Proceed. 11th International Conference on Software Engineering, 1989.

[Rolland87] : Rolland C., Foucault O., Benci G., *Conception des systèmes d'information : la méthode REMORA,* in Conceptual modelling, Database and CASE, an integrated view of information systems development., Eyrolles (pub), 1987.

[Rolland91] : Rolland C., Proix C., *Natural language approach to Conceptual Modelling,* in Conceptual modelling, Database and CASE, an integrated view of information systems development., Ellis Horwood (pub), 1991.

[Royce70] : Royce W.W.; *Managing the development of large Software Systems;* Proc. IEEE WESCON 08/1970.

[Rueher88] : Rueher M., Ladret D., Legeard B., *Capturing Software Process through the generated Objects;* Proc. 4th Software Process Workshop; 1988.

[Takala88] : Takala T.; *Development Transactions and Retrospective Planning, Tools for Conceptual Development;* Intelligent CAD Systems II, Springer Verlag, 1988.

[Tomiyama89] : Tomiyama T., Kiriyama T., Takeda H., Xue D., Yoshikaya H.; *Metamodel: A Key to Intelligent CAD Systems;* Research in Engineering Development Vol 1, pp 19-34, 1989.

[Williams88] : Williams L.G.; *Software Process Modelling: A Behavioral Approach;* Proceed. 10th International Conference on Software Engineering, 1988.

3.

REUSE I

Information System Development Process (A-30)
N. Prakash, C. Rolland and B. Pernici (Editors)
Elsevier Science Publishers B.V. (North–Holland)

© 1993 IFIP. All rights reserved.

Mechanisms of Standardized Reusability of Objects (MCO methodology)

X. Castellani

Laboratoire CEDRIC IIE (CNAM), 18 allée Jean Rostand, 91025 Evry, France
Tel (16 1) 60 77 97 40 - Fax (16 1) 60 77 96 99 - Email: castellani@viie.iie.cnam.fr

Abstract

This paper describes mechanisms of standardized reusability of object characteristics. These mechanisms can be used during the integration of new object types or of new instances in an object system. These mechanisms use object reusability gauges.

Seven results of object reusability are presented and show how objects of an object system can be built in a standardized manner using these gauges. These mechanisms allow an incremental and automatizable design of object reusability.

These mechanisms belong to MCO methodology. They are presented by using the concepts and the vocabulary of this object-oriented analysis and design methodology. But these mechanisms are general; they can be used with concepts of other object-oriented analysis and design methods, of object-oriented languages and of data base management systems.

Keyword Codes: H.1.0; D.2.10.
Keywords: Models and Principles, General; Software Engineering, Design.

1. INTRODUCTION

According to B. Meyer [1], *reusability is the ability of software products to be reused, in whole or in part, for new applications.* Reusability is a quality factor of object-oriented information systems, that we call called object systems.

Concepts of the object approach facilitate the reusability in an object system: the inheritance, the reusability by declaration, the masking, the renaming, the polymorphism, ... But it is difficult to define in which cases components may be reused. So it is necessary to precise their conditions of use so that the object systems will be designed with objects built using concepts of reusability in the same cases, that is to say standardized. In practise, some reuse components whereas, in the same conditions, others consider that it is not necessary to reuse these components. What's more, some create objects with two or three variables and two or three methods whereas others create objects only with an important number of variables and methods. So the designs are heterogeneous.

Object-oriented analysis and design methods do not propose recommendations to define the objects and to use the concepts of the reusability.

Several works on the reusability relate to the concepts and the methods which allow the reusability and not to the conditions of use of these concepts and of these methods [2] [3]. Other works, for example the OTGen project ("Object Transformgen") by B. Staudt Lerner and N. Habermann [4], relate to the reorganisation of data bases by helping the administrators so that they understand the effects of their modifications on some classes and that the DBMS proposes transformations to realize particularly in the sub-classes. Other works, such as the Software Information Base (SIB), developed within the ESPRIT project ITHACA [5] and the SIRIUS project [6], also propose organisations of libraries but with user-friendly systems of object research.

To avoid a plurality of solutions, and so design heterogeneousness of an object system, MCO methodology proposes normalized designs of which objects and their characteristics are calibrated by using object reusability gauges. This paper shows how these gauges are defined using metrics to measure the object characteristics and how these gauges are used with the proposed reusability mechanisms; the choice between different solutions of object reusability is thus rationalized and optimized.

Seven results of the object type reusability may be obtained when creating object types or instances, using reusability mechanisms according to the sizes of object reusability gauges.

These gauges may be defined and these mechanisms may be used on specifications or on the code of the object characteristics. These gauges may be measured with any metric; but it is necessary to use the same metric to measure the gauges and the object characteristics.

The idea of using metrics to normalize the object reusability has been proposed by several object-oriented specialists. We can mention B. Cox [7], R. Chidamber and F. Kemerer [8], and M. Griss who has indicated in [2] that metrics would be used in the "Corporate Engineering Software Reuse HP' program". But, to our knowledge, there is no rational utilisation of metrics to normalize objects, that is what propose the mechanisms of object reusability presented in this paper.

Only the principal concepts of the MCO model which allows to understand the mechanisms of reusability are defined in Section 2 because these mechanisms are usable with ever object-oriented analysis and design method, or object-oriented DBMS or object-oriented language. The principal concepts of the reusability are defined in Section 3. The standardized reusability of the objects is presented in Section 4. An example of results of object type reusability is presented in Section 5. Indications on the use and on the implementation of the algorithms of standardized reusability of objects are given in Section 6. The use of the mechanisms of reusability during the integration of new instances is presented in Section 7.

- Brief presentation of MCO

MCO is a systemic methodology of software engineering for analysis and design of object systems and object specifications.

MCO proposes a model to represent the object systems, model presented and whose basic concepts are recalled in Sections 2 and 3 and object systems development processes which are not presented in this paper. MCO is a parameterizable methodology which allows the definition of customizable methods.

The aim of this paper is not to present MCO because the mechanisms of reusability may be used with the models of other methods. Only the principal concepts of MCO useful to present the mechanisms of reusability are defined in Sections 2 and 3. The reader interested by more informations on MCO may in particular report him to [9] and [10].

2. REMINDER OF THE PRINCIPAL CONCEPTS OF THE MCO MODEL (except the concepts of reusability which are presented in Section 3)

These concepts concern both the conceptual level and the organizational level.

- ***Service.*** A service is a required and/or provided treatment.

Examples: Provide statistics monthly. Create a customer. Modify the shape of a window. Display a scrolling menu.

The services are implemented with procedures (with methods), or with rules of expert systems.

- ***Object.*** An object is a concrete or abstract entity having acquaintances in a certain state at a given time, and that provides or requires some services.

- ***Acquaintance.*** An acquaintance of an object is a characteristic which delivers a value.

The concept of acquaintance in MCO is taken with its general meaning by considering the object's point of view: a man knows his Name, his Address, his Age, ..., his Wife, his Children, his House, his Car.

The *internal acquaintances* of an object are useful locally to define the instances of this object, i.e. without the need of other objects. Examples: for a customer his code, his turnover.

The *external acquaintances* of an object OB-a are the objects, distinct or not from OB-a, whose OB-a instances know instances. Examples: for a customer: the products he bought, the bills he has not paid. The external acquaintances are implemented with references with the object-oriented languages.

- ***Object characteristics, object types, instances, classes***

The object characteristics are their acquaintances and their services.

An object type is defined by the types of its characteristics: the types of its acquaintances and its services. Example: customer type.

An instance of an object type is a value of the type of this object type.

A class is defined by an object type and by the set of the instances which are of the type of this object type.

An abstract object is an object for which no instance, other than instances of its sub-types, can be create. Example: the object Vehicle is abstract if the instances of vehicle are only the instances of its sub-types Car, Lorry, etc.

- ***Semantic objects, technical objects, construction objects***

Semantic objects are objects which have a meaning for the end-users. Examples: Customer, Employee, Order, Invoice.

The technical objects are the non semantic objects which are necessary so that the semantic objects may be usable. Examples: the sets, the sorted lists, the windows with vertical palettes on the left.

The construction objects are objects only defined to put into common factor characteristics of several objects. Example: the object Identification defined with the common characteristics of the objects Employee and Customer. The construction objects cannot be instantiated; so they are abstract objects. The objects of construction are inherited by the objects which reuse their characteristics.

3. MAIN CONCEPTS OF OBJECT REUSABILITY

The main concepts of object reusability are the inheritance and the reusability of object characteristics by declaration. These concepts are used by languages. A reminder of their definitions is given below.

3.1. Inheritance

The inheritance of an object is the set of the object's characteristics which can be reused to define objects.

An object type OB-b inherits from an object type OB-a if characteristics of OB-a contribute to define instances of OB-b.

- Specialization inheritances, construction inheritances

The specialization inheritances are inheritances which represent semantic links of specialization "Is a".

An object type OB-b inherits by specialization of an object type OB-a if the set of the characteristics de OB-a is included in the set of the characteristics of OB-b and if the instances of OB-b are elements of the set of the instances of OB-a.

This definition is conform with the definition of the specialization-generalization links of J. J. M. Smith and D. C. P. Smith [11].

An object type OB-b which inherits from an object OB-a with an inheritance of specialization is a sub-type of OB-a.

The construction inheritances are inheritances which have no semantics, and are such that the instances of an object type which inherits from an other object type do not belong to the set of the instances of the inherited object type.

The construction inheritances are defined only with the aim of reusing characteristics of objects in other objects. The construction inheritances do not concern the end-users. They are called "implementation inheritances" by C. Delobel, C. Lecluse and P. Richard [12].

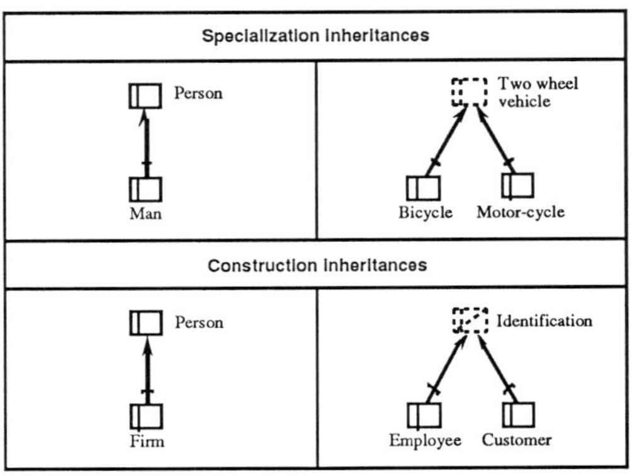

Figure 1: Examples of specialization inheritances and construction inheritances

MCO allows to define simple and multiple inheritances.

3.2. Reusability of object characteristics by declaration

The reusability of object characteristics by declaration allows the reuse of characteristics of objects (the types of the acquaintances, the services), considered one by one, directly, independently from inheritances.

The reusability by declaration is used with languages as Ada, Pascal, and so on.

4. THE STANDARDIZED REUSABILITY OF OBJECTS

4.1. General presentation of the seven results of the object reusability

Taking into account the concepts of reusability that can be used, the seven results of reusability presented below during the creation of an object type can be obtained. The conditions in which these results are obtained, will be explained in Section 4.3.

THE SEVEN RESULTS OF REUSABILITY DURING THE CREATION OF AN OBJECT TYPE OB-b

1 - OB-b is of the type of an existing object type: so it is identical to this existing object type.

2 - OB-b is merged with an existing object type.

3 - OB-b inherits from one or several existing object types.
4 - One or several existing object types inherit from OB-b.

5 - Creation of abstract objects of which OB-b and other objects inherit.

6 - Characteristics of OB-b are of the types of characteristics of existing object types.
7 - Characteristics of existing object types are of the types of characteristics of OB-b.

4.2. The object reusability gauges

These gauges fix the minimum of common characteristics of two objects types and the maximum of particular characteristics to study the reusability of their characteristics.

Two object reusability gauges are used: the first is used for the merges and the simple inheritances, the second is used for the multiple inheritances. We do not present the second gauge because we do not explain the creation of multiple inheritances for reasons of concision.

These gauges suppose that metrics allowing the measurement of the characteristics of the object types are defined. These metrics are presented after the first object reusability gauge.

- The first object reusability gauge

The first object reusability gauge which is used to define the merges of objects types and the simple inheritances, fixes:

. the weight of the minimum of common characteristics of two objects (WeightMinCCOB) in order that two objects may be merged or in order that one may inherit from the other;
. and the weight of the maximum of particular characteristics of an object OB-b (WeightMaxPCOB) with regard to an other object OB-a in order that it may be merged with this other object OB-a or in order that this other object may inherit from it.

The particular characteristics are masked in the objects which inherit from it but they are deducted of the measures of these objects when they are considered to be reused by other objects.

The common conceptual characteristics of two objects are:
. the acquaintances which are of the same type,
. and the services which provide the same processing: they are the services which have the same signature and of which the specifications are syntactically identical or the services not defined with syntactically identical specifications but for which an analyst or a tool certifies that they ensure the same processing.

The common implementation characteristics of two objects are:
. the attributes which are of the same type,
. and the procedures, the functions or the methods which provide the same processing: they are the procedures, the functions or the methods which have the same signature and of which the codes are syntactically identical or the procedures, the functions or the methods not defined with syntactically identical codes but for which an analyst or a tool certifies that they ensure the same processing.

The particular (conceptual or implementation) characteristics to an object OB-b compared with an object OB-a are the characteristics of OB-b which are not common to OB-b and OB-a.

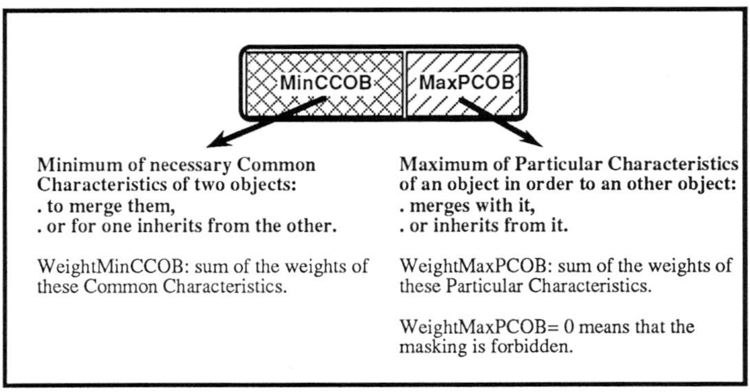

Figure 2: First object reusability gauge: merge and simple inheritance gauge

This object reusability gauge is difficult to define.

If the reusability is studied on conceptual specifications defined with an object-oriented conceptual model, and if the objects are defined with a number of characteristics between 5 and 50, it is possible to consider for example that:

. WeightMinCCOB may be at less between 5 and 15 characteristics not weighted: for example 10,
. and WeightMaxPCOB may be at most between 1 and 8 characteristics not weighted: for example 5.

If the reusability is studied on an implementation with a programming language, it is also possible to consider the same values of WeightMinCCOB and WeightMaxPCOB. But it is better not to only count the number of characteristics, but to measure them with the metrics above-mentioned. This is obligatory for the procedures (the functions, the methods).

Generally, the average size of a non object program written in C, Pascal, Cobol, ..., is comprised between 800 and 3000 lines; some programs even pass beyond 5000 lines. With these languages, the sequences of statements which are stored in libraries to be (re)used in several programs with the statements "Include" in C or Pascal, "Copy" in Cobol, ..., have generally minimal sizes comprise between 30 and 100 lines according to the programming recommendations: "it is forbidden to store too little sequences of statements in a library". These minimal sizes (30 and 100), are possible values of WeightMinCCOB. With a non object-oriented programming language, the masking being not usable, WeightMaxPCOB is null by default.

The programs written with object-oriented programming languages: C++, Eiffel, Smalltalk, ..., are smaller than non object-oriented programs because they ensure a service of an object. The extreme case is represented by the Smalltalk methods which are associated to variables and which allocate or read their values : these methods have only one line.

The values of WeightMinCCOB and of WeightMaxPCOB depend of the object-oriented language used and of the programming recommendations. So, with an object-oriented language, it is for example possible to consider that :
. WeightMinCCOB may be at less between 100 et 500: for example 200,
. et WeightMaxPCOB may be at most between 30 et 100: for example 50, value not null which supposes that the masking is used.

The object reusability gauge allows the comparison of objects so as to know if they are *similar* by measuring their common characteristics and their differences, that is to say their particular characteristics. This gauge is so used to define a very simple "distance" between the objects which is an indication of likeness, and so of unlikeness, of the objects in terms of clustering analysis. We have not adopted the solution which consists in measuring the likeness between objects with percentages of common characteristics and percentages of particular characteristics because this approach does not allow the comparison of objects to a reference (a gauge).

- Metrics of measurement of object characteristics

Numerous software experts have proposed metrics to measure software components. Some of them are mentioned by N. E. Fenton [13]. He indicates that the most used measure of source code program length is the number of lines of code. He considers that without a careful definition of a line of code, there will be many ways in which this measure may be calculated, i.e. it is ambiguous, and he proposes the following definition:

"A line of code is any line of program text that is not a comment or blank line, regardless of the number of statements or fragments of statements on the line. This specifically includes all lines containing program headers, declarations and practicable and non-practicable statements."

Other authors prefer the statements to measure the code of the programs. This is in particular the case of B.W. Boehm in the COCOMO method (COst COnstructive MOdel) [14], in which he recommends to measure the code of the programs with the number of the significant statements.

Software engineering specialists have defined other metrics than the sizes of the programs to measure the quality of the software. Among the most used:

. the metrics to measure numbers of operators and numbers of operands, the whole number of operators and the whole number of operands of a program; mention the metrics of M. H. Halstead [15] which are the number of distinct operators, the number of distinct operands, the whole number of operators and the whole number of operands of a program;

. the metrics to measure program control graphs (graphs which are graphic representations of the logical structures of the programs, every node represents a block of sequential statements, every arrow represents a connection between two blocks); mention the metrics of of T. J. Mac Cabe [16]: the cyclomatic number which is the number of independent cycles of an allied control graph of a program, the cocyclomatic number which is the number of elementary statements, the control density which is the average number of decisions by node, the maximal number of levels which is the maximum number of interleavings of structures;

. and the metrics to measure program call graphs (graphs which are graphic representations of the global architectures of the programs, every node represents a module, every arrow represents a call between two modules); the hierarchical complexity which is the average number of modules by level (number of modules divided by the number of levels), the structural complexity which is the average number of calls of a module (number of calls between modules divided by the number of modules).

Specific metrics of the object oriented approach exist. R. Chidamber and F. Kemere propose six metrics in [8]: weighted methods per class, depth of inheritance tree, number of children, coupling between objects, response for a class and lack of cohesion in methods.

- Which metrics will be used for the measurement of common characteristics of two objects types and of their particular characteristics?

The metrics which are easier to use to study the reusability of the objects are those which allow the measurement of the sizes of their characteristics. Examples of such metrics are presented below. But the mechanisms of reusability can be used with any metrics.

The mechanisms of reusability are usable on the conceptual representations and on the implementation representations of the object systems. Two metrics types are generally required because the conceptual characteristics and the implementation characteristics of the objects are not defined with the same concepts and are not specified with the same formalisms.

- *Examples of metrics to measure the conceptual object characteristics*

- *Metrics to measure the sizes of the acquaintances*

If at the conceptual level, only the names of the acquaintances are declared, the acquaintances can only be measured with counting them.

If, on the other hand, the acquaintances are defined, that is to say if their types and their sizes are defined, then the metrics below may be used:

. *size of an atomic acquaintance:*

. *internal* :. *single-valued:* . of boolean type, integer or real = number of digits,
. of string type, text or date = number of characters,
. of sound type or image = number of kilobytes which are necessary to store it;
. *multivalued* = size of every one of its elements measured as it is above-mentioned multiplied by its average repetition degree;
. *external* :. *single-valued* = number of digits of the maximal number of instances of an objet type (of a class) of the object system, because an external single-valued acquaintance refers an instance of an object type;
. *multivalued* = size of every one of its elements measured as it is above-mentioned multiplied par its average cardinality;
. *size of a composed acquaintance:*
. *single-valued acquaintance* = sum of the sizes of the composed acquaintances and of the atomic acquaintances which compose it;
. *multivalued acquaintance* = sum of the sizes of the composed acquaintances and of the atomic acquaintances which compose it, multiplied by its average repetition degree.

- *Metrics to measure the sizes of the services*
The conceptual specifications of the services may be:
. informal specifications defined with a natural language;
. formal specifications defined with languages as VDM (Vienna Development Method) [17] [18] [19], and Z [20] [21] [22] ; these languages are not object to day in particular because they do not allow to represent the inheritances ; object versions of these languages, VDM++ and Object Z, are studied;
. or algorithmic specifications defined with an extended algorithmic language ; today, with MCO, the conceptual specifications of the services defined with the LCO language, are algorithmic and object ; they are structured and they are defined with a natural language and/or with algorithmic and object extended statements presented in [10].

Formal specifications may be defined mapping specifications LCO to validate them. R. Laleau and P. Facon propose rules to represent semantic concepts with VDM [23]. These rules are usable to define concepts of the conceptual model of MCO with formal specifications VDM.

It seems impossible to measure informal specifications defined with a natural language; in this case it is only possible to count the number of services.

We consider that a simple and usable metric to study the reusability of the services of the objects *specified with a formal language or with an algorithmic language is their size measured with the number of lines or with the number of statements of their specifications.*

- <u>Examples of metrics usable to measure the implementation characteristics of the objects</u>

The size of an atomic attribute (a variable, a reference) may be defined as the size of an atomic acquaintance (cf. above-mentioned).

The size of a composed attribute (a variable, a reference) may be defined as the size of a composed acquaintance (cf. above-mentioned).

The size of a procedure (of a function, of a method) of an object is measured with the number of the lines or the number of statements of its code.

- The weight of reusability of a characteristic *(conceptual or of implementation) of an object is equal to its measure possibly weighted with a coefficient which represents its importance in reuse.* The degrees of these importances must be taken in a scale of values.

- The weight of reusability of a set of characteristics *is the sum of the weights of reusability of these characteristics.*

The inherited characteristics by an object are to consider in the set of characteristics to take into account for the reusability of this object because they define the object and so are to carry when the object is reused.

The most simple metric to measure any characteristics of the objects consists in counting the number of their characteristics: the number of their atomic acquaintances (or attributes) added with the number of their services (or of their procedures, functions or methods), without weighted them. This is equivalent to consider that the size of each characteristic is equal to 1.

This unrefined metric is usable in particular to measure the conceptual object characteristics on which non formal specifications, very difficult to measure, had been defined.

4.3. Synthetical presentation of the mechanisms of object reusability

The mechanisms of standardized reusability of objects optimize the reusability *of their characteristics with the following criteria:*

. a characteristic used by several objects must be defined in only one of these objects,

. the reusability must be done in priority with groups of characteristics (with re-using objects) if the characteristics satisfy the reusability gauges constraints, otherwise with performing an individual reusability by declaration of the characteristics,

. and the number of objects must be minimized.

The conditions to obtain the seven results of object reusability presented in Section 4.1 are specified in the decision table represented in Figure 3.

The existing object which has the weight of common characteristics the most important with a new object to create is researched. This weight may be superior or equal to the minimum fixed by the first reusability gauge so as to be able to carry out a merge or simple inheritance (including the creation of an abstract object from which the two objects inherit).

The weight of particular characteristics of the new object or of the existing object which has the weight of common characteristics the more important with the new object, are studied and compared with the maximum weight of particular characteristics fixed by the first reusability gauge.

The order used to perform the actions of this decision table results from the above-mentioned optimization criteria.

This decision table precises only how to perform the reusability mechanisms using the first reusability gauge (used for the merges and for the simple inheritances). It does not consider other conditions, explained below, to decide of reusability between two object types. It does not use the second reusability gauge used for the multiple inheritances.

For the case of object identity and for the case of object merge, the decision table does not consider the use of the instances of the object types. So, if an object type to create, OB-b, is such that its instances know several instances of an existing object type OB-a, OB-a and OB-b cannot be considered as identical and do not be merged. Two different object types

- The characteristics of OB-b are the same (are of the same types) that the characteristics of OB-a.	Yes	No					
- Weight of common characteristics of OB-a and of OB-b: **Weight (CCOB-ab)** compared with the minimum weight of common characteristics fixed by the first reusability gauge: ***WeightMinCCOB.***	/	≥				<	
- Weight of particular characteristics of OB-a: **Weight (PCOB-a)** compared with the maximum weight of particular characteristics fixed by the first reusability gauge: ***WeightMaxPCOB.***	/	≤		>		/	/
- Weight of particular characteristics of OB-b: **Weight (PCOB-b)** compared with the maximum weight of particular characteristics fixed by the first reusability gauge: ***WeightMaxPCOB.***	/	≤	>	≤	>	/	/
- The reusability by declaration is allowed.	/	/	/	/	/	**Yes**	**No**
1 - OB-b is of the type of OB-a: it is identical to OB-a.	**X**						
2 - OB-b is merged with OB-a.		**X**					
3 - OB-b inherits from OB-a.			**X**				
4 - OB-a inherits from OB-b.				**X**			
5 - Creation of an abstract object of which OB-a and OB-b inherit.					**X**		
6 - Characteristics of OB-b are declared to be of the types of characteristics of OB-a. **7 - or characteristics of OB-a are declared to be of the types of characteristics of OB-b.**						**X**	
OB-b does not reuse OB-a and OB-b is not reused by OB-a.							**X**

Figure 3: Decision table which defines conditions relating to the first object reusability gauge to obtain the 7 results of reusability of studying an object type OB-b with an existing object type OB-a with which the weight of common characteristics is the more important

must be created and a multivalued external acquaintance must be defined in OB-b towards OB-a.

Example: we suppose that the object types Car model and Car are defined with the same types of acquaintances and with the same services; these object types cannot be merged because several cars correspond to a car model; two different object types must be created and a multivalued external acquaintance must be defined in the object Car model towards the object Car.

We can say that the object types cannot be merged only if their instances are in a one-to-one correspondence. This case is classical in the data entity-relationship representations [24] [25] with which the merge of entities must be envisaged if they are linked with a relation of which the maximal cardinalities are equal to 1. This merge is realized if it does not set problems of use of these entities occurrences. In the same way, the merge of two relations of the relational model the tuples of which are in a one-to-one correspondence may be merged. But with the entity-relationship model and data bases the merges of entities and of relations are only considered in the case of a one-to-one correspondence without taking attribute types into account.

A merge between two object types OB-a and OB-b can also be realized if OB-a is an abstract object and OB-b is the only object which inherits of OB-a, case not considered by the decision table. Example: let us consider the abstract object type "Vehicle" and the object type "Motor vehicle" supposing that it is the only object which inherits of "Vehicle"; these two objects must be merged because the existence of the object "Vehicle" does not be useful to create instances because it is abstract and its existence does not be useful to define other object types than "Motor vehicle".

5. EXAMPLE OF RESULTS OF THE STANDARDIZED REUSABILITY OF OBJECTS

Let us study the reusability of conceptual representations defined with acquaintances and services. We consider the object Firm which is to be created in an object system. The object Person is the existing object in this object system of which the weight of common characteristics with the object Firm is the most important (see Figure 4). The acquaintances and the services of the objects are measured with the most simple metric presented in Section 4.2, that is to say by counting the characteristics. We consider several values of the first object reusability gauge and we examine their incidence on the reusability during the creation of the Firm object. Three different results of reusability are obtained according to the value of the first object reusability gauge (see Figure 5): the merge of Firm with Person, Firm inherits from Person or an (abstract) object of construction PersonFirm is created from which Person and Firm inherit.

6. USE AND IMPLEMENTATION OF THE ALGORITHM OF STANDARDIZED REUSABILITY OF THE OBJECTS

The mechanisms of standardized reusability are successively applied between a new object and the existing objects which have with this new object weight of common characteristics superior to the minimal weight fixed by the first reusability gauge, objects considered in the decreasing order of their common characteristics with the new object. The conditions of the mechanisms of reusability are respectively studied in order they have been presented.

This order allows to find one of the 7 results with the below order:
1: object of the type of an existing object type,
2: object merged with an existing object,

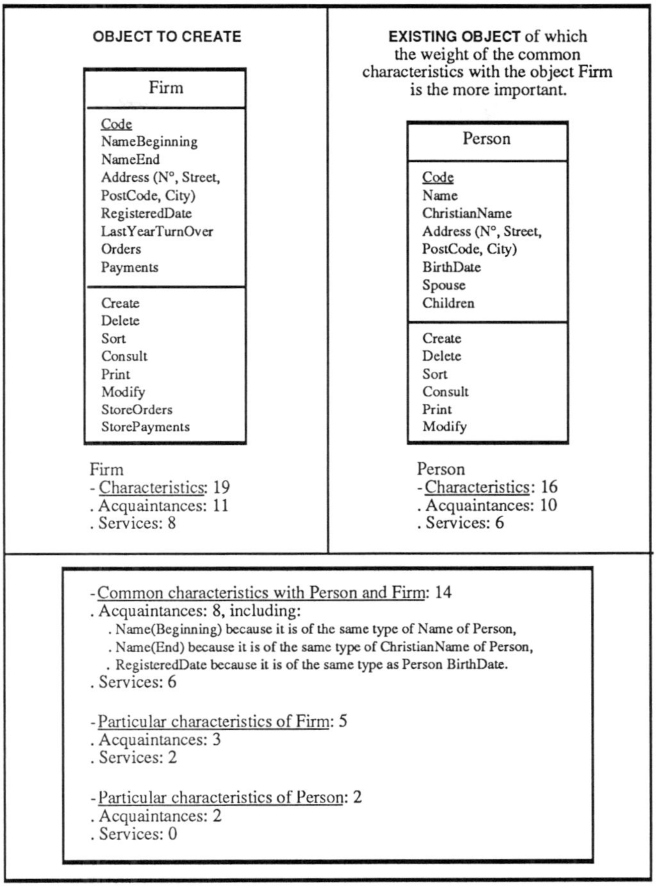

Figure 4: Example of object reusability

3: object which inherits from one or several existing objects,
4: existing object(s) which inherit(s) from the new object,
5: creation of abstract object(s) from which the new object inherits with other existing object(s).

The mechanisms which generate the results 6 and 7 (obtained when characteristics of a new object are declared to be of types of characteristics of existing objects and vice versa), are only used if the other mechanisms cannot be applied.

The creation of an abstract object with the common characteristics of a new object and of an existing object, abstract object from which the new object and the existing object inherit, allows to study this abstract object with the mechanisms of reusability. This abstract object may itself be involved in reusability with other objects. So the algorithms of the reusability

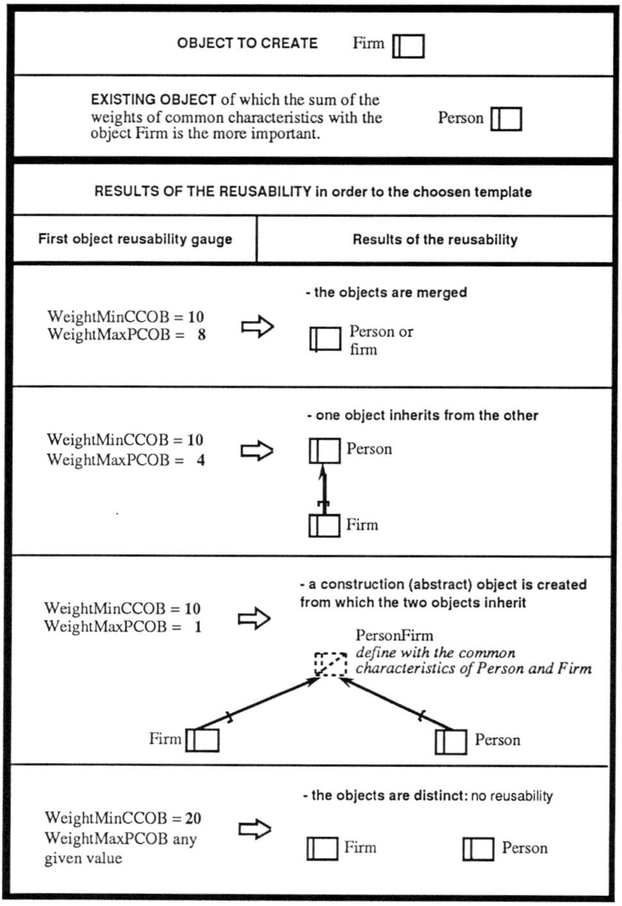

Figure 5: Examples of results of standardized reusability of objects

mechanisms are recursive. These algorithms have been defined. G. Blaise has validated and implemented them in Smalltalk-80 [26].

7. USE OF MECHANISMS OF STANDARDIZED REUSABILITY DURING THE INTEGRATION OF NEW INSTANCES

The mechanisms of standardized reusability may be used to integrate new object types in an object system and to integrate new instances by comparing the types of the characteristics of these instances with the types of the characteristics of the existing object types.

The seven results obtained (which are the results presented in the previous Sections), are commented below with the point of view of an instance integration:

1 . the identity between the types of the characteristics of a new instance and the types of the characteristics of an existing object type generates an instanciation of this object type;

2 . a merge is realized by adding the types of characteristics of the new instance to the types of the characteristics of an existing object type, which is thus modified;
3 . an object type may be created for a new instance and an inheritance link may be defined between this created object type and an existing object type;
4 . an object type may be created for the new instance and existing object types may inherit from this new object type;
5 . an object type may be created for the new instance and abstract objects may be created which the new object type and existing objects inherit;
6 . an object type may be created for the new instance with declaring the types of its characteristics to be of the types of characteristics of existing object types;
7 . an object type may be created for the new instance with declaring that characteristics of existing object types are types of characteristics of the new object type.

8. STEPS WHERE THE OBJECT REUSABILITY IS STUDIED

The mechanisms of reusability must be used on the conceptual representation of an object system and on its organizational representation which defines the structure of its implementation.

The mechanisms of reusability do not preserve the semantic of the objects which are created. So, the end-user conceptual representations are created with a not standardized reusability and therefore are not optimized. The optimization of the reusability on the conceptual representations is made by the analysts during the first part of the detailed study. The correspondences between the semantic conceptual objects, which are known by the end-users, and the detailed conceptual objects defined by the data processing personnel by optimizing the reusability, may be managed by the used tool CASE.

The organizational representations which define the implementation structure of an object system is directly defined with a standardized reusability by the data processing personnel during the second part of the detailed study.

Conceptual reusability gauges and implementation reusability gauges, generally different, are thus respectively defined to optimize the reusability of the conceptual representation and of the organizational representation of the object system.

The optimized conceptual representation and the organizational representation of an object system are obtained using twice the mechanisms of reusability.

The steps where is studied the object reusability are summed up on the Figure 6.

9. CONCLUSION

The mechanisms of standardized reusability are mechanisms of pattern recognition because they allow to compare objects and to study their resemblance.

These mechanisms allow the optimization of object systems in terms of normalization of the use of the concepts of merge, of inheritance and of reusability by declaration. The optimization of an object system is equivalent to try to obtain an important coupling inside the objects and a weak coupling between the objects. Objects weakly coupled are obtained by minimizing the number of objects, that means creating more independent objects because their external acquaintances and their inheritances are less numerous. The implementations of the objects are more efficient and their reusability is easier. But optimizing the reusability is equivalent to minimize the common characteristics often with the creation of objects to the detriment of the minimisation of the number of objects. So the mechanisms of standardized

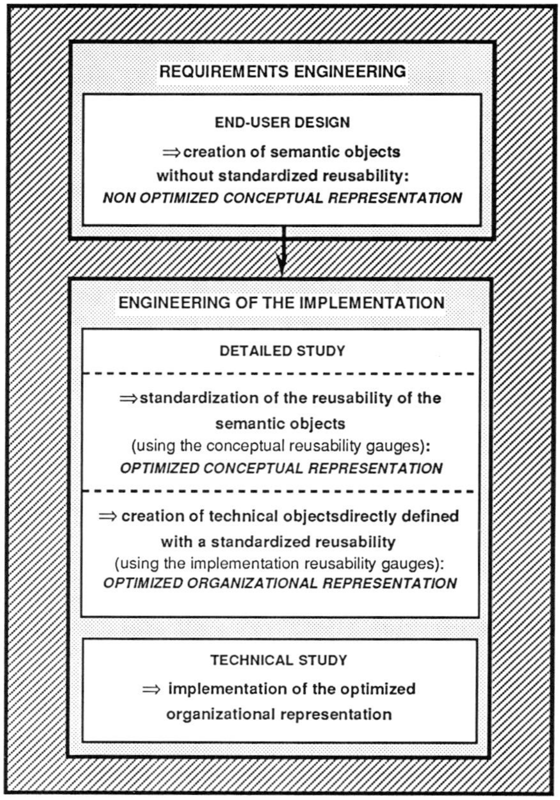

Figure 6: Steps where the object reusability is studied

reusability contribute to optimize the design of object systems, but without the guarantee that the "optimum" will be reached.

The use of these mechanisms supposes that "good" metrics allowing to measure the objects and their characteristics had been chosen. These metrics, and after, the object reusability gauges must be carefully defined before applying the mechanisms presented. As for each measure it is necessary to study the pertinence, the cost and the possibility of calibration [27].

Allowing an incremental automatized design, the presented mechanisms should be implemented in aided design of object systems tools (CASE tools), and also in object-oriented DBMS, and in the programming environments of the object-oriented languages.

As these mechanisms allow an automatized design of the objects, the users of these tools, including the analysts, can ignore the concepts of reusability. These concepts and the object reusability gauges are chosen by a manager of the studies. The analysts and the software developpers create after the objects. These objects are automatically insert in the object system with a standardized reusability.

The mechanisms of standardized reusability may be improved with using frequency object activities of the objects and of their characteristics weighting the measures of the objects and of their characteristics with these frequencies. Taking into account these frequencies supposes a precise definition of the activities to be measured.

Measures of activities frequencies are possible with some DBMS. With object-oriented DBMS, to our knowledge, these types of measures of frequencies do not exist. What's more, taking into consideration of these frequencies requires the use of the reusability mechanisms in a pre-existing object system to reorganize it either because the values of the gauges have been modified, or because it has not been created with these mechanisms. The mechanisms being usable during the creation of objects, the reorganizations of object systems must be realized by recreating them. This is possible for the types. On the other hand it is also necessary to transform the instances, and this difficult problem supposes the use a sophisticated management system of versions in the case where the transformation of instances is impossible.

The mechanisms of standardized reusability search and use identical specification or code sequences of which the sizes are checked with gauges. An outstanding research is on the possibility to take into account the specification or code sequences syntactically different but semantically identical. Furthermore this research considers the fact that the objects of some libraries (in particular external) cannot be modified.

Acknowledgments: I should like to thank David Allen (IIE), Hong Jiang (CEDRIC-IIE), Jean-Yves Lafaye (IUT La Rochelle), Marie-Christine Lafaye (IUT La Rochelle), and Régine Laleau (CEDRIC-IIE) for their critical appraisal of this paper.

REFERENCES

1. B. Meyer, Object-oriented Software Construction. Prentice Hall international, Series in computer science, 1988.
2. P. M. Cullough, B. Atkinson, A. Golberg, M. Griss and J. Morrinson, Reuse : Truth or Fiction (PANEL), OOPSLA '92, Seventh annual Conference on Object-Oriented Programming Systems, Languages, and Applications, ACM SIGPLAN NOTICES, Volume 27, Number 10, October 1992.
3. Sofware Re-use, Proceedings of the Software Re-use, Workshop 23-24 November 1989, Utrecht, L. M. Dusink and P. A. V. Hall editors, Springer-Verlag.
4. B. Staudt Lerner and N. Habermann, Beyond schema evolution to database reorganization. ECOOP/OOPSLA ' 90 Proceedings, October 21-25 1990.
5. P. Constantopoulos and E. Pataki, A Browser for Sotware Reuse, Advanced Information Systems Engineering, 4th International Conference CAISE '92, Manchester, UK, May 1992, Proceedings, Springer-Verlag.
6. M. Boughanem, C. Chrisment, E. Rames, R. Razouk and F. Sédes, SYRIUS: Un système d'information pour la classification et la recherche de composants logiciels réutilisables, Fourth International Conference on Software engineering & its applications, Toulouse, France, December 9-13, 1991.
7. B. Cox, Planning the software industrial revolution, IEEE Software, 7(6), November 1990.

8. R. Chidamber and F. Kemerer, Towards a metrics suite for object oriented design, OOPSLA '91, Conference on Object-Oriented Programming Systems, Languages, and Applications, ACM SIGPLAN NOTICES, Volume 26, Number 11, November 1991.
9. X. Castellani, Le modèle de la méthode MCO d'analyse et de conception des systèmes d'objets, INFORSID Conference, Paris, June 5-7 1991.
10. X. Castellani, MCO: Méthodologie générale d'analyse et de conception des systèmes d'objets, Tome 1: L'ingénierie des besoins, 1993, Tome 2: L'ingénierie de l'implantation, to be published, Masson.
11. J. M. Smith and D. C. P. Smith, Database Abstractions: Aggregation and Generalization. ACM Transactions on Database Systems, vol 2, n 2, june 1977.
12. C. Delobel, C. Lecluse and P. Richard, Bases de données: des systèmes relationnels aux systèmes à objets. InterEditions, 1991.
13. N. E. Fenton, Software metrics, A Rigourous Approach, Chapman & Hall, 1991.
14. B.W. Boehm, Software Engineering Economics, Prentice-Hall, New York, 1981.
15. M. H. Halstead, Element of Software Science, Elsevier, North Holland, 1975.
16. T. J. Mac Cabe, A complexity measure, IEEE Transactions on Software Engineering, SE-2(4), December 1976.
17. C. B. Jones, Systematic Software Development Using VDM, Prentice Hall, London, 2d edition, 1990.
18. D. Andrews and D, Ince, Practical Formal Methods with VDM, Mac Graw Hill, Series in Software Engineering, 1991.
19. J. Dawes , The VDM-SL reference guide, Pitman, 1991.
20. J. R. Abrial , Data semantics in data management, North Holland, 1974.
21. J. M. Spivey, The Z notation. A Reference Manual, Prentice Hall international series in computer science, C.A.R. Hoare series editor, 1987.
22. Potter, Sinclair et Till, An introduction to formal specification and Z, Prentice Hall, 1991.
23. R. Laleau and P. Facon, Modeling semantic data concepts with VDM, SEKE'93 : Fifth International Conference on Software Engineering and Knowledge Engineering, San Francisco, June 16-18, 1993.
24. P. P. Chen, The entity-relationship model, ACM transactions on database systems, vol 1, n°1 March 1976.
25. H. Tardieu, C. Deheneffe and J. L. Hainaut, The Individual Model, International Workshop on Data Structure Models for Information Systems, May 1974.
26. G. Blaise, Implantation de l'algorithme de réutilisabilité uniforme d'objets MCO en Smalltalk 80, engineer cycle C thesis CNAM, 1992.
27. J. P. Martin, La qualité des logiciels (du bricolage à l'industrialisation), Afnor gestion, 1987.

Information System Development Process (A-30)
N. Prakash, C. Rolland and B. Pernici (Editors)
Elsevier Science Publishers B.V. (North–Holland)

© 1993 IFIP. All rights reserved.

Reuse of Specifications and Designs in a Development Information System

R. Bellinzona[a], *M. G. Fugini*[b], *V. de Mey*[c]

[a] Dipartimento di Elettronica e Informazione, Politecnico di Milano
Piazza L. da Vinci, 32, I-20133 Milano, Italy
e-mail: bellinzo@ipmel2.elet.polimi.it

[b] Dipartimento di Informatica e Sistemistica, Università di Pavia
Via Abbiategrasso, 209, I-27100 Pavia, Italy
e-mail: fugini@ipmel1.polimi.it

[c] Centre Universitaire d'Informatique, Université de Genève
24, rue du General-Dufour, CH-1211 Geneva 4, Switzerland
e-mail: vicki@cui.unige.ch

Abstract

This paper describes the approach to application specification and design via reuse at the basis of the Development Information System of the ITHACA[1] environment. Requirements and detailed design of a specific application are incrementally composed by aggregating available reusable components stored in the Software Information Base repository. The paper reviews the Development Information System, then focuses on two tools of the system: RECAST (Requirements Composition And Specification Tool) and Visual ADL, which help the developer in selecting reusable artifacts from the Software Base and in composing and tailoring them according to the specific needs of the application. The paper illustrates the composition approach and describes how reuse is supported via meta classes incorporating suggestions for component reuse and tailoring, and for detailed design.

Keyword Codes: D.1.7; D.2.1; D.1.5

Keywords: Visual Programming; Requirements/Specifications; Object-oriented programming

---

1. ITHACA (Integrated Toolkit for Highly Advanced Computer Applications) is a 4 years EEC-ESPRIT II project started January 1989 and completed in December 1992

1. Introduction

Within ITHACA [1], where an environment and a method are provided to develop new applications by reusing artifacts of old applications, the requirements specification phase and the detailed design phase aim at composing existing reusable software artifacts. According to the object-oriented approach to application development assumed in ITHACA, the target application is object-oriented, as well as the development method: objects are used in all the phases of an application development cycle. Therefore, the environment stores and makes available for reuse requirement objects, design objects, and implementation objects. The developer incrementally builds a Specific Application Frame (SAF) by reusing as many software artifacts as possible. Software artifacts, organized in Generic Application Frames (GAFs) are stored in the Software Information Base (SIB) [5].

Various approaches exist aimed at providing automatic support for application development; they range from specialized tools for development and for project management, through covering the whole life-cycle via a unique support paradigm (e.g., [7]), to integrated CASE tools and Software Factories [30] [12]. The idea of storing development information about all the development steps in a core repository is under investigation; aspects related to the contents, the organization and the access methods for the repository, together with schema evolution control techniques are to be solved, although some standardization process is ongoing [21]. Recent approaches focus on guided software development via process modelling and intelligent tools. In DAIDA [18], the design cycle is assisted through a process model and the development steps are recorded in multi-layered design histories. In [2], reuse information is organized in frameworks used mainly for the design phase. In LaSSIE [10], information relating to software development is stored in frames structures, and a retrieval system is provided on the basis of frame contents. In [23], multi-agent development is explicitly represented as a meta model using a knowledge-based formalism; knowledge acquisition and query mechanisms are taken into account as a basis for simulation of software behaviour.

The approach presented in this paper consists of tools supporting requirements specification, design, and implementation of SAFs by reusing information in the SIB. The underlying method [9] considers that requirements specification, detailed design, and implementation are phases to be performed back and forth, reusing classes in each phase. Classes are formalized differently for each phase, and are put in relationships that lead the developer from requirements to more detailed application frames where composed elements can be selected and prototyped; eventually, software modules, implemented in the target object-oriented language, can be aggregated into the final software system. The method outlines a development strategy oriented to objects and to reusability from the early phases. In particular, specifications are formalized considering the possibility of reusing them, and to build automatic tools supporting object-oriented analysis [25]. Among the tools comprising the ITHACA Development Information System are: RECAST (Requirements Composition And Specification Tool) supports the composition, via guided selection [26][13], of requirements specified in the object-oriented specification model, called Functionality in the Objects with Roles Model (F-ORM) [28][8]; Visual ADL supports the detailed design specification phase according to the Activity Definition Language (ADL) [17]; Vista (Visual Composition Tool) provides composition functionality to the Development System.

The paper is organized as follows. Section 2 briefly illustrates the composition approach and focuses on the Development Information System tools [13] for requirements and design specification. In Section 3, the reuse model is analysed. In Section 4, the application specification and design tools are described in some more detail.

2. Development Information System

The architecture of the Development Information System provided in ITHACA is depicted in Figure 1. It is composed of tools for application specification (RECAST), for detailed design (Visual ADL), for composition support (Vista), and for storage and extraction of development information (SIB system [6]). The underlying paradigm considers that applications are developed mainly by reusing development data (specifications, detailed design information, executable objects, etc.). Reuse affects all the stages of the development cycle and development information is available in the Development Information System for any development stage. A method for development under reuse has been defined [9]. Applications are developed by accessing old applications stored in the system repository, the SIB System.

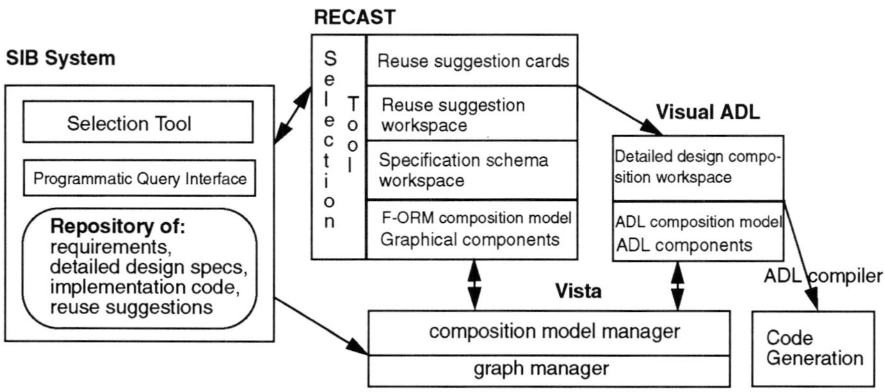

Figure 1 Architecture of the Development Information System

Tools are based on the "key" idea of visual composition [26]: applications are built out of components; every component has a composition interface according to which components are interconnected; the allowed interconnections are defined in a composition model. The basic composition functionality is provided by the **Vista** tool [22]. Component sets and composition models are defined for requirements and detailed design specification.

The composition approach is at the basis of **RECAST**; this supports the requirements specification task based on an object-oriented specification model [8] and on the ITHACA Object-Oriented Methodology [9]. RECAST also supports the retrieval of reusable requirements from the SIB system through the SIB Selection Tool and its own Selection Tool, and provides reuse suggestions that describe the reuse of selected requirements.

The **Visual ADL** tool supports the detailed design phase for workflow applications. The Activity Definition Language (ADL) notation [17] for office workflow specification is at the basis of the tool. ADL specifications are directly mapped into implementation classes via the ADL compiler [20]. Implementation is given in the CooL[1] object-oriented programming language.

2.1. Visual composition: Vista

Visual composition [26] is the interactive construction of applications from pre-packaged, plug-compatible software components by direct manipulation and graphical editing. This approach allows both the internal behaviour of applications, as well as their user interfaces, to be directly edited and manipulated. For visual composition to work, *component sets* and *composition models* must be available.

Visual composition is a technique for application development that fits into the more general context of *component-oriented software development* [27], an approach to software engineering that shifts emphasis in the software life cycle from the development of individual applications to the engineering of reusable frameworks [11] of software components.

In order to evaluate visual composition as an approach to application construction, we developed *Vista*, a prototype visual composition tool, and we applied the tool to a number of selected application domains. Vista supports visual composition in two ways: (1) by imposing a reasonably flexible structure for component definition, and (2) by defining a framework, referred to as the Component-Port-Link (CPL) framework, for component composition. In order to use Vista, composition models and component sets must be provided for particular application domains. It is through the composition models and component sets that Vista can support the creation of specific applications.

A *component set* consists of the objects with which the developer will work, for example user interface components, and a composition model determines the way in which components may be connected. A component is made up of three parts: a *presentation*, a *behaviour* and a *composition interface*. The presentation of a component is how it looks on the screen. The presentation can be the actual user interface the component will have in the final application or just a visualization for tool purposes. The behaviour of a component consists of whatever it has been designed to do. The most critical part, however, is the composition interface, which allows the behaviour of the component to be bound to a given context. The composition interface of a component consists of a set of *ports*, each of which has a name, a type and a polarity. It is also possible to define a group of components as a *composite component*, thereby promoting hierarchical composition. To define a composite component, one must provide (1) a composition interface (by specifying which ports of the constituent components are to become ports of the

1. CooL is the object-oriented programming language developed in the ITHACA project.

composite component), and (2) a visual presentation (which can be composed of existing presentation components). The behaviour of a composite component is defined by the behaviour of the components it contains.

A *composition model* declares what port and link types are valid in a particular application domain and which ports are *compatible*, i.e., which may be linked together. Composition models can be related to each other by inheritance allowing the reuse of models in the declaration of other models. By decoupling composition model from component sets, a variety of different software composition paradigms can be supported. Components share information with each other once they are linked together. A composition model is dynamically loaded into the tool at run-time. Usually, considerable effort must be put into the design of a useful and reusable set of components, ports and links.

2.2. Requirements specification: RECAST

The main aim of RECAST is the reuse of requirements; this is supported by composition and reuse suggestions. The Functionality in the Objects with Roles Model (F-ORM) [28] represents the formal basis for requirements specification. Application requirements are represented as classes, objects are created as class instances, and messages are used to access the services provided by objects. The *concept of role* extends the object-oriented paradigm [25] to model the different behaviours an object can have during its life time [28]: thus an object can send and receive different messages at different stages of its evolution. The role dynamics is represented via state/transition diagrams; role data are described as a set of properties. In the context of office applications, F-ORM [8] contains *process* and *resource classes*. The former represent sets of tasks and the latter define agents and information.

An example of a F-ORM specification related to an order processing application is illustrated in Figure 2. The main tasks of order processing are represented by the OrderProcessing process class. The involved resources are the classes Client, Employee, OrderAdministrator, and Order. Role connections represent message exchange. An IsA relation is defined between OrderAdministrator and Employee.

A *component set* has been defined to represent F-ORM requirements. Its graphical notation is as depicted in Figure 2. Class and role components are used to achieve the requirements representation. Role components are in effect composite components that include a state/transition diagram definition representing the role behaviour.

The *composition model* for F-ORM defines the allowed interconnections among class, role and state/transition diagram components. In particular, IsA and PartOf relations derived from the used object-oriented paradigm [25] can be established among classes. Role composition is based on the *role message interface*; each role can receive and send a fixed set of messages (see Figure 2) and can be connected only to roles having a compatible message interface. State/transition diagram composition involves the connection of diagram components (e.g., states and messages) according to the possible flows of execution among role states.

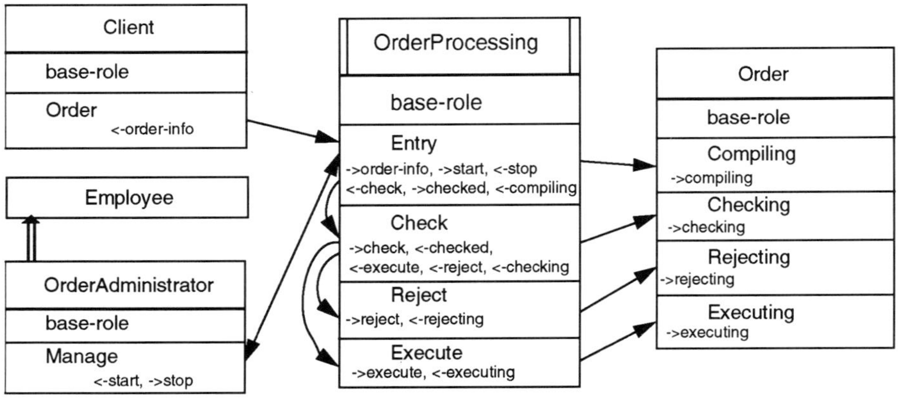

Figure 2 F-ORM classes for order processing specification

RECAST enhances the composition support provided by Vista functionality introducing *reuse facilities*. Reusable classes stored in the SIB have associated *reuse suggestions* that drive the specification task [13].

Requirements specification is based on the ITHACA Object-Oriented Method (IOOM) [9]. According to IOOM, requirements are organized at various detail levels and their specification includes definition actions at a given detail level (*schema definition*) and transformation actions mapping a given level into a new detail level (*schema transformation*). The specification of requirements at a given level involves the identification of reusable classes from the SIB repository and their composition in the RECAST workspace.

2.3. Detailed design: Visual ADL

An Activity Definition Language (ADL) [17] has been defined to describe coordination procedures (workflows). *Coordination procedures* specify the flow of a number of (office) objects through a number of *coordination steps*. The workflow application depends heavily on reuse. *Activity types* are defined and then tailored and reused as *steps* to build procedures. Figure 3 is a sketch of a procedure that processes order forms. When an activity type is instantiated as a step, it is given a step name (i.e. step1, step2 etc.), a person responsible for the step (i.e. OrderAdministrator) and inputs and outputs. The inputs of each step are bound to inputs of the procedure or to outputs of some other step. The procedure itself may have several output alternatives, depending on the outcome of its constituent steps.

Defining activity types and procedures is supported by visual composition. In the *ADL component set*, each component representing an office object, activity, etc., is equipped with methods for generating various ADL code fragments. An office procedure is then defined through visual composition by connecting existing code generation components. A complete composition can then be packaged as an office procedure, and requested to generate its own ADL specification. The ADL code, generated by ADL components, is translated into CooL

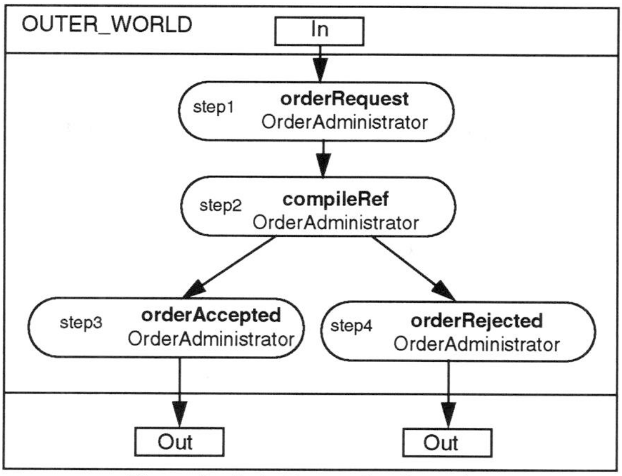

Figure 3 OrderProcessing Procedure

code and executed within a run-time system for coordination procedures. Activity definitions are visually represented as activity components which are composite components. Procedures are compositions of steps (instances of activity components) connected together to represent the data that flows between each step as pictured in Figure 3.

The *composition model for ADL* is simple and checks to make sure that only ports of the same type are connected as a user interactively creates an activity definition or a procedure. The composition model declares the component port types, and a link type for checking port types before a link is made. This link consults the composition model to make sure that the types of the "from" port and the "to" port are of the same or compatible types. Other constraints could be added to the composition model to reflect more of the ADL semantics.

ADL is useful to perform the *detailed design* out of the requirements schema when coordination procedures must be analysed. F-ORM requirements are mapped into detailed design objects specified through a notation suitable for the domain of the application and supported by Vista. In this paper we focus on ADL. The mapping is based on correspondences between F-ORM concepts and ADL concepts. In particular, each F-ORM task (a role of a process class) is detailed into a set of ADL activities; agent and resource roles involved in task execution represent the activity responsible and the input and output data; task activation and data manipulation are represented as a coordination procedure; activities are enriched with information about preconditions, actions and postconditions, directly defined using CooL classes. The preconditions are particularly important since they support the elimination of the non-deterministic behaviours represented in F-ORM state/transition diagrams.

2.4. SIB System

The SIB system [5] consists of objects representing information about software, including requirements, designs and code, organized in *descriptions*. The structure of each description is strongly dependent on the description model that is used in each case. A *description model* is a set of meta-classes of entities and relationships between these entities with specific semantics associated with the way their instances are interrelated. All SIB descriptions are represented in Telos [24], a knowledge representation language supporting a multi-level class specification and class attributes, inheritance and instantiation. The SIB system establishes a semantic network of software descriptions: each description is a node in the network; links specify class necessary and possible dependencies, class specialization / decomposition, classes similarities, class correspondences, class transformations, hyper-media links among class documentation. The semantic net is displayed via the SIB Selection Tool [6] browser.

Although the retrieval of reusable classes via the SIB browser is useful, *query functionality* has been considered relevant for the specification tools. RECAST is enriched by a query manager oriented to requirements retrieval. Each reusable class is classified by the application engineer (the ITHACA user typology in charge of SIB maintenance) according to *Functional Descriptions* [14], that is, semiformal descriptions of class services. Query formulation is based on a developer provided functional description; a fuzzy-logic based algorithm [19] is used to compute the similarity between the requested features and the reusable class features.

3. Reuse model

The reuse approach is based on the reuse information stored in the SIB which includes generic classes and reuse suggestions. This section first describes how the information stored in the SIB is organized. The "genericity" properties are examined and an example of a F-ORM generic class is provided. Reuse suggestions are then examined and the reuse process considered.

3.1. Generic Application Frames

Reusable software artifacts are grouped in the SIB as Generic Application Frames (GAFs). A GAF can be seen as a framework that provides a skeleton for developing applications in specific application domains [16]. Reusable classes related to requirements, detailed design and implementation phases are provided in GAFs. *Generic* behaviours are defined in reusable classes in order to make them easily adaptable to specific application needs.

GAFs also include reuse suggestions that provide knowledge to reuse GAF classes. Reuse suggestions are *meta classes*, formalized in F-ORM, where the concept of role is used to specify various reuse strategies. In our approach, reuse suggestions are given for requirements reuse and for mapping of requirements into detailed design. It is assumed that these phases include the most of the reuse issues.

GAF classes and their relationships are shown in Figure 4. A set of F-ORM classes has an associated pair of meta classes:

- a *reuse-related meta class*: this specifies how the F-ORM classes can be reused (*describe-reuse-of* link); reuse occurs basically by specifying necessary dependencies (depends-on link) and optional, suggested dependencies among F-ORM classes (can-depend-on link);

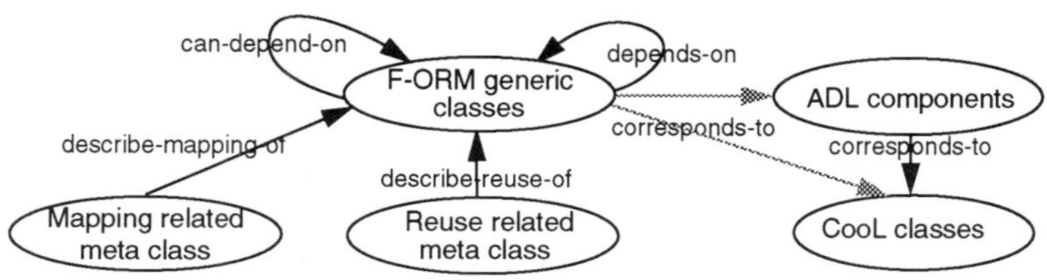

Figure 4 GAF classes and relations among classes

- a *mapping-related meta class*: this guides the developer in the identification of the design classes (e.g. ADL procedures and activities) related to the F-ORM classes, and in producing design specifications corresponding to requirements specifications. A *describe-mapping-of* link specifies the association between the F-ORM class set and its mapping related meta class. The mapping of the F-ORM class set into a set of design classes is described in the mapping-related meta class contents; the associations among F-ORM classes and design classes are defined via *corresponds-to* links, abstraction of the meta class contents.

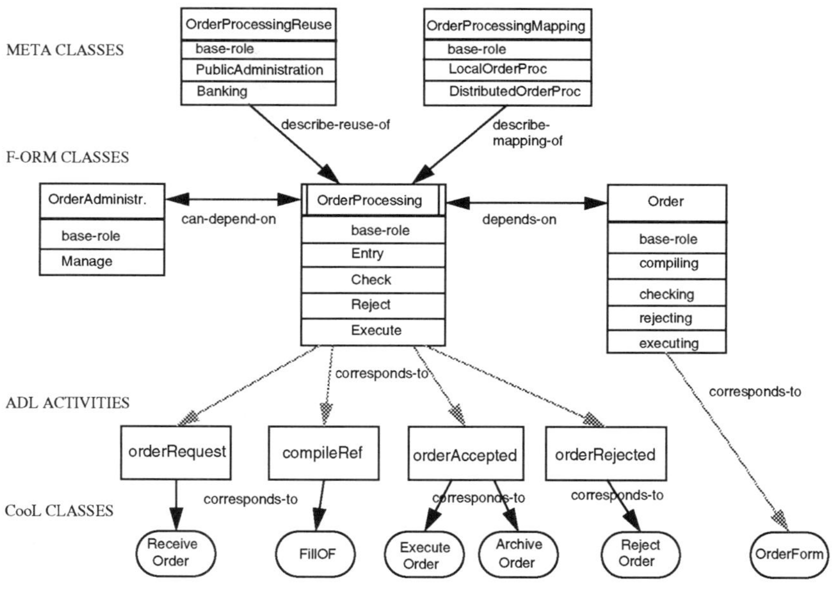

Figure 5 Example of an "order processing" GAF

An example of a GAF related to "order processing" is pictured in Figure 5. It contains three of the F-ORM classes of Figure 2: the OrderProcessing process class, the agent that is in charge for order management (OrderAdministrator resource class), and the order document (Order resource class). The OrderProcessingReuse meta class describes the reuse of the OrderProcessing class and of dependent classes; the meta roles PublicAdministration and Banking identify different reuses of OrderProcessing in two application domains. For mapping strategies, the OrderProcessingMapping meta class describes mapping in centralized and distributed order management systems. The contents of OrderProcessingMapping is used to establish corresponds-to links from F-ORM classes to ADL and CooL classes.

3.2. Generic requirements

In order to be suitable for reuse, SIB classes must be easily adaptable to various application contexts. To this purpose F-ORM classes stored in the SIB are made "generic" [2] by inserting parametric parts. Parameters relate to:

- *dependencies among classes*: the message exchange among the roles of F-ORM classes is made parametric; a task can be connected to other tasks / agents / resources according to the application needs;
- *dependencies within classes*: only a subset of the class behaviours represented by roles can be useful for an application. The dependencies among roles of generic classes are so parametric;
- *base elements and optional elements*: state/transition diagrams can specify a base behaviour and some optional issues. Optional issues can be alternative.

During class reuse, parameters are filled on the basis of application needs guided by meta classes.

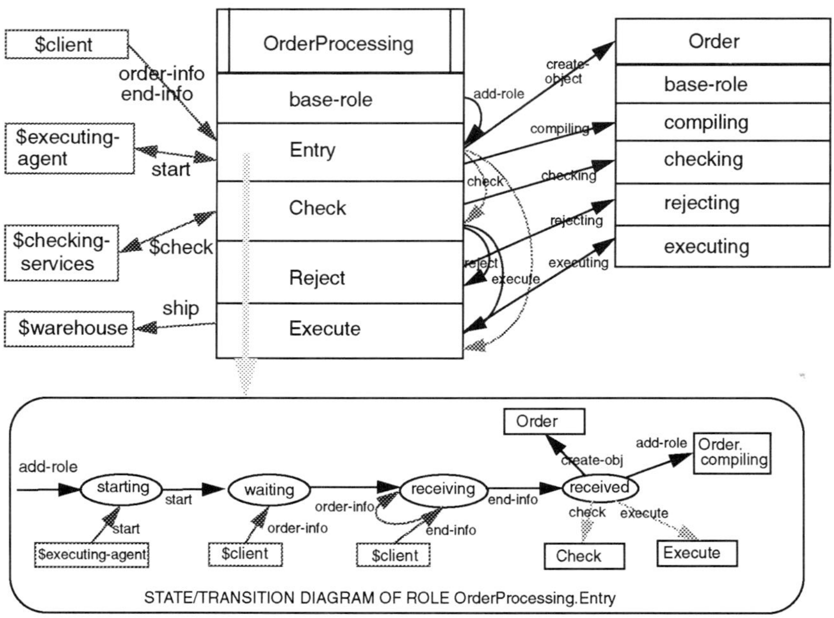

Figure 6 Example of OrderProcessing generic class

The generic class OrderProcessing in Figure 6 is built from the OrderProcessing class of Figure 2 by introducing genericity parameters. Many dependencies between roles can vary from one application to another and are so substituted by parameters. All parameter names are prefixed by the $ character and parametric message source/destination roles are represented by boxes with a dotted border.

The state/transition diagram of the Entry role is also represented in Figure 6. An extended notation is used: source roles of incoming messages are represented and are connected to the states that precede the transitions they activate; messages triggered after each transition are also represented, together with the destination roles. The reception of order information, the creation of the Order document, and the activation of new roles are defined in the state/transition diagram of the Entry role.

3.3. Reuse Suggestions

Meta classes describe the reuse and the mapping processes. A class can be reused, in principle, in various ways. Meta classes represent the invariant reuse strategies [2] of generic classes and specify reuse suggestions to guide the developer in the reuse process according to developer selectable reuse strategies. Reuse strategies correspond to the application domains (and subdomains) in which a class can be reused, to the different specialization / decomposition / transformations of a class, etc. Meta classes are specified by the application engineer.

A role of a meta class specifies a reuse strategy and includes a state/transition diagram representing the *reuse rules* associated with a reuse strategy. The incoming messages of the diagram are design actions executed by the developer. Messages triggered by the diagram include: design actions, directly executed on the requirements schema; meta role instantiation / termination, corresponding to the selection of reuse strategies; display of suggestion cards, representing reuse suggestions. The dynamics of the reuse process is described in meta classes, while the reuse data are contained in suggestion cards.

Suggestion cards include descriptions of reuse tasks and contain lists of design suggestions about actions to be executed to accomplish the reuse tasks. Design suggestions can be *necessary* (must be executed to make requirements consistent), *possible* (actions whose execution is useful but that does not concern consistency), *eventual* (actions that, although deferred, must be executed to produce the final version of the application). Cards can also contain *selection buttons* whose semantics is usually associated with the selection of reuse strategies. The selection of a button causes the select-option design action to be sent back to the meta role that activated the suggestion. Suggestion of dependencies can be difficult when the SIB system is populated with many classes (as it should be), particularly when dependencies cross GAFs; *retrieved functionality* is directly accessed through cards in order to propose classes on the basis of needed class features.

Reuse process

When the developer selects a generic class for reuse, new objects are created as instances of the meta classes associated with the generic class. Only the base-role is instantiated; usually, it guides the developer in the selection of a specific reuse strategy, and instantiates the roles that describe the selected reuse strategy. The execution of design actions causes information about the actions to be sent to the objects created from meta classes associated with the class on which the action is executed; new design actions and suggestions can be triggered by reuse rules as described above. Card execution causes all suggestions, marked as N or P and selected by the developer, to be executed on the requirements schema. Suggestions marked as E are moved into a global card that groups all eventual design actions; these can be examined and executed before the production of a final release of the requirements schema.

Reuse related meta classes

Reuse related meta classes are used to guide the developer in the reuse of F-ORM requirements. These meta classes describe, via suggestion cards, the following specification tasks:

- composition: necessary and useful dependencies of selected classes are retrieved and copied into the composition workspace. Role selections and interconnections are performed. Alter-

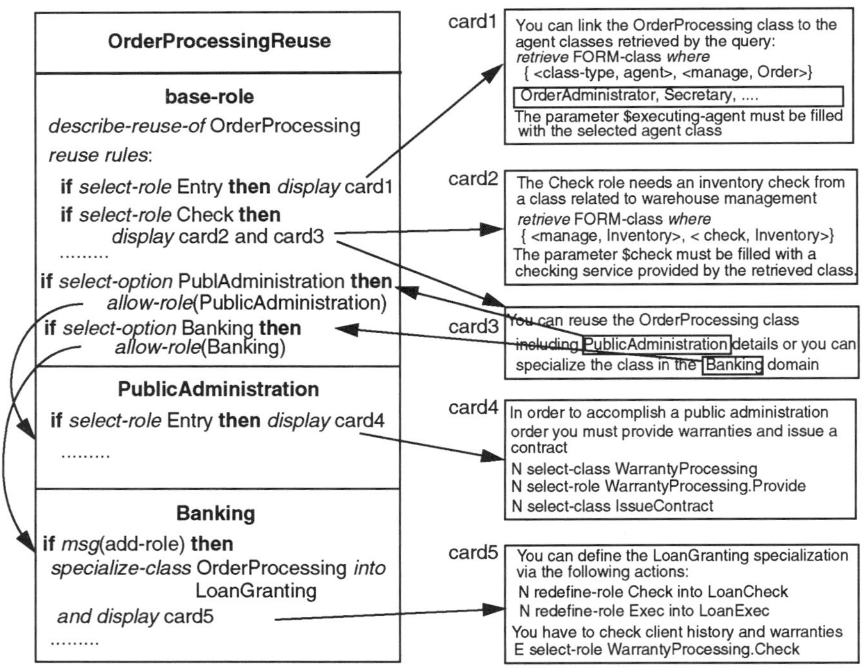

Legend: N = necessary action, P = possible action, E = eventual action

Figure 7 Reuse related meta class of the generic class OrderProcessing

native paths contained in state/transition diagrams are selected. Classes are specialized and decomposed;

- tailoring: tailoring actions can be suggested in order to make composition actions possible. These involve the change of state/transition diagram behaviours to define compatible message interfaces and the instantiation of parameters;
- transformation: refinement actions are suggested. SIB classes are directly proposed as refinements. The developer can start by analysing abstract classes and is then guided in the retrieval of new classes (or whole GAFs) that refine the previously selected ones.

Figure 7 is an example of a meta class related to the reuse of the F-ORM generic class OrderProcessing illustrated in Figure 6. The base role specifies "default" reuses: some parameters must be instantiated and some reuse strategies can be selected. Since the Entry role needs an agent, the meta class displays a card that activates a SIB query searching for an agent with proper functional characteristics. A class for inventory check services is provided in an analogous way. The specialization of OrderProcessing in the public administration and banking domains are also suggested by the meta class.

Mapping related meta classes

The structure of mapping related meta classes is similar to that of reuse related meta classes; they are composed of roles partitioned by mapping alternatives and including rules for suggestion production.

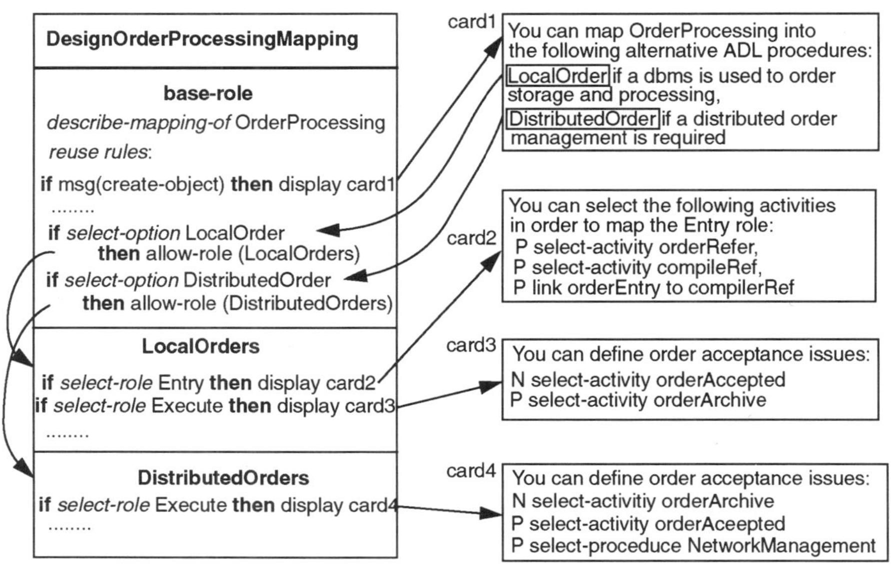

Figure 8 Mapping related meta class of the generic class OrderProcessing

In particular, information included in meta class roles relates to:

- *selection of reusable design classes* from a set of alternative design specifications: the described specifications map into design classes i.e. the F-ORM classes to which the meta class is linked;
- *composition of design classes*; analogous to F-ORM classes, design classes need other classes to work according to their interfaces.

An example of a mapping-related meta class is illustrated in Figure 8. It shows two alternative mappings of OrderProcessing into the ADL procedures LocalOrders and DistributedOrders whose construction is incrementally suggested to the developer.

4. Application Specification Session

The developer uses RECAST and Vista in an interleaved way and produces, starting from the reusable components selected from the SIB, a requirements schema and a design schema of the application. This section describes how the Development Information System tools can be used to compose an order processing application.

Requirements composition

A requirements schema is incrementally composed through RECAST on the basis of retrieved classes and reuse suggestions. Various composition windows are provided by RECAST in order to produce multi-level requirements specifications. Each composition window contains graphical components directly managed by Vista. For requirements specification class, role, state and message components have been defined.

Figure 9 represents a snapshot of a composition window related to an order processing application. The window can be produced via the following specification steps:

1. *select-class RequestProcessing*: the SIB is searched for classes suitable for the specification of the order processing application; a RequestProcessing GAF is identified at level 0 and its main class (RequestProcessing) is selected; this task is performed via SIB browsing;
2. *compose RequestProcessing*: a requirements schema at level 0 is produced; the dependencies of the RequestProcessing class are retrieved from the SIB on the basis of meta class suggestions; request related classes are then specialized to manage order requests;
3. *transform RequestProcessing*: the level 0 schema is transformed and order specific issues are detailed at level 1; an OrderProcessing class is built from the level 0 specialization of RequestProcessing;
4. *compose OrderProcessing*: new classes are retrieved from the SIB to represent warehouse and account tasks involved in order processing; the classes WarehouseProcessing and AccountProcessing are then composed with the OrderProcessing class;
5. *specialize OrderProcessing in the public administration domain*; the OrderProcessing class is specialized to manage orders coming from public administrations.

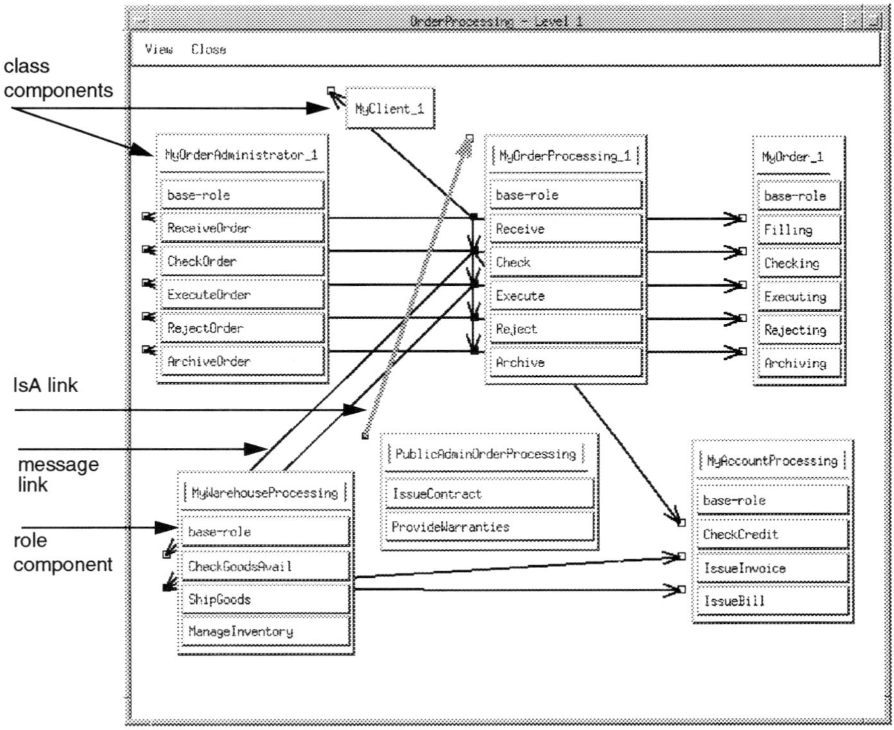

Figure 9 Example of a composition window of the order processing application

Application design

Once the requirements for the application start to be fixed, detailed design can start. To use visual composition for the detailed design of the order processing application, components for the composition tool must be supplied. Since the detailed design should correspond to an implementation in ADL, components for activity creation (Input, Variable, Activity, Alternative, Output) were defined to be used with Vista. These five components are linked together to create activity composite components which will ultimately generate ADL code.

The composite component for the activity definition of compileRef is pictured in Figure 10. The window containing the definition has an extra command menu, called ADL, where the “print code” function is found. The composite component contains one Activity component. Since this composition is only the activity type definition, the bottom two text fields are filled. The other two fields are filled in when the definition is reused as a step. The composite component for compileRef also contains one Input component (labelled In) and two Output components (labelled Accept and Reject). One Variable component is needed in the definition for the orderForm variable. The Input and Output components are connected to the Variable component. The activity definition has one Alternative component connected to the Output components. To build

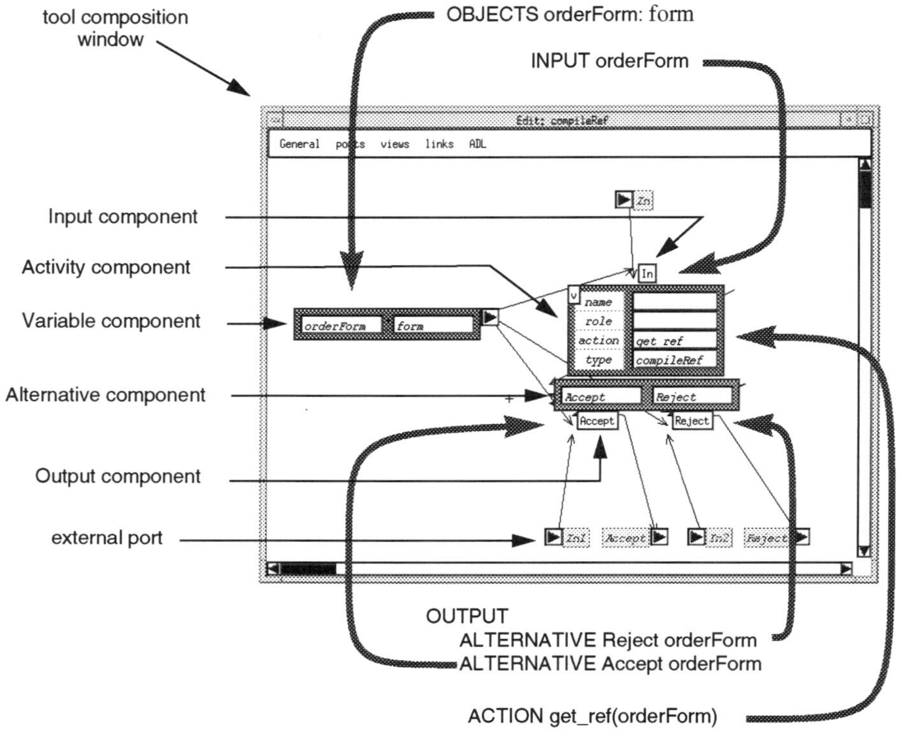

Figure 10 Activity type definition composition for the compileRef activity of the OrderProcessing procedure. Components responsible for particular parts of the code are labelled along with the ADL code they generate.

the OrderProcessing procedure definition (see Figure 3), this composite component would be reused as step 2. The compileRef activity can be stored in the SIB and directly suggested by RECAST as suitable to define the compilation of the orderForm document with order information, that is, to represent a part of the Entry task of the OrderProcessing class.

5. Concluding remarks and future work

In this paper, an approach to requirements specification and detailed design through reuse and composition has been described. Two tools, RECAST and Vista with the Visual ADL extension, have been illustrated. All tools of the ITHACA Development Information System run of SUN/4 workstations and are implemented using GNU C++, X Window, and Motif.

Vista provides a mechanism for the creation of new components and for composition model definition. Visual ADL is a direct experiment with Vista: an ADL component set and composition model are defined. Vista and Visual ADL have been developed at University of Geneva [22] in cooperation with other ITHACA partners especially IFATEC who worked on defining the ADL component set.

RECAST is based on a F-ORM component set and composition model; it adds new features to the basic Vista composition facilities related to retrieval and reuse support; the Vista user interface has been redefined in order to provide the RECAST specific functionality. RECAST has been developed at Politecnico di Milano [3].

The environment repository, the SIB system, has been developed at FORTH (Foundation for Research and Technology - Hellas). The storage of classes is supported by the generation of Telos descriptions [24]; these are then retrieved via a programmatic query interface. RECAST uses the interface to implement its own retrieval functionality.

The development of the RECAST and Vista tools demonstrated the importance of the merge of reuse and composition functionality into a new general composition tool. In an ideal scenario, the developer interacts with the composition tool for application specification; he can use various specification notations for the requirements, design and implementation phases; he can use a selection tool in order to retrieve reusable classes; he is guided by suggestions in the composition, in the refinement along detail levels, and in the mapping of classes into other specification notations. To progress toward this ideal scenario, Vista will be enhanced by including RECAST facilities.

Acknowledgments

We acknowledge all the ITHACA partners in this work and particularly the ITHACA Tools Group. Barbara Pernici and Valeria de Antonellis from Politecnico di Milano, and Oscar Nierstrasz from University of Geneva contributed directly with common work.

References

[1] M. Ader, O. Nierstrasz, S. McMahon, G. Muller, A-K Pröfrock, "The ITHACA Technology: a Landscape for Object-Oriented Application Development", Proc. ESPRIT'90 Conf., Kluwer Academic Publisher, November 1990

[2] K. Becker, F. Bodart, "Reusable Object-Oriented Specifications for Decision Support Systems", IFIP WG 8.4 Working Conf. on Object Oriented Aspects in Information Systems, Quebec, October 1991

[3] R. Bellinzona, M. G. Fugini, "RECAST User Manual", Technical Report ITHACA.POLIMI.92.E.2.9.#3, Politecnico di Milano, December 1992

[4] R. Bellinzona, M. G. Fugini, B. Pernici, "An environment for requirement reuse", Report n. 92_082, Politecnico di Milano, December 1992

[5] P. Constantopoulos, M. Jarke, J. Mylopoulos, Y. Vassiliou, "Software Information Base - A Server for Reuse", Technical Report ITHACA.FORTH.92.E2.#1, Forth Computer Science Institute, Iraklion, Greece, January 1992

[6] P. Constantopoulos, E. Pataki, "A Browser for Software Reuse", 4th Int'l Conf. CAiSE '92, Manchester, U.K., May 1992

[7] J. L. Cybuski, K. Reed, "Hypertext-based Software Engineering Environment", IEEE Software, March 1992

[8] V. De Antonellis, B. Pernici, P. Samarati, "Object-Orientation in the Analysis of Work Organization and Agent Cooperations", Int. Conf. on Dynamic Modeling in Information Systems, Washington D.C., July 1991

[9] V. De Antonellis, B. Pernici, P. Samarati, "F-ORM METHOD: A F-ORM Methodology for Reusing Specifications", IFIP WG 8.4 Working Conf. on Object Oriented Aspects in Information Systems, Quebec, October 1991

[10] P. Devanbu, R. J. Brachman, P. G. Selfridge, B. W. Ballard, "LaSSIE: A Knowledge-Based Software Information System", Communication of the ACM, Vol. 34 N. 5, May 1991

[11] L. P. Deutsch, "Design Reuse and Framework in the Smalltalk-80 System", in Software Reusability, Vol. II, (eds. T. J. Biggerstaff and A.J. Perlis) ACM Press, 1989

[12] C. Fernström, K. Närfelt, L. Ohlsson, "Software Factory Principles, Architecture and Experience", IEEE Software, March 1992

[13] M. G. Fugini, M. Guggino, B. Pernici, "Reusing Requirements through a Modeling and Composition Support Tool", Third International Conference CAiSE'91, Trondheim, Norway, May 1991

[14] M.G. Fugini, S. Faustle, "Querying a Software Information Base for Components Reuse", IEEE Workshop on Software Reusability, Lucca, Italy, March 1993

[15] M.G. Fugini, O. Nierstrasz, B. Pernici, "Application Development through Reuse: the Ithaca Tools Environment", ACM SIG-OIS Bulletin, August 1992

[16] R. Girardi, "Application Engineering: Putting Reuse to work", in "Object Frameworks", D. Tsichritzis eds., Centre Universitaire d'Informatique, University of Geneva, June 1992

[17] A. Graffigna et al., "ADL Syntax Description", Technical Report ITHACA.Nixdorf.90.U.2.#7, Siemens Nixdorf Informationssysteme AG, Paderborn, December 1990

[18] M. Jarke, J. Mylopoulos, J. W. Schmidt, Y. Vassiliou, "DAIDA: An Environment for Evolving Information Systems", ACM Transations on Information Systems, Vol. 10, No. 1, January 1992

[19] G. J. Klir, T. A. Folger, "Fuzzy Sets, Uncertainty, and Information", Prentice Hall, 1988

[20] J. Li, "ADL and its Compiler", Technical Report ITHACA.Bull.91.U2.#3, Bull SA, June 1991

[21] V.T. Mercurio, B.F. Meyers, A.M. Nisbet, G. Radin, "AD/Cycle strategy and Architecture", IBM Systems Journal, 29, 2, 1990

[22] V. de Mey, B. Junod, S. Renfer, "Vista User's Manual", Technical Report ITHACA.CUI.92.Vista.#2, Centre Universitaire d'Informatique, University of Geneva, December 1992

[23] P. Mi, W. Scacchi, "A Knowledge-based Environment for Modeling and Simulating Software Engineering", IEEE Trans. on Knowledge and Data Engineering, vol. 2, n.3, Sept. 1990

[24] J. Mylopoulos et al., "Telos: Representing Knowledge about Information Systems", ACM Trans. Information Systems, October 1989

[25] O. Nierstrasz, "A Survey of Object-Oriented Concepts", in "Object-Oriented Concepts, Databases and Applications" ed. W. Kim and F. Lochovsky, Addison-Wesley/ACM Press, 1989

[26] O. Nierstrasz, D. Tsichritzis, V. de Mey, M. Stadelmann, "Objects + Scripts = Applications", Proc. ESPRIT'91 Conf., Kluwer Academic Publisher, November 1991

[27] O. Nierstrasz, S. Gibbs, D. Tsichritzis, "Component-Oriented Software Development", Communication of the ACM, Vol. 35, No. 9, September 1992

[28] B. Pernici, "Objects with Roles", Conf. on Office Information Systems, April 25-27 1990, Cambridge, Massachusetts

[29] R. Prieto-Diaz, "Implementing Faceted Classification for Software Reuse", Communications of the ACM, Vol. 34, N. 5, May 1991

[30] W. Scacchi, "The USC System Factory Project", Proc. Soft. Symp., Software Engineers Associates, ACM Press, January 1989

4.

REQUIREMENTS ENGINEERING

Information System Development Process (A-30)
N. Prakash, C. Rolland and B. Pernici (Editors)
Elsevier Science Publishers B.V. (North-Holland)

© 1993 IFIP. All rights reserved.

Use of Domain Knowledge for Requirements Validation

A.G. Sutcliffe and N.A.M. Maiden

Department of Business Computing, City University, Northampton Square, London EC1V 0HB,United Kingdom.

This paper reports reuse of generic domain knowledge in the form of templates, patterns or clichés to aid requirements capture and validation. These templates are retrieved through machine-based analogical matching. A cooperative paradigm for domain knowledge reuse is proposed. Human interpretation of templates is needed to maximise benefits from knowledge reuse, necessitating explanation and exploration of domain templates.

Keyword Codes: D.2.1
Keywords: Requirements/Specifications

1. INTRODUCTION

Domain knowledge is acknowledged to be important for the acquisition and validation of requirements specification. Unfortunately this is one of the most error prone and costly activities in system development which has led a number of researchers to investigate how the process of requirements capture and validation may be improved.

Previous approaches have varied from development of powerful specification languages [14], to investigation of declarative, rule based paradigms [10] and embedding domain knowledge in CASE tools to allow intelligent requirements validation [15]. While more powerful languages can help expression of requirements and verification of specifications, they do not in themselves help validation. Embedded domain knowledge can give better leverage on validation but at a considerable cost in acquiring and representing such knowledge in a machine processable form. It is doubtful whether tools with embedded domain knowledge could ever keep pace with the development of new systems in changing domains.

A possible solution to the domain knowledge acquisition dilemma is to use more generic domain knowledge in the form of templates, patterns, or cliches. This approach has been primarily explored in software reuse [6, 16], and could be applied to requirements validation, although matching of appropriate generic templates to new applications is problematic. Concepts of analogy based matching, also employed in specification reuse [11, 20] could be used to solve this problem.

This paper extends our work in analogical matching for specification reuse, by extending models of domains into a wider theory for requirements capture and validation. A preliminary theory of domain knowledge is proposed which describes abstract domain classes, rules which discriminate between domain classes and a matching process which takes descriptions of new applications and finds their generic domain class. Requirements of a new application are then validated against a model of the domain class. The paper is organised into four sections. First the domain theory is presented then the matching process is described. This is followed by use of the domain models for a case study in requirements validation and the paper concludes with a brief discussion.

2. A PRELIMINARY THEORY OF DOMAIN KNOWLEDGE

The assumptions that the theory rests upon are drawn from cognitive models of memory, in particular the hierarchical models of natural categories [17], hierarchical memory schemata [1] and categories of dynamic memory [21]. These assert in slightly different forms that human memory is organised in an informal hierarchy of classes. Generally there is good evidence that memory for several different types of knowledge (e.g. objects, procedures and plans) is organised hierarchically and applied theories of knowledge representation embody classification structures (e.g. Task Knowledge Structures [9]). We propose that domain abstractions are modelled as classes which are specialised by addition of further knowledge to achieve appropriate targeting in terms of generalisation/specialisation. This leads to the basic propositions:

- domain knowledge is organised into a hierarchy of models, each domain model is defined by a finite set of shared features. Each class level adds more specialised features;
- domain knowledge is aggregated by association with a problem that exists in the universe of discourse, that is some state in a system which should be changed;
- differences between domain classes can be distinguished by a small number of key determining features;
- most software engineering problems can be ascribed to one of a tractably small set of domain models.

The first distinction the theory makes is between object models and information system models:

- object models are the basic processing of the system composed of objects, actions, and constraints. Objects models describe what we more readily call transaction processing;
- information system models describe processing which is itself dependent upon the existence of the object model. Information systems feed off the object model and are more familiar as report-generating sub systems or online queries.

Both models describe problem spaces, that is collections of knowledge which relate to a system requiring change. Problems are conceived as a future state of affairs that the user wants the system to achieve. Initially these may be linguistically expressed functional requirements. As analysis progresses ambiguous expression in language can be more formally expressed as description of system behaviour and the desired (solution) state of system objects. For instance 'the library should control book loans' is expressed as an invariant that each book which is loaned must be returned. This approach is similar to ideas employed on the KAOS project [3]. The problem is therefore the domain's rasion d'etre. From this we hypothesise that the fundamental aspects of domain are objects and transitions to achieve change from initial (problem) to final (solution) states. To this we add the components which are fundamental to modelling object transitions. These we term system structures which represent the physical or abstract sets containing objects. These predictions accord with our empirical knowledge of systems analysts [20], cognitive studies of problems solving in other domains and the fact gathering strategies employed in structured system development methods. The basic semantics of the domain are therefore structure, objects, transitions with respect to the structure and states to be achieved.

The basic models are augmented with further knowledge about the environment, e.g. organisational knowledge and causal reasons for behaviour in the domain. This leads to two further models:

- an organisation framework describes the superstructure within which domain models exist;
- models describing the casual relationships between objects and structures in the domain model in order to explain their behaviour. Causal relationships can also explain how the system relates to its purpose, i.e. how behaviour is linked to the system's goal state.

The organisational framework gives a means of structuring knowledge for validation, although such knowledge will probably require human interpretation. A payoff will have to be established between the effort of recording such knowledge and possible benefit in validation, and this is one focus of our ongoing work. A further justification may, however, be in explanation. We believe that an important part of requirements engineering is understanding the application by reference to its immediate context and by reference to similar contexts. The organisation framework could prove invaluable as a explanatory setting linking a problem-oriented domain to an organisation, its place within the organisation structure, and relevance to organisation policy.

Explanation prompts the final component of the theory, capture of causal knowledge about the problem domain. Experience with abstract domain models has shown that while people can understand them [12], there was a need for explanation about the object structure and for linking goals with the problem abstraction. This suggests a validation role for causal knowledge about 'why things happen as they do'. Inspiration for this work comes from the concept of causal stories in knowledge engineering [2]. The need is for explanation of the observed transitions of objects and laws governing them. For example in air traffic control causal explanation would provide knowledge about structural components (air corridors, manoeuvring areas, airports, flight paths), objects and their properties (types of aircraft, flight speeds, manoeuvring capabilities) rules governing transitions (direction, height, speed, instructions) and system invariants (separation distance). The corresponding abstract causal model describes spatial object management with objects following paths according to rules governing movement and separation. A generic model of spatial object management can be applied several applications in its class (e.g. air traffic control, ship navigation control, railway signalling, etc.). Causal knowledge is represented in informal semantic networks to help tracing of causal links. This part of the theory is the subject of further investigation to look at the stopping problem, i.e. at which point is the causal story sufficient for explanation. For instance, does the system need basic physical laws about aero dynamics ? Again there will be a trade off between the effort of capture and benefit of understanding for reuse and explanation for validation.

To summarise the theory as it currently stands has three main components as shown in Figure 1:

- a set of abstract domain problem classes, a meta-schema which defines the modelling language and rules for determining class membership. These form the object and information system models of the application;
- the organisation framework;
- causal models for explanation of abstract problem classes.

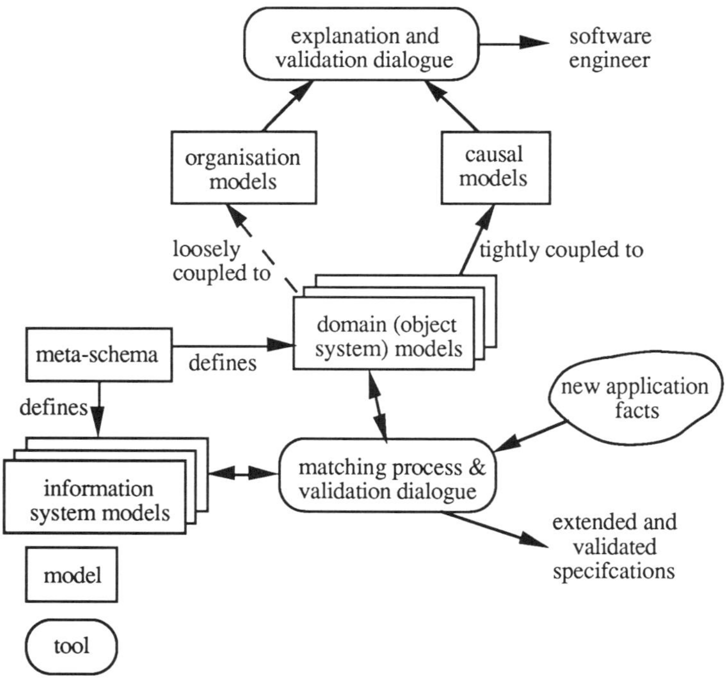

Figure 1. Components of the domain theory and their interaction.

Constraints of space in this paper preclude further description of the whole theory. Instead we shall concentrate on the domain theory and its matching process, and attempt to demonstrate how validation fits into this component.

We shall return briefly to the wider picture in the discussion by suggesting how further validation and explanation can be delivered by using other components by virtue of their links to the abstract domain models. The components of the theory are a meta-schema which defines the modelling language for abstract domain models, an initial set of domain models and rules for matching facts describing application problems to one or more domain models. The rules have been developed as a computational matching process. Each component is elaborated in the following sections.

2.1. Meta-Schema of Domain Knowledge

The meta schema describes our modelling language. We hypothesise that seven key knowledge determine software engineering domains:

- objects. These are the prime modelling primitive which represent constructs of interest in the universe of discourse;
- the structure of the system. This is knowledge of the objects within the systems and the sets they naturally fall into. The prediction is that people will perceive sets which pertain to physical structures in the real world. Hence the term 'containment' may be a familiar cue for system structure, e.g. stock objects-contained-in warehouse; students are-contained-in a school. The system structure describes the object sets implicated in input and output (i.e. changes in object status across the system boundary) and any major physical entity sets within the system itself. Most of the system structure should be apparent from an entity relationship diagram;
- state transitions which cause objects to change set membership with respect to the system structure. Inter-domain class differences are critically determined by these state transitions more than any other feature;
- events which trigger state transitions. Internal and external events (with an origin outside the system) are recognised. This enables description of the scope or boundaries of the system;
- object properties. High level properties of an object, focusing on roles within the system (e.g. resource, mechanism), movement, and other high level abstract or concrete qualities. Properties are essentially a type definition of objects, which although currently not formalised, are amenable to such treatment;
- requirements/purpose. This is the goal or solution state that the system exists to achieve goals and statements of purpose often differ between users and may be expressed with different degrees of precision, more formal definition is in terms of future states which the system must attain;
- conditions. Stative information or values held in attributes of an object and other non-object states (e.g. time, duration) which are evaluated before a state transition can occur.

Users are predicted to use requirements and purpose as the most 'natural' descriptors of domains, hence these features will be more easy to elicit. However, given the ambiguity inherent in many teleological descriptions, system structure and state transitions are predicted to be the most reliable determinants of domains. A composite of system structure and related transitions could be taken as the domain/class 'key' in database terms.

Another modelling component, although not part of the meta-schema, is the transformation. These are set of actions leading to a state change of system objects within a single procedure. In other words transformations can not be halted midway and all the operations must execute to change the object's state. Transformations may result in state transitions in set membership in the system structure. To illustrate the concept, common transformations in information systems are scheduling, allocation by constraint satisfaction, searching for objects, reservation, etc.. These result in conceptual-stative changes to objects such as 'reserved, found, sorted, scheduled.' Transformations are similar to 'methods' in object oriented specifications or procedures in structured methods.

The relationship between meta-schema components is shown as an informal entity relationship diagram in Figure 2. Space limitations preclude discussion of the many of the schema primitives which elaborate the above principal modelling components. Most of the schema primitives are familiar from the modelling languages of structured developments methods (e.g. JSD, NIAM, SADT, etc.). The additions made by the domain theory is to emphasise system structure as a modelling concept, to link system structure to system purpose and differentiate between object and information system models.

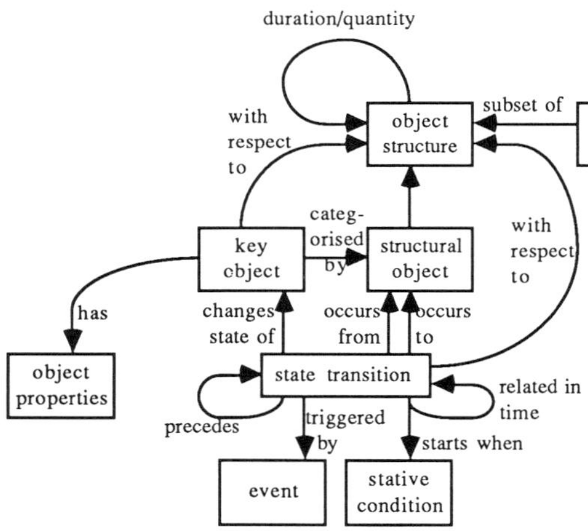

Figure 2. Domain theory meta-schema.

2.2. Matching applications to domain models

The abstract domain classes for object hiring and object containment share similarities in their basic system structure however they are differentiated by the key state transition of a return from the client to the system.

The resource hiring abstraction may appear to fit a standard stock control problem in which stock items are matched to customers orders, and stock is replenished; however two key transitions differentiate resource hiring from stock control. First, in stock control objects are dispatched and the majority never return and new-resources arrive. A return in the library changes an object's state from on-loan to in library, whereas this transition is not common in stock control, return of damaged stock non withstanding. In contrast, some actions do not discriminate between abstract classes; for instance, reservation of objects can lead to a status change in either abstraction.

The architecture and algorithms of the domain matcher are described in three parts. First the components of the matcher are described, then the matching algorithms are followed by the role of the domain matcher in an example. The aim of the domain matcher is to determine a degree of similarity between a target domain description and one or more candidate domain abstractions, then use inferred fact mappings to identify equivalences between objects in the domain and its abstraction.

2.3. Architecture of the domain matcher

The matcher's architecture shown in Figure 3 has five components, namely a match controller, structure matcher, rule-based matcher, domain discriminator and computational analogical matcher. These components access three knowledge sources, the target domain description, domain abstractions and domain discrimination rules. The target domain description represents facts about the new application while domain abstractions and discrimination rules are defined by the domain theory.

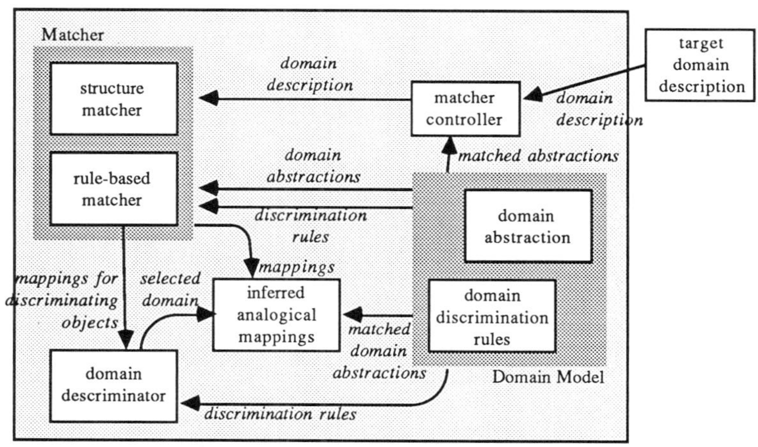

Figure 3. Architecture of the domain matcher.

The match controller decides how a target description is mapped to domain abstractions. It sends this description to the structure or rule-based matcher depending on the current state of the match. Structure matching identifies mappings between state transitions and object structures while other knowledge types are mapped by the rule-based matcher. This distinction is dictated by the knowledge structure defined in the domain theory. State transitions in respect to object structures are central to the theory and are matched structurally because of the inter-relatedness of such facts.

The structure matcher uses an analogical matching paradigm [22] to match object structures and state transitions and outputs a quantified match between input facts and each abstract domain model. Rule based matching calculates the degree of mapping between facts not related to the system structure and extend an existing match inferred by the structure matcher. First, events and stative conditions for state transitions are matched, then actions, then domain requirements. The domain discriminator reasons heuristically about key differences between two or more candidate domain models using rules defined by the domain theory. The quantified result of this reasoning discriminates between borderline matches.

Matching between a domain description and candidate abstractions at one level in the domain specialisation hierarchy is achieved in five phases:

phase 1: examine candidate type mappings for the likelihood of a structure or rule-based match. The total of type mappings defines the potential of a match and acts as a filter to avoid unnecessary and time-consuming computational matching;

phase 2: rule-based or structure matching for each object and fact needed to infer key differences between two or more candidate abstractions;

phase 3: reasoning about key differences between candidate abstractions using the object and fact mappings inferred in the previous stage;

phase 4: further rule-based matching between the domain description and the selected abstraction to calculate the full extent of the match with the abstraction;

phase 5: comprehensive structure matching between the domain description and each candidate domain abstraction.

Operation of the matching process is best described in the following example scenario which demonstrates both structure and rule-based matching. Structure matching is used to infer an initial degree of match with a candidate abstraction while rule-based matching refines the match to specialisations of the abstract domain class. The algorithm maps pairs of facts which belong to a coherent knowledge structure in preference to those which do not. The matching process is repeated for each application fact until a degree of match between it and each candidate abstraction has been calculated. Resulting mappings between objects are calculated from the total scores of fact mappings which include these object pairs in equivalent positions.

In the first phase of matching, the structure matcher attempts to map a target application description to the object containment domain shown in Figure 4. The structure matcher infers an interrelated knowledge structure shared by the application and top-level abstractions, in this case the OC abstraction. Details of the matching mechanism are given in [22]. As the software engineer enters further facts, the domain matcher matches these facts against the lower level OM and OR abstractions. The domain theory dictates that the OM and OR abstractions are differentiated by state transitions with respect to object structures, and defines two discriminating rules between the OM and OR abstractions. Each rule defines one difference between two abstractions, a difference being constrained to the inclusion of one or many instances of a fact type in domain abstraction but not in the other.

Rule-based matching in next stage validates the agreed match with the OM abstraction. It takes new application facts (events, conditions and domain requirements) and matches them to the abstract models in a predefined order dictated by the domain theory, e.g. events, conditions, etc. Rule-based matching reveals several omissions from the stock control description, for instance, there are no facts describing domain requirements or situations. Previous structure and local mappings are used to infer the omitted facts and to produce validation guidance for the software engineer.

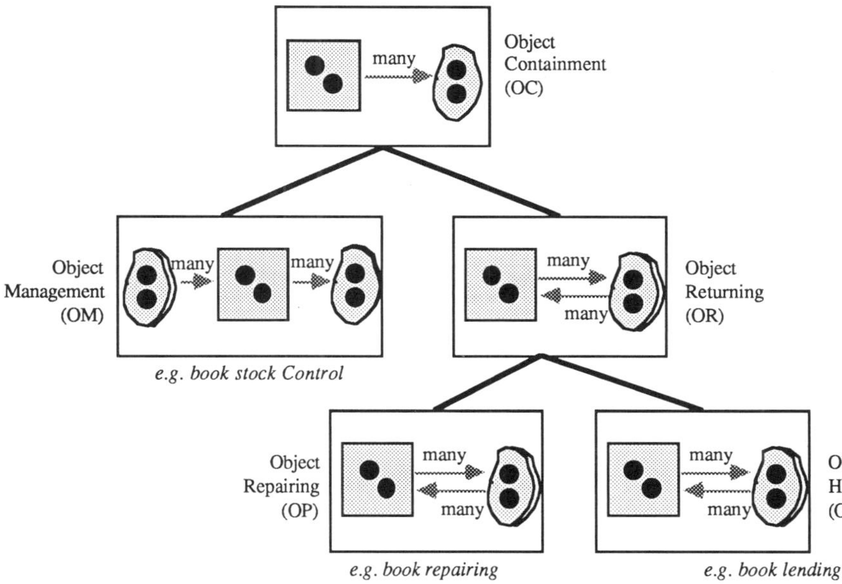

Figure 4. Example specialisation hierarchy of domain abstractions, showing specialisation of basic object containment abstraction through addition of state transitions, object structures, and events to distinguish the object repairing and object hiring abstractions.

3. VALIDATION AND THE DOMAIN THEORY

The intention of the following scenario is to demonstrate how the domain theory assists derivation of a more complete and consistent requirements specification. Validation is envisaged as a cooperative task in which the machine matches facts describing a new application to existing generic models of domains and then provides assistance by pointing to likely omissions, inconsistencies and contradictions to the software developer. The scenario also reveals how the theory may help move from an informal to formal representation of requirements. Informal requirements are usually represented as narrative descriptions. The system permits requirements to be entered as a formal representation using frames describing knowledge types, similar to those used in a previous prototype developed for reusable component matching (Maiden & Sutcliffe 1992).

The scenario examines the need for stock control capabilities within a library and illustrates the transition from an informal and incomplete statement of stock control requirements to a more formal and complete domain description. This is achieved by:

- using the meta-schema of domain knowledge types to capture key facts as formal domain predicates;
- matching this domain description to known domain classes represented as abstract conceptual models;
- validating and guiding the domain description in light of agreed matches with these abstractions.

The scenario illustrates the domain matcher component which is implemented in Prolog. However, some of the fact capture dialogue is simulated in the current version of the prototype because we intend carrying further usability testing on the user interface before fully implementing the fact acquisition and validator component. A revised implementation is in progress using TELOS [14], an object oriented deductive database language, and its implemented form the ConceptBase [8]. The classification structure of Telos allows meta-classes hence the domain theory modelling language is implemented using the class constructs provided. The TELOS implementation allows inferences to made about facts entered as queries and domain models held in the database.

The domain matcher can be used in two different modes of cooperation:

(i) the user enters application facts and the system matches these against its domain models and selects an appropriate class. This is presented to the user who can then validate their understanding of the domain against that of the system. Further validation by extension of the specification may be possible by the system bringing further related facts to the the user attention;

(ii) the user first selects an abstract domain model and then enters application facts. In this case the system acts as a validator on fact capture. If the entered facts do not conform to the abstraction selected by the user then the system rejects them.

These two modes can be used interchangeably so the software engineers can make assumptions about the nature of the problem and ask the system to confirm them or alternatively ask the system to select the appropriate domain class. In both modes the system can import further knowledge from linked domain models to help validation and augmentation of the specification.

3.1. Initial requirements capture: the incomplete problem statement

The problem statement defines the required system functionality and describes what happens in during stock control in the library domain. This problem statement is both incomplete and overspecified (c.f. Meyer 1985) to demonstrate typical problems encountered when refining the requirements specification:

The computerised library lending system is to be extended by a stock control facility with the following needs:

- *to identify missing or damaged books which are no longer in the library;*
- *to permit a stock take of books within parts of the library.*

Limitations on this functionality include:

- *the system must support both automated and staff identification of missing books;*
- *books cannot be purchased without staff authorisation entered to the system.*

In the current library stock control books can be on the library shelves to be lent, in the archive store or with borrowers. Damaged or out-of-date books are taken from the library to the archives store. Missing books are assumed to be stolen by borrowers. There is only library and one archive store. It is known that some borrowers steal books.

3.2. Transformation of informal to formal requirements statement

The aim of this first stage is to capture informal requirements as semi-formalised domain descriptions. This is achieved using requirement definition frames. Each frame provides a restricted set of terms for defining the application. Terms are defined by the meta-schema of domain knowledge types and individual tokens in the system lexicon.

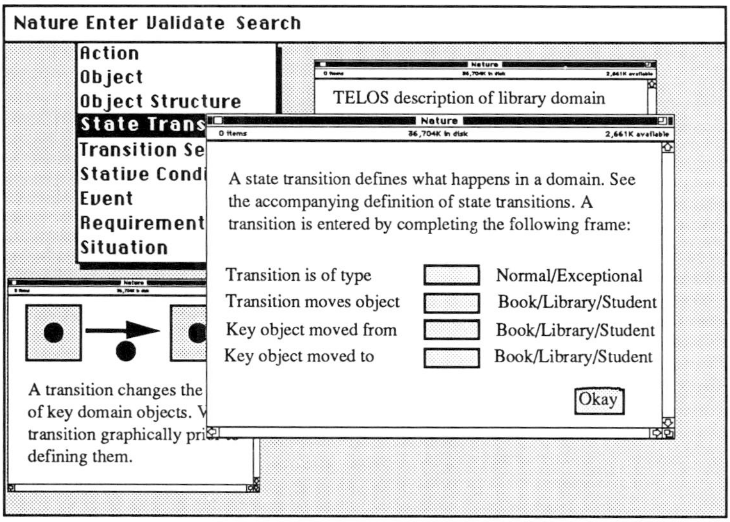

Figure 5. Dialogue screen showing fact capture for state transitions.

Figure 5 illustrates the first stage when the user enters key state transitions with respect to object structures. Fact capture is aided by description of state transitions and explanation by analogical examples. The initial problem statement is incomplete because it does not mention stock replenishment actions. Fact entry at each stage is validated by matching against candidate domain models and then suggesting possible omissions and inconsistencies to be repaired by the user. Key fact types are captured early in the dialogue to identify the most important requirements and assist problem scoping, two tasks known to be difficult for less experienced software engineers [23]. The dialogue actively encourages better domain understanding by presenting examples, partial views of abstract domain model and new fact types linked to the requirement engineer's current mental model of the domain.

The interface has four parts. A definition of state transitions uses both narrative and spatial diagrams. Such definitions are supported by presentation of concrete examples of state transitions. A frame permits entry of the state transition from options. Finally a TELOS definition of existing library objects is presented to avoid duplication domain description.

3.3. Retrieve and present appropriate domain abstraction

The partial domain description is sufficient to match the Object Containment (OC) abstraction since it describes depletion of books from the library but not their renewal. This inferred match is explained to the requirements engineer for checking and confirmation, see Figure 6. This explanation can be in four parts. First, a formal Telos definition of the abstraction is supported by narrative explanation and spatial diagrams representing the domain. Familiar concrete examples of the OC abstraction can also assist comprehension. A fourth window instructs the requirements engineer to select or reject the OC abstraction as a partial match for the stock control domain.

3.4. Further fact acquisition

The tool explains that the current application should be specialised to either an Object Management (OM) or Object Resource (OR) domain. The two abstractions are represented using spatial diagrams which highlight key state transitions with respect to object structures. Selection of the OM abstraction permits the tool to provide further hints for extending the stock control domain description. These hints are controlled to ensure that the domain description is extended according to the domain theory. The requirements engineer is encouraged to elaborate the stock control description in a specific order:

- state transition linked to the replenish action;
- object structures describing the supplier concept;
- events and stative conditions controlling the state transition;
- elaboration of action definitions linked to the key transition;
- situations and domain requirements.

The dialogue is sufficiently robust to identify omission of fact in the entry order and return to the requirements engineer for such facts. As in earlier stages, fact acquisition is supported by explanation of the matched domain abstraction, intelligent hints based on a match with the abstraction.

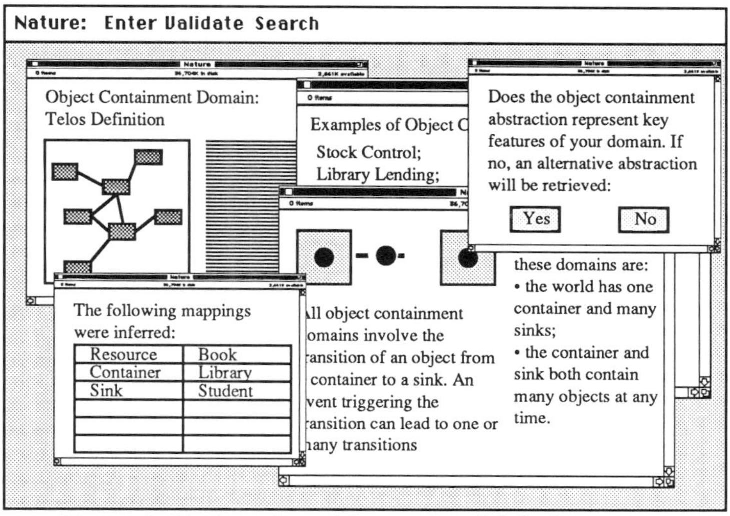

Figure 6. Explanation of the retrieved OC abstraction

3.5 Validating and extending the domain description

The domain matcher uses rule-based matching with the OM abstraction to validate the application description, revealing several omissions from the description. These omissions provide the basis for guiding the requirements engineer to extend the stock control description in the next stage. Figure 7 demonstrates inference of a possible omission of a domain requirement from the stock control description and the subsequent dialogue encouraging entry of the required fact(s). The result of this final stage is a more complete and consistent domain description for the library's stock control domain according to key facts in the domain theory.

Validation is currently driven from the structure of abstract domain models contained in the domain theory. Hence if the tool expects a certain transition to be present in an abstract domain classes and this fact has not been entered, it suggests there may be an omission to the user. Further validation is driven from the type structure and meta-schema, hence the tool prompts for conditions to be added to state transitions. So far validation rules perform structure and type checking which enables at least limited semantic validation of requirements and specification. However more can be achieved and in the final section we return to the causal and organisation models.

4. FUTURE WORK ON VALIDATION

Once a domain class has been recognised by the matcher further stored knowledge can be employed for validation purposes. First, the causal model, which is tightly coupled to the domain model, can be used to explain certain causal effects on system behaviour and thereby helping development of requirements. For instance in the library domain the link between fines and the effect of causing users to return books on time can be explained or the causal relationship between authorisation for purchase of new books and the necessary discipline in accounting procedures. Causal models can be used in two ways, as a repository of wisdom about the reasons of domain behaviour, and secondly as descriptions about the behaviour of systems given their relationship to physical, biological, or social laws. Causal models therefore represent knowledge which may be useful for determining requirements in a system and for understanding why systems behave as they do.

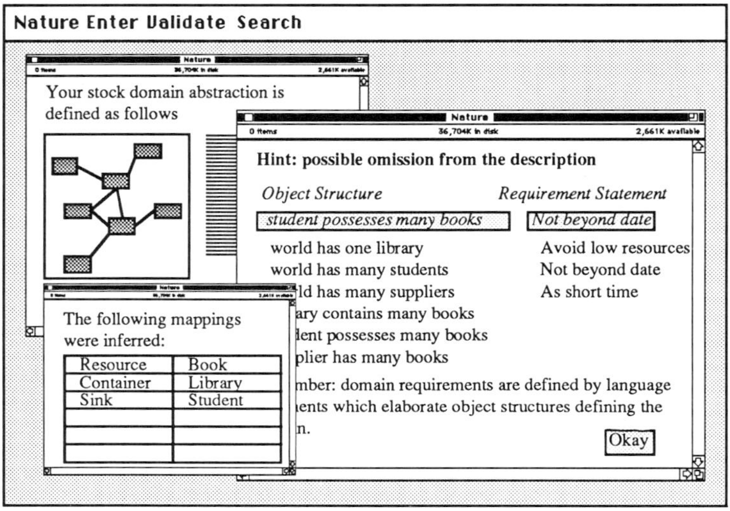

Figure 7. Validation of the domain description, revealing a possible omission which the requirement engineer is requested to reason about and enter if correct.

Organisation models are less closely coupled. The same domain model may be found in several different organisation environments, so organisation models can only be used as general advice. Some tighter coupling may be possible when organisation types can be identified as reliably co-occuring with specific domain types, as may be found in command and control systems in military organisations. However, we generally consider organisation models to be a 'framework of thought' within which we intend to develop further work extending the concept of goal backwards from the domain models towards business goals and organisational policy.

Finally, information systems model are amenable to the same matching and validation process as the abstract domain models for the object system. We are developing a set of abstractions of typical information systems needs in line with the philosophy of our theory, hence the definition of the model is linked to its purpose. In information systems models the purposes at the abstract level are progress tracking, status checking, and valuation; in more concrete terms these are reporting functions such as age of debt reports, stock status, and financial cost control.

5. CONCLUSIONS

The theory and description of domain classes is still in its preliminary stages. So far 40 abstract problem domain classes have been described ranging from object hiring (e.g. library, car hire, video hire) to spatial object management (e.g. air traffic control). Each class has approximately three levels of specialisation. However several problems which remain to be solved:

(i) the granularity between levels in one class;
(ii) the naturalness and usability of key features in determining the identity of domains by users;
(iii) goodness of fit of natural problems into domain classes;
(iv) formal properties of domain abstractions and how they related to design abstractions.

So far we have some preliminary, encouraging results on the second problem [12]. The granularity issue does have a partial answer in terms of system purpose and the organisation framework. Our studies continue on extending the number of problem abstractions and examining the fit between applications and abstract problem classes. The theory as it stands describes the problem domain. It therefore models requirements specification and current system description. One future direction is to examine how solutions (designs) may be linked to specifications (problem description). Other workers have studied abstract classes of design problems [6, 18] and proposed classes of solutions. Extension of our current work in analogical matching envisages matching abstract domain models to software solutions belonging to the same problem class.

The domain theory represents an alternative view of the Subject, Usage and Development worlds espoused in [17]. The domain abstractions give a richer view of the subject world than captured in conceptual models of structured development methods (e.g. JSD, SSADM). Furthermore it adds the dimension of abstraction to models of problems which, with a machine assisted matching process [11] can support validation. The need for explanation in requirements engineering has been partially recognised by interest in argumentation models and design rationales. A further extension of our work is to look at modelling how decisions are made when requirements specifications are transformed into software designs. We believe explanation of requirements documents has an important function in decision making and validation.

In conclusion, the domain theory provides a systematic means for defining models of domain knowledge. It also gives a mechanism for empowering validation at several levels. We believe the future for validation in requirements analysis lies in creating more formal, knowledge intensive models which grow with corporate CASE repositories and our work in the NATURE project will progress in that direction.

ACKNOWLEDEGEMENTS

This work was partially funded by the European Commission's Esprit programme in Basic Research Project P6353 NATURE (Novel Approaches to Theory Underlying Requirements Engineering). It is a pleasure to acknowledge the stimulus and help of partners Matthias Jarke, Klaus Pohl, Stephan Jacobs, University of Aachen, Germany (project coordinator); Collete Rolland, Georges Grosz, Jean-Roch Schmidt, University of Paris 1, the Sorbonne; Yannis Vassiliou, Panos Constantopoulos, Giorgios Spanoudakis, FORTH research institute, Crete, Greece; Janis Bubenko, Benkt Wangler, Peter Holm, SISU, Sweden and David Till, Sara Jones, City University.

REFERENCES

1. Anderson J.R., (1985) Cognitive psychology and its implications. W.H. Freeman, New York.
2. Chandrasekaran B., Keuneke A. & Tanner M., (1992), Explanation in Knowledge Systems, The roles of the Task structures and Domain Functional Models. In Proceedings of Workshop on task based Explanation, Samos, Greece, Univ of the Aegean.
3. Dardanne A., Fickas S. & van Lamsweerde A., (1991) Goal directed acquisition in requirements elicitation. Proceeding 6th International Workshop on Software Specification and Design, Como Italy, IEEE Computer Society Press, 14.
4. Gentner D., (1983) Structure-Mapping: A Theoretical Framework for Analogy, Cognitive Science 7, 155.
5. Gick M.L. & Holyoak K.J., (1983), Schema Induction and Analogical Transfer, Cognitive Psychology 15, 1.
6. Harandi M.T. & Lee M.Y., (1991), Acquiring Software Design Schema: A machine learning perspective. Proceedings 6th Conference on Knowledge Based Software Engineering, Syracuse, NY, IEEE Computer Society Press, 188.
7. Jarke M., Rolland C., Sutcliffe A.G. & Vassiliou Y., (1993), Theories underlying requirements engineering: An overview of NATURE at genesis. Proceedings 1st International Symposium on Requirements Engineering, San Diego CA, IEEE Computer Society press, 19.
8. Jarke M., (1992), ConceptBase V3.1 User Manual, Aachener Informatik Berichte 92-17.
9. Johnson P., Johnson H., Waddington R. & Shouls A., (1988), Task Related Knowledge Structures: Analysis, Modelling and Application. In People and Computers IV (HCI-88); (eds) Jones D.M. and Winder R., Cambridge University Press, 35.
10. Loucopoulos P., Papamastatiou G., Pantazis D. & Diakonolaou G., (1991), Design and execution of event/action DB applications. Proceedings 2nd International Workshop on Deductive Approach to Information Systems and Databases., Aiguablava, Spain.
11. Maiden N.A.M & Sutcliffe A.G. (1992); Exploiting reusable specification through analogy. Communications of the ACM 35(4), 55.
12. Maiden N.A.M & Sutcliffe A.G., (1993), Requirements Engineering by Example: an Empirical Study. Proceedings of 1st International Symposium on Requirements Engineering, San Diego, CA, IEEE Computer Society Press, 104.
13. Meyer B., (1988), Object oriented software construction. Prentice Hall.

14. Mylopopoulos J., Borgida A., Jarke M. & Koubarakis M,, (1990), Telos: Representing Knowledge about Information Systems. ACM Transactions on Office Information Systems 8(4), 325.
15. Punchello P.P., Torrigiani P., Pietri F., Burion R., Cardile B., & Conti M., (1988) ASPIS, a knowledge based CASE environment. IEEE Software March 1988, 58.
16. Reubenstein H.B., 1990, 'Automated Acquisition of Evolving Informal Descriptions', Ph.D. Dissertation (A.I.T.R. No. 1205), Artificial Intelligence Laboratory, Massachusetts Institute of Technology.
17. Rosch, E., (1985), Prototype classification and logical classification: The two systems. In E.K. Scholnick (ed), New trends in conceptual representation: Challenges to Piaget's theory? New Jersey: Lawrence Erlbaum.
18. Shaw M., (1991), Heterogeneous design idioms for software architecture. Proceedings 6th International Workshop on Software Specification and Design, Como Italy, IEEE Computer Society Press, 158.
19. Sutcliffe A.G. & Maiden N.A.M., (1990), Software reusability: Delivering productivity gains or short cuts. Proceedings Interact'90, (eds) Diaper, D., Gilmore D., Cockton G. & Shackel B., North Holland, 895.
20. Sutcliffe A.G. & Maiden N.A.M., (1991), Analogical software reuse: Empirical investigations of analogy based reuse and software engineering practices. Acta Psychologica 78(1-3), 173.
21. Schank R.C. & Leake D.B., (1989), Creativity and learning in a case-based explainer, Artificial Intelligence 40, 353.
22. Maiden N.A.M & Sutcliffe A.G., (1991), Analogical Matching for Specification Retrieval, Proceedings 6th Knowledge-Based Software Engineering Conference, IEEE Computer Society Press, 108.
23. Sutcliffe A.G. & Maiden N.A.M., (1992), Analysing the novice analyst: cognitive models in software engineering, International Journal of Man-Machine Studies 36, 719.

Information System Development Process (A-30)
N. Prakash, C. Rolland and B. Pernici (Editors)
Elsevier Science Publishers B.V. (North-Holland)

© 1993 IFIP. All rights reserved.

Utilizing Scenarios in the Software Development Process

Kevin M. Benner, Martin S. Feather, W. Lewis Johnson and Lorna A. Zorman*

USC/Information Sciences Institute, 4676 Admiralty Way, Marina del Rey, CA 90292, USA
e-mail: {benner,feather,johnson,lorna}@isi.edu

Abstract

Scenarios play an important role throughout the information system development process. Scenarios are partial descriptions of system and environment *behavior* arising in restricted *situations*. They are instrumental to the following activities: describing and clarifying the relevant properties of the application domain, uncovering system requirements, evaluating design alternatives, and validating designs. This paper will describe these roles in the context of an example and explain how computer-based tools can support the use of scenarios throughout the development process. The thesis of this paper is based on experience with three such computer-based tools.

Keycodes: D.2.1; D.2.6
Keywords: Requirements/Specification; Programming Environments

1 Introduction

This paper argues that scenarios have an important role to play in the information system development process. Scenarios are partial descriptions of system and environment behavior arising in restricted situations. Both the behaviors and the situations are expressed in concrete terms. Using scenarios in information system development usually involves an interplay between describing situations and describing behaviors; e.g., an analyst might propose a situation and decide what behavior would be appropriate to that situation, or suggest a behavior and determine in what situations that behavior might arise.

Conventional specification and implementation languages are not designed to support the description of systems via scenarios. Specifications describe the requirements that the system must satisfy in all cases. Likewise, source codes are sets of instructions sufficient to handle all possible inputs that the system will encounter. This emphasis on general, all-encompassing descriptions in software engineering stands in stark contrast to most human expertise. Cognitive science has demonstrated that human expert knowledge is organized in chunks, which recognize and respond to specific situations [1]. Human problem solving tends to be highly situated, i.e., people respond to details of the situation as it unfolds

*The authors have been supported in part by Rome Laboratory contract F30602-89-C-0103 and in part by Defense Advanced Research Projects Agency contract DABT 63-91-K-0006. Views and conclusions contained in this document are those of the authors and should not be interpreted as representing the official opinion or policy of RL, DARPA, the U.S. Government, or any other person or agency connected with them.

rather than carry out detailed plans that have been worked out in advance [19]. This incompatibility between software engineering notation and human expertise causes severe difficulties in requirements elicitation and system validation. System analysts must elicit from domain experts general properties of the application domain, and general rules of behavior that the system should follow. Experts may be able to offer such rules, but when they are presented with particular hypothetical situations the experts are likely to raise issues that are not accounted for in the general rules. Likewise, validating the implemented system against client intent involves evaluating the system's behavior in specific situations.

Scenarios have attracted interest lately in the human-computer interaction (HCI) community, as a way of describing sequences of interactions between systems and users [5, 16]. Campbell notes [4] that they can be used to illustrate how a user might accomplish particular tasks with the system, to evaluate system usability, to guide interface design, and to test theories of human-computer interaction. There has been limited discussion in the software engineering community of their use for describing, critiquing and explaining system behavior [2, 8]. Empirical studies have shown that designers evaluate designs by mentally simulating scenarios [9].

We claim that the significance of scenarios is greater than even these studies suggest. Scenarios are pervasive throughout the software development process, and are important for any system that is situated in a complex environment, not just systems with human-computer interfaces [12]. Furthermore, computer-based tools can enable scenarios to be realized as explicit artifacts. Automated retrieval, execution, etc. of scenarios can supplement and support the activities that software engineers perform mentally on scenarios at the present time.

In what follows, four different uses for scenarios will be discussed:

- describing and clarifying the relevant properties of the application domain,
- uncovering system requirements,
- evaluating design alternatives, and
- validating designs.

The rest of the paper is structured as follows: Section 2 introduces the example that we will use as illustration, the design of a traffic-light control system for a 4-way intersection. Section 3 elaborates our definition of a scenario. Section 4 introduces some scenario processing capabilities that we are developing. Section 5 illustrates our points regarding the different uses for scenarios by appealing to the 4-way intersection example. Section 6 enumerates the kinds of automated support that computer-based tools might be able to provide for scenarios in these activities, and describes and assesses the tools that we have developed so far for scenario processing. Section 7 summarizes and concludes the paper.

2 An Example Application

The following problem will be used throughout this paper as a focus for discussion.

Consider an intersection between two roadways of two-way traffic. At the point of intersection each roadway has one or more approach lanes for through traffic in each direction, and an approach lane for traffic turning left through the intersection. Design a system to control the traffic lights at this intersection in such a way as to optimize traffic flow. The system can utilize sensors to sense passing vehicles, and computers to analyze the traffic flow and adjust light timing and sequencing as appropriate.

This problem is quite simple compared to the problems that designers of large software systems must face nowadays; nevertheless it provides abundant illustrations of scenarios in use. It is also an area of current active technological development. The British Government's Road Research Laboratory has recently developed a system called Microprocessor-Optimized Vehicle Actuation (MOVA) that alters light timings to minimize the amount of time vehicles have to wait at intersection [10]. The City of Los Angeles has designed and implemented a system called Automated Traffic Surveillance and Control (ATSAC) that is currently being used to control traffic at over one thousand intersections [20]; by 1998 all 4,000 signalized intersections in the city will be integrated into the system [18]. Computer-controlled traffic signals are increasingly being recognized as having a critical role to play in relieving congestion, and reducing fuel consumption and emissions, and offer a cost-effective alternative to building new freeways and rail lines in urban settings.

Although individual traffic signal control systems have limited complexity, they must interact with a complex environment, namely vehicular traffic flow. The designer of such a system must make sure that the important characteristics of this environment have been taken into account.

3 A Scenario is ...

This section will elaborate upon our high level, initial characterization of scenarios, namely that scenarios are partial descriptions of system and environment behavior arising in restricted situations.

Scenarios are *partial* descriptions because they need not completely specify all the states that comprise a behavior, nor need they completely specify all the attributes of any given state. The intent is to allow the communicator of a scenario to provide only those parts of the description that are relevant to the scenario. For example, it is this characteristic that allows one to describe a scenario of a car moving through an intersection, without mentioning the number of passengers, or describing the buildings located around the intersection.

Scenario descriptions are formed of two parts — *behavior* and *situation*. These are expressed using the same constructs, but kept separate for purposes of focus, a distinction we will explain shortly. The behavior and the situation are each a partial ordering of states and transitions. Ordering between states and composition of partially ordered states are specified by means of the following common relations [11]: sequentiality (e.g., one state must follow another, or one behavior must follow another), partial and total concurrency (e.g., two events must take place at the same time), repetition, permutation, inclusive and exclusive or (e.g., event1 or event2 but not both), negation (e.g., event3 is not to occur) etc. For example, the behavior of a car moving through an intersection may be specified as a sequence of states (car in front of intersection, car inside intersection, car beyond intersection). Note that the scenario communicator has a variety of options for describing such a behavior — as an alternative to the sequence of *states* just mentioned, he/she could instead provide a sequence of *transitions* (car approaches the intersection, car enters the intersection, car leaves the intersection), or a combination of states and transitions (e.g., car is to the north of the intersection, car enters the intersection, car is to south of the intersection). These alternatives allow the communicator in each case to describe the same partial behavior, but with respect to different attributes of the system and environment. This illustrates how the communicator may describe partial behaviors so as to *focus* on desired portions of system and environment behavior.

Another aspect of *behavior* which is separate from the aforementioned partial description of states and transitions is the *rationale* of the scenario. Rationale is formalized in terms of a completely distinct set of relations among states and transitions. Such relations include triggering, enabling, and restraining. The effect of these is to further restrict the behavior described by the scenario. Again considering any of the previous scenarios about cars moving through an intersection, we know that entering the intersection is not an unconstrained transition. Rather, there are both enabling conditions which make entry into the intersection possible (green lights, ...), as well as restraining conditions which prevent it (red lights, ...). Such conditions on the temporal orderings within scenarios are common.

A scenario's *situation* is specified using the same constructs as its behavior, but is kept separate from that description in order to distinguish *focus*. Typically, the situation is where we would state background assumptions on the initial state of the scenario, and on the progress of the scenario (e.g., invariants that must hold throughout). For example, in the above the scenario communicator has focused on the movement of the car. The situation is the state of the traffic light. The situation expresses how the traffic light changes (red to amber to green to red ...). A change of focus by the scenario's user (e.g., focusing on how the traffic light responds to the presence or absence of cars) will cause behaviors to be reclassified such that the car's activity becomes part of the situation and the traffic light's activity becomes part of the behavior of interest. Although the basic formalism we use is similar to that in other scenario-based research, the separations we make between behavior and situation, and between rationale and temporal orderings, are relatively novel.

The focus of a scenario is often a consequence of the scenario's intended communicative function. That is, when a scenario is being used to demonstrate some point about system functionality, either the situation or the behavior is being demonstrated. The scenario may be describing the behavior expected in a given situation, or a situation in which a given behavior is expected to occur.

Distinct from the above discussion is the abstraction level at which a scenario is described. It is crucial that scenarios be expressible in concrete terms, yet at arbitrary levels of abstraction. This is accomplished by reifying abstract concepts as concrete instances. For example, suppose a hierarchy of concepts included "moving-vehicle," "car," and "Ford

Taurus," then any one of those abstract concepts could be "reified" into an object (or multiple such objects) to be used in scenarios. This capability allows the analyst to describe a behavior at the highest level of generality, rather than at a lower level which might require details immaterial to the intent of the scenario communicator. With regard to our example, the intersection concept has been reified as a generic instance of an intersection which is used instead of some specific intersection. Alternatively, if the attributes of a specific intersection were important to the scenario communicator, then the more specific instance would be used. This illustrates once again the pervasive role *focus* plays in determining what is important and thus what should and should not be included in a scenario.

Although scenarios can incorporate abstractions, it is important that scenarios not be too abstract or general, lest they ignore important factors in the situation. It is not always obvious a priori what factors in a situation have impact on a scenario. For example, one might imagine that it is unnecessary to describe the buildings surrounding an intersection when designing a traffic light controller, but this is not always the case. Driveways into and out of the surrounding buildings can influence traffic flow; so can displays in surrounding store windows. Scenarios are used to make these influences explicit in realistic situations, so that designers can take them into account. We will see numerous examples of this throughout the paper.

4 Three Example Systems

As part of our overall effort at understanding and supporting the use of scenarios, we have developed or are developing three scenario processing capabilities. These have all been integrated with the our knowledge-based system for supporting requirements acquisition, called ARIES (Acquisition of Requirements and Incremental Evolution into Specifications) [13, 14]. This section introduces the systems briefly, so that the reader may have some understanding of how automated tools can make use of scenarios. At the end of the paper, after the uses of scenarios have been surveyed, we will revisit these systems and further categorize their capabilities.

The Requirements Acquisition by Demonstration (RAD) system is intended to be used by non-programming application domain experts to create application domain scenarios in which multiple objects are interacting with their environment [15]. The scenarios are constructed by manipulating a graphical depiction of a situation into which the system being designed will be introduced, such as the depiction of a traffic light system shown in Figure 1. A user can construct or modify domain specific objects, assign behaviors to individual objects in the situation, and describe the rationale among the objects interacting in the situation. An interactive forms-based dialog is used to describe the behavior so that the scenario can be animated. RAD also allows the domain expert to describe scenarios at different levels of abstraction as well as describe the focus for the scenario being demonstrated.

The ARIES Simulation Component (ASC) addresses validation of specifications to make sure they encompass the right behaviors. In particular, ASC allows an analyst to state

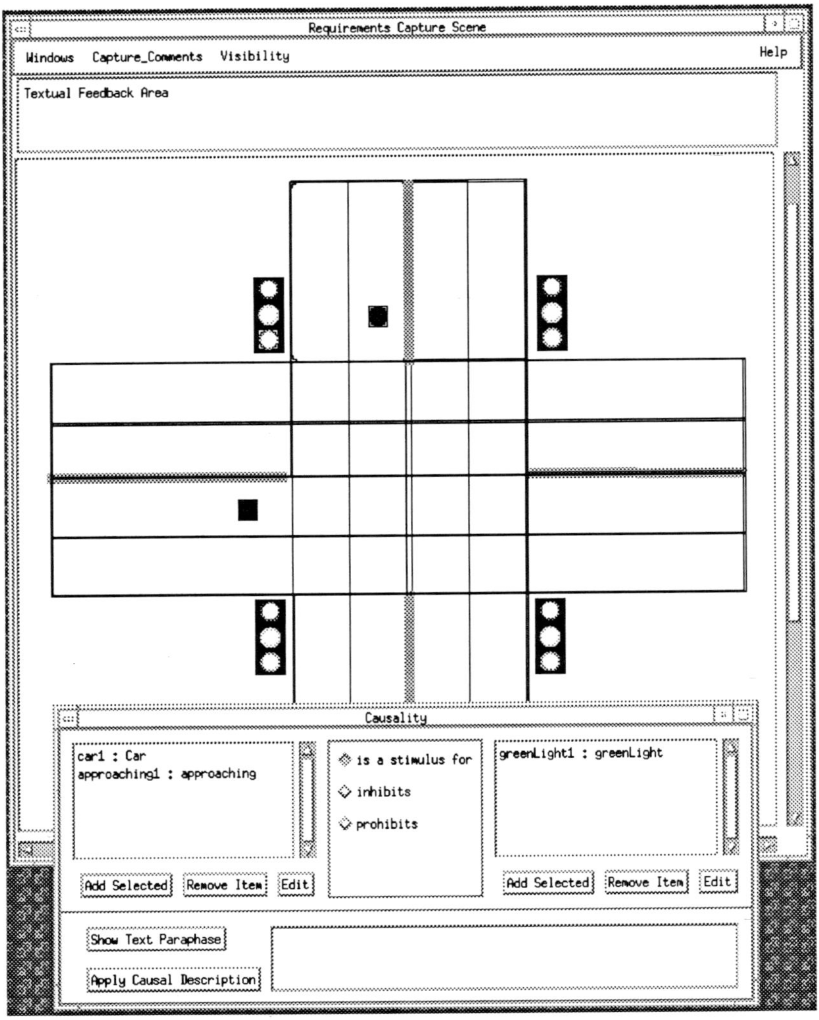

Figure 1: RAD demonstration interface

validation questions as scenarios which ASC then answers via simulation. The general form of the validation question is: "Does some specific behavior happen in the given situation." The ASC simulator answers this question by determining if the behavior is realizable, sometimes realizable, not realizable, or sometimes not realizable in the current specification. ASC differs from other simulation based tools in that it uses scenarios to address the problems of reducing irrelevant simulation data, simulating incomplete specifications, and reducing the size of the behavior space to consider.

ASC aids an analyst in abstracting out of the specification an appropriate simulation model, called a *specialized specification.* The specialized specification — based on the context of the validation question's behavior and situation — preserves the details of system behaviors that have a bearing on the validation question scenario, and suppresses other details. If the specification is incomplete, the specialized specification is augmented in order to make it executable, as in the PAISLey simulator[21]. This augmentation is incorporated as part of a validation question's situation. Finally, scenarios may be used to capture simplifying assumptions, also as part of a validation question's situation. In general, the specialized specification can be thought of as a slice through the specification's overall behavior space which includes only those behaviors concerned with the validation question scenario.

ARIES has an on-line instruction facility that employs scenarios to train users of the ARIES system. Each scenario describes a sequence of actions that a user might take in performing some task when using the system. The system automatically sets up a situation in which the task is appropriate to perform: it initializes the user's workspace, and displays on the screen those elements of the workspace that the user will manipulate while performing the task. When the user activates a training scenario, the system brings up a window that shows the steps in the scenario, as shown in Figure 2. The display shows a three-level hierarchy of structure in the examples: tasks to be performed (e.g., "Perform a complex evolution"), actions to complete as part of the task (e.g., "Find transformation"), and individual buttons to mouse on or text to type (e.g., "modify-spec"). When the mouse is placed over one of the action descriptions, a detailed description of each input required appears in a documentation window. The left column of the display indicates the analyst's progress through the example:"C" indicates that the action has been completed, and an arrow indicates the action that should be performed next. The instructional system tracks the user's progress through the scenario, and allows him or her to make detours from it at any time.

5 Roles of scenarios

We use the controller for traffic lights of a 4-way intersection as a common example throughout this section. This is intended as an intuitive example (of a system we are all familiar with) that illustrates the activities and corresponding capabilities we are postulating are useful.

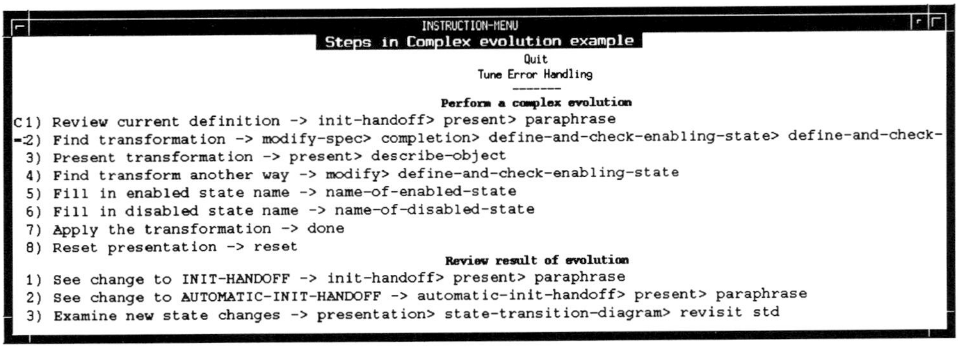

Figure 2: An instructional scenario

5.1 Describing and clarifying the relevant properties of the application domain

Curtis et. al. [7] cites "the thin spread of application domain knowledge" as an important cause of development effort and mistakes in large software systems. Capturing domain knowledge in the form of scenarios can alleviate this problem. Scenarios are also useful to validate our understanding of domains.

In the context of our 4-way intersection example, examples of domain properties that we would wish to ascertain include vehicular flow and velocity profiles of vehicles approaching, traversing and departing intersections, safety requirements in the form of bounds on amber light times, the lengths of time it takes the traffic in an intersection to clear out (when the lights change), etc. We examine these in more detail in the following subsections.

Vehicular flow around intersections: Vehicle behavior in the vicinity of intersections can be ascertained by considering a variety of typical situations (when approaching a clear intersection with a green light, when in a line of traffic, when approaching a red light, when accelerating on exit from an intersection, etc.).

From this we would determine, for example, lower bounds on the typical distances before and after intersections at which vehicles are flowing at full speed (i.e., have not begun decelerating in approach to the intersection, and are not still accelerating having traversed an intersection).

We would also determine that, in general, the longer the green light time (i.e., the longer each light stays green before turning to red and the next light in the sequence turning to green), the better the average throughput (because each change of lights necessitates the expense of stopping all traffic from entering until traffic within the intersection has cleared out — i.e., "context switching" in our domain). An actual scenario supportive of this is that of the traffic lights that used to be on highway 101 in California (a very busy route — freeway most of its length but interrupted in a few places to allow cross traffic) as it passed through Santa Barbara; anyone who has driven highway 101 through this intersection knows the additional delays incurred by bringing freeway traffic to a halt, and anyone who has waited to use one of the streets crossing highway 101 at this point knows the potentially long wait (several minutes) for a green light (indeed, signs advised drivers to turn off their engines while waiting!).

Bounds on light times: Scenarios can be applied in deriving quantitative safety bounds. For example, consider the task of finding the lower bound on the duration of the amber light, in the transition from a green light to a red light. The following is a relevant scenario:

> Consider the situation of a vehicle approaching an intersection at the time the light changes to amber. The behavior required of the vehicle is that it either comes to a halt before entering the intersection, or enters the intersection prior to the signal changing to red. This can be used to determine a lower bound on the amber period — too short a period would make it impossible for a vehicle approaching at the legal speed limit to either stop (based on driver reaction time and vehicle braking capacity) or have entered the intersection (assuming continued movement at maximum legal speed).

Time for the intersection to clear: In a similar manner to determining bounds on light times, scenarios can be used to determine the time it will take for an intersection to clear of vehicles after a light change:

> Consider the situation of a vehicle that enters an intersection at the last possible instant of an amber light, and compute the time required by the behavior in which the vehicle exits the intersection.
>
> Consider the situation of several vehicles waiting in the intersection to turn left (as many as can fit in the intersection) and compute the time required by the behavior in which they go from their stationary positions, through their turn, and out of the intersection.

Analytic techniques come into play to perform the actual calculations, but note that a scenario (or several scenarios) provides context within which to do these calculations.

In all these examples, it is the concrete nature of scenarios that identifies what domain properties are relevant, and suggests means to clarify their details.

5.2 Uncovering Requirements

Given a candidate design, the domain expert may draw upon scenarios from the real world to uncover further requirements that might impinge upon the design. Failure to consider these scenarios makes it much more likely that these requirements will be overlooked. In other words, the context provided by real-world scenarios is useful in bringing into consideration issues that lie outside the idealistic boundary we might otherwise have been tempted to draw around a system description.

Placement of loop detectors: Consider the following description on the choice of placement of loop detector (sensors that detect the passage of vehicles) (Figure 3), taken from Rowe [18]:

> "System detectors are placed in either of two configurations: in each marked lane at least 250 feet upstream of the signalized intersection or 100 feet on the departure side of the nearest upstream intersection which is signalized. The second option is more economical because of shorter conduit runs to the nearest intersection controller, but can only be used where there are no significant additions or losses of traffic between the detector and the downstream intersection and where the distances between intersections are not too great."

First, note the quantitative bounds on detector placement: ... *at least 250 feet upstream of the signalized intersection or 100 feet on the departure side of the nearest upstream intersection which is signalized* ... — presumably these bounds were arrived at from an analysis of typical traffic flow to determine where "normal" traffic flow could be measured by sensors (the vehicular-flow example of section 5.1).

Second, note the qualification: ... *but can only be used where there are no significant additions or losses of traffic between the detector and the downstream intersection and* .... This is precisely the sort of requirement that would be uncovered by considering real-world scenarios, e.g., a parking lot between the two intersections that feeds extra traffic into the road downstream of the point where the 100 foot sensor would go. We see the extracted description as the *codification* of a mix of domain knowledge and special-case reasoning.

Third, note that the depiction of this configuration employs *problem domain notation*, further enhancing the ease of human perusal and understanding. The RAD system's depiction of the situation in Figure 3 has precisely this characteristic of employing problem domain notation. For the purposes of this paper, in this static rendering of the RAD depiction we approximated the dynamic nature of the actual RAD interface, — e.g., mouse-sensitive labeling of objects — by hand-augmenting the scene with labels for the objects.

Downstream blockage / shortcutting: Domain considerations (section 5.1) suggested that the the longer the green light time the better; at this point, therefore, we might expect a domain expert to seek "stress" scenarios illustrating disadvantages of a very long green light. Two such scenarios that the domain expert might come up with are:

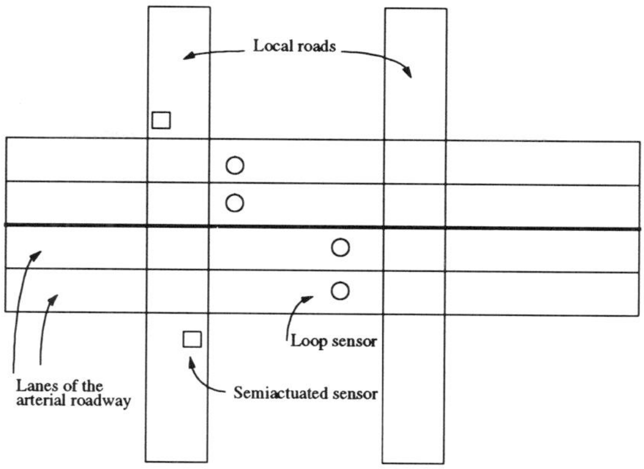

Figure 3: Placement of system detectors

Downstream blockage — a too-long green light lets so much traffic through so quickly that it backs up at the next intersection down the street, nullifying the advantage of the lengthy green light time.

Detouring — a too-long green light, and therefore too-long red light in some other direction(s), leads to people finding alternative routes around the intersection, e.g., residential side streets, thus nullifying the intended use of major thoroughfares.

Notice that both these scenarios uncover pertinent aspects from activities beyond the single intersection that is our primary concern — the first expands consideration to include the next intersection along the street, while the second deals with how drivers might react to circumvent the behaviors we had planned for them.

5.3 Evaluating Design Alternatives

Scenarios help while investigating alternative designs and requirements. Specific scenarios are especially useful for highlighting the crucial differences between design alternatives; they aid both in establishing what the differences might be (as in the other sections, through consideration of specific cases), and in serving as focal points around which to discuss relative importance (i.e., taking into account the relative frequencies at which scenarios occur, and the relative (dis)advantages of each).

Whether or not to have a left-hand turn arrow? A scenario that demonstrates the utility of a left-hand turn arrow is one in which during the time of a complete light cycle, more than three vehicles arrive along some direction wishing to turn left, and while that direction's light is green, there is continual heavy traffic in the opposing direction (meaning that left turns can be done only on the light changing to red, when the opposing traffic halts, and the three vehicles already in the intersection can complete their left turn). Ultimately, the accumulation of traffic wishing to turn left fills the left hand turn lane and backs up into the straight lane, impeding the flow of all traffic through the intersection.

Applying this same traffic flow behavior to a different situation, that of an intersection with a separate left-hand turn arrow, shows how the left hand turning traffic is allowed through, and does not therefore back up.

Conversely, a scenario in which there is sporadic traffic flow in the opposite direction, or only occasional vehicles wishing to turn left, illustrates how traffic flows satisfactorily even without a left-hand turn arrow, and may even demonstrate better overall throughput for the intersection (because of not having to devote some of the light cycle time aside specifically for left hand turns).

Balancing the considerations that arise in each of these scenarios provides the analyst with the motivation for choice of one design over another.

Whether to coordinate closely spaced signals? We have already observed that traffic blockage can occur when traffic waiting at one signal backs up as far back as another signal. This is especially likely in the case of closely spaced signals. Two alternative designs to dealing with this are to either coordinate the light cycles of those two signals, or to leave those signal cycles uncoordinated, but have short cycle times.

The choice will depend on the situation. The former design — coordinated cycles — is appropriate for scenarios of heavy traffic flow, with an objective of maximizing throughput. For example outside our office building is a lot of commuter traffic flowing along a short cross street that intersects two parallel, heavily traveled streets; since the objective of traffic planners in this situation was (presumably) to maximize throughput, the light cycles at the intersections of the cross street with the two other streets are carefully coordinated, allowing long green lights (and thus good throughput), but avoiding downstream blockage along the cross street by coordinating those green light times. Conversely, another Los Angeles situation is that of the Wilshire shopping district; here, the roadside stores welcome stop-and-go slowly moving traffic, because it gives people the opportunity to notice the stores they are passing. Thus in this area, short light cycle times avert downstream blockages (it is still an objective that traffic flow, albeit slowly) and produce the kind of traffic flow desired for a shopping district.

5.4 Validating Designs

Analysts and domain experts often use scenarios informally to validate designs throughout the development process. They employ their knowledge of the domain and the current design to develop and reuse individual scenarios which selectively stress the current design while insuring that the requirements are satisfied. This approach differs from exhaustive testing in that it neither requires the design to be complete, nor requires the commitment of resources necessary for exhaustive testing. The following paragraphs demonstrate the use of scenarios which stress important parts of a design.

Amber light duration: Restating the issues relating to the duration of an amber light: If it is too short, cars will end up in the intersection when the light turns red. If it is too long the intersection becomes idle unnecessarily or the amber may be ignored by motorists. To address these problems an analyst has selected a design in which the amber duration is as short as possible, yet sufficiently long to ensure our safety concerns. Given a specification with this bias, an analyst might construct the following validation scenario to stress the safety portion of the requirements:

> Situation: A car is approaching an intersection and the controlling light turns amber. Consider the expected speed of the car and the rate at which the car can decelerate.
>
> Behavior: Does the car have time to either continue through the intersection before the light turns red or come to a stop before entering the intersection?

While the above scenario represents a whole class of behaviors, analysts and domain experts do not exercise all possible instances of this class. Instead one or more representative behaviors are selected. In this case, since the concern is safety, the analyst selects the worst case one, i.e., the highest expected speed and the slowest expected deceleration rate. Confidence that this executes properly translates into confidence that the entire class of scenarios executes properly.

Coordinated lights vs. short lights: Selection of one design over the other in the case of coordinated lights verses short duration lights depends on the performance of these designs under varying, expected traffic conditions. Scenarios allow the analyst to quantify these conditions as alternative situations and then via simulation stress each of the designs with respect to these situations to determine whether the desired behavior occurs.

The above examples illustrate how scenarios serve three roles in design validation. First, scenarios are used to state user expectations (i.e., in a given situation, what behaviors does the analyst expect?). These expectations may either be bad behaviors which should not occur or be good behaviors that should occur. ASC refers to this class of scenario as a Validation Question.

Second, a scenario situation is used to justify focusing execution on specific parts of the behavior space to the exclusion of others. That is, with respect to a validation question, some parts of the specification are more relevant than others. This realization allows the analyst to expend significantly less effort in order to achieve executability as opposed to making the entire specification executable and then having to deal with the resulting myriad of data.

Third, scenarios can be used to approximate behavior via concrete depictions at an appropriate level of detail. This idea is based on the thesis of this paper, that acquisition, formalization, and reasoning (in this case, execution) of scenarios, within well constrained situations, is easier than doing the same for abstract descriptions of behavior. Such approximations allow the analyst to facilitate early executability and hence design validation.

The utility of each of the above validation scenarios is that the analyst is able to validate the design during the development process rather than waiting until the entire design has been completed, thus uncovering latent requirements and design errors and reducing the amount of rework necessary because of errors discovered late in the development process. Guindon in [9] describes this process with respect to mental simulations. ASC [3] provides computer support for this same activity.

6 Computer-Based Support for Scenarios

We have seen many ways that people use scenarios in the previous examples. There are also many ways that computer-based tools can support scenario processing. The following is a summary of the major kinds of computer-based processing of scenarios that we believe are feasible, and a discussion of the contributions of the systems that we have built in each area.

6.1 Recording scenarios

The most fundamental function that computer-based tools can provide is the means to record scenarios; this serves as a prerequisite for any other computer-based support. Argumentative hypermedia tools such as gIBIS [6] can serve this purpose. Such tools use hypertext nodes to record the arguments for or against particular design choices. One form of argument can be whether or not the system supports a particular scenario, described in natural language. Unfortunately, recording scenarios in natural language limits their usefulness, since computer-based tools cannot provide much assistance in processing the scenarios. Tools that can record scenarios formally in some fashion are likely to be more useful.

Our work has focused more on specialized notations that formalize the *situation* and *behavior* in the scenario. In ASC scenarios are expressed as path expressions [11], a notation designed to describe sequences of events. The ARIES representation for states and events [14] may be used to describe scenario situations. In RAD users first create a domain-oriented model (an interactive depiction) of a situation which contains objects in their environment, and then describe the behavior exhibited by the objects in that situation.

6.2 Retrieving scenarios

Once a group of scenarios has been collected and recorded, it is important to be able to retrieve them whenever they are relevant. For example, when a designer is trying to develop an algorithm for selecting the duration for the left-turn signal, he or she should be able to retrieve all scenarios involving left-turning traffic, or which assign particular durations to the left-turn signal.

At the present time we have made no special provision for retrieving scenarios or pieces of scenarios beyond the general mechanisms within ARIES for storing and retrieving requirements information in a knowledge base.

6.3 Executing scenarios

Executing scenarios can uncover missing or inconsistent information in the scenarios, and in the system being designed. By walking through the scenario and comparing it to a domain model one can determine whether the scenario is missing key steps, and whether implicit assumptions are being made that were not recorded in the scenario. Computer-based testing tools can also use scenarios to drive system execution, and check whether or not the system behaves as indicated in the scenario.

ASC can drive the execution of a specification using scenarios. ASC uses scenarios to model the external environment (external relative to the current focus, i.e., validation question). This enables the analyst to force the simulation to react to specific situations, and validate those reactions. RAD is designed to animate the execution of scenarios, so that domain experts can validate and critique examples of behavior. The completed RAD system will be able to check for violations of requirements and domain axioms automatically as the scenario is being executed, and point out the problems to the user.

6.4 Visualizing scenarios

The power of scenarios in highlighting concrete details of system and environment behavior is further enhanced if the scenarios can be visualized in domain terms. For example, representations of vehicles moving through intersections are more perspicuous to most viewers than animated state-transition diagrams of the same scenarios. Computer graphics tools for animating behavior within situations are an important means for supporting this visualization process.

The domain-oriented depictions in RAD are intended to provide this visualization capability. We expect that giving domain experts such domain-oriented depictions to work with will help uncover important domain properties and requirements that might otherwise be overlooked or ambiguous if the scenarios were described using text. For example, depending on the frame of reference, there are three interpretations for the phrase, "The truck in front of the car." The intended frame of reference might be the car or some outside observer. Each interpretation has a unique visual depiction.

6.5 Monitoring scenario execution

Scenario monitoring involves watching the system as it runs, and detecting whether or not behavior patterns described via scenarios occur.

The ASC simulator is designed to monitor validation question scenarios. In general this is a pattern matching activity in which all simulation events are matched against the validation question scenario as they occur. ASC is then able to inform the analyst of matches, partial matches, and contradictions as they occur. The analyst then uses this knowledge to decide whether or not the specification is behaving properly with respect to the current validation question scenario.

The ARIES instructional system also performs scenario monitoring—however, it monitors actions by users rather than actions by the system. Each scenario's behavior is encoded as a sequence of user inputs, where each user input may be a keystroke, a sequence of keystrokes, or some class of keystrokes. The user's keystrokes are matched against the scenario description to determine adherence to the training scenario.

6.6 Developing requirements and designs from scenarios

We envision that automated tools will ultimately be able to generate requirements and designs directly from scenarios. It will then be unnecessary to develop scenarios and designs separately and compare one against the other. Some systems that demonstrate such capabilities already exist. For example, the WATSON system can take as input a scenario describing a proposed feature for a telephone system, and derive from it a complete specification of the feature [17].

We are providing some capabilities along these lines in RAD. The system provides a set of generic building blocks to let domain experts express the domain specific concepts that represent the objects and their situation as well as the behavior of the objects in the scenario. They will be able to express the triggering and restraining conditions in the scenarios that must be satisfied at particular states in the scenario. In this way the scenario can be gradually transformed into a rule specifying a particular class of system behavior. Further work would be required to recognize and resolve conflicts between such rules, combine specific rules and generalize them into more complete specifications of behavior.

6.7 Processing scenarios effectively

The extent to which such automated support for scenario processing is effective depends heavily upon being able to refer to some existing body of formalized domain knowledge. Without such domain knowledge, scenarios are cumbersome to state, and automated reasoning on scenarios is likely to yield nonsensical conclusions. Suppose, for example, that in writing the scenarios described in the previous section, it was necessary to define each time what a vehicle was, what a roadway was, what traffic flow was, etc. Recording the scenarios would quickly have become a very burdensome process. The RAD system provides a set of useful scenario building blocks that the user can employ and further compose, easing the task of capturing scenario descriptions. Retrieval of scenarios presupposes some sort of content-oriented classification of scenarios; a knowledge base of terminology for classification would be needed for this purpose.

If a design has already been developed, it may be possible to write scenarios in terms of the concepts already identified and defined in the design description. This does not help for scenarios that are being articulated prior to design, however. In such cases it is necessary to rely upon some preexisting domain model or knowledge base describing the domain.

7 Summary

This paper has demonstrated the importance of scenarios in the software engineering process. They are useful throughout the process, not just in specific activities such as testing. They are important not just for systems with human interfaces, but for any system that interacts with a complex environment, and most likely for complex systems in general. We believe that they have been neglected in part because tools that support the recording and processing of scenarios as first-class artifacts have been lacking. This in turn may be a consequence of a tendency within computer science to emphasize the general over the specific, and the abstract over the concrete.

Tools are being developed by us as well as others that support scenario processing. They are beginning to provide enough in the way of processing support to make them worth using. Evaluation studies with domain experts and software engineers need to be conducted in order prove their effectiveness.

References

[1] J.R. Anderson. Acquisition of Cognitive Skill. *Psychological Review*, 89(4), 1982.

[2] J.S. Anderson and B. Durney. Using Scenarios in Deficiency-Driven Requirements Engineering. In *RE'93: IEEE International Symposium on Requirements Engineering*, pages 134–141. IEEE Computer Society Press, January 1993.

[3] K.M. Benner. Specification Reformulation During Specification Validation. In *Proceedings, Workshop on Problem Reformulation and Representation Change, Asilomar Conference Center, Pacific Grove, CA*, April 1992.

[4] R.L. Campbell. Will the Real Scenario Please Stand Up? *SIGCHI Bulletin*, 24(2):6–8, April 1992.

[5] J.M. Carroll and M.B. Rosson. Getting Around the Task-Artifact Cycle: How to Make Claims and Design by Scenario. *ACM Transactions on Information Systems*, 10(2):181–212, April 1992.

[6] J. Conklin and M.L. Begeman. gIBIS—A Hypertext Tool for Exploratory Policy Discussion. *ACM Transactions on Office Information Systems*, 6(4):303–331, 1988.

[7] B. Curtis, H. Krasner, and N. Iscoe. A Field Study of the Software Design Process for Large Systems. *Communications of the ACM*, 31(11):1268–1287, November 1988.

[8] S.F. Fickas and P. Nagarajan. Critiquing Software Specifications: A Knowledge Based Approach. *IEEE Software*, 5(6):37–49, November 1988.

[9] R. Guindon. Knowledge Exploited by Experts During Software System Design. *Int. J. Man-Machine Studies*, 33:279–304, 1990.

[10] M. Hamer. Traffic Lights Learn To Go With the Flow. *New Scientist*, 1715:35, May 1990.

[11] W. Hseush and G.E. Kaiser. Modeling Concurrency in Parallel Debugging. In *Proceedings of the ACM SIGPLAN Symposium on Principles and Practices of Parallel Programming*, pages 11–20. ACM Press, March 1990. Published in *SIGPLAN Notices*, Vol. 25 No. 3, March 1990.

[12] W.L. Johnson. Specification via Scenarios and Views. In *Proceedings of the 3rd International Software Process Workshop*, pages 61–63, Breckenridge, CO, 1986. IEEE Computer Society Press.

[13] W.L. Johnson, M.S. Feather, and D.R. Harris. Integrating Domain Knowledge, Requirements and Specifications. *Journal of Systems Integration*, 1:283–320, 1991.

[14] W.L. Johnson, M.S. Feather, and D.R. Harris. Representation and Presentation of Requirements Knowledge. *IEEE Trans. on Software Engineering*, 18(10):853–869, October 1992.

[15] W.L. Johnson and L. Zorman. Supporting Groups Involved in Software Specification and Design. In *Proceedings of the 1992 CSCW Workshop on Understanding and Supporting Successful Group Work in Software Design*, 1992. Available from John Karat, IBM Watson Research Center.

[16] J. Karat and J.L. Bennett. Using Scenarios in Design Meetings - A Case Study Example. In *Taking Software Design Serious Seriously: Practical Techniques for Human-Computer Interaction Design*, pages 63–94. Academic Press, 1991.

[17] V.E. Kelly and U. Nonnenmann. Reducing the Complexity of Formal Specification Acquisition. In *Proceedings of the AAAI-88 Workshop on Automating Software Design*, pages 66–72, St. Paul, MN, 1988.

[18] E. Rowe. The Los Angeles Automated Traffic Surveillance and Control (ATSAC) System, September 1992. Los Angeles Department of Transportation.

[19] L.A. Suchman. *Plans and Situated Actions: The Problem of Human-Machine Communication.* Cambridge University Press, New York, 1987.

[20] J. Walters. Los Angeles: Technology and Traffic. *Governing*, page 43, October 1992.

[21] P. Zave. An Insider's Evaluation of PAISLey. *IEEE Trans. on Software Engineering*, SE-17:212–225, 1991.

Information System Development Process (A-30)
N. Prakash, C. Rolland and B. Pernici (Editors)
Elsevier Science Publishers B.V. (North-Holland)

© 1993 IFIP. All rights reserved.

Assessment and control of the requirements elicitation process in a CASE environment

József Györkös, Ivan Rozman

University of Maribor, Faculty of Technical Sciences
Smetanova 17, SLO-62000 Maribor, Slovenia
e-mail: gyorkos@uni-mb.si

Abstract

In the computer aided software engineering environments a wide range of data about the development process can be collected. Basing on these easy - collected data our aim is to upgrade a CASE tool to bid such an information on the basis of past activities to the subjects of the software development team which can be interpreted as an estimation of the development process. This information must be evaluated upon the dynamics of the system specification in progress. The dynamic of this process is influenced by the needs of the user. The needs are mostly based on his/her assumptions about the planned system. In this paper studies on the unsteadiness of requirements specification with special attention to identification and assessment of the requirements risk are presented. Results of assessment can be used for management, control and avoidance of requirements risk detected during the system analysis phase.

Keyword Codes: D.2.1; D.2.8; D.2.9
Keywords: Software Engineering, Requirements/Specifications; Metrics; Management

1. INTRODUCTION

The software development process became strongly influenced by CASE (Computer Aided Software Engineering) tools. In our examination the effective use of data in software project dynamics gathered by a used CASE environment is emphasised. The evaluation and interpretation of these data is the topic of different research works [1]. In these projects the Software Process Capability Maturity Model by Software Engineering Institute (SEI) is the key reference [2], [3]. The projects on process evaluation are based (beside this model) also on the ISO standard 9000-3 for quality assurance and quality management [4]. The presented research can be placed between the project dealing with the third, fourth and partly fifth maturity level of the SEI model. In summary the implementation and use of proposed approach can *improve* the mentioned *Defined, Managed* and *Optimising* maturity levels. The automated data collecting is a prime characteristic of the fifth level, but it can be spread to all other levels too. In a CASE environment the effort for collecting data should be minimal or none, the effort should be paid to the finding or adapting of appropriate metrics. In the reference [1] a figure describes the relation between key terms used in this introduction: the CASE environment is a subset of the metrics envelope that is the subset of the software process model. The developer and the project manager interact with the software process model. Please consider that the subject of this paper is limited to the system requirements analysis phase of software project development. The results and conclusions should be interpreted within this scope.

One of the most accurate and formal descriptions of the characteristics of a good software requirements specification is the source IEEE Std 830-1984 [5]. This guideline declares that a good software requirements specification is: *unambiguous, complete, verifiable, consistent, modifiable, traceable and usable during the operation and maintenance phase*. It is quite simple to imagine the negative influences on the required characteristics, but all those characteristics are not measurable directly from the software requirements specification document. There are no metrics to assess the usability, completeness etc. In [6] the requirements specification is defined as a source of risk. In the dictionary risk is defined as a possibility of loss or injury, alternatively also a degree of probability of loss. With the assessment and control of the risk we can never guarantee the success in the widest sense, but the crisis situations in the software project development can prevented. The risk areas defined in the software project development [6] are: *schedule, budget, requirements, personnel, technology, resources, externals and operation*. Requirements risks are just one of the risks, endangering the software project development. All other risks (personnel, environment, ...), declared by the same source will not be considered in this paper, neither the interrelation from the requirements risk to them. We will consider the specific risks that are those attributes of requirements risk which build a complete entity - the risk, produced by requirements. The specific requirements risks are: *volatility, miscommunication, hidden complexity, imprecision and ambiguity*. The requirements risk should be seriously assessed and controlled because it is embedded into the further development process.

Both mentioned classifications of the properties of requirements specification documents are close to each other, they are complementary. The first classification deals with the required characteristics and the second one with constraints. The subject of this paper is to show which characteristics and constraints could be assessed directly from the requirements specification document in the form of numeric values. These numeric values cannot be used in their absolute form. They must be normalised and used in a comparative manner with other events in the software development process. Graphical presentation is required with the possibility of predictable interpretation. In the next paragraph the environment for the production of software requirements specification will be described. The required characteristics - the specific risks - will be expressed by the proposed metrics. The construction of a database with requirements analysis process data is emphasised as a testbed for metrics evaluation. Collecting of data for this database is essential while the metrics should be at this stage of our research modifiable in the sense of possibility of experimentation. At the end of this paper results are evaluated and some directions for the further research and implementation are shown.

2. AN UPGRADED CASE ENVIRONMENT

In our research different CASE tools were used for the production of software requirements specifications. In the wide range of available commercial CASE tools also a theoretical model of an upper CASE tool named *aSet* was included [7]. CASE tools were selected by a common criterion: for the system/requirements analysis phase those structured techniques must be supported, which cover at least two extensions of the three dimensional view of the requirements analysis phase [8]. Instead of different names for life cycle models the meaning of views is common and well declared as a description of the system regarding *processes, information and events*. Our final aim, regarding the research framework, was to upgrade the used environment for the production of software requirements specification with a presentation and decision support system. The general feature of this decision support system should be *to give the subjects of the software development team such information on the basis of past activities which can be interpreted in the predictable manner*. A concept of a CASE environment, upgraded with the decision support system is shown in the Figure 1. The needed information is extracted from the CASE environment with a CASE-dependent module EXM (EXtraction Module). All obtained data are modified into the data base under the logical model CREDO (both parts CGP (Consolidation of Global Parameters) and ICRS (Inter-Components Relationships Space) will be described). This model is the source of data for the expressions for assessment of the requirements risks. The assessment is done in the module RRAM (Requirements Risk Assessment Module). This module is a user interface of the decision support system. At the users questions, the interpretation of the past activities throughout specific risks are given. This interpretation is a support for the actions which will influence the further development process.

2.1. Extraction of data from repositories

The module EXM is the only CASE-dependent component of the system, presented in Figure 1. The complete understanding of the extraction process demands a knowledge about the logical data base model of CREDO. In the present discussion we can simplify this demand: from the CASE environment information about the creation, update and deletion of notation components and of their description can be extracted. The kernel of CASE tools is a repository which contains different amounts of information. The amount and the structure of the information depends on the concept, class and quality of the tool. Repositories have different commercial names (e.g. central/system dictionary, encyclopedia, XL dictionary) and different formats. The different formats are the reason why the EXM module is CASE-dependent.

2.2. CREDO

CREDO (Consolidation of Requirements Elicitation Data mOdel), a logical model of the development process is a set of two data bases: *CGP* (Consolidation of Global Parameters) and *ICRS* (Inter-Components Relationships Space). Data are added into both data bases in cycles. The time between cycles (called evaluation interval) can be determined: *(a) manually:* the length of intervals is measured by days, hours or by the duration of a relatively concluded phase of work (this phase of work must be shorter than the software life cycle phase), *(b) automatically:* the length of the intervals is previously defined by the intensity of work; intensity of work can be measured by the quantity of added and/or updated components of system specifications. *Activity points (AP)* are placed at the end of each evaluation interval. At activity points data about changes in the system specification process are collected.

The detailed description of the CGP data base follows in the next subsection. In this paper the concept of the ICRS data base is not explained. The importance of ICRS from the functional view is in its ability of tracing the development process and in the possibility to evaluate a historical analysis of influence of particular notation components regarding the obtained structured technique.

We can find some functions of ICRS already embedded in the more sophisticated CASE tools (eg. encyclopedia or repository services). Among others our aim is to give an equal platform for comparison of development processes using different tools including different performance levels. ICRS can be used for a fine identification of specific risks and for a control of them. The need for redundant data regarding the CASE environment is the weakness of ICRS. The extraction and the unification of data at every activity point requires manual operations. By large models it can be time and memory consuming. The need for comparability and unified acquisition of events in development process is paid with this (reasonable) limitations.

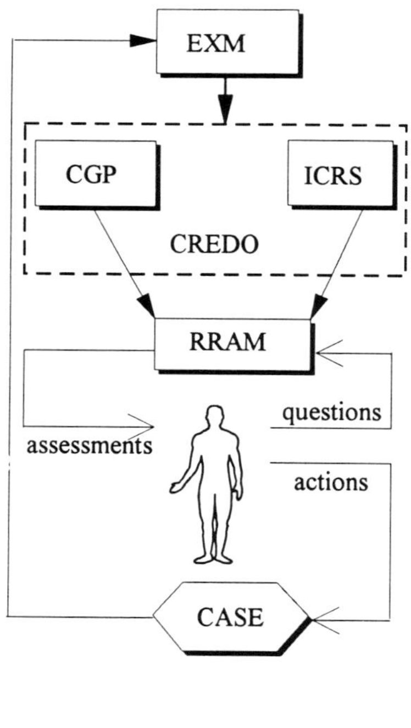

Figure 1. The concept of an upgraded CASE environment.

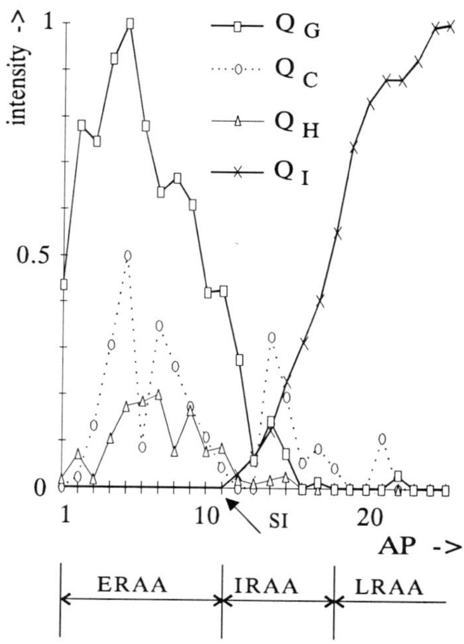

Figure 2. A sketch of CGP diagram.

2.3. The consolidation diagram

In Figure 2 a sketch of the CGP diagram is presented. Different areas of risk assessment are defined regarding the value of single parameters: early risk assessment area ERAA (quite similar to the beginning of requirements analysis phase in a waterfall life cycle model), intensive risk assessment phase IRAA (late requirements analysis phase including transformation/

transaction analysis and overlapping with the beginning of system design phase) and late risk assessment area LRAA (system design). Names to the areas were assigned due to the possibility and suitability of risk assessment. The value of the parameters depend on the unsteadines of system specification, stored in CASE environment.

In the early risk assessment area all estimations are only of informative nature because of the expected volatility of parameters in expressions (the growth of quantity of notation components - the graphical objects - of used structured techniques is intensive). Most important is the intensive risk assessment area. It is most easy to express the risk in late risk assessment area, but from the view of the user this assessment is done too late. This is also the paradox of the proposed method. This paradox has to be solved with the expressions presented later for the assessment of specific requirements risks.

2.4. The parameters in CGP diagram

In the CGP data base the quantitative data about consolidation of requirements elicitation process are stored. The consolidation process is described by four fundamental parameters: Q_G, Q_C, Q_H and Q_I. Follows the description of single parameters with their full names and properties.

Parameter of consolidation of the system specification (Q_G). Q_G depends on the intensity of work by requirements elicitation and on the project size. Influences of subjective skills and of tools used should be evident in the gradient of the curve, articulating Q_G. These influences are evident in the form of continuous quantitative growth of the documentation, generated by the upper-CASE components of the CASE tool. The main problem in quantification of Q_G parameter is the determination of the importance (in the form of weights) of the sub components within the mentioned notation components. For the purpose of calibration 27 different projects from different environments were analysed (up to medium size; e.g. 160 entities in the data model). The introduction of the term *"the main notation component"* of the single method is required. All weights are determined in relation to the main notation component. As the main notation components the process (process view), the entity (information view) and the state (event view) were chosen. The correlation of the quantity of notation sub-components with the main notation component is expressed by the parametrical correlation coefficient r_p. The weights are most stable (reliable) for those components which are in the greatest correlation with the main notation component. Table 1 shows the results of the analysis.

Parameter of intensity of changes made in the system specification (Q_C). Q_C depends on the quality of job, done in the first draft of requirements elicitation. The dynamics of changes in requirements can be seen from the intensity of this parameter. The intensity of Q_C is *casual* in the Early Risk Assessment Area, *interesting* in the IRAA and *undesired* in LRAA. The changes in the system specifications in most cases are not re-documented, they are a part of the design and implementation documentation. The loss is not only in the interrupted development process but also in the unusability of development results for the purpose of full-document supported reusability.

The weighting of Q_C is influenced with the hierarchical level of change (HLC). The effect of change to the specific risks assessment is greater if it is made on the higher hierarchical level in documentation (e.g. changes in the context diagram in data flow diagrams is acute to the whole system of data flow diagrams). The normally calculated part of parameter Q_C will be modified to its final value (Q_{CF}) in those components where the hierarchy is evident (1).

$$Q_{CiF} = Q_{Ci} \frac{1}{HLC} \tag{1}$$

Homogeneity of system specification (Q_H). The homogeneity of the system specification is defined as the degree of integration of integral components. The introduction of Q_H issues from the empirical statement that the documentation of different views is not developed simultaneously. Integration shows the synthesis and consolidation of system specification. An example of integration: an entity, depicted in the entity-relationship model as a part of information view is used in the data store of process view representing data flow diagrams.

Table 1
Quantitative correlation between the components of structured techniques.

View	Number of patterns	Critical correl. coef. (0.01)	Components in correlation	Pearson's coef. r_p
process (analysis)	15	0.6411	process/data flow process/data store process/external entity	0.90889 0.72543 0.29457
information (analysis)	14	0.6614	entity/attribute entity/association	0.85336 0.92511
event (analysis)	5	0.8587	state/transition	0.94403
design	12	0.7079	module/couple	0.98796

Parameter of growing of the implementation documentation (Q_I). Q_I is a typical pre-implementation activity parameter which depends on the subjective decisions about the beginning of the design, coding and about the intensity of these tasks. The Q_I parameter will be roughly determined, because in our expressions for risk assessment we need only the activity point, where Q_I starts. The influence on this parameter can be detected more precisely by counting new modules in the structured design document or by counting the lines of the code.

It should be known that the intensity of the single parameter is important only in separate observation of this parameter; the intensity of different parameters is not directly comparable. The purpose of presentation of all parameters in the same diagram is only symbolic and illustrative. Figure 2 must be observed as a sketch and visualisation of an idea.

The parametrization system is evaluated on the quantity of new or modified notation components. Weights from 1 (low influence) to 10 (important influence) are added to each notation component of used structured techniques. Evaluating the parameters Q_G and Q_C the weights are multiplied with the number of adequate components occurred (new, modified) in the observed evaluation interval. The value of the parameter is the sum of all those products. Let us use Q for any of parameters Q_C or Q_G. Equation (2) shows how the final value considering the weights is calculated.

$$Q(AP) = \sum_{i=1}^{CMPMAX} WQ(CMPQ_i) \tag{2}$$

If this simple expression is used and the type of the developed system is not considered, the value of the parameter can not be real. This problem is solved by separate observing of each view of system specification, which requires the introduction of coefficients of the type of the developed system (3). With the value of coefficients k_{IV}, k_{PV} and k_{EV} the type of the system is denoted.

$$Q(AP) = k_{IV} \sum_{i=0}^{CMPMAXIV} WQ(CMPQ_i) + k_{PV} \sum_{i=0}^{CMPMAXPV} WQ(CMPQ_i) + k_{EV} \sum_{i=0}^{CMPMAXEV} WQ(CMPQ_i) \tag{3}$$

The sum of coefficients must always be 1. Some guidelines for the values of coefficients could be derived from the experience gained with Bang model [9]. The calibration of these coefficients is the aim of our future work, when at least 7-10 different projects will be collected. It is obvious that the change of coefficients k_{IV}, k_{PV} and k_{EV} must be affected in all activity points. Significant alternations can be seen on the value of the parameter if the proportion between coefficients is changed due to the orientation of the project (data, process or event driven).

3. CALCULATION OF SPECIFIC RISKS

Specific risks are calculated at all activity points in the process of requirements specification consolidation. It has not been established yet if the absolute values of specific risks are comparable. For this thesis more examples of projects completely documented on CREDO must be evaluated. That is the reason for the observation of the normalised values of specific results. Normalisation can be done also on the basic parameters from the CGP diagram. In these cases the character *N* is added to the index of the parameters (e.g. the normalised value of the parameter Q_G is depicted as Q_{GN}). In the figures following, all the assessed specific risks will be shown in the normalised form. The normalisation is done considering the greatest value of the specific risk regarding the actual *activity point* (AP). The enduring adjustment of the diagram (if new peaks are calculated) is the consequence of normalisation.

3.1 Volatility

The system specification is volatile when permanent changes can be identified. Changes are expected in ERAA. In and after intensive risk assessment area changes introduce specific risk - volatility. CASE tools use on-line syntactical checking of the produced documentation, which means: all changes made in system specification are clear indicators of volatility.

Because of the different meaning of changes in different risk assessment areas the *sensitivity border* (SB) was introduced into the expression for the assessment of volatility (R_{VO}). When the activity point of the development process moves away from *sensitivity border* SB (that is in IRAA and LRAA), the assessed risk will be multiplied with relative difference from the SB, measured in number of activity points. As the expression shows (4), the volatility is basically assessed by the sum of parameters Q_G and Q_C. The sensitivity border SB is fixed at the point Start of implementation (SI) in the diagram CGP (see also Figure 2).

$$R_{VO} = \begin{cases} Q_{GN};[ERAA > \\ (Q_{GN} + Q_{CN}) * (AP - AP(SI - 1));[IRAA >,[LRAA > \end{cases} \tag{4}$$

3.2. Hidden Complexity

The source of hidden complexity is a too-large abstraction in requirements specification. From our experience, mostly neglected parts are external entities, which define the border of the system. The insufficiently detailed functional primitives can be also a source of hidden complexity. All this can be produced because of improper use of structured techniques, also known as a paradox *how methods change problems* ("first, problems amenable to formal methods are eliminated, leaving a higher percentage of messy problems; then, because of the promise of the formal methods, ambitions grow, leaving more problems of every kind" [11]). Hidden complexity is mainly expressed by the sum of the absolute difference of Q_G and Q_C between tthe last two activity points (expression 5 (R_{HC}), Figure 4). This sum is multiplied with the degree of integration (Q_H) and with the number of modules without "parents" in system specification. The consequences of hidden complexity is a demand for modification of already validated system specification. In this cases re documentation is required for comprehensive system specification.

$$R_{HC}(AP) = (Q_G(AP) - Q_G(AP-1) + Q_C(AP) - Q_C(AP-1)) * (Q_H(AP) + 1) * (NMOD + 1);[\text{ERAA,IRAA,LRAA} > \tag{5}$$

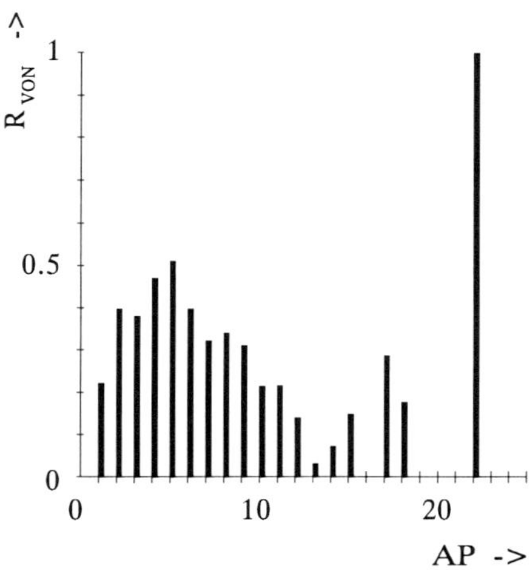

Figure 3. Assessment of volatility.

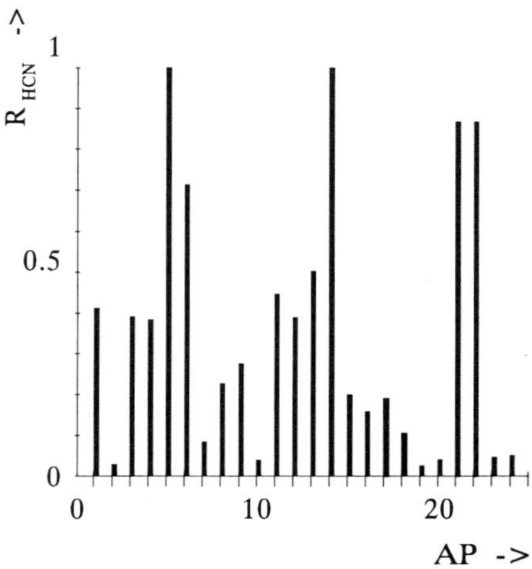

Figure 4. Assessment of hidden complexity.

3.3. Imprecision

The assessment of imprecision is presumed on the characteristics of the design documentation. Normally, the modules of structured design are derived from the processes in data flow diagrams using the transformation or transaction analysis. If modules which do not have their source in system specification can be defined, then the hidden complexity and imprecision are produced. The number of new modules (NMOD), multiplied with the processes, unused for the transformation or transaction analysis (UPROC) will build the expression for the assessment of imprecision (expression 6 (R_{IM}), Figure 5). The imprecision is not defined in the ERAA. It could be assessed by observing the parameter Q_C, but we did not find this correlation strong enough. Instead of that, Q_C could be used for the assessment of imprecision by manual "reading" of the CGP diagram. The reliability of this manual estimation depends on the user and on his experience and recognition. In the IRAA the peak of imprecision will be encountered. This peak is expected because all transformations are not made yet. The assessment does not give a real insight into imprecision until a late risk assessment area is reached. That is the weakness of the model for assessment of imprecision in system specification; the user can see the state of some specific risk after finished key phases, where some significant changes could still be made.

$$R_{IP} = \begin{cases} undefined; [ERAA] \\ (UPROC+1)*(NMOD+1); < IRAA], [LRAA > \end{cases} \quad (6)$$

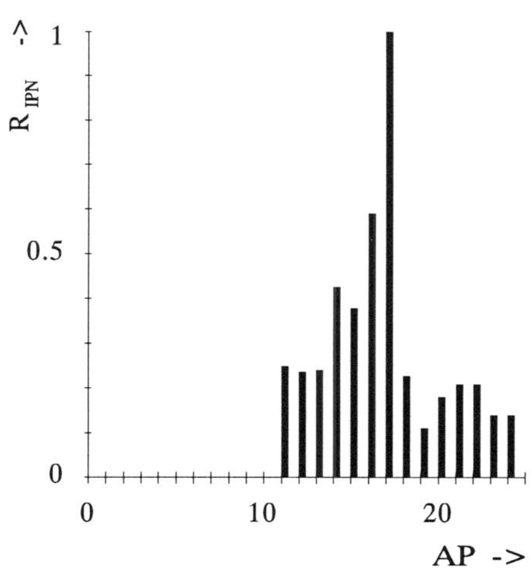

Figure 5. Assessment of imprecision.

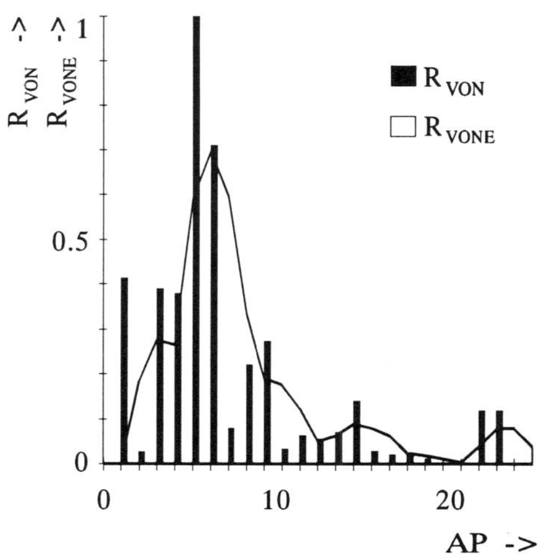

Figure 6. Extended presentation of specific risk

3.4. Not Assessed Specific Risks

Three of specific risks defined by SEI remain not assessed: miscommunication, ambiguity an requirements creep. Here will be given just few hints, what the influences on the specific risks which can not be measured are. Miscommunication is an error in the user/reader dialogue cycle [12]. This dialogue is formalised in the use of CASE tools as much as possible. All communications which can not be formalised and stored in a CASE environment introduce possibility of miscommunication. Ambiguity is a specific risk in which requirements statements can be interpreted in several different ways. The receiver has to clarify these statements based on the surrounding context. A software requirement specification is unambiguous if the requirement stated has only one semantic interpretation [5].

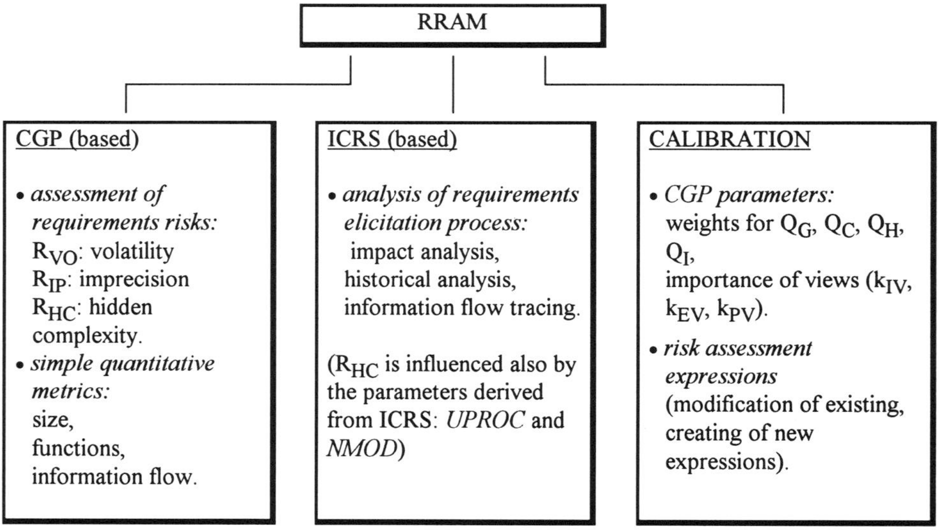

Figure 7 Functions of Requirements Risk Assessment Module (RRAM).

3.5. Extended presentation of specific risks

All three assessed specific risks (volatility, hidden complexity and imprecision) depend on events between the last two activity points. They are eventually influenced by the position of the actual activity point regarding the risk assessment area. For the visualisation of the risk assessment for different subjects in software project development, an extended presentation will be introduced. The aim of the expressed presentation is to add an envelope to the values of specific risks. This envelope has to hide all peaks and to preserve the intensity of assessed risk in previous activity points (Figure 6). The real and the extended value of specific risk must be presented simultaneously at the same diagram. The expression for the extended value of specific risk is empirical and it can be modified according to the needs of the user. In our example, presented in figure 6, the extended value is calculated as an arithmetic mid-range of specific risks in the last three activity points including the actual one, too.

The non existing referential values for single parameters is the weakness of the proposed expressions. The results can be obtained in the comparative manner regarding the previous values or the final value (predictable only if zero is required). The subject of the further research will be an attempt of encapsulation of the proposed model into some formal planning method. As most suitable the *Planguage* [13, 14] was found. The management of results and their dissemination to the subjects in software development team should be clear and non ambiguous.

4. CONCLUSIONS

The objective of our research is to present the information obtained on the basis of past activities to the members of the software development team. This can be interpreted in a predictable manner and must be evaluated on the data from the earliest phases of software development.

What has been done. A model of an environment was developed to upgrade the existing CASE tools. Problems regarding the extraction of data from different CASE tools are a the part of this upgraded environment. The extracted data are stored in two data bases (CGP and ICRS). These data bases have a unique independent form regarding the starting CASE environment. The quantitative changes in the notation components of used methodologies are considered as an issue for the interpretation of events in the development process. Figure 7 shows the comprehensive view of the possibilities given by upgraded CASE tool.

Intermediate solutions and proposals. One possible interpretation of events in the development process was presented. The specific requirements risks (volatility, hidden complexity and imprecision) were assessed. The visualisation of the activities in the system specification creating process should be useful in many aspects of the software project development. The team of software technicians uses it as a *risk - assessment* and *risk - control* support system. This support gives a picture about undesired events in the requirements analysis process. The management team gets an up-to-date information about activities in the initial phase of the project by observing the requirements elicitation consolidation process. Indirectly, the presented measurements should be used also as an estimating media for the "objects which do not exist (yet)". This kind of estimation activity in the presented environment is a prediction of the behaviour and thr requirements fulfilling the *future system* using the results collected in the earliest development period.

Further directions. In the assessment of specific risks just a limited part of responsible data were used. Building of new expressions for the assessment of other mentioned required characteristics of system requirements specification and of non - expressed specific risks is possible. The number of examples of software systems, developed under required conditions should be increased. Experiments with weights and weigt-correction-expressions should be done until reliable comparative results will be achieved. At this point different expressions for the estimation of the development time and effort will be introduced.

REFERENCES

1. G. Tate, J. Verner, R. Jeffery, CASE A Testbed for Modeling, Measurement and Management, Communications of the ACM, April 1992, Vol. 35, No. 4, pp. 65-72.
2. W.S. Humphrey, Characterizing the Software Process: A Maturity Framework, IEEE Software, March 1988, 73-79.
3. W.S. Humprey, T. R. Snyder, R. R. Willis, Software Process Improvement at Huges Aircraft, IEEE Software, July 1991, pp. 11-23.
4. V. Haase, R. Messnarz, R.M. Cachia, Software Process Improvement by Measurement - BOOTSTRAP/ESPRIT Project 5441, Shifting Paradigms in Software Engineering (Ed. R Mittermeier), Springer Verlag Wien New York, 1992, pp.32-41.
5. M. Dorfman and R.H. Thayer (Eds.), Standards, Guidelines, and Examples on System and Software Requirements Engineering, IEEE, Computer Society, 1990.
6. R. Fairley, COCOMO Based Risk Management, ECUG - Europecan COCOMO Users Group Meeting (working papers), Botley, Hampshir, 1990, pp. 23.1-23.41.
7. J. Györkös, I. Rozman, T. Welzer, The Concept of an Efficient Computer Aided Software Engineering Tool, Annual Review in Automatic Programming, Volume 14, Part II, pp. 89-94, Oxford Press, Oxford, 1990.
8. P. Peters, Advanced Structured System Analysis and System Design, McGraw Hill, 1988.
9. T. DeMarco, Controlling Software Projects - Management, Measurement & Estimation, Yourdon Press, Inc., 1984.
10. B. Bollinger, C. McGowan, A Critical Look at Software Evaluations, IEEE Software, July 1991, pp. 25-41.
11. D.C. Gause, G.M. Weinberg, Exploring Requirements - Quality Before Design, Dorset House Publishing, New York, 1989.
12. D.T. Ross, "Applications and Extension of SADT", IEEE Computer, April 1985.
13. T. Gilb, Principles of Software Engineering Management, Addison-Wesley Publishing Company, 1988.
14. T. Gilb, Result Planware, NordData'92 Conference Workshop working papers, 1992.

5.

METAMODELING

Information System Development Process (A-30)
N. Prakash, C. Rolland and B. Pernici (Editors)
Elsevier Science Publishers B.V. (North–Holland)
© 1993 IFIP. All rights reserved.

A Meta-Model for Representing Software Specification & Design Methods

Motoshi Saeki, Kazuhisa Iguchi, Kuo Wen-yin, and Masanori Shinohara

Dept. of Electrical & Electronic Engineering, Tokyo Institute of Technology
Ookayama 2-12-1, Meguro-ku, Tokyo 152, Japan, E-mail : saeki@cs.titech.ac.jp

This paper discusses a meta model for representing various software specification & design methods, and a supporting tool for development of specifications by using the multiple methods. This tool is called *method base*, which has various catalogued methods so that a software designer can select an adequate method for his problem domain by consulting with it. The designer will be navigated throughout his design process, according to the selected method. Subsequently, a method base system can hold the information about the produced documents and about the activities performed in the specification process. It is an essential point how to integrate sub specifications developed by the multiple methods into a final specification. The information about the semantical relationships among the methods is needed. It can be represented by the meta model because it is constructed from the atomic concepts common to the methods, such as *object*, *association*, *event*, *state*, *data*, and *process*. The meta model and the formal representations of the methods can be described in Entity Relationship Diagram. The representations of Object Oriented Analysis (OOA) and Structured Analysis (SA) are presented as the examples. Furthermore we introduce how to construct a specification of an example problem by using three methods, OOA, SA, and State Transition Diagram.

Keyword Codes: D.2.1; D.2.2; D.2.10
Keywords: Requirements/Specifications; Tools and Techniques; Design

1. INTRODUCTION

Designing software specifications effectively is important for developing high quality software since specification & design phases are the early steps in the software development process. Several specification & design methods (shortened to methods or design methods) and supporting environments based on them have been developed to aid analysis and design work. However, these methods work well in some problem domains and fall over in other domains. It is very difficult to create an universal design method which works well in all problem domains. Therefore it is more feasible that the designers can select the adequate design methods and the supporting environments for their problem domains. To reduce the management effort of many supporting tools, we need an integrated supporting tool which holds various kinds of design methods.

Recently, several researches introduced the specification methods from multiple viewpoints to develop large and complex software systems. Statemate is an example of *multi-view* specification methods[8]. It has three viewpoints : structural, functional, behavioral viewpoints, and the designers describe three types of charts according these three viewpoints. Shlaer's and Melor's Object Oriented Analysis[12] can be considered to be based on multiple viewpoints, since its framework consists of an information model (Entity Relationship Diagram), a state model (State Transition Diagram), and a process model (Data Flow Diagram). Specifications described with the different design methods from the multiple viewpoints are useful. It, however, is a problem how to integrate the multiple specification documents into a final version of the specification. To support *multi-view specification*, only the information of methods is not enough, the mechanism for integrating specifications written in the different methods is also necessary.

One of the solutions to solve the above requirements to our supporting tool is *meta systems* or *meta model* approach[2]. Meta model is a data model or scheme for representing design methods, and also expresses a concept structure common to the various methods. In our tool, design methods are stored following the structure of the meta model. This paper introduces a new meta model and meta modeling technique based on the common concepts included in the methods. It allows the designers to integrate multi-view specifications into a specification. We also discuss a supporting tool, called *method base*[17], based on our meta model.

The organization of this paper is as follows. In the next section, we discuss the requirements for meta models to achieve the above goals. We will introduce a powerful meta model based on the common concepts in section 3. Section 4 presents two examples of formal representations of the methods, Object Oriented Analysis (OOA) and Structured Analysis (SA), based on the meta model. In section 5, other related work will be briefly discussed and compared with our meta model. The supporting tool for development of specification by using multiple methods is introduced in section 6.

2. REQUIREMENTS TO META MODEL

Our supporting tool, called *method base*, should hold three types of information to support the software designers as follows :

- documents produced throughout the development (called *products*), and
- histories of the activities performed by the designers, and
- design methods and semantical relationships among them.

The first and second types of information can be used to navigate the designers according as the methods they chose. The third one is necessary for integrating products developed by the different methods into one specification. We should develop a meta model and the representations of the methods to be stored in a method base system. In particular, it is crucial how to formalize semantical relationships among the methods for the effective intergration.

Figure 1 shows the structural relationships among a meta model, formal representations of design methods (called *object models*), and actual specification processes. The first and second information are stored in the actual specification process level, i.e. instance level. The object level has the representations of the design methods belonging to a part of the third information. The other part of the third information, semantical relationships among the methods, is included in the meta model. Thus we should develop a meta model which can represent these semantical relationships.

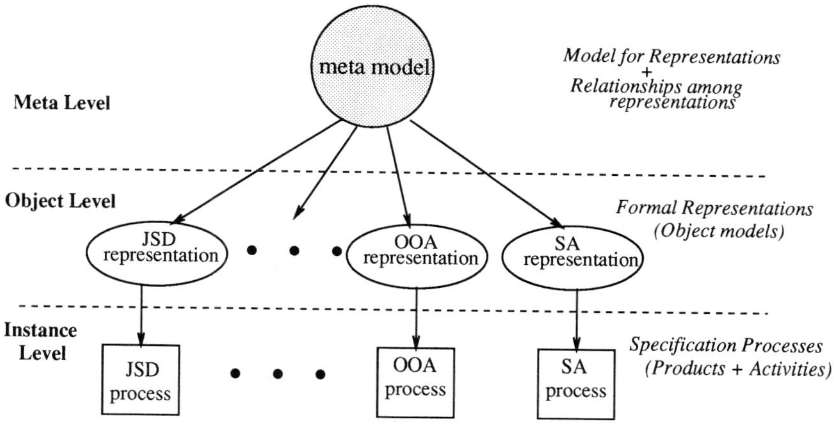

Figure 1. Logical Structure of Method Base

Let's consider the relationships among the multi-view specifications. There are several types of the relationships as shown in Figure 2. The first type is a whole-to-whole relationship. It is the case that a system is described by two specifications. This relationship can be managed by using the names or identifiers of the specification documents. The second case is a part-to-part relationship. The names of the two documents are different and a constituent of the products is related to a constituent of the other products developed by the different method. This type of relationships can be formalized by using the semantical relationship between the two methods. In the example, objects in OOA can correspond to data stores in SA, and this semantical relationship between objects in OOA and data store in SA establishes the relationship of the second case. The last type is a part-to-whole relationship. It is the case that we refine the constituents of the products by using other methods. In the figure, an object developed by OOA is refined into a SA specification. This type of the relationships is concerned with the hierarchical structure of the multi-view specifications. The meta model can manage these hierarchical structures also.

3. META MODEL

3.1. Development of the Meta Model

In this section, let's consider how to develop the effective meta model to satisfy the requirements mentioned in the previous section.

The major aim of the design methods is the user-navigation of design activities. The design methods tell the users what documents they should produce in a design process and what activities they should perform for producing the documents. For the example, Coad's OOA[5] tells us that its users start the procedure "identifying objects" and produces a list of the objects. So we can model the methods from two perspectives — product perspective

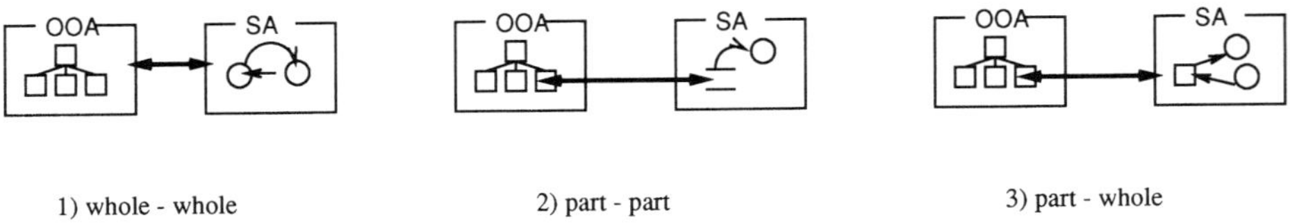

Figure 2. Relationships among Multi-view Specifications

and procedural perspective. From the product perspective, the structures of the produced products (including intermediate products) are specified, and the performed activities can be modeled from the procedural perspective of the method. Our meta model is described from these two perspectives, that is to say, it consists of two parts : one is product part and the other is procedural part.

We use the common concepts in the various methods so that our meta model can represent the semantical relationships among the methods easily and effectively. Though design methods contain many constitutional concepts which are expressed by the different technical terms, there are several common concepts among them. For example, the "object " concept in OOA can semantically involve a "source & sink (external entity)" or a "data store" concepts in SA[3]. Thus we can consider that these concepts have the same concept type. We named this type *object* type. The product part of our meta model has six common concept types including *object*, and five types of the relationships among the concept types. In the next section, we discuss these types of the concepts and the relationships in detail.

3.2. Product Part of the Meta Model

The product part of this meta model has six concept types which are common to various methods — *state*, *event*, *process*, *data*, *object* and *association*, and they can be classified into three categories as follows :

1. Behavioral Concept : The behavioral concept types *state* and *event* are used to capture behavioral properties of a problem domain.

2. Functional Concept : The functional concept types are used to describe what functions are being performed. In this category, a problem space is decomposed into *process*, which represents functions, and *data* that flows among them.

3. Structural Concept : Structural concept types represent physical components and the interactions or the relationships among them. We use the concept types *object* and *association*.

We also call these six concept types *meta concepts*.

We can also generalize the relationships among the meta concepts into six types as *Has_a*, *Defines*, *Input*, *Output*, *Is_a* and *Next-to*.

1. *Has_a* relationship : *Has_a* relationship represents ownership among the instances of the concepts. In the example of OOA, the concept "Object" *has* "Attributes", thus this type of the relationship is *Has_a* relationship.

2. *Defines* relationship : A concept may be defined by the other concepts. In this case, the equivalence relationship between the defined concept and the defining concepts is established. In Structured Analysis, a mini spec (or a process description) *defines* a detail of a "Process". This type of the relationships plays an important role of the management of product hierarchies.

3. *Input/Output* relationship : A concept may be a source or a destination of the other concepts. "Data Flows" are inputs to or outputs from "Processes" in SA. Thus the data flows have input/output relationship to the processes.

4. *Is_a* relationship : *Is_a* relationship represents the generalization/specialization structure of the concepts. In OOA, "Object" has a relationship "Inherit-from" to "Object" and this relationship represents generalization/specialization structure among objects.

5. *Next_to* relationship : *Next_to* relationship represents the successor relationships among the ordered concepts. For example, the concepts "State" has an order "next-to" which expresses the relationship between the current state and its next state.

The possible types of the relationships depend on the meta concepts which participates in them. Figure 3 shows the meta concepts and the possible relationships among them in the form of Entity Relationship Diagram, and it is a product part of our meta model. In the figure, the relationships between the concept types *object* and *process* are restricted to two types of the relationships *Defines* and *Has_a*. Only one type of the relationship between *object* and *state* is allowable.

3.3. Procedural Part of the Meta Model

A design method restricts an allowable set or sequences of activities. In the design method, we need the descriptions informing us what activities are performed in the design method and when they are done. Furthermore we specify what products should be produced in the activities.

The procedural part of the meta model consists of an *procedure* concept, and four types of relationships as shown in Figure 4. The procedure class stores all steps of the procedures of the design methods. A procedure could be directly applied to a part of the products in the product model part. The *input* and *output* relationships mean which constituents and their relationships in the product part are inputs and outputs of the procedure respectively. The *Has* relationship explains what sub procedures belong to a procedure and also represents their hierarchies. The *precede* type relationships involve the execution order of the procedures.

3.4. Hierarchical Structure

To represent the hierarchical structure within different kinds of products, i.e. part-whole relationships mentioned in section 2, we embed a new relationship "refine" to the product part of our meta model as show in Figure 5. We can have the relationship "refine" between the concept types and the whole of the product part of the meta model.

4. REPRESENTING METHODS BY USING META MODEL

We have developed formal representations of the methods such as OOA[12, 5], SA[6], State Transition Diagram (State Chart)[8], Real time SA[16], Jackson System Develop-

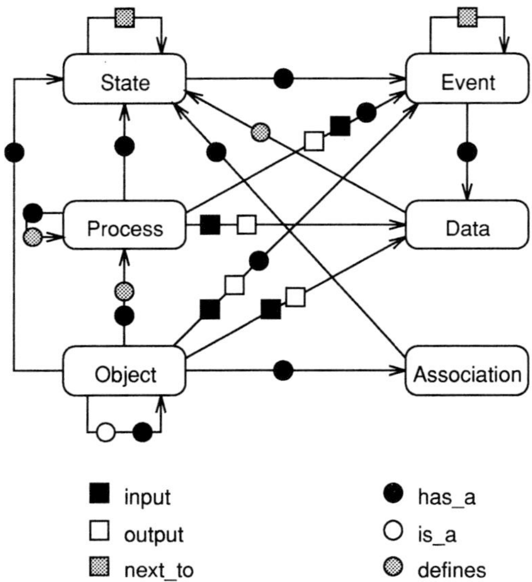

Figure 3. Product Part of the Meta Model

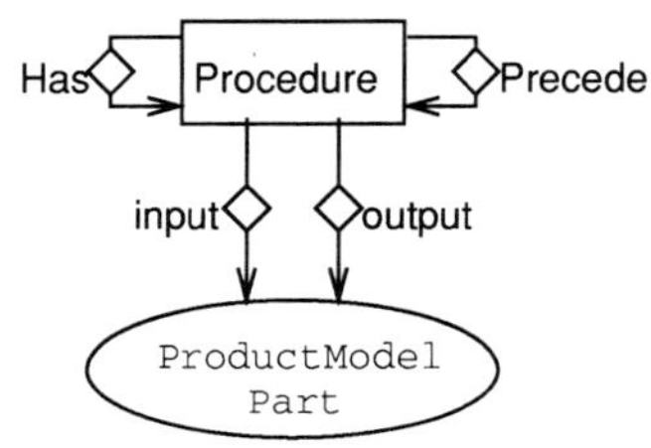

Figure 4. Procedural Part of the Meta Model

ment[9] and so on. In this section, we will introduce two examples : OOA description and SA description.

4.1. Coad's Object Oriented Analysis (OOA)

Figure 6 shows a product part of the OOA description. The entire structure of produced documents in the OOA method can be expressed in the form of Entity Relationship Diagram as shown in the figure. Parenthesized words in the round boxes stand for the meta concepts which the concepts belong to. For example, the meta concept of messages are considered as *event* on our meta model. In OOA, the problem domain to be specified may consist of a set of objects communicating to each other with messages. The objects have their attributes which denote their internal states. A service is an encapsulated function of the object. It changes the values of attributes of the object or sends messages to objects when a message comes from the environment. Properties of objects can be inherited from an ancestor object. This inheritance mechanism allows us to specify common attributes and common services once.

An "Object" is directly related to five concepts of product constituents — "Subject", "Message", "Instance Connection", "Attribute", and "Service", and has eight kinds of relationships — "receive", "send", "has (between Object and Service)", "has (between Object and Attribute)", "has (between Object and Subject)","has (between Object and Instance Connection)", "aggregation", and "inherit-from". The two relationships "send" and "receive" between "Object" and "Message" express message connection between two

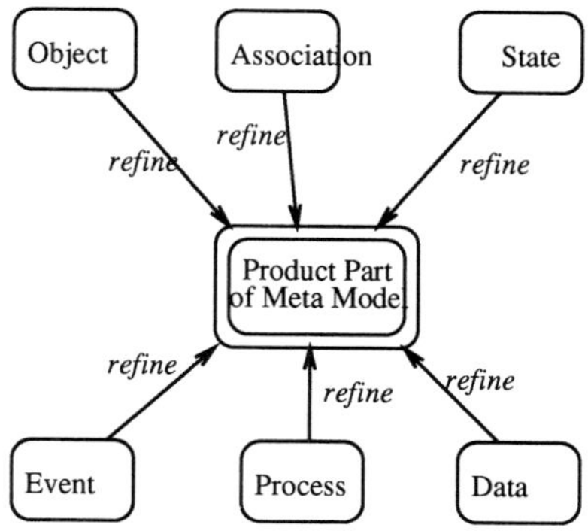

Figure 5. A Part for Representing Hierarchical Structure

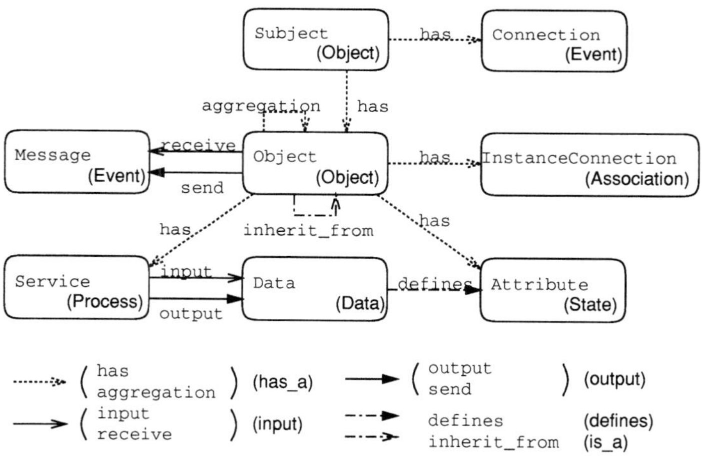

Figure 6. Product Part of OOA Representation

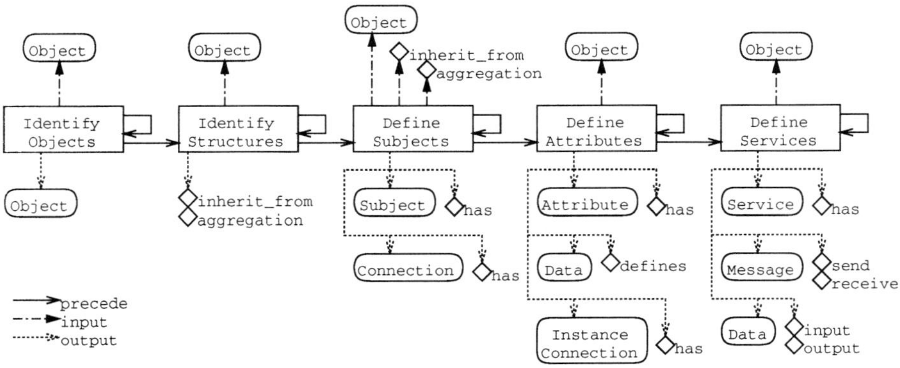

Figure 7. Procedural Part of OOA Representation

objects, i.e. what objects are senders or receivers of a message.

Furthermore we should add the procedure (the sequence of activities, i.e. procedural part) to this product part, and then complete a formal representation of the OOA method. This procedural part is emphasized in Figure 7. Rectangles and round boxes stand for procedures and product constituents respectively. Top level of the OOA procedure consists of five procedures : "Identify Objects", "Identify Structures", "Define Subjects", "Define Attributes", and "Define Services". The relationships "input" and "output" express what products are inputs to the activity and what products are outputs respectively. In the figure, we begin with the procedure "Identify Objects", which is for identifying the objects in the problem domain to be specified and outputs a set of the identified objects. The designer may identify new objects from the already identified objects, so the input of the activity is a set of objects. The next procedure "Identify Structures" decides the classification and the aggregation structure of the identified objects, and its results can be represented as inheritance and aggregation relationships.

According to Coad[5], furthermore we can decompose the procedure "Define Subjects" in Figure 7 into four sub procedures "Add Subjects", "Refine Subjects", "Show Connections", and "Number the Subjects", as shown in Figure 8. The figure shows the example of hierarchical structure of procedures, and the "Has" relationships of the procedural part of the meta model are used here.

The produced products and the performed activities in a design process should be recorded according to the OOA representation of Figure 6 and Figure 7. Suppose that we design the lift control system mentioned in [1]. Figure 9 illustrates the part of an actual design process of the lift control system. It holds produced documents and a history of the actual design activities.

We identified the objects "lift" by the activity "identify object #1", and "lift button" by "identify object #2" in order. The next procedure is "identify structures" and its performance is based on the previously identified objects. For example, we focus on the

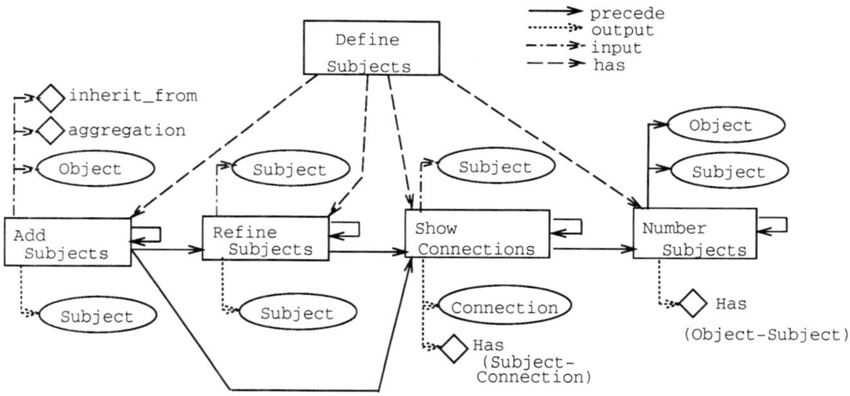

Figure 8. Sub Procedure Description of OOA

identified objects "lift" and "lift button", and identify a relationship instance "aggregation #1", which represents an aggregation structure between "lift" and "lift button", by an activity "identify structure #1".

4.2. Structured Analysis

Figure 10 shows the product part of Structure Analysis[6], i.e. the structure of Data Flow Diagrams. It has six concepts : "Process", "DataFlow", "DataStore", "MiniSpec (structured text for explanation of the process)", "Source/Sink (external entity or interface)", and "DataDictionary (definitions of data structures)". Parenthesized words in the figure expresses the types which the concepts or relationships belong to on the meta model. For example, "DataFlow" and the "describe" relationship belong to the meta concept *event* and to the *defines* type relationship of the meta model respectively. Thus the data flow concept in SA corresponds to the message concept of OOA because their types are the same, i.e. *event type.* The concepts and relationships having in the same type of the meta model play an important role of the integration of the products developed by the different methods.

The procedural information is shown in Figure 11. The first procedure "IdentifyInputs&Outputs" identifies the source&sinks and data flows connected to them. That is to say, in SA, the designers should establish the boundary to the external environment of the system to be developed. The figure tells the designers that they can perform three procedures, "LabelDataFlows", "LabelDataStores", and "LabelProcesses" in parallel after the procedure Fill in DFD Body.

5. RELATED WORKS

Several researchers constructed excellent meta models for software specification & design methods. Table 1 summarizes the other meta models, and their features from the

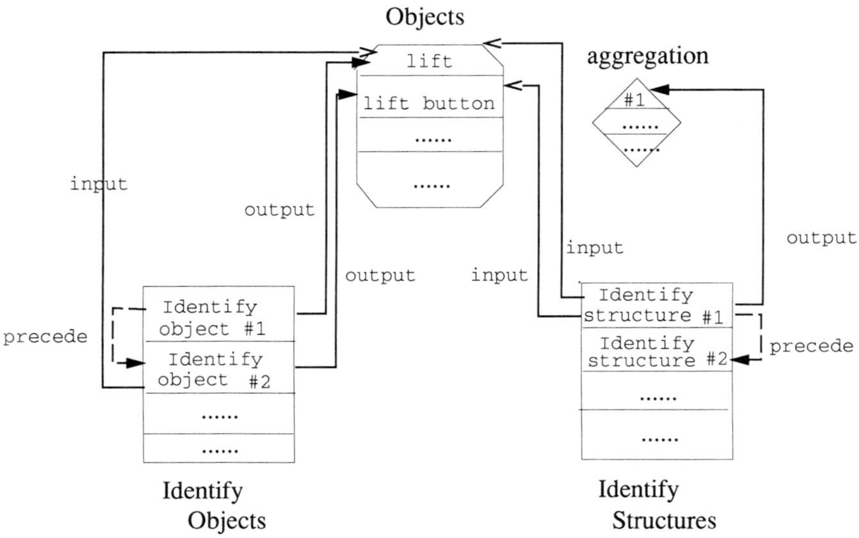

Figure 9. An Example of Design Process according to OOA Method

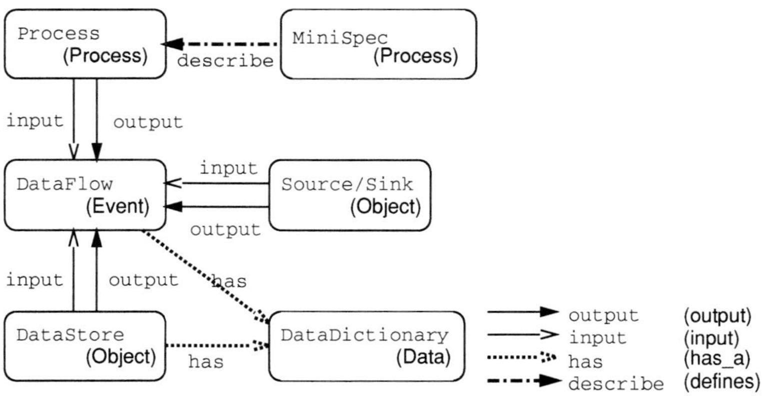

Figure 10. Product Part of SA Representation

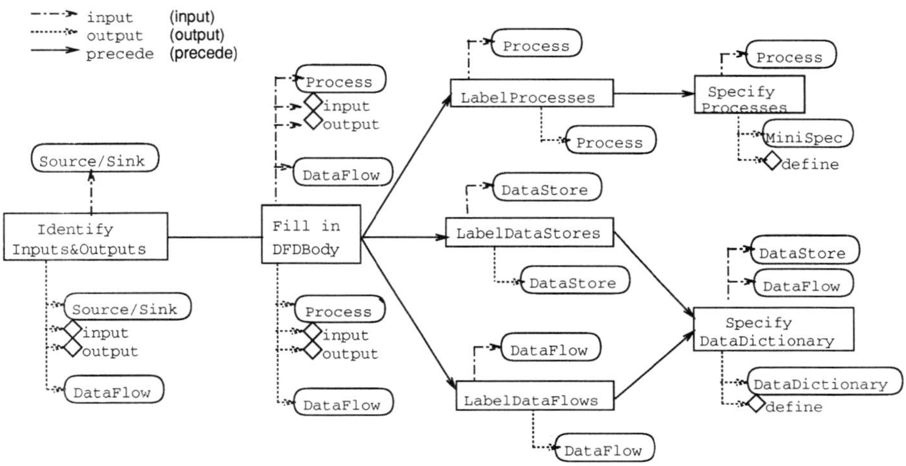

Figure 11. Procedural Part of SA Representation

several viewpoints :

1. *Notation* : The methods have various kinds of graphical notations. For example, the processes in SA are described in circles. This viewpoint involves the possibility of the meta models to define these graphical notations of the concepts. The Viewpoints Approach[7] and the MetaEdit[13] have the facility to define the graphical notations of the method concepts expressed by ER model. Their facilities, however, is restricted to the simple graphical elements, so it seems difficult to describe the complex graphical elements and their correspondence to the concepts such as the Coad's and Rumbaugh's OOA diagrams[11].

2. *Procedure* : To support software specification development under multiple methods, the tool holds information about what activities were performed in each of the methods. This viewpoint is concerned with the facility to specify the procedural information of the methods and to record the actual design activities. Most of the meta models have no consideration for the design activities in the methods. That is to say, they pay attention to a model only for the structures of the products produced in the methods. The Viewpoints Approach holds the information about the activities as *work plans* and *work records*. These, however, seem to be too simple and too informal to represent the methods precisely and to record the activities usefully.

3. *Hierarchy of Products* : We have two types of the product hierarchies – one is the hierarchy within the products developed by the same method, and the other one is the hierarchy in the products developed by the multiple methods. The latter

hierarchy was organized by the relationships of the third case in Figure 2. Our meta model can manage this type of hierarchy by using the "refine" relationship.

4. *Constraints of Products* : The products may contain inconsistency within themselves (inner-inconsistencies), or may have inconsistency to the other products developed by the different methods (inter-inconsistencies). The constraints of the products allow us to avoid these inconsistencies. Brinkkemper has proposed a technique of meta modeling from three perspectives — event, data, and task[4]. He used ER model and first order predicate logic to describe these three meta models. The constraints can be described in predicate logic, however, the evaluation of the constraints written in predicate logic may be inefficient for practical systems. The facility of representing the constraints is not embedded to the model of MetaView[14] or our model, but the constraints are efficiently supported in their tool environments. In the method base system, the user interface parts support the check of these inconsistencies as will be mentioned in the next section.

5. *Applicability* : The expressive power of the meta models, i.e. what kind of method can be expressed by the meta models, is one of crucial factors. Brinkkemper's model have expressive power enough to describe some methods precisely. It, however, can apply only to the kind of methods, such as Data Flow Diagrams (a part of Structured Analysis) and Entity Relationship modeling, for information systems. Jordan & Davis also discussed a meta model for Data Flow Diagram, Coad's OOA, and State Transition Diagram[10]. Thus their meta model is restricted to these three methods. If they enlarged their meta model to describe other design methods, the enlargement would have made their model complex.

6. *Base Model* : Almost all of the meta models have been described in Entity Relationship Model or its variant ones. The usage of predicate logic increases the expressive power of the meta model, but on the other side, it provides the difficulty of implementing the efficient systems.

MetaEdit[13] has a function for its users to define various meta models. This function results from the existence of a "meta-meta-model". It, however, is difficult for the users to construct a suitable meta model without some guidelines such as "meta-methods".

6. METHOD BASE SYSTEMS

6.1. Architectural Overview of A Method Base System

The prototype of our method base system is implemented in client/server style on UNIX workstations as shown in Figure 12. The server part is a kernel of the system and it interacts with the method base schematically depicted in Figure 1. It also navigates software designers following the methods they selected, and records the products and the performed activities. The client parts provide user friendly interface suitable for the methods. For example, the client of OOA can display the products in Coad's OOA diagram form, and the client of JSD can generate Entity Structure Diagram from the stored products. It also supports graphical representation of the products and consistency check in the products. The system has a client for each method which is stored in it.

Table 1
Comparison of The Existing Meta Models

Meta Model	Notation	Procedure	Hierarchy of Products	Constraints of Products	Applicability	Base Model
Viewpoints[7]	○	△[1)]	○	○	○	Template with 5 slots (incl. ER)
Jordan & Davis[10]	–	–	–	–	–	ER
MetaEdit[13]	○	–	–	–	○	OPRR
MetaView[14]	–[2)]	–	–	–[4)]	○	ER
Brinkkemper[4]	–	–	–	○	△[3)]	ER + Predicate Logic
Method Base	×[2)]	○	○	×[4)]	○	ER

– : not referred × : not included
ER : Entity Relationship Model
OPRR : Object Property Role Relationship Model (Extended version of ER model)
1) : Informal description only
2) : The definition of graphical notation can be implemented in the tool environment, not included in meta model part
3) : Special purpose of methods for information system development
4) : The constraints can be specified in the tool environment and checked by the tool.

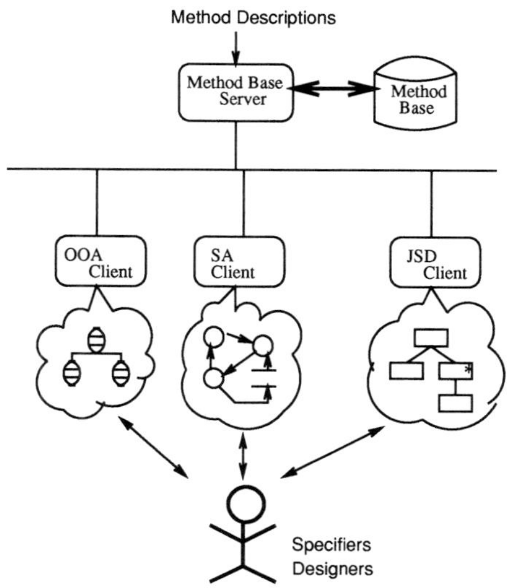

Figure 12. Prototype of the Method Base System

6.2. Method Description

We use PSL[15] like language to describe the methods according our meta model. The descriptions are inputted to the method base server as shown in Figure 12. The following is an example of the OOA description of Figure 6 and 7 in our PSL like language. The words written in upper-case letters such as OBJECT, EVENT, HAS_A are reserved and stand for the terms of the meta model.

```
METHOD OOA   %Coad's Object Oriented Analysis
   OBJECT    Object ;
     HAS_A   Aggregation : Object ;
     HAS_A   Has : Service, Attribute, InstanceConnection ;
     IS_A    Inherit_from : Object ;
     INPUT   Receive : Message ;
     OUTPUT  Send : Message ;

   OBJECT    Subject ;
     HAS_A   Has : Object, Connection ;

   EVENT      Message ;

   PROCESS    Service ;
     INPUT   input : Data ;
     OUTPUT  output : Data ;

   STATE      Attribute ;

   DATA       Data ;
     DEFINES  Defines  Attribute

   ACTIVITY   Identify_Objects ;
     INPUT : Object ;
     OUTPUT : Objects ;
     PRECEDE : Identify_Objects, Identify_Structures ;

   ACTIVITY   Identify_Structures ;
     IN : Object ;
     OUT : Aggregation, Inherit-from ;
     PRECEDE : Identify_Structures, Define_Subjects ;
   ...

ENDMETHOD
```

6.3. Example

We explain our method base system by using the example of the design of a lift control system. At first, the worker decomposed a lift control system to three objects : lift box (shortened to lift), floor button, and scheduler in Shlare & Mellor's OOA method citeooa and describes the message flow diagram. Thus the top level specification of the system is described as shown in Figure 13. He decided to design the lift by using Coad & Youdon's OOA, SA, and STD. The method base system holds the refine relationships of the lift for the three specifications to be developed.

After the worker invokes the method base system, it opens an *OverviewWindow* as shown in the right window of Figure 14, where the activities and the methods used in his development are displayed. This window is used for getting the multi-view specifications to be developed or being developed as shown in the figure. He has three activities to be performed : Lift design, Floor button design, and Scheduler design. The black area tells

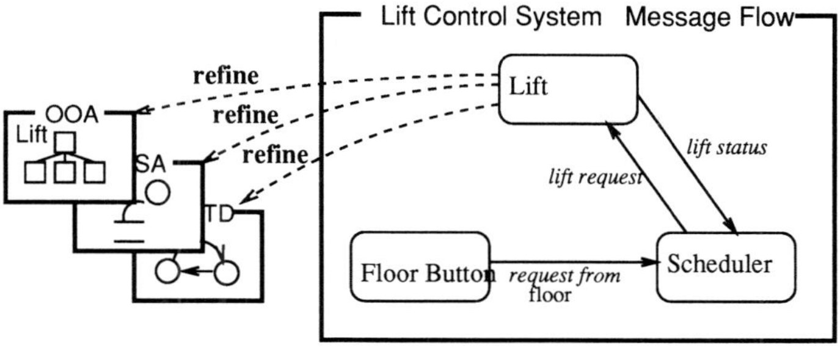

Figure 13. An Example of Refine Relationship

us the completed activities and the gray ones are for the on-going ones. So, from this window, we know: the user have finished two design activities by using OOA and SA, and he is trying to complete the document of the state transition diagram.

The method base system has another type of windows, called *EditWindows*, where the user can input and edit his products. Each EditWindow is for one design activity and opened by clipping the menu from the OverviewWindow. When the user points to the Lift-OOA area on the OverviewWindow with the mouse to open an EditWindow, the lift specification in OOA form will be displayed as shown on the left window of Figure 14. An EditWindow consists of two areas : one is for the products and the other one is for procedures. The products are displayed on the left side of the window, and the user can edit the displayed products with the commands on the upper line of the window. By using the commands, the user can do the usual editing work such as creation, deletion, movement of graphical objects, resizing and text input. On the right side, the flow chart of typical procedures of OOA is displayed. This flow chart is generated according to the procedural description of Figure 7, which is stored in the method base. It plays an important role of navigating the worker to use OOA design method. Each oval in this area stands for a procedure of OOA, and he is currently performing a procedure expressed by the black oval, which is surrounded with a larger oval in the figure, i.e. identifying structures. These ovals can be used as menu commands for manipulating the displayed product elements. Let's suppose that the user points to the oval "identifying structures" with his mouse. He can create or delete solid lines expressing aggregation relationships between objects, e.g. a line between the lift and the sensor objects.

The user opens his editing windows for SA (Data Flow Diagram) and STD successively. Figure 15 shows four editing windows for a specification of lift control system. Thus he has been developing a lift specification from three viewpoints : OOA, SA, and STD. The product elements which have the same identifier and belong to the same type can be *bridges* to integrate these three products into a specification. Lift button, door button, and door are examples of the *bridge* elements because they belong to *object type* of our meta model both in OOA and SA.

In the MessageFlow window, the rightmost top window of Figure 15, the top level

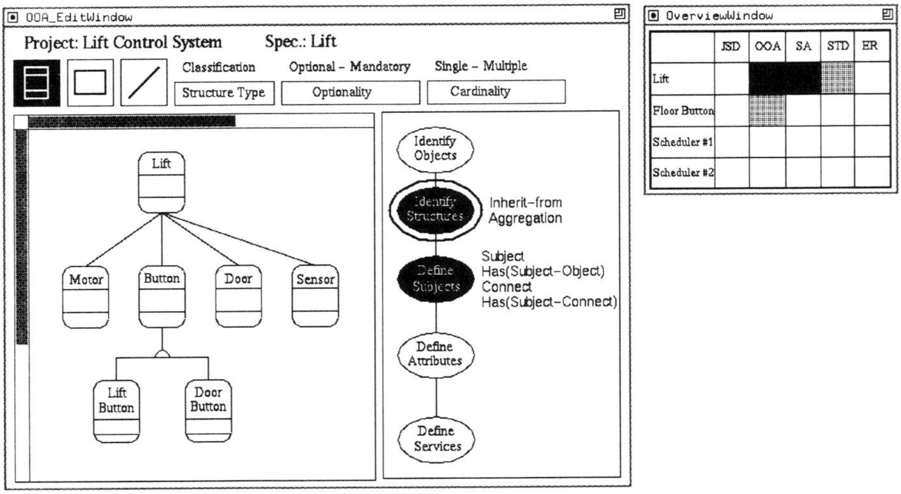

Figure 14. An Example of A OverviewWindow and An EditWindow

specification is displayed and he can also open his editing windows by selecting a refine command displayed on the upper line of the window.

7. Conclusion

This paper has discussed a method base system to manage software specification & design methods for supporting the development of software specifications. Actual design processes are recorded according to the object model of the adopted design method, so we can reuse them to improve our design process and to extract particular knowledge or know-how which design experts have. Furthermore we should clarify the relationships between design methods and the problem domains where they can be applied effectively. These will be researched later.

REFERENCES

1. *Problem Set for the 4th International Workshop on Software Specification and Design: Proc. of 4th International Workshop on Software Specification and Design*, 1987.
2. A. Alderson. Meta-CASE Technology. In *Lecture Notes in Computer Science 509*, pages 81–91, 1992.
3. G. Booch. *Object Oriented Design With Applications.* Benjamin Cummings, 1991.
4. S. Brinkkemper. *Formalisation of Information Systems Modelling.* Thesis Publisher, 1990.
5. P. Coad and E. Yourdon. *Object-Oriented Analysis.* Prentice Hall, 1990.

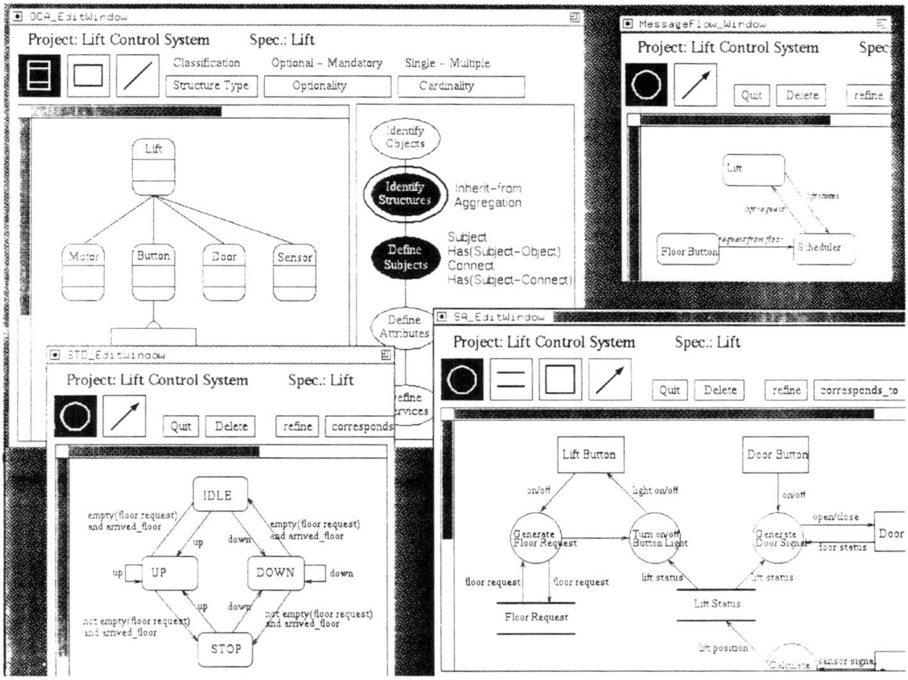

Figure 15. Example of Multiple Edit Windows

6. T. DeMarco. *Structured Analysis and System Specification.* Yourdon Press, 1978.
7. A. Finkelstein, J. Kramer, B. Nuseibeh, L. Finkelstein, and M. Goedicke. Viewpoints : A Framework for Integrating Multiple Perspectives in System Development. *International Journal of Software Engineering and Knowledge Engineering,* 1(2):31–58, 1992.
8. D. Harel, H. Lachover, A. Naamad, A. Pnueli, M. Politi, R. Sherman, and A. Shtul-Trauring. STATEMATE : A Working Environment for the Development of Complex Reactive Systems. In *Proc. of 10th ICSE,* pages 396–406, 1988.
9. M.A. Jackson. *System Development.* Prentice-Hall, 1983.
10. A.K. Jordan and A.M. Davis. Requirements Engineering Metamodel : An Integrated View of Requirements. In *Proc. of 15th COMPSAC,* pages 472–478, 1991.
11. J. Rumbaugh, M. Blaha, W. Premerlani, F. Eddy, and W. Lonrensen. *Object-Oriented Modeling and Design.* Prentice-Hall, 1991.
12. S. Shlaer and S.J. Mellor. An Object-Oriented Approach to Domain Analysis. *ACM SIGSOFT Software Engineering Notes,* 14(5):66–77, 1989.
13. K. Smolander, K. Lyytinen, V.P. Tahvanainen, and P. Marttiin. MetaEdit — A Flexible Graphical Environment for Methodology Modelling. In *Proc. of 3rd International Conference CAiSE91, LNCS 498,* pages 168–193, 1991.
14. P. Sorenson, J. Tremblay, and A. McAllister. The Metaview System for Many Specification Envirnments. *IEEE Software,* 2(5):30–38, 1988.
15. D. Teichroew and E.A. Hershey III. PSL/PSA : A Computer-aided Technique for Structured Documentation and Analysis of Information Processing Systems. *IEEE Trans. on Software Engineering,* 1(3):6–15, 1977.
16. P. Ward. The Transformation Schema : An Extension of the Data Flow Diagram to Represent Control and Timing. *IEEE Trans. on Soft. Eng.,* 2(12):198–210, 1986.
17. K. Wen-yin and M. Saeki. Method Base : Database of Software Design Methods & Specifications. In *Joint Conference on Software Engineering '92,* pages 311–318, 1992.

Information System Development Process (A-30)
N. Prakash, C. Rolland and B. Pernici (Editors)
Elsevier Science Publishers B.V. (North-Holland)

© 1993 IFIP. All rights reserved.

A Method Engineering Approach to Information Systems Development

Kees van Slooten[a] and Sjaak Brinkkemper[b]

[a]University of Twente, School of Management Studies, P.O. Box 217, 7500 AE Enschede, The Netherlands, E-mail: C.vanSlooten@sms.utwente.nl

[b]University of Twente, Dept. of Computer Science, P.O. Box 217, 7500 AE Enschede, The Netherlands, E-mail: sjbr@cs.utwente.nl

Abstract

Method Engineering is introduced as an approach to configure project specific methods for the development of information systems. We propose to support method engineering with a formal procedure to configure development scenarios from project characterizations. The project characterization is defined by a number of project contingency factors and determines the interest of aspects considered during the development of information systems. Process-, information-, behaviour-, organization-, and problem-oriented aspects constitute one dimension of a framework facilitating the selection of fragments of methods as components of the required scenario. The other dimension of the framework consists of two levels for the analysis and design process related to the levels of decomposition of the object system, or universe of discourse. Also, a development strategy is derived from the project characterization which means selecting a route map for information systems development. The available fragments of methods, and the route maps, will be stored in what we call a method base.

Keyword Codes: D.2.0; K.6.0
Keywords: Software Engineering; Management of Computing and Information Systems

1. Introduction

Numerous methods and tools supporting information systems development have already been published [OLL 82, OLL 86, HIR 85, FAL 89]. That means there are many ways, depending on a large number of factors [DAV 84, BUR 85, OLL 91], for developing information systems. In practice, it is difficult to select the right methods, tools, and development strategy. Different circumstances, e.g. as a consequence of different application domains, interest groups, business strategies, cultures and skills, require a different approach, a different collection of methods and tools and the performance of a different set of development tasks in a different sequence. In other words, the contingency factors, as characteristics of the situation, influence the scenario for information systems development. Many information system development teams, from organizations using a standard systems development method, feel a need for a more flexible configuration procedure for a scenario that matches the situation. Necco [NEC 87] already perceived, after a study about practices in systems analysis and design, the need for something like method engineering by stating:

"Guidelines should be developed for the systems analyst within the organization to provide direction for the use and integration of the various approaches, techniques and tools which the organization selects for its systems development process".

Due to negative experience with existing methods for information systems development, method engineering recently became an interesting topic for research. Adaptability of methods depending upon variables describing the project context, was proposed by Welke and Kumar [WEL 91]. Our definition of *method engineering* is as follows:

The process of configuring a project scenario for information systems development using existing methods, or fragments thereof, to satisfy the factors that define the project context

The goal of our research and this paper is to support organizations in configuring a specific scenario matching the specific project characteristics as well as possible.

Figure 1. illustrates the global structure of the configuration process of a project scenario. Note, that project management is not included in this figure, due to the generic nature of planning and control of resource assignment to systems development tasks. Scenario configuration consists of the following stages.

1. First, the project characterization is determined by assigning values and weights to contingency factors. Contingency factors are defined in [WEL 91] as characteristics of the development situation. We have categorized the contingencies into domain characteristics (i.e. related to the contents of the application), external factors (such as legal and social norms), technical factors (related to particular hardware and software dependencies), and the development expertise (internal, external and end-users). We have started a field study to investigate this process in the IS development practice.
2. Based on the project characterization, the method engineer determines the aspects, levels, constraints, and development strategy. This is related to a set of possible route maps and method fragments in the method base. Route maps are development strategy plans consisting of development activities and products. Method fragments are parts of methods, techniques and tools that can be incorporated in a route map forming a complete project approach.
3. A first project scenario is composed by selecting the most appropriate route map and a corresponding number of method fragments. These are finely tuned to the project characterization. For instance, the development expertise is related to the choice of tools and techniques.
4. The actual project performance is started using the scenario as guide line. The scenario is further refined during the course of the project, and possibly adapted in the case of unforeseen contingencies. The project characterization is made more precise and, where necessary corrected. Thus additional method fragments are added to the scenario. The complete performance leads to more development expertise, which, in turn, can be exploited for future projects.

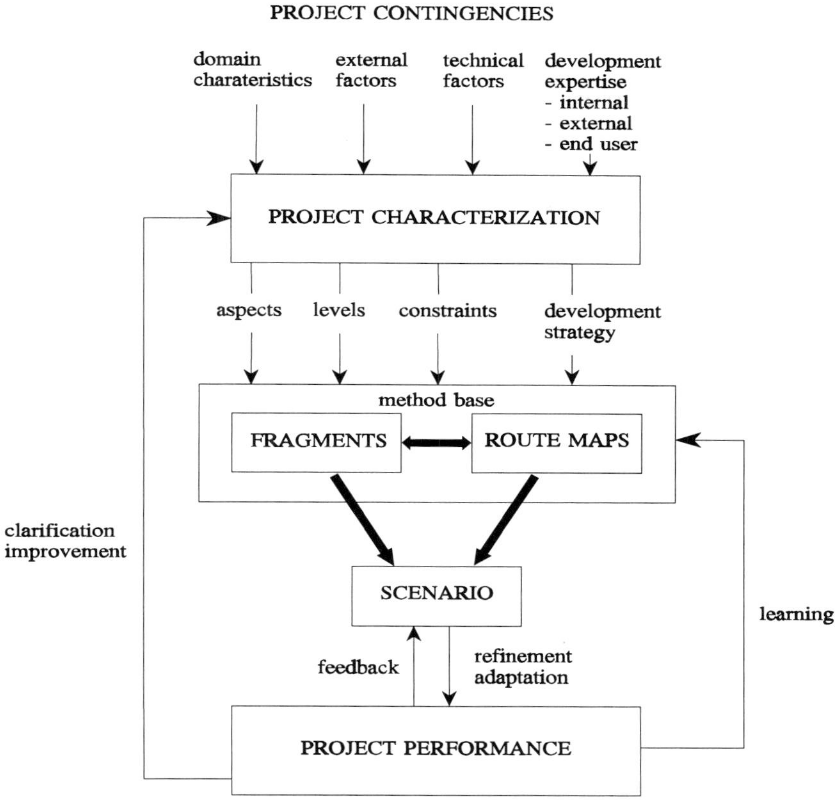

Figure 1 Configuration Procedure for a Scenario

This paper introduces a framework from which the two dimensions: aspects and levels, can be used for selecting fragments of methods.

The first dimension, aspects, emphasizes the way of looking at the object system. The object system, or universe of discourse, is defined here as the part of reality considered as problem area for the development of an information system. An example of an object system, namely "project work", will be used in section 3 of this paper. Other examples are a business function or process, an office etc. The boundaries of the object system must be defined during the early stages of the analysis and design process. A few examples of well-known aspects are the process-, data- and behaviour-aspects (perspectives called by Olle et al. [OLL 91]) derived from existing information systems development methods. Process-oriented methods, emphasize the modelling of object system functioning and decomposition, e.g. ISAC [LUN 82] activity analysis. Information- or data-oriented methods emphasize the modelling of information-entities and the relationships between them, e.g. ER-modelling. The temporal aspects and the dynamic sequencing of processes are addressed by the behaviour-oriented aspect, e.g. dynamic modelling of MERISE[TAR86].

The second dimension of the framework, levels, distinguishes two levels for the analysis and design process: the object systems level and the computer based systems level. The structure and functioning of the object system is the focus of the object systems analysis and design level. Only the functioning of potential computer based information systems is important during object systems analysis and design, which means that the potential computer based information systems remain black-boxes during this stage. The analysis and design of computer based information systems, identified at the object systems level, is the focus of the computer based systems level, the second main level of the framework.

In which way the aspects and levels influences the selection of fragments of methods is a topic of our research. Another topic is the assembly of the route map, with the selected set of method fragments, into a suitable format (i.e. manual, tool or mixture of both) for supporting the project performance. As route maps and fragments can be adequately manipulated and stored by means of meta-models [BRI 90], method assembly with corresponding completeness and consistency checks is under investigation.

The selection of a *development strategy* was elaborated by Davis and Olson [DAV 84] and Burns and Dennis [BUR 85]. The first authors presented a one-dimensional model for the selection of a strategy for information systems development, which was extended by the last two authors. Burns and Dennis distinguish three main strategies:

- Linear systems development without prototyping.
- Linear systems development with prototyping during the analysis phase. The prototype is deleted.
- Non-linear systems development with up-grade-prototyping.

The selection of one of these strategies is based on two groups of contingency variables: project uncertainty and project complexity. The relationship between contingency factors, development strategy and route maps, is an interesting topic of our research.

Organizational and practical constraints, as a consequence of organizational strategy and the presence of skills, may influence the application of possible scenarios for information systems development. So far we have highlighted the role of aspects, levels, development strategies and constraints in the context of the configuration procedure of figure 1. The main focus of the paper is on the framework, aspects against levels, that will be applied in the context of method engineering.

The paper is organized as follows. Section 2. introduces the proposed framework in short. The relationship between the decomposition process and the levels of the framework is elaborated in section 3. Section 4. explains the aspects of the framework. Section 5. presents an example of an instantiation of the framework. The final section formulates some conclusions and issues of our research.

2. The Framework

In the context of the selection process of a scenario for information systems development (figure 1.), the framework of aspects against levels plays an important role. The framework connects the project characteristics and the selected fragments of methods, which means support for method engineering. To describe the focus of the proposed framework we mention the kind of models required to represent the architecture of an information system as defined by Zachman [ZAC 87], namely:

- Scope models.
  Modelling the scope of the object system and the underlying strategy for an information system.
- Business models.
  Modelling the exact functioning of the object system.
- Design models.
  Modelling the information systems functions for information input and output.
  The conceptual specification of a computer based information system.
- Implementation models.
  Modelling the computer based information system as it is implemented in a particular technology.

Although all levels are important for method engineering, this paper will only deal with methods concerning the construction of Business models and Design models. We name analysis and design at the Business models level: Object Systems Analysis and Design (OSAD), and at the Design models level: Information Systems Analysis and Design (ISAD).

OSAD aims to design a new object system through analysis of the old system by articulating and solving the problems of the old one. ISAD aims to design a computer based information system through the analysis of that part of the object system selected by OSAD for that purpose. During OSAD, more than one computer based information system may have been selected, which means more than one ISAD process related to the same OSAD process (figure 2).

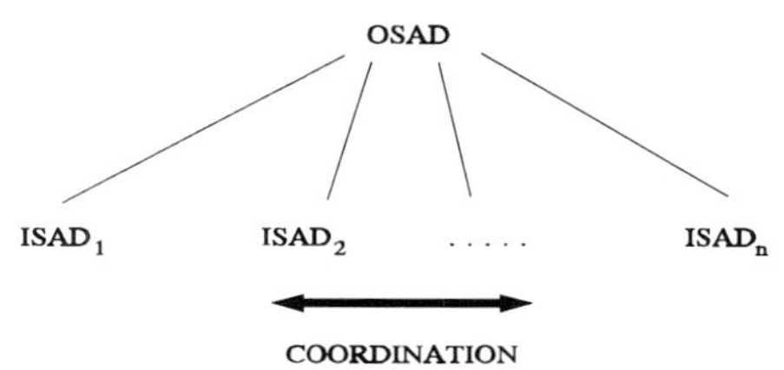

Figure 2. The Levels of the Analysis and Design Process

Be aware of the fact that coordination of the various computer based information systems is guaranteed by the process at the OSAD level. During OSAD, as well as during ISAD, a decomposition process of the object system may be necessary to investigate the object system and the computer based information system at an appropriate level of detail. There is a precise relationship between the decomposition levels and the analysis and design levels, OSAD and ISAD, used by the framework. This relationship will be elaborated in section 3. So far, we explained the "levels" dimension of the framework. Subsequently, it is the turn of the "aspects" dimension.

An aspect is a way of looking at the object system. Examples of aspects are the process-, data-, and behaviour aspects defined by Olle et al. [OLL 91]. These aspects were derived from existing information systems development methods. There are methods emphasizing the process aspect or the data aspect; other methods combine two or more aspects. *Process*-oriented methods structure the functions of the object system, e.g. markteting, production or distribution. *Functions* may be considered as processes or activities at a higher level of decomposition of the object system. Modelling of information entities, as done by Entity-Relationship-Diagrams, and the relationships between them from *messages* between activities, is the focus of *data*- or *information*-oriented methods. The behaviour-oriented aspect encompasses the *temporal* characteristics of the object system, e.g. the maximum duration of a process, and the dynamic sequencing of processes by synchronization of *events*, e.g. starting a process by clock-interrupt as an event. The integration of the well-known process, data and behaviour aspects may be realized by the application of object-oriented modelling approaches [BOO 86, RAM 91, HEN 90], which is especially useful during ISAD.

Mumford [MUM 85] has already proposed a structured design approach that covers organizational, adminstrative and quality-of-working-life factors. Solutions invented during object systems analysis and design, may affect the organizational *structure* and *culture*. That is why the organization-oriented aspect has been added to the framework. Elements, e.g. organizational functions, processes and events already covered by the other aspects, are excluded from the organization-oriented aspect. Till now, the process-, information-, behaviour- and organization-oriented aspects may be used to describe the existing and desired situation of the object system according to these aspects.

However, more specific domain-oriented methods, techniques or tools may be useful to *articulate* and *solve* the problems and needs of the object system, e.g. the application of simulation techniques to analyze the consequences of some changes. We name this the problem-oriented aspect. Often, a process of creative thinking is necessary to find feasible solutions for the problems of the object system. Summing up we have distinguished five aspects, each depicted by two terms (figure 3.).

process	information	behaviour	organization	problem
function activity	message data	event time	structure culture	articulation solving

Figure 3. The five aspects.

The process-, information-, behaviour-, organization-, and problem-oriented aspects constitute one dimension of the framework, but not every aspect deserves the same attention at each level, the other dimension of the framework, e.g. detailed information analysis techniques are less useful at the OSAD level. The construction of tables containing data classes against processes will suffice.It may even be necessary to differentiate between upper and lower levels of detail at the OSAD level. The differentiation between levels of detail or levels of decomposition is elaborated in section 3, e.g. the behaviour-oriented aspect is more useful at lower levels of decomposition.

The importance of an aspect depends very much on the characteristics of the object system, and the computer based information system as part of the object system. Behaviour-oriented modelling may be very important with respect to the order-processing procedures of a wholesale company, but less important for a report generation system to support project management. Important criteria for the selection of methods, techniques and tools are:

- level of analysis and design and/or level of decomposition (a dimension of the framework) (figure 1.).
- aspects depending on the object system characteristics (a dimension of the framework) (figure 1.).
- presence of skills inside or outside (involved external expertise) the organization, and the policies of the organization (constraints in figure 1.).
- requirements with respect to characteristics of the methods, techniques and tools (constraints in figure 1.).

The requirements of the object system concerning the characteristics of methods, techniques and tools may include: completeness, consistency, clarity, simplicity and the possibility of integrating the various methods, techniques and tools. In this context, it is valuable to be aware of studies which have compared and evaluated methods, techniques and tools [OLL 82, MAL 83, WOO 82, NAU 82, COL 84, HIR 85, SOL 83, IIV 83]. It was further suggested that a fitting approach would depend on contingency factors of the problem situation [DAV 82, NAU 82, OLL 91, EPI 86, IIV 83]. So far, we have discussed the role of the framework in the context of figure 1.

3. The Decomposition Process

3.1 The two levels of the Analysis and Design Process

In section two it has been said that the functioning of the business is the subject of Object Systems Analysis and Design (OSAD), and the functioning of a Computer Based Information System (CBIS) will be handled by Information Systems Analysis and Design (ISAD). Before starting a process of decomposition, we have to define the boundaries of the object system: the problem area to be analyzed and the environment of the object system. Generally, a process of decomposition of the object system is required to describe the functioning of the business at a level of detail needed to recognize and to articulate the problems of the object system. Another goal of the decomposition process may be the identification of business processes suitable for computerization. At a certain level of decomposition one or more computer based information systems may be identified; this level is named the CBIS-level.

The CBIS-level is used to split up the analysis and design process of the object system and is defined as the lowest level of decomposition during OSAD. A decomposition of a CBIS will elaborate the functioning of the CBIS and is always part of ISAD. This means that OSAD, as well as ISAD, deal with various levels of decomposition and that one OSAD process might be followed by more than one ISAD process if more than one CBIS has to be developed. The coordination between different computer based information systems must be guaranteed by the related OSAD-process (figure 2.). In the sections 3.2 and 3.3, we want to explain the decomposition process of OSAD and ISAD in much more detail by using a simple business example. The decomposition process will be supported by so called *decomposition matrices*.

The decomposition matrix is based on the N^2 chart of Lano [LAN 79]. The N^2-chart is a matrix representation of a system. The system elements are put on the diagonal of the matrix: E_1, O_1, O_2, O_3, E_2 in figure 4. The object system of figure 4. consists of the sub-object-systems O_1, O_2, O_3, and the environment of the system elements E_1, E_2. The off-diagonal matrix elements represent mutual relationships between the system elements.

Two system elements, S_1 and S_2, may be related in two ways, namely from S_1 to S_2 and from S_2 to S_1. In the first case the relationship is represented by the matrix element above the diagonal identified by the row number of S_1 and the column number of S_2. In figure 4., a relationship A has been specified from $S_1 = E_1$ to $S_2 = O_1$, and furthermore, X from $S_1 = O_1$ to $S_2 = O_2$. In the second case, the relationship is represented by the matrix element below the diagonal identified by the row number of S_2 and the column number of S_1. In figure 4., a relationship Y has been specified from $S_2 = O_3$ to $S_1 = O_2$. The relationships may represent physical and information objects. It is possible that a relationship is complex and consists of more than one information object. After this, an example will show the usage of these kinds of decomposition matrices.

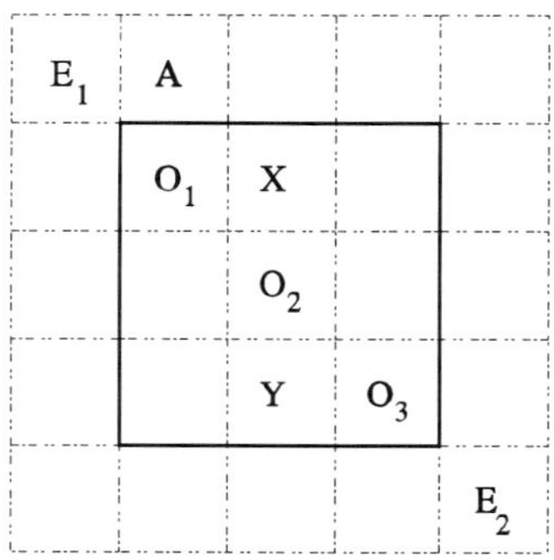

Figure 4 N^2 chart of object system, environment and relationships

The example can be described as follows:

Departments are responsible for projects initiated by management of the company. The work of an employee, at a department on various projects, will be charged against a rate per hour depending on his function. Expenses are calculated per project. Every employee may be requested to generate a report on his task within the project. Departmental management has the task of controlling the expenses of departments and projects, and requires information about the progress of the projects.

3.2 Decomposition at the OSAD-level

The business situation described in section 3.1, is represented by the matrix of figure 5. concerning the first level of decomposition of the object system "project work" and the related environmental components. Similar matrix notations to represent a decomposition product are applied by various systems development methods, e.g. PRISMA [LAA 83]. In this case, the object system can be identified as "project work" and the environment of the object system is decomposed into "company management" and "employee administration". Information about "projects" and "budgets" is directed from "company management" to "project work", and information about the organization (employees, department, functions, rates per hour, etc.) is sent by "employee administration" to "project work". All input to "project work" is specified in the column of "project work", and all output of "project work" is specified in the row of "project work".

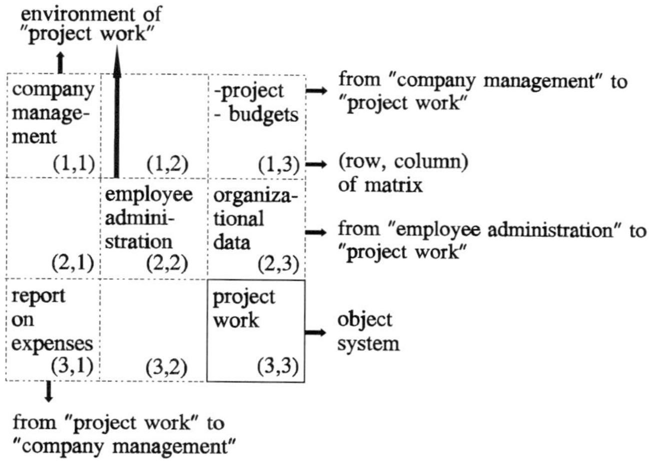

Figure 5 First level of decomposition of "project work" and environment

Subsequently, it is the responsibility of management at departmental level to manage the operational project work. From this point of view, we are able to divide "project work" into two sub-object-systems, namely "project management" and "operational project work", n.b. be aware of the applied criterion for decomposition of "project work". In practice, this business situation requires the existence of the regulatory process "project management" and the regulated process "operational project work". This kind of systems management modelling represents a well-known way of thinking in the systems theory discipline, and may be used to support the problem-oriented aspect (problem-articulation and problem-solving) of the proposed framework. One can find more on this subject in section 3.4. After this decomposition of the object system "project work" into the sub-object-systems "project management" and "operational project work", we are able to construct the second level decomposition matrix (figure 6.).

A study of the activities of the sub-object-system "project management", may show an activity to generate a "report on expenses" monthly for each project per department by using information about projects, budgets, organizational data and hours worked (figure 6.). This "report on expenses" is also required by "company management". Furthermore, a file of abstracts is maintained by "project management", which contains relevant data about the progress of tasks carried out by operational project workers. Such activities may be substituted by a computer based information system. A study of the activities of the sub-object-system "operational project work", may show the generation of a monthly list of tasks for each operational project worker with the hours worked on each task. A task is defined as the work to be done by a worker for a particular project. The proposal is to change the structure of the object system "project work" by replacing the mentioned activities by a computer based information system. The structure of the new object system is given by figure 7. By introducing a CBIS to replace some activities of the object system, the communication structure of the object system has been changed. Moreover, the organizational task structure and the contents of various jobs may be influenced. This kind of problem will be addressed by methods, techniques and tools classified by the organization-oriented aspect: structure and culture.

Other possibilities in defining a CBIS may exist. For example, a computer based system to support the planning activity of the sub-object-system "project management" or a computer-based system to facilitate conversations between the project manager and project workers. But such applications require a more detailed analysis of the business situation, which is not the purpose of this paper. We consider the decomposition process at the OSAD-level as finished.

company manage-ment		-project -budgets	
	employee administra-tion	org.data	
reports on expenses		project manage-ment	-planning -orders -requests
		-hours worked -report on progress	operatio-nal project work

Figure 6. Second level of decomposition of the object system "project work"

project manage-ment	-org. data -projects -budgets	-planning -orders -requests
-report/ expenses -report/ progress	CBIS report generation	report/ tasks
report on progress complete	-hours worked -abstract/ progress	operatio-nal project work

Figure 7. Object system with CBIS without environment and without input- and output messages of the object system

3.3 Decomposition at the ISAD-level

The decomposition matrix with one or more CBIS black boxes is the lowest level of decomposition during the decomposition process at the OSAD-level, if no further decomposition of sub-object-systems is required, which may bring about another CBIS. This lowest level of decomposition is called the CBIS-level. During OSAD the function of a CBIS in the broader context of the object system has been clarified, which includes the potential coordination and tuning of different computer based systems. During ISAD, the analysis and design process is focused on a particular CBIS. To analyse the structure of the CBIS we have to continue the decomposition process concerning the CBIS. In the column of the CBIS of figure 7., we find the inputs of the CBIS, and in the row of the CBIS the outputs. The inputs and outputs are user oriented categories of data, the so-called User Oriented Data Classes (UODC).

An User Oriented Data Class is a class of data considered by the user, who is the involved human actor of the object system, as a coherent collection of data, e.g. the data of an order or invoice.

Such user-oriented-data-classes play an important role during the decomposition process of the CBIS at the ISAD-level. The input processing sub-object-systems of the CBIS take care of storing and updating data and the output processing sub-object-systems produce the required outputs from the stored data, e.g. reports. The input processing sub-object-systems of the CBIS are defined by the input-boxes of the matrix of figure 7., namely:

- registration of organizational data, information about projects and budgets.
- registration of hours worked and abstracts about progress.

The output processing sub-object-systems of the CBIS are defined by the output-boxes of the matrix of figure 7, namely:

- generation of reports on expenses and progress.
- generation of report on tasks.

Sometimes the input- or output-boxes have a rather complicated structure, which means that further decomposition is required. e.g. the input-box containing the user-oriented-data-classes "hours worked" and "abstracts/progress" requires further decomposition, namely:

- registration of "hours worked".
- registration of "abstracts/progress".

The same procedure may be applicable to other input- or output-boxes. The levels of decomposition are represented by matrices of a similar structure as exposed during OSAD. Figure 8. is a *partial* representation of the decomposition of the CBIS so far.

A database management system takes care of the storage, retrieval and control of the data. The database management system may also contain functions for the storage and maintenance of conceptual schemata of the data, including the specification of constraints, rules, dictionaries etc. In figure 8., a report about expenses over a certain period is required by "project management". Data about hours worked over a certain period, perhaps a week, is added to the sum of hours worked for a certain task, that is stored by the database management system as the new sum of hours worked for that particular task. Such a decomposition process at the ISAD-level can be continued until every sub-object-system of the CBIS processes one single user-oriented-data-class. In that case, we get so-called *elementary subsystems* of the CBIS. The database management system mediates the communication between elementary subsystems of a CBIS. If direct communication between elementary subsystems is necessary, then we have to put them together in one

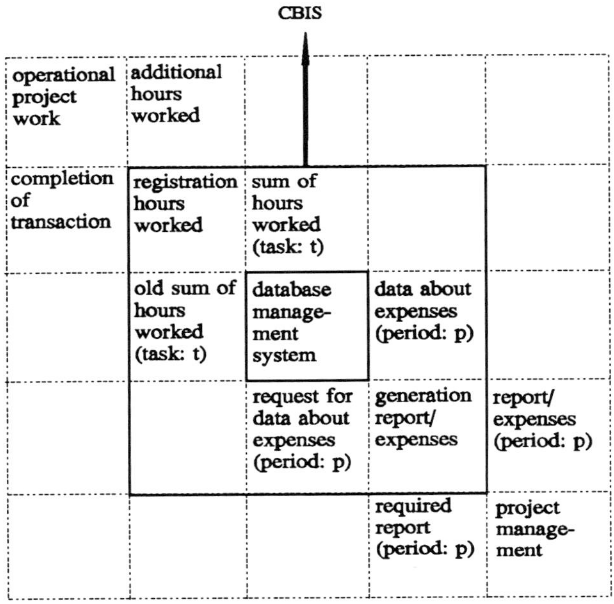

Figure 8 Part of the decomposition product during ISAD

subsystem. Consequently, the boxes of the matrix of figure 8., indicating communication between the subsystems "registration of hours worked" and "generation of report/expenses", must stay empty. Due to the fact that communication with the database management system is only possible through the subsystems of the CBIS, we conclude that the boxes for communication between the database management system and the environment of the CBIS (project management and operational project work) are intentionally empty. Moreover, the direct communication between "project management" and "operational project work" is not specified by figure 8., because the focus is on the CBIS and not on the communication between sub-object-systems outside the CBIS.

3.4 Criteria for decomposition

During the decomposition process at the OSAD level, we demonstrated an approach to decomposition by splitting up "project work" into the regulatory process "project management" and the regulated process "operational project work". The application of the systems management perspective is very useful at any level of the organization hierarchy.

The former section has already indicated the importance of the user-oriented-data-classes as a criterion for decomposition of the subsystems of a CBIS. But also at the OSAD-level, the user-oriented-data-classes may be important as a criterion for decomposition, e.g. a purchaser could divide his work into two processes:

- collection and maintenance concerning the class of suppliers data.
- determination of orders concerning the class of order data.

In figure 7., a "request", done by "project management", indicates the presence of conversations between the project manager and the operational project workers. A request made by the project manager may be followed by a promise, a counter-offer, a refusal, or another type of speech act by the operational project worker. The conversation between the project manager and operational project workers may be analyzed, and a network of communication acts may be constructed. Knowledge from speech act theory and conversation analysis is used to study the structure of the conversations between actors of the object system [SEA 69, WIN 86, LEE 91, AUR 88].

There are other approaches with respect to the decomposition of the object system, e.g. executive processes like planning and control; processes of the value chain according to Porter [POR 80]; processes to support the separation of responsibilities from the discipline of administrative organization; the arrangement of a number of collateral systems around a focal system to bring it into existence, provide maintenance, back-up and recovery, supply its inputs and outputs and give it any value it may have, after which, each collateral system can be treated as a new focal system [STA 88]; systems morphology subdivides a system into three functional areas, namely the substantive, the procedural and the control [STA 88].

All these approaches have their own way of looking towards the object system and are valuable for comprehending the business processes. It is sometimes fruitful to apply more than one of these approaches to get to the bottom of the problems of the object system, which may be useful to support the problem-oriented aspect of the proposed framework.

4 Aspects of the Framework

4.1 The Process-Oriented Aspect

Most has been said about the process-oriented aspect, because the decomposition process in section 3 is focused on the decomposition of the object system into subsystems, which may be processes. The label *process* emphasizes the dynamic character of the subsystem: a transformation process. A (business) *function* is a grouping of processes considered by the researcher as one system, which means that a function in this context is a process at a higher level of decomposition. Functions and processes are related by physical flows (e.g. raw material, capital, goods) and information flows. Information and physical flows may be specified in the communication boxes of the decomposition matrix (row index not equal column index). The *environment* of an object system consists of systems (e.g. organizations, individuals) outside the object system, but related to the object system. An object system may often be an organization. According to Boer [BOE 91], an *organization* is a purposeful system of people and resources. In order to achieve its objectives, an organization transforms inputs into outputs which are useful for the environment of the organization. These transformation processes are labelled *primary processes.* To be effective, the primary processes have to be regulated by *regulative processes* like policy-making, planning and control. Moreover, *maintenance processes* are necessary to obtain and to maintain the means (e.g. staff, machines) of the organization. The classification of regulatory, maintenance and primary processes may be used as a decomposition mechanism at the OSAD level for a complete organization. The decomposition matrix of the former section may be used to represent the decomposition of the organization into regulatory, maintenance and primary processes, including their interrelationships.

4.2 The Information- or Data-Oriented Aspect

The off-diagonal matrix elements of a decomposition matrix may be considered as communication boxes. A communication box may contain more than one specification referring to more than one user oriented data class.

The decomposition process, discussed in section 3, may also cause a decomposition of relationships between subsystems, e.g. the relationship between "operational project work" and "project management" of figure 6., namely "hours worked and report on progress", is replaced in figure 7. by "report on progress", and "hours worked" and becomes part of the relationship between "operational project work" and the CBIS. Furthermore, we have seen that a decomposition of a relationship may be used to decompose a (sub)system.

Decomposition of relationships is finished if the relationships consist of single user-oriented-data-classes, which is always applied at the ISAD level. In short, creative thinking about the contents of the communication boxes, with respect to the specification of the required relationships, yields the basic elements for the information architecture. Because the decomposition matrices will be designed for any level of decomposition, it is possible to determine the information structure of each level of decomposition. Often, Entity-Relationship-Diagrams are applied to specify the information structure. We shall describe the process of constructing an information structure for the level of decomposition of figure 8., the CBIS with the processes "registration of hours worked" and "generation of report on expenses". The user-oriented-data-classes determining the information structure are "hours worked" and "report on expenses". Usually, it is possible to show instances of the various data-classes. According to the adopted specification method, each separate data-class is converted into an information structure. The entire information structure of the CBIS is the union of the separate information structures derived from the involved data-classes. The union is constructed by looking for common elements of the separate information structures, e.g. common entity types. Information structures like this may be constructed for higher levels of decomposition as well. However, at higher levels it will often be enough to construct less detailed models, like the decomposition matrices.

4.3 The Behaviour-Oriented Aspect

During behaviour-oriented modelling, we have to determine sequences of processes, their start- and end-conditions, possibly their duration and delay. We propose to apply the usual basic concepts like *events*, preconditions, postconditions and a few *time*-related concepts.

An event is something that happens or arises inside or outside an object system and which influences the execution of a process of the object system, e.g. at the end of the month (event) the execution of the process "generation of report on expenses" (figure 8.) is started, in which case a single event is enough to start the process. Generally, the start of a process depends upon a precondition, which is defined by logical propositions in which events appear as logical variables. More than one postcondition may be defined at the end of a process, indicating different end-states for a process. Postconditions are also defined by logical propositions which cause the occurrence of new events if satisfied. Sometimes a certain process has to be finished within a certain time period: the duration of the process, or a process has to be delayed a certain time period after the precondition has been satisfied: the delay of the process.

The behaviour-oriented models of all processes may be integrated if there are common events between the processes; an event may be output of process **a** and at the same time input of process **b.** The need for a behaviour-oriented model depends upon the dynamic nature of the object system and/or the CBIS. Behaviour-oriented modelling is especially important at lower levels of decomposition of dynamic object systems.

4.4 The Organization-Oriented Aspect

The object system is often an organization or a coherent part of an organization. In section 4.1 it was already mentioned that an organization may be considered as a purposeful system of people and resources. Based on contingency theory, Krabbendam [BOE 91] developed a process model of organizations, which was interpreted as follows:

"for the organization to be effective, a consistency is required among the component elements of the organization (people, resources, processes, organizational arrangements) and its environment".

The important relationships between these elements are elaborated by the before mentioned authors. Identification of the most important relationships for a specific business situation will be very useful for object systems analysis and design, because the introduction of computer based information systems in organizations will influence various component elements of the organization.

People in organizations hold positions. The responsibilities and competences of these positions are often recorded in an organization chart. Positions are charged with tasks, which can be related to organizational processes. What we may do is describe, specify or model the *structure* of the organization. Furthermore, mutual relationships between people are characterized by differences with respect to power and knowledge or information.

The *culture* of an organization consists of a set of more or less coherent values, norms, goals and opinions. The coherence between structure and culture is defined by the concept social role, the expectations about the behaviour of people in certain situations. The interaction between structure and culture takes place through social processes. Changing the structure influences the culture and vice versa. A social process may be defined as the on going interaction between structure (position, power, knowledge) and culture (values, norms, goals, opinions). Unnecessary to say that these elements are extremely important for object systems analysis and design.

4.5 The Problem-Oriented Aspect

The existing, as well as the new object system, may be described by the process-, information-, behaviour- and organization-oriented aspects, but a process of creative thinking is necessary to articulate and solve the problems and needs of the object system. We do not want to make a sharp distinction between methods, techniques or tools for problem articulation and problem solving, because getting the problem straight often means the solution is at hand. A process of creative thinking needs two types of support:

- procedural support (the process).
- support for the analysis process (creative thinking).

Before describing a procedure and giving some explanation of the analysis process, it must be emphasized that the actual approach depends a lot upon the characteristics of the specific object system to be analyzed.

A Global Procedure

Starting from the formulation of *experienced* problems, needs, goals and constraints of the object system, the new situation must be specified through a process of analysis. The consequences of the proposed solutions (the outcome of the analysis process) must be described exhaustively, because the object system should be able to anticipate in time. Such an analysis process has to be started by the people of the organization if one realizes bad functioning. The objective is to construct a common view for all people involved of the object system concerning the *actual* problems and their solutions.

Often, the expertise of more disciplines is required to solve the problems. Sometimes, it is important to oppose views of various groups of people to achieve a view acceptable for everybody. Probably, organizational measures are necessary if a common view is not possible. Finally, a strategy has to be determined with which the new situation can be achieved.

The Analysis

Of course, the way of thinking and modelling described by the former sections may support the analysis process, but often more specific problem-oriented methods, techniques, tools and knowledge is necessary to solve the problems of the object system. A few examples are:

- Specific techniques are available to support the process to identify the *actual* problems, e.g. the analysis of cause and effect relationships.
- Mistakes made by people within an organization can be detected if separation of functions and responsibilities is applied more strictly. Principles from administrative organization are useful for this kind of problems.
- Reference models of similar object systems may be available for comparison.
- A specific kind of interview technique may be useful to articulate the problems of the object system.

5. Instantiating the Framework, an Example

By the former sections of this paper the two dimensions of the framework have been clarified, namely:

- the two levels of analysis and design OSAD and ISAD tightly related to the decomposition process.
- the process-, information-, behaviour-, organization-, and problem-oriented aspects, each labelled by two words (figure 9.).

During OSAD, the new situation of the object system concerning all aspects will be specified, including the functioning of computer based information systems in the context of the object system. For the specification of a computer based information system at the ISAD level process-, information- and behaviour-oriented models may be necessary, but the organization- and problem-oriented aspect will not be applied, because that kind of aspects has been completely settled by OSAD. Each remaining box of the framework may be filled up with methods, techniques and tools. Figure 9., as an example, shows such a combination of methods, techniques and tools, which has been applied many times in practice. Filling up the framework has to be done very carefully, because the used (fragments of) methods may overlap, and the definition of comparable concepts of different methods may be slightly different. Special attention is necessary for the transition from the OSAD level to the ISAD level (vertical connection), if different methods are involved at these levels, and for the horizontal connection of aspect models at each level. Meta-modelling, elaborated in section 6, may help to recognize and to overcome these problems. Subsequently, we explain the contents of figure 9.

Aspects / Levels	process	information	behaviour	organization	problem
	function activity	message data	event time	structure culture	articulation solving
OSAD	decomposition process	decomposition process	MERISE dynamic modelling	-org. chart -resp. matrix -valuation framing	-ISAC analysis of change
ISAD	decomposition process	NIAM information structuring	MERISE dynamic modelling		

Figure 9 The Example

The problem-Oriented Aspect (articulation, solving)

ISAC [LUN 82] stands for: Information Systems work and Analysis of Change. The Analysis of Change maintains a strict procedure for problem solving, although problem analysis is hardly addressed. Referring to the business situation of section 3, systems management modelling may be helpful to study the regulating processes at the company- and the project-level, and also knowledge and models from the discipline of project management may be useful. These specific topics are not mentioned in figure 9. The Analysis of Change will be supported by the decomposition process (process- and information-oriented aspects) of section 3 and the organization-oriented aspect.

The Organization-Oriented Aspect (structure, culture)

Specification of an organization chart and the modelling of responsibilities of organizational positions for the business processes, also called the responsibility matrix. The development of a responsibility matrix may be supported by the problem-oriented aspect, i.e. the use of knowledge and models derived from the discipline of administrative organization. To specify the cultural effects of an innovation, one may apply the technique of Valuation Framing, which offers a framework for identifying and describing cultural changes [STA 88].

The Behaviour-Oriented Aspect (event, time)

The dynamic modelling approach of MERISE [TAR 86] may be applied to address the behaviour-oriented aspect at the OSAD- and ISAD-level. The basic concepts of MERISE for dynamic modelling are comparable to the concepts mentioned in section 3.3. The dynamic model is related to a certain level of decomposition during OSAD or ISAD, which means that the processes of the dynamic model can also be found in the process-oriented aspect model of the same level. Furthermore, there is often a correspondence between the event types of the dynamic model and the user-oriented-data-classes at the OSAD level, or the entity types at the ISAD level, with respect to the information-oriented aspect model.

The Information-Oriented Aspect (message, data)

The decomposition process of section 3 offers enough modelling capabilities at the OSAD level. NIAM [NIJ 89] offers a detailed way of information structuring which is adequate at the ISAD level. The user specifies examples of user-oriented-data-classes and describes the examples with the help of natural language sentences. NIAM prescribes a very structured procedure for the transformation of the examples into a so-called information structure diagram including many types of constraints, subtyping, a language for the specification of rules, n-ary relationships and indicators for redundancy.

The Process-Oriented Aspect (function, activity)

Enough has already been said about the process-oriented aspect because the framework is filled up completely with the decomposition process of section 3, at least, if we only consider the process-oriented aspect.

Finally, we can say that the process-, information-, and behaviour-oriented aspects are completely supported by CASE-tools and that the organization-oriented aspect is supported partly (only the organization chart and the responsibility matrix). The procedure for the analysis and design process of figure 9. is:

- OSAD, following the steps of the analysis of change with a continuation of the decomposition process if computer based information systems must be developed including the support of all aspects.
- ISAD, a decomposition process for each computer based information system including the development of the information- and behaviour-oriented aspect models.

6. Conclusions and further research

So far, we have discussed our thoughts about method engineering and the determination of a scenario according to the project characterization. Part of the framework has already appeared valuable in practice, but more research will be done to investigate the interdependencies of aspects, levels and fragments of methods. The determination of the most interesting contingency factors of the project characterization and in which way they are related to aspects of the framework has our special attention. Determination of contingency factors includes their identification, dimension, estimation, grouping, weight and space. There are already examples of investigations with respect to the relationship of project characterization and development strategy and route map, but a research project has started to clarify this relationship by collecting empirical data at two financial institutions and a national computing service centre.

The storage, selection and assembly of method fragments and route maps is currently under investigation. The metaCASE tool MAESTRO II of Softlab is chosen as the kernel of a Computer Aided Method Engineering (CAME) tool. This tool offers basic functionality for the specification of diagram editors in a dedicated language, called Prolan II, and for the input and traversal of a project work breakdown structure, called PCMS. These functionalities are being extended with a high level method specification aid, a method assembly tool, and a consistency and completeness checker of assembled methods. The CASE tool capabilities of MAESTRO offer the possibilities of fast enactment of the assembled methods [HAR 93].

In the course of a project, it may be necessary to refine or to improve the initially derived scenario, and even the project characterization may be clarified or improved during the project. An other research issue is the implementation of a learning cycle for scenarios, by adding scenarios applied in practice to the method base.

References

[AUR 88] Auromaki, E., Lehtinen, E., Lyytinen, K., A Speech-Act-Based Office Modelling Approach, In: *Transactions on Office Information Systems*, 6 (2), 126-152.

[BOE 91] Boer, H., *Organising Innovative Manufacturing Systems*, Aveburg, Aldershot, United Kingdom.

[BOO 86] Booch, G., Object-Oriented Development, In: *IEEE Transactions on software Engineering*, vol. se-12, nr. 2, pp. 211-221.

[BRI 90] Brinkkemper, S., *Formalisation of Information Systems Modelling*, Thesis Publishers, Amsterdam.

[BUR 85] Burns, R.N., Dennis, A.R., Selecting the Appropriate Application Development Methodology, In: *Database*.

[COL 84] Coller, M.A., A Comparative Analysis of Systems Analysis Techniques, In: *MIS Quarterly*, March, 51-66.

[DAV 82] Davis, G.B., Strategies for Information Requirements Determination, In: *IBM Systems Journal*, 21, 1.

[DAV 84] Davis, G.B., Olson, M.H., *Management Information Systems*, New York.

[EPI 86] Episkoupu, D., Stokes, N., Wood, J.R.G., Towards a Framework to Choose Appropriate IS Approaches, In: *The Computer Journal*, 29 (3), 222-228.

[FAL 89] Falkenberg, E.D., Lindgreen, P. (eds), *Information System Concepts: An In-depth Analysis,* North-Holland.

[HAR 93] Harmsen, F., Brinkkemper S., Computer Aided Method Engineering based on existing Meta CASE technology, working paper Centre for Telematics and Information Technology, University of Twente.

[HEN 90] Henderson-Sellers, B.H., Edwards, J.M., Object-Oriented Systems Life Cycle, In: *Communications of the ACM*, vol. 33, nr. 9.

[HIR 85] Hirschheim, R.A., *Office Automation: A Social and Organizational Perspective*, John Wiley and Sons, Chicester.

[IIV 83] Iivari, J., Kerola, P., A Socio-Cybernetic Framework for Feature Analysis fo Information Systems Design Methodologies, In: Olle, T.W., Sol, H.G., Tully, C.J. (Eds.), *Information Systems Methodologies: A Feature Analysis*, North-Holland.

[LAA 83] Laagland, P.T.M., *Modeling in Information Systems Development*, dissertation, Free University Amsterdam, Muller's Drukkerij.

[LAN 79] Lano, R.J., *A technique for software and systems design methodologies*, Noth-Holland, Amsterdam.

[LEE 91] Lee, R., Stamper, R.K., *Doing Business with Words: Performative Aspects of Deontic Systems,* Working Paper.

[LUN 82] Lundeberg, M., The ISAC Approach to Specification of Information Systems and its Application to the Organization of an IFIP Working Conferenc, In:

Olle, T.W., Sol, H.G., Verrijn-Stuart, A.A. (eds), *Information Systems Design Methodologies: a comparative review*, North Holland.

[MAL 83] Malouin, J.L., Landry, M., The Mirage of Universal Methods in Systems Design, In: *Journal of Applied Systems Analysis*, 10, 47-62.

[MUM 85] Mumford, E., Defining System Requirements to meet Business Needs: A Case Study Example, In: *The Computer Journal*, 28 (2).

[NAU 82] Naumann, J.D., Palvia, S., A Selection Model for System Development Tools, In: *MIS Quarterly*, March, 39-48.

[NEC 87] Necco, C.R, Gordan, C.L., Tsai, N.W., Systems Analysis and Design: Current Practices, *MIS Quarterly*, 11, 4.

[NIJ 89] Nijssen, G.M., Halpin, T.A., *Conceptual Schema and Relational Database Design*, Prentice Hall.

[OLL 82] Olle, T.W., Sol, H.G., Verrijn-Stuart, A.A. (eds), *Information Systems Design Methodologies: A Comparative Review*, North-Holland.

[OLL 86] Olle, T.W., Sol, H.G., Verrijn-Stuart, A.A. (eds), *Information Systems Design Methodologies: Improving the Practice*, North-Holland.

[OLLE 91] Olle, T.W., et al., *Information Systems Methodologies: A Framework for Understanding*, Addison-Wesley.

[POR 80] Porter, M.E., *Competitive Strategy: Techniques for Analyzing Industries and Competitors*, New York: Free Press.

[RAM 91] Ramackers, G.J., Verrijn-Stuart, A.A., Integrating Information System Perspectives with Objects, In: Van Assche et al. (eds), *Object-Oriented Approach in Information Systems*, North-Holland.

[SEA 69] Searle, J.R., *Speech acts: An Essay in the Philosophy of Language*, Cambridge University Press.

[SOL 83] Sol, H.G., A Feature Analysis of Information Systems Design Methodologies: Methodological Considerations, In: Olle, T.W., Sol, H.G., Tully, C.J. (Eds.), *Information Systems Design Methodologies: A Feature Analysis*, North-Holland.

[STA 88] Stamper, R.K. et al., MEASUR: Method for Eliciting, Analyzing and Specifying User Requirements, In: Olle, T.W., Verrijn-Stuart, A.A., Bhabuta, L. (Eds), *Computerized Assistence During the Information Systems Life Cycle*, North-Holland.

[TAR 86] Tardieu, H. et al., *La Méthode Mérise*, tome 1, Les Editions d'Organization, Paris.

[WEL 91] Welke, R.J., Kumar, K., Method Engineering: A Proposal for Situation-Specific Methodology Construction, In: WW. Cotterman, J.A. Senn (eds.), *Systems Analysis and Design: A Research Agenda.*

[WIN 86] Winograd, T., Flores, F., *Understanding Computers and Cognition*, Ablex.

[WOO 82] Wood-Harper, A.T., Fitzgerald, G., A Taxonomy of Current Approaches to Systems Analysis, In: *The Computer Journal*, 25(1).

[ZAC 87] Zachman, J.A., A Framework for Information Architecture, *IBM Systems Journal*, vol.26, no. 3.

6.

COOPERATIVE APPROACHES

Information System Development Process (A-30)
N. Prakash, C. Rolland and B. Pernici (Editors)
Elsevier Science Publishers B.V. (North-Holland)
© 1993 IFIP. All rights reserved.

The Role of Interaction Analysis in Requirements Engineering

A.J.C. Blyth and J. Chudge

Department of Computing Science, University of Newcastle upon Tyne, Newcastle Upon Tyne, NE1 7RU. United Kingdom

Abstract

We describe the technique of interaction analysis which we have developed as a model capable of representing and reasoning about the requirements on information technology systems and the implications for organisational change. We then present the results of an actual case study on which the model has been applied.

Keyword codes: C.5.m; D.2.1; I.2.m
Keywords: Computer System Implementation, re: Organisational Change; Requirements/Specifications; Artificial Intelligence, re: Interaction Analysis

1. INTRODUCTION

1.1. Introduction

In this paper we shall examine one particular aspect of the design of computer supported collaborative work (CSCW) systems which we believe has been under represented in traditional systems analysis for software design, namely the representation of the conversations that take place in an organisational context and which mediate the co-operative work and bear the mutual creation of, commitment to, and discharge of the obligations that arise. Our justification for adopting this position is that underlying each and every organisation are its communication procedures. That is to say, how information, of whatever type or description, is passed around within an organisation. It is our belief that these communications, whether they be verbal, written, via phone, e-mail, fax, or whatever, can all be described as interactions capable of being modelled or represented in speech.

We seek to address this problem by first presenting some background material necessary to understanding the context within which interaction analysis operates, namely the enterprise modelling scheme. Our approach to modelling and representing interactions is largely diagrammatic and we discuss our building blocks in Section 2. The case study on which our analysis has been applied is presented in Section 3, briefly in Section 4 we outline some further developments, and finally in the Summary we review the merits, or otherwise, of interaction analysis.

1.2. The Enterprise Projection

Our view of an organisation is put forward in the enterprise projection whose objective, as defined in [Ansa 1989], is to interpret the role of a computer system within an organisation. Essentially it provides a framework for representing and reasoning about the IT system as a component of a wider environment which is the organisation whose needs it is designed to serve. We have found that this form of modelling [Dobson and McDermid 1990] ensures an adequate representation of the structural and organisational aspects of the problem making explicit policy issues and assumptions which cannot so easily be stated. The Enterprise projection describes the overall objectives of a system in terms of agency, actions, resources and policies. It makes explicit the roles and interactions that can exist within the system and the organisation at the enterprise level. We use the language of responsibilities and obligations to tie these concepts down making the connection between the organisation as an abstract entity modelled in design and the organisation as a body with its own goals and objectives. Indeed, one of the main characteristics of our approach is that we model responsibilities and relationships rather than activities and base our understanding of the architectural framework on these models and not on the current implementation. Thus systems designers can examine and explore the implications of a proposed system design with the problem owners themselves. Design decisions made using the enterprise projection are concerned with *what* the system is to do rather than *how* it is to do it. The requirements that are expressed in the enterprise projection are expressed in both system and environmental terms.

Furthermore, the enterprise modelling language has been devised to represent the structure of the organisation in order to serve two related but distinct purposes: 1) to identify the requirements owners and their positions and roles within the organisation in order to demonstrate completeness of the requirements elicitation process, and 2) to identify the user community (and others affected by the proposed IT system) and their roles and responsibilities within the organisation in order to demonstrate completeness of the requirements modelling process.

The three essential elements of the Enterprise Model are agents, actions and resources. The relations between these entities are defined in Figure 1. Agencies (embodied in agents) are regarded as primary manipulators of the state or structure of the system, and agency is the only object that can create, modify or destroy other objects. Actions are the operations that change the state of the system, and they are performed by agencies. All actions must induce state changes in the system that are visible to one or more agencies. The resources can be of two types: physical or logical, where physical resources are tangible objects such as nuts and bolts, and logical resources include information, time etc. When modelling organisations at the enterprise projection level, resources may act in one of two ways. They may act as tokens of responsibility signifying that an agency has a binding responsibility upon it, or they may act as objects for which some agency is said to be responsible. An important type of logical resource is data. When data are passed from one action to another interactions occur, the data being the bearer of those interactions.

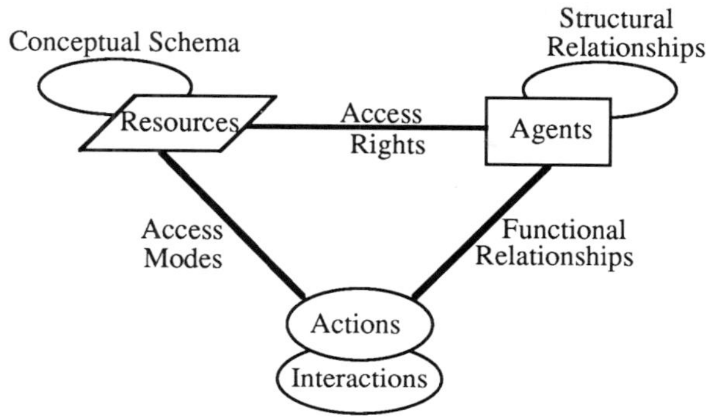

Figure 1. The Enterprise Model

The enterprise model enables us to examine relationships between entities of different types. An examination of these relationships will assist the problem owner and solver in understanding how the basic objects influence and are related to each other. In our enterprise modelling we have chosen to concentrate on the concepts of 'agency' and 'role' as being central to our procedure and the emphasis on the flow of responsibilities and obligations provides the ideal level of description at which we can discuss the human and technical aspects of a problem.

1.3. Socio Technical Systems

The philosophy behind the creation of socio-technical systems is based on the belief that it is important to consider human as well as technical issues in the design of IT systems. Socio-technical theory developed out of the work of organisational theorists such as [Emery and Trist 1965], who discovered that many of the issues that determined the success or failure of work systems were social in nature rather than specifically attributable to the physical working environment. Emphasis was placed on the need to consider work in social as well as technical terms, and, for change to be effective, it was argued that both human organisation as well as technology need to be considered. The early research in this field did not investigate settings where information technology was being applied, but more recently the value of using a socio-technical approach has also been demonstrated in this area [Pava 1983, Mumford 1986, Eason 1988]. However, it is not sufficient to create only a framework whereby such issues can be identified, as designers also need a suitable language with which to discuss the human requirements of socio-technical systems, and to demonstrate how these are linked to the technical features of the system design. History is littered with incidents where the technical aspects of a problem were considered in isolation from the social aspects and consequently, the proposed solution failed to address the real scope of the problem, omitting altogether user related issues such as information transfer rights, or change control.

2.0. INTERACTION ANALYSIS

2.1. Introduction

When modelling the interactions that can exist within an organisation a clear comprehension of the types of questions that such models will attempt to solve is required in order not to misuse the notation. The types of questions that the model of interaction will attempt to address can be classed into two broad categories. The first category is concerned with the establishment and discharge of obligations and the creation and fulfilment of responsibilities. Hence problem solvers and problem owners may begin to address such questions as *when does X become responsible for Y* ? The second class of question is concerned with the accessing of objects, such as resources, that act as tokens for the fulfilment of responsibilities and obligations.

Figure 2 depicts the basic building blocks from which an interaction diagram can be constructed. For a more detailed explanation of speech act theory and conversation analysis techniques the reader is referred to [Austin 62, Searle 69]. There are several approaches that have been developed to aid in the analysis and specification of organisational information technology systems that draw upon speech acts and illocutionary logic as their basic formalism [Lyytinen 88, Winograd86, Stamper 88, Finkelstein 89]. The problem with all of the current techniques is that they are either too graphical or too textual in nature. They all attempt to take raw problem statements from the problem owners and process them via a series of iterations and refinements so as to produce a complete and consistent problem statement that can then be fed into the classical software development model.

The process that we present in this paper is in essence a dialectical one, [Blyth, Chudge *et al.* 1993] where both the problem and the solution space are analysed at the same time by the construction and analysis of the interaction model. Our approach is essentially cyclical. Exploration of the problem space with the problem owners, through the models we will describe, slowly evolves into the exploration of the solution space. The ongoing involvement of the problem owners in this process serves not only to clarify and broaden the target but also to enhance the sense of ownership and commitment to the eventual solution amongst the stakeholders in the client organisation.

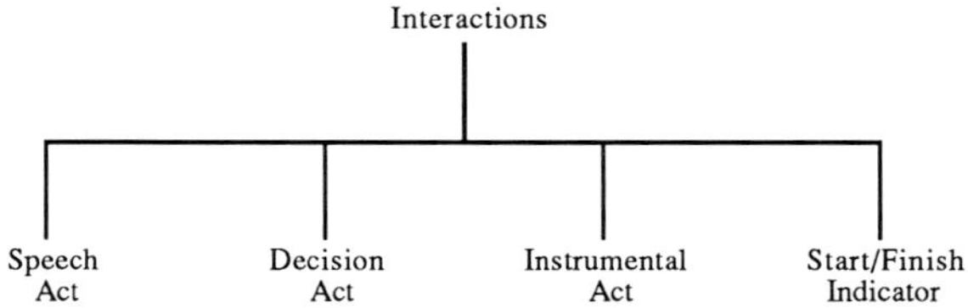

Figure 2. Building Blocks of a Conversation.

Figure 2 shows the basic building blocks of an interaction which are called, from left to right, a speech act, a decision act, an instrumental act and a start/finish indicator. Each of these basic building blocks is now explained in more detail.

2.2. Speech Act

A speech act object aids in the elicitation, comprehension and formalisation of how, when and where organisational attributes such as responsibilities and obligations are either brought into being or fulfilled. A speech act object has four distinct attributes, the first expresses the idea of an agent owning a speech act object, this being the agent that makes the utterance. The second attribute is the type of utterance being made in the object, this, in classical speech act theory [Austin 62, Searle 69] is called the *speech act* and may be of the following types, commissive, directive, assertive, declarative, and expressive. In practice, we have extended this list to include negation to allow for a more clearer exposition avoiding some of the ambiguity inherent in the theory. The third attribute is the enterprise attribute that the utterance manipulates in some way and this attribute is optional. Finally the fourth attribute is the enterprise object (e.g. a resource) that is accessed in some way as a result of the utterance and this attribute is also optional. The thick black lines shown on the diagram denote that the inclusion of these attributes is optional to the model.

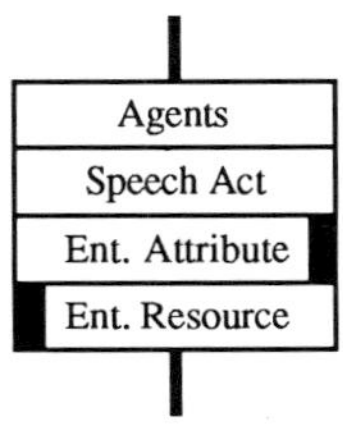

Figure 3. A Speech Act Object

2.3. Decision Act

A decision act is used to identify when a role holder has to make a decision of some kind. Thus it is used to allow the problem solvers and problem owners to examine when, where and under what conditions decisions are made and by whom. In addition conditions that are necessary for the role holder to make the decision can be explored as well as the circumstances under which the decision is taken.

Figure 4. A Decision Act

The primary purpose of a decision act is to aid in the comprehension of what a decision means and thus what its implications are, i.e. what decisions are critical or not for the fulfillment of the organisations responsibilities. In addition, decision acts facilitate the elicitation of what resources are not only necessary, but also sufficient for the role holder to make the decision. The notion of a decision act is the only concept that combines issues of data flow with control flow and for this reason this act should have special attention paid to it, particularly in safety-critical systems.

2.4. Instrumental Act

Instrumental acts not only facilitate in the examination and formalisation of when, where and by whom an instrumental act (or task) is performed, but they also aid in the elucidation and identification of what enterprise objects and attributes are required and manipulated by the agent entity performing the act. An instrumental act can either be decomposed down into small instrumental acts or sets of interactions depending upon the degree of detail required. An example of an instrumental act is when, for instance, an electrician agent fixes an appliance for a house-person agent. In performing this act the agent is not only discharging his obligations but also consuming a resource.

Figure 5. An Instrumental Act

2.5. Start/Finish Indicators

The start/finish indicators are used to denote when an interaction begins and when it terminates. They are thus used purely as control points to denote the entry and exit points of the interaction.

2.6. The Flow of Control

The easiest way to model the flow of control is as a black box with a set of inputs and a set of outputs and this is depicted in Figure 6. In this diagram the inputs are shown on the top of the black box and numbered from left to right j1,j2,..,jn and denoted by a semi-circle at the bottom of the input arc. The outputs are shown emerging from the black box and are numbered from left to right k1,k2,..,km.

The black box facilitates the problem solvers and problem owners in the examination and comprehension of the relationships that can exist between the inputs and the outputs without having to be concerned about the various types of speech acts. Thus a distinction is drawn between the data flow and the control flow parts of the interaction. It is important that when modelling an interaction each control block be carefully examined and its structure explored. This examination and exploration is to make sure that both the problem solving and the problem owning parties understand the implications of the various structures used to represent the flow of control.

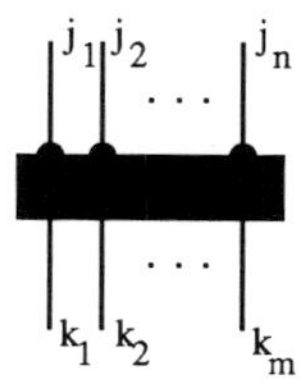

Figure 6. A Control Block

An example of the control block construct being used to aid in the process of interaction analysis can be constructed quite easily. Consider a clerk in a dispatch office, the clerk makes a request to two engineers and then waits for a reply from both of them. The control box allows us to explore the conditions under which the clerk may perform certain actions such as make another request. Hence questions such as what does the clerk do if none of the engineers reply, and what does the clerk do if just one engineer replies can all be examined, and their answers explored by means of the control box.

2.7. Arcs and Conditionals

The arcs are the means by which the notion of control is said to flow though the model as they link together the basic objects that form an interaction diagram. Along with each arc and each object a conditional will be associated, if no conditional is specified then the default conditional of true will be adopted, i.e. that of *True if No-Action*. If the conditional holds then the action is applied to the environment.

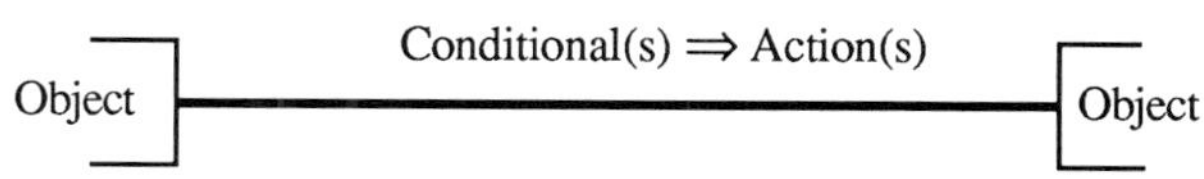

Figure 7. Arcs and Conditionals

Figure 7 illustrates that with every arc and every object it is possible to associate a set of conditionals and actions. The conditionals and actions associated with an object are used to express the concepts of the pre- and post- conditions and invariants. So, for example, the amount of time that it takes for a message to pass though a communications medium can be clearly expressed. Hence, by attaching conditionals and actions to arcs and objects temporal and conditional aspects of the model may be explored and elucidated upon. In addition by using conditional as pre and post condition of objects one may be able to investigate and clarify the set of conditions under which a set of interactions may be entered into and exited from.

2.8. Scripting

Scripting is the name given to the language we have used to denote the speech acts used in the interaction analysis. It is basically a form of abbreviation sufficient to convey the structure and meaning of the interaction or discourse. Its origins lie in the work of [Schank and Abelson, 1977] on scripts which were designed to help explain understanding of stereotypical event sequences. Hence, the interactions we examine have to be representative of the conversations that actually take place between agents in the course of their everyday work.

3.0. CASE STUDY

3.1. Introduction to the Case Study.

The problem presented in this paper is taken from the real world, it has however been slightly simplified to limit the scope of the problem for this paper and thus aid understandability and comprehension of the techniques and notations applied to elicit organisational requirements. Electricians in the Area Board provide a wide range of services on customer premises, such as repairing appliances and restoring supply. This can be a costly and wasteful process with electricians in vans inefficiently deployed, clerical staff unable to process customer requests quickly, and long delays in communication. One problem is that the communication to arrange visits to premises for emergency work is undertaken by radio. This can often be sub-optimal, e.g. when the electrician is not in the van, the radio operator has to stack calls and keep trying. This case is concerned with the installation of mobile data terminals (MDT's) in vans which can receive and store calls. The purpose of the study is to examine the organisational implications of setting up a technical system of this kind.

3.2. The System as it Exists

Customer Service in the Area Board is organised as depicted in Figure 8. The Senior Customer Service Engineer is directly responsible to the Area Commercial Manager for a Customer Service Unit based at Area Offices. The Customer Service Unit consists of a team of clerks and a radio operator controlling communications with the fleet of service vans, each service van belonging to an electrician. There are four depots each with a foreman supervising the work of a team of electricians who are of two types. Day electricians mostly undertake specialist activities requiring specialist knowledge, e.g. fixing and maintaining washing machines whilst the shift electricians are responsible for the statutory duties of the Board, e.g. to attend to main fuses on a property to restore supply.

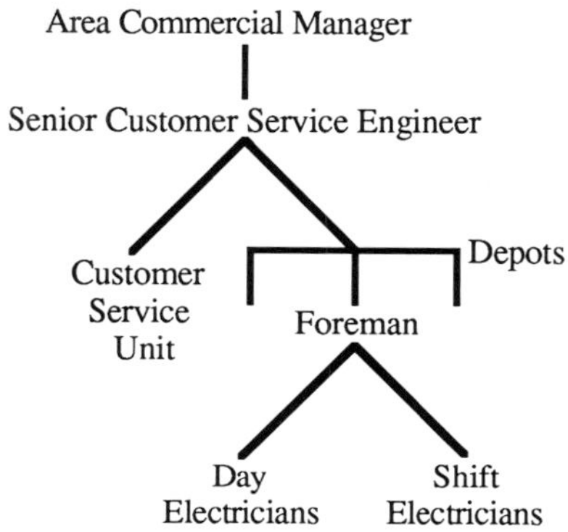

Figure 8. Customer Service Organisation

In a simplified form the main work flow of the Service Unit is presented in Figure 9. Each customers call is routed to a clerk in the Customer Service Unit (1). If it requires a visit to a customers premises it is programmed as a task for the electricians, and is classified as non-emergency (requiring a visit in three days) or as an emergency (requiring immediate action). For non-emergency calls the clerk raises a Work Instruction Sheet (W.I.S) and allocates it to an electrician at the appropriate depot (2). The W.I.S. is logged on an on-line computer system by the clerk which can be accessed at any time by the foreman (3). The foreman checks the content of the W.I.S's, raises the appropriate parts from the store, discusses jobs with electricians and reallocates if necessary. Emergency W.I.S's are passed to the radio operator (4) who allocates them by radio primarily to the shift electricians.

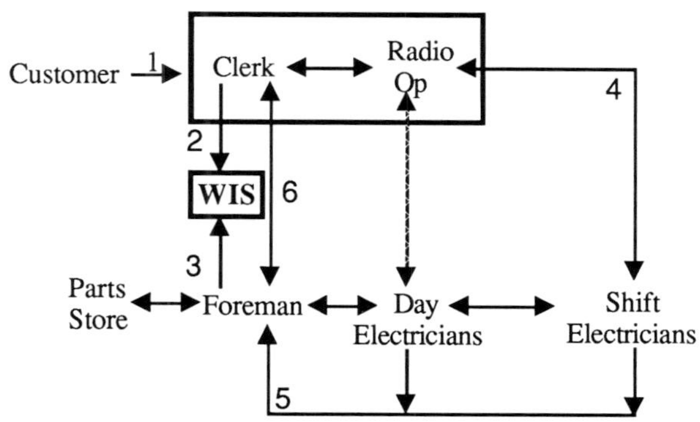

Figure 9. Main Work Flow in the Customer Service Unit

If the electrician is out of the van or the radio is busy, it may take a considerable time to make this contact. When the work is done, the electricians complete job sheets that the foreman at the depot checks (5). The foreman then sends the W.I.S. by courier to the Customer Service Unit (6) for de-programming, e.g. billing, arranging the next visit, etc.

3.3. The System as Proposed

The management of the Board plans to introduce a computer-based mobile communications system with a mobile data terminal in each van. The terminal will be capable of receiving and storing up to 25 complete job messages. These can be displayed on a screen or printed at the electricians discretion. The messages will be transmitted from a computer terminal operated by the radio operator in the Customer Service Unit.

The management are looking for the following kinds of benefit from the system: faster response time to emergencies, prompter response to non-emergencies, better customer services, better utilisation of electrician resources and more efficient use of office staff.

To this end the Customer Service Unit clerks will not only pass emergency W.I.S's to the radio operator but also non-emergency requests which the clerks records show electricians could undertake that day. The radio operator will then send them to the terminal in the van of the appropriate electrician and from this point on the jobs are treated as the electricians responsibility.

3.4. Interaction Analysis of the Case Study

In this case study the communications occur in the first instance between the consumer (the problem owner) and the Electricity Board itself (the problem repairer). Then, through the Boards own internal channels of communication, the nature of the problem is received by the electrician, whose task it is to repair it. Supervision occurs between the foreman and both the emergency (shift) electricians and the ordinary (day) electricians.

In the Electricity Board System described in section 3.2, a clerk receives the customers call at the Customer Service Unit (CSU) and makes a decision of whether it is a emergency or not. If the customers premises have to be visited, the problem is recorded as a task for the electricians. If the task is non-emergency, the Clerk raises a Work Instruction Sheet and allocates it to a day electrician at the appropriate depot. The foreman has access to the Work Instruction Sheet via a computer. When the foreman has checked it, he may then discuss the job with the day electrician and raise the necessary parts from the store. Under certain conditions the Foreman may even reallocate the job. If the task is urgent the radio operator allocates the job to a shift electrician at an appropriate depot via radio. When work is completed the electricians complete job-sheets, which are checked by the foreman at the depot, and are then sent to the Customer Service Unit for billing and suchlike.

At this stage we are concerned only with the conversations arising out of non-emergency situations. From the point of view of analysing them by interaction analysis, their dynamics make them more interesting and therefore they are likely to prove more insightful. Since the structural relation between the two agents is one of supervision, we want to be able to assess whether the notation is able to represent this adequately.

Figure 10 shows us the state in the conversation at which the foreman offers the job to the electrician. This diagram serves to point out the three possible ways in which the electrician may respond to the 'job offer' speech act made by the foreman. The electrician may either 'postpone' the job, 'reject' the job, or, 'accept' the job. In performing the latter speech act the electrician is entering into an obligation with the foreman to perform the specified job.

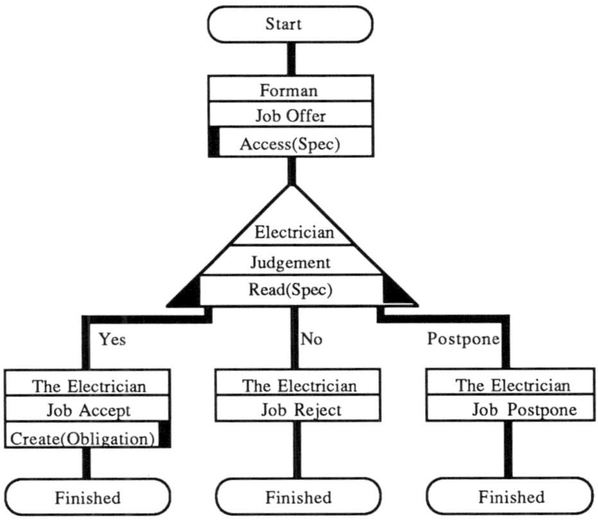

Figure 10. The Offer Stage

Starting at the top of the diagram and working down we note that the beginning of the interaction is depicted with a start/finish indicator. The next component in the interaction diagram is a speech act, and this object is depicted as a rectangle. The speech act is composed of three components, the first is the agent entity making the utterance and the second is the type of utterance being made. The third component is the enterprise object that is being accessed in some way by the utterance. Since the expression of the enterprise object's manipulation is an optional component of the speech act it is denoted by a black line in the left hand side of the component.

The largest of the basic building blocks that is shown in Figure 10 is the decision act. This act is also composed of three components, the first of which express the type of decision that is being made. The second is an optional component (denoted by two black shaded areas on either side of the condition) to the act and expresses what conditions are necessary for an agent entity to make the decision. The third and final component of the act is the agent entity that is engaged in making the decision.

Figure 11 represents how the interaction between the foreman and the electrician further develops. In this diagram the electrician is shown accepting the job offer made by the foreman and thus entering into an obligation with the foreman. The electrician then performs the task specified by the foreman and in so doing consumes some spare parts. Upon completion of the task the electrician reports back to the foreman and raises a work sheet (WS).

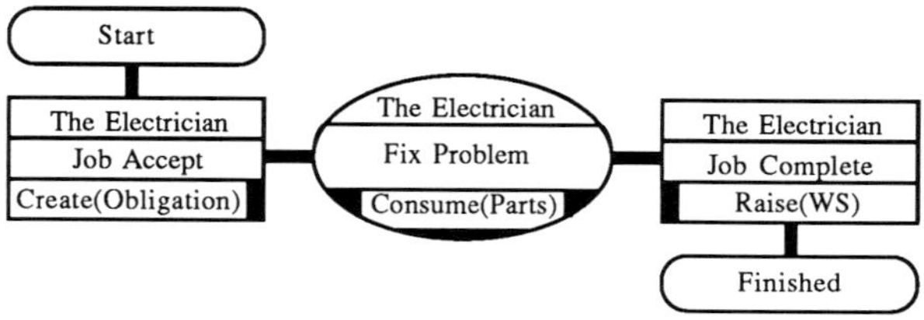

Figure 11. Performing the Task

The speech act on the far left of Figure 11 is noteworthy in that it depicts the creation of an enterprise attribute. This optional component is denoted by a black line in the right hand side of the component. The building block that is subsequently created is shown as an ellipse and is called an instrumental act; it allows for the expression of the task that an agent entity is required to perform. The optional component 'Consume (SpareParts)' is shown by shaded lines either side of it; and it allows for the representation and examination of the enterprise objects and attributes required for, or altered by, the performance of the instrumental act.

Once the electrician has raised a work sheet (WS) the foreman then reads it and decides if the electrician has successfully completed the task. The foreman can decide either 'yes' or 'no' and this is depicted in Figure 12. If the foreman chooses the former, then he agrees to the electricians appraisal of the situation and thus the obligation created by the acceptance of the electrician is discharged. In Figure 12 we have shown that it is the act of the foreman that discharges the obligation that was held by the electrician. If the foreman chooses the latter, then the job sheet must be amended to the satisfaction of both of them before being passed to the CSU.

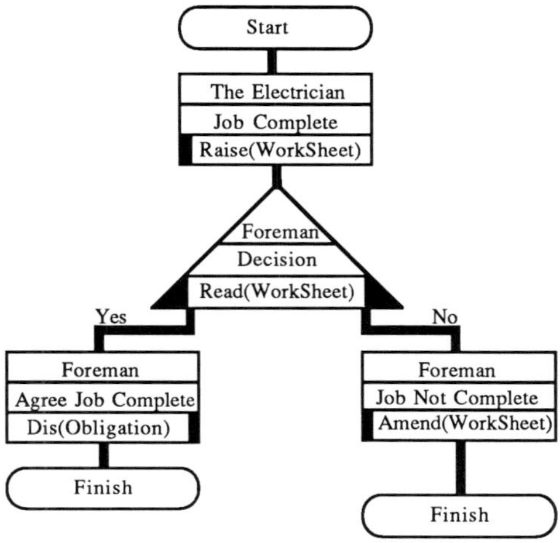

Figure 12. Discharging the Obligation

When the job is allocated to the electrician and the electrician either rejects it, or, postpones it, then the foreman may request an explanation from the electrician. For the sake of brevity we have shown the conversations as stopping but in reality it would be the problem solvers and problem owners that would dictate when the interaction modelling should stop.

The beginning of the process of scheduling the electrician is shown in Figure 13. This process starts with the clerk making a job offer to the electrician and filling out a W.I.S. and is expressed in the enterprise component of the speech act as *Write(Spec)*. Once the job offer has been made by the clerk the electrician then has to make a decision similar to the decision act shown in Figure 9 where the decision has three possible outcomes. Having made a decision the electrician then has to generate the appropriate response.

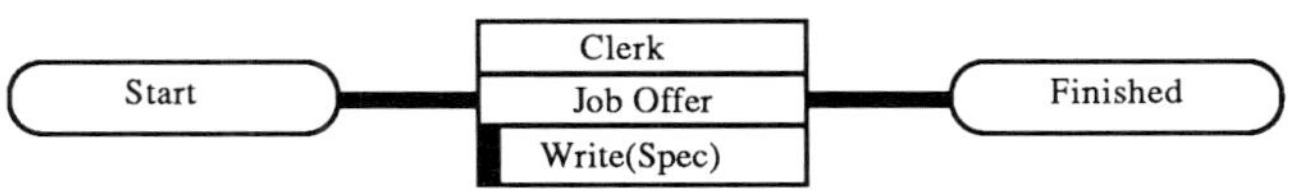

Figure 13. Beginning the Scheduling

Figure 14 shows the electrician making a job rejection utterance followed by the foreman making a job rejection acknowledgement utterance. When we use interaction diagrams to examine the scheduling of the electrician we notice that after the initial job offer made by the clerk all interaction takes place between the electrician and the foreman. So, in this case, understanding the relationships that can exist between the foreman and the electrician is vital to comprehending how the organisation discharges its obligations and responsibilities to the house-holder.

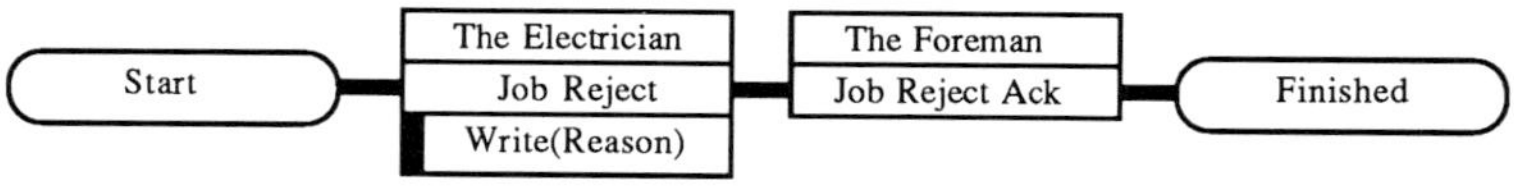

Figure 14. The Job Rejection

4.0. FURTHER DEVELOPMENTS

In the past our rule for dealing with complex (i.e. involving more than 2 agents) relationships has been to split them down into relationships involving just two agents. For instance, if there was a tri-partite relationship between agents A, B, and C, we would effectively have to examine three relationships, between A and B, A and C, and B and C. The problem of many-to-many relationships emerged from case studies where group-working or the need for a number of agents to discuss and share information was the norm across a number of different organisations each with their own particular culture. We propose the following proforma as a tool which may assist in the task of representing and reasoning about the nature of these relationships.

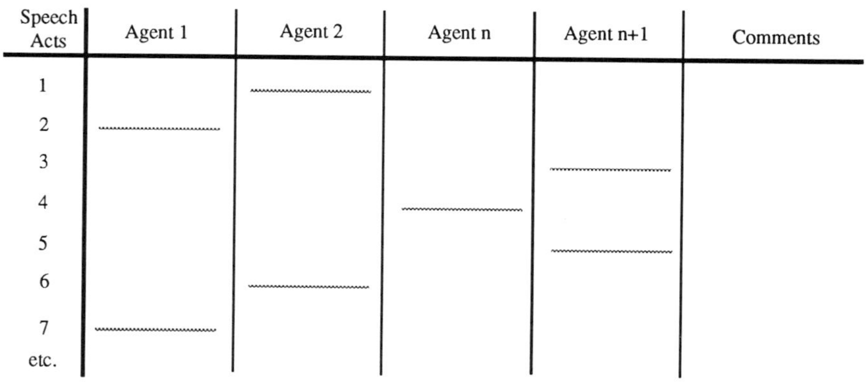

Figure 15. The Many-to-Many Relationships Proforma

The form is basically a means of capturing the conversation exchange between a number of agents. The number of agents form columns along the horizontal plane and the speech acts they employ are listed vertically providing a sequence of ordering in time. The column at the extreme right is left blank to record notes and comments pertaining to the analysis being undertaken. Therefore this may be used to record information regarding responsibilities, obligations, and commitments; structural and functional relationships etc.

This form can represent a number of scenarios involving many-to-many relationships, from meetings, group or collaborative work, to multi-agent conferencing. In each of these, structural relationships between agents can be determined; the effectiveness of teams can be examined in light of what responsibilities are assigned to role-holders in view of their conversation exchanges; and interaction analysis could also be used to examine the 'hidden' power structures often at play in a group discourse.

5.0. SUMMARY

The problem of determining system boundaries of complex IT systems has meant that mistakes have occurred where the boundaries turned out to have been drawn in the wrong place, often at great cost. We claim that our representation-cum-modelling technique of interaction analysis provides a sufficiently rich environment in which organisational structure and the roles of agents, responsibilities, information flow, resource management, and the relationships between all of these are capable of being represented, and we are therefore able to capture the complexities of organisational structure and requirements.

Used in the context of the enterprise projection, interaction analysis has shown, through the use of the case study, its usefulness in dealing with an organisations requirements and policies. A major advantage is the degree of flexibility it places within the analysts control. For instance, it may be evident that in taking an object-oriented view, both of the organisation and of the concepts we use to model it, that enterprise modelling is capable of describing an organisation at any number of different levels, and the power of interaction analysis as a tool lies in being able to support this. However, because it is a time consuming exercise its most important domains of use may well be safety-critical systems, or wherever security and privacy is at a premium.

From an examination of the case study it can be seen that interaction analysis allows us to "zoom" in on particular aspects of cases, problems, or organisations. Hence, the detailed analysis that this provides may be vital in ascertaining where responsibilities lie, the procedures necessary to carry out actions in the system, weaknesses in communication chains etc. In addition, it allows us to examine an actors responsibilities in a more dynamic way since the conversation exchange is a dynamic on-going process. Furthermore, the responsibilities are examined in direct relation to other agents' responsibilities and this greatly enhances the capacity to check for conflicts within and between agents with regard to their respective roles and requirements. Responsibilities can now be allocated to agents or roles in the knowledge that questions of conflict, job satisfaction and so on, have been considered and addressed.

The diagrammatic representation we have developed is adept not only at capturing the dynamicism inherent in a conversation but is also capable of conveying change-control from one agent to another, iteration, decision points and so on. Currently, we believe our representation technique to be the most powerful and flexible conversation representation tool. It has the added advantage that it can be used in systems or organisational design to construct scenarios of possible future states describing the relationships between agents, responsibilities, and resources.

Interaction analysis, we believe, significantly narrows the gap between what the user wants and what the analyst can represent. Because of its emphasis on communication and interaction the system design it facilitates is very much a case of 'what you see is what you get'. The modelling language it is supported by facilitates a more open discussion of organisational requirements of both a technical and a human nature. As always though, there is no substitute for experience - any modelling language or tool, no matter how powerful, if it is in inexperienced hands will not be well used.

REFERENCES

[ANSA 1989] ANSA, *ANSA Reference Manual, Release 01.00,* Architecture Projects Managements Ltd., Cambridge, (1989).

[Auramaki 88] *A Speech Act Based Office Modelling Approach,* by E.Auramaki, E.Lehtinen and K.Lyytinen, ACM Transactions on Office Information Systems, Vol 6, No 2, (1988).

[Austin 62] *How to do Things with Words,* by J.L.Austin, published by Clarendon Press (1962).

[Blyth, Chudge *et al.* 1993] *A Framework for Modelling Evolving Requirements* by A.J.C. Blyth, J. Chudge, J.E. Dobson & M.R. Strens, submitted to COMPSAC '93 ' The Seventeeth Annual International Computer Software and Applications Conference'.

[Dobson and McDermid 1990] *An Investigation into Modelling and Categorisation of Non-Functional Requirements,* by J.E. Dobson and J.A. McDermid,Report No. YCS 141, University of York, (1990).

[Eason 88] Eason K D, *Information Technology and Organisational Change,* London, Taylor and Francis, (1988).

[Emery and Trist 1965] Emery F E and Trist E L, 1965, *The Causal Texture of Organisational Environments,* Human Relations, V18, P21-32.

[Finkelstein 89] *A Cooperative Framework for Software Engineering,* by Anthony Finkelstein and Hugo Fuks, Hawaii International Conference on Systems Sciences, (1989).

[Mumford 1986] Mumford E, *Using Computers for Business Success, The Ethics method,* Manchester Business School, (1986).

[Pava 1983] Pava C, *Managing New Office Technology: An Organisational Strategy,* New York, Free Press, (1983).

[Schank and Abelson 1977] Schank, Roger C. and Abelson, Robert P., *Scripts, Plans, Goals, and Understanding,* Lawrence Erlbaum, Hillsdale, N.J. (1977).

[Searle 69] *Speech Acts - An Essay in the Philosopy of Language,* by J.R.Searle, published by Cambridge University Press, (1969).

[Stamper 88] MEASUR: *Method for Eliciting, Analysing and Specifying User Requirements,* by Ronald Stamper, K.Althans and J.Backhouse, Computerized Assistance during the Information Systems Life Cycle, North-Holland, (1988).

[Winograd and Flores 1986] Winograd T and Flores F, *Understanding Computers and Cognition: A New Foundation for Design,* Addison-Wesley Publishing Company Inc, (1986).

ACKNOWLEDGEMENTS

We gratefully acknowledge the support provided by the ORDIT (Organisational Requirements Definition in Information Technology) project to this work. The project is supported by the Commission of the European Communities under its ESPRIT programme (Project no. 2301). The project consortium consists of Algotech (Rome), HUSAT Research Institute (Loughborough), MARI (Gateshead), University of Newcastle upon Tyne, and Work Research Centre (Dublin).

Information System Development Process (A-30)
N. Prakash, C. Rolland and B. Pernici (Editors)
Elsevier Science Publishers B.V. (North-Holland)

© 1993 IFIP. All rights reserved.

Conflict Management in Systems Development Groups

Rudolf Andersen and Arne Sølvberg
Department of Computer Science and Telematics
The Norwegian Institute of Technology
University of Trondheim
N-7043 Trondheim
Norway

Abstract

Contemporary computerised information systems are usually large and complex. Modifications of such systems require significant efforts. The work is usually done by a group of developers. Contemporary CASE tools offer limited support for working in groups. The standard CASE tool require that you are able to split the system into disjoint subsets that are modified separately by each member of the group.

This paper proposes an improved approach to systems development in groups. The approach has three stages: (1) Allow for controlled chaos by true sharing of the specifications among the members in the group. This implies that all members of the group are allowed to check-out any development object, even if it is checked out by somebody else. (2) Monitor potential conflicts among developers by keeping track of the different local versions of a development object. The local versions are not allowed to update the shared specification database as long as there is a potential conflict between two or more members of the group. (3) Help resolve conflicts through negotiations. This implies that the specification database is updated by an object that is the result of a merging operation. The objects that are merged are the conflicting local versions. The negotiations are supported by groupware functionality, e.g. joint editing, video conferencing, voice mail.

1. INTRODUCTION

Development and maintenance of computerised information systems are characterised by continuous modifications to the specifications. Requirements to the modification's process are usually only expressed in qualitative terms. E.g. according to [4] modifications should be performed

- in a short time
- with high productivity
- with high quality

- under good control
- solving the right problem
- giving the right solution

Modifications to information systems of some size require significant efforts. The systems are usually large, complex, and imperceivable [14][20]. Modifications of imperceivable systems within a short time and with high productivity usually require coordinated efforts of several people. Coordination covers aspects of organisation and the management of resources (people and systems), control of the use of resources, and the provision of and oiling of the interaction links that are required [18].

Contemporary CASE (Computer Aided Software Engineering) technology offers limited support for working in groups. The standard CASE tool consists of analysis and design workbenches, code generators and other standalone tools. The primary focus of ICASE tools is on integration across development stages. For that reason the tools relate to a specification repository. The existence of a specification repository makes sharing of specifications possible among tools. However, facilities for the sharing of specifications are still limited which makes them difficult to be used in a group context.

Specification repositories are also called encyclopaedias, dictionaries, or simply specification databases. The repositories are either offered as standalone systems, e.g. Repository Manager from IBM [9], or as the hub of an integrated systems development environment, e.g. the Central Encyclopedia in Information Engineering Facility, IEF [22].

The group interaction patterns that are offered by the tools are still restricted. Contemporary repositories are based on the assumption that it is possible to undertake systems development in teams by splitting the system specification into disjoint subsets. Each subset is further developed by individual team members. For example, in IEF [21][22], subsets of the specification are checked out during each “development transaction”. The checked out subsets of the specification are marked in the repository as being locked. The revised specifications are checked back into the repository when the development transaction is over. During a development transaction the development objects in the repository that are locked cannot be modified by others.

Arguments and empirical evidence exist to support the hypothesis that achieving independence between development objects is extremely difficult if not impossible [13][4]. This may of course be so because one has not been sufficiently clever in choosing the disjoint subsets. However, it is our opinion that it is impossible to determine these disjoint subsets unless a detailed analysis has been performed. One simply can not know what possible dependencies exist among the development objects without doing a detailed analysis. To be able to do this detailed analysis it is necessary to do a split of work and consequently a split of development objects into disjoint subsets, due to the size and complexity of the average problem. This is the classical chicken and egg situation.

We offer a three stage approach to improved systems development done in groups:

- Allow for controlled chaos

  We permit a completely distributed development situation where the system specifications are shared among the developers. A relaxed set of authorisation rights is proposed, such that objects may be checked out to many transactions, thus creating potential update conflicts. It may well be that several transactions modify the same object. Several transactions may subsequently all wish to update the repository.

- Monitor potential conflicts among developers

  Our strategy is to keep track of the different local versions existing in the different transactions such that potential conflicts can be detected and managed. The publish and subscribe facilities provide for exchange of local versions of objects among transactions. As long as there is a potential conflict, no single transaction is allowed to update the repository.

- Help resolve conflicts through negotiations

  An update conflict will have to be resolved in one of two ways: (1) The developer responsible for the object in question unilaterally dictates a solution to the other interested parties. (2) A negotiation process among the transactions with potentially conflicting local versions of the same object is initiated. The negotiation process should be supported by groupware technology, e.g. joint editing functions, and multi media technology, e.g. video conferencing and voice mail.

A note on terminology

The usability of the functionality for conflict management presented in this paper is dependent on adequate version and configuration management support. Such functionality will is described in a forthcoming thesis [1]. This section gives a brief presentation of the terminology necessary for the discussions in this paper.

An information system is perceived to consist of a set of related *development objects*. A development object may be *flat*, e.g. Entity Relationship diagrams, or *hierarchical*, e.g. Data Flow diagrams.

Flat development objects have no inherent hierarchical structure. Components of varying significance and multiple levels of detail are logically placed on the same level of abstraction, i.e. in the same diagram. For example, entities and attributes, entities and specialised entities, entities and relationships, would all be depicted in the same Entity Relationship diagram. Flat development objects generally have no concept of decomposition, e.g. entities are seldom decomposed.

The hierarchical models are characterised by hierarchical decomposition. Decomposition of a component is a refinement of the component in terms of a more detailed structure of lower level (i.e. more detailed) components. Hence, every system component is either atomic or compound. An atomic component has not been further decomposed, while a compound component has been further decomposed into a set of system components.

Development objects may exist in multiple *versions*. A version of a development object is an immutable, identifiable edition of that object. There are two classes of versions: *Revisions* are versions that are meant to replace previous versions, and *variants* are versions that are meant to coexist with previous versions. A version of an object may thus be either revision related or variant related to another version.

Versions are given unique names based on the name of the development object followed by a version number, e.g. *Replenish Stock 1.0* would be version 1.0 of an object named *Replenish Stock*. Versions that are meant to exist in parallel, variants, are separated by adding a variant specific name in brackets just after the version number, e.g. *Replenish Stock 1.2[Monopoly]* would be version 1.2 of a variant of *Replenish Stock* identified by *Monopoly*.

The paper is organised as follows: In chapter 2 we introduce the ideas through an informal scenario. In chapter 3 we describe the conflict management including the functions for check-in, check-out, synchronisation among transactions, and support for merging of development object versions. Chapter 4 presents future work.

2. A WAY OF WORKING

This chapter describes a scenario of a distributed development session.

Select your development objects

Version graphs reflect on the various versions of a development object. Component graphs reflect on the structural relationships among development objects. A specific version of a development object may be selected through browsing of the component graphs in combination with browsing of the version graphs.

For example, to check out version 1.2 of an object named *Replenish Stock* from the specification database one simply selects the appropriate object in the version graph and chooses the check-out command from a pop-up menu. This results in the creation of an empty placeholder in the version graph. The placeholder is related either as a revision or as a variant to the version that was checked out.

An elaboration on version and component graphs is given in chapter 4.

The development transaction

When a version of a development object is checked out for further development, it is copied to a private workspace where it may be modified. Modifications will only have effect within the private workspace. Modifications may take time, in the order of days and weeks. When the modifications are completed the object is checked in to the specification database. The task of developing a new version of a development object, i.e. from check-out till check-in, is termed a development transaction.

Since development transactions may be arbitrarily long lived, facilities for sharing of specifications between transactions are provided. Several transactions are permitted to concurrently access and check-out the same version of a development object. Thus, several copies of the same version may be in the process of being modified simultaneously by different transactions.

The alternative is to lock the development object for everybody but the one responsible for the object. This is not an attractive solution.

Modifications made to the development object by the different transactions are by default considered private and kept separate until check-in time. Synchronisation among transactions is provided by the publish/subscribe mechanism that allows one transaction to subscribe to local revisions of development objects developed and published by other transactions.

Check-in time is determined by the developer responsible for the development object.

Suppose that two different developers were interested in modifying *Replenish Stock 1.2* with the intention of creating a new version. Both developers would check out the development object in separate development transactions, say *Trans-1* and *Trans-2*. For each development transaction a *transaction log* is created. Each transaction log contains data about the development objects that have been checked out by the transaction.

Check-out Contract
Object id: Replenish Stock 1.3 Status: Checked out ...
Transaction id: Trans-1 Date: 06.01.92 : 09:45:20 Publish: Yes Subscribe: None
Transaction id: Trans-2 Date: 08.01.92 : 12:05:10 Publish: No Subscribe: (Object id = Replenish Stock 1.2, Transaction id = T1)
...

Figure 1. Check-out contract for *Replenish Stock 1.3*

When, e.g. *Trans-1* checks out the development object, a placeholder for the new version is created and a *check-out contract* for the new version of the object (the placeholder) is created. The check-out contract will be updated with information on date and time of check-out, transaction identifier, whether local revisions created during the transaction are to be published or not, subscriptions to local revisions of development objects that are created by other transactions, and an estimated check-in time. Assume that the first transaction that checks out version 1.2 of *Replenish Stock* defines the new placeholder to be a revision of version 1.2. The placeholder will thus be named *Replenish Stock 1.3*. Figure 1 depicts the check-out contract for *Replenish Stock 1.3*, after transactions *Trans-1* and *Trans-2* have checked out the object.

Checking in a new version of a development object

At check-in time the development object is returned to the specification database with the purpose of updating the database with a new version of the development object. If there are several candidates for the new version, i.e. if the development object was checked out by several transactions and these transactions have modified the object, the candidate versions must be merged. All developers having a copy of the development object are notified, and a suitable time to attempt the merging is negotiated. Some developers may need an extra day or an extra week before being ready to merge with the others. In the end, the time of merging will have to be determined by the developer responsible for the development object.

When the merging of the candidate versions is attempted, conflicts among the candidate versions may be detected, and a cooperative session among the developers of the candidate versions will have to be initiated. The purpose of the cooperative session is to negotiate a new version of the development object.

The negotiations are based on the conflicting candidate versions. The session may be synchronous or asynchronous. Tool support is provided through multi-user editing capabilities.

In the synchronous case all candidate versions are available through a multi window interface to the involved parties during the negotiation session. A developer may comment on all proposals. Various candidate versions may be compared, both on a non-executable (textual or diagrammatic) and an executable (by simulation or execution) basis. Cut and paste among windows to achieve a reconciled version is supported.

In the asynchronous case one has to rely on written communication in the form of comments added, and cut and paste versions, to convey opinions among the developers that are involved in the negotiation process.

A successful negotiation session results in an agreement on the next version of the development object. This version will be stored in the specification database, and the development transaction is terminated.

Suppose that development transaction *Trans-1* is ready to check-in the development object at "Date = 13.01.92 : 15:05:50". Additionally we assume that the developer responsible for transaction *Trans-1* is also responsible for *Replenish Stock*. This means that in the end it is the owner of *Trans-1* who determines the time of check-in. When *Trans-1* issues the request for check-in, the check-out contract for the development object is inspected. All transactions that have checked out the development object are notified of the request for check-in. Suppose that transaction *Trans-2* requests a one week postponement before merging. The owner of *Trans-1*, being the developer responsible for the development object, is at liberty to grant or reject the request. When merging is needed, i.e. when several candidates for the next version of the development object exist, there are two possible outcomes:

- The developer responsible for the object picks one of the candidate versions. The selected candidate will be checked back into the repository to become the next version of the development object.
- The developer responsible decides to merge the candidate versions. The two major approaches are:
  - Try an automatic merging of the candidates. If overlap is detected, initiate a cooperative session to negotiate a new version.
  - Initiate a cooperative session to negotiate a new version directly without trying to merge automatically first.

When the merging process is finished, the result is checked back into the specification database as *Replenish Stock 1.3*, i.e. filling the placeholder for this version of the development object.

3. DEVELOPMENT TRANSACTIONS

A development transaction is the task of developing a new version of a development object. A development transaction is initiated, controlled and terminated by a developer. It takes as input a version of a development object, and involves the use of several automated tools by intelligent human agents, to produce an output in the form of a new version of the development object. This version will update the specification repository. The development transactions closely reflect the work task structure of the development project. Development transactions may therefore be of considerable length.

3.1. Development transaction are different from database transactions

Development transactions differ from database transactions in several ways [17]:

- The controlling agent for a development transaction is human.
- Strict serialisability of transactions is not achievable.
- Rollback is normally not feasible.
- Update conflicts cannot generally be handled automatically.

The development transaction provides a framework to perform consistent updates of the specification repository by several developers [13][3]. In determining a working practise for the development transaction we firstly touch briefly upon the concept of long and nested transactions.

Long transactions

Development transactions are examples of transactions where elapsed time from check-out till check-in may be in the range of days and weeks, e.g. the task of performing a modification in a development object may take a couple of weeks. During this time the development object in question is unstable. It is in the process of being replaced by a new version. When a development object is in an unstable state, access to it by other developers is normally prohibited.

However, the potentially extensive duration of the transactions indicates that one must provide adequate facilities for sharing of specifications during transactions. In the case of overlap between specifications worked on by different developers, the strategy of locking utilised by standard database systems is clearly too restrictive and thus not feasible.

Nested transactions

Development transactions will reflect the work task structure of the development project. Most development projects will be organised into a hierarchy of tasks with associated milestones. It is therefore necessary to support nested transactions, i.e. transactions and sub transactions, to properly reflect the hierarchical organisation of development projects.

A sub transaction is constrained relative to its superior transaction both in elapsed time and in scope. All sub transactions must terminate before their superior may terminate. However, a sub transaction may be wider in scope than its superior provided that the new objects checked out aren't going to be modified. The scope is in terms of the specifications checked out by the transaction.

A transaction cannot terminate before all sub transactions have terminated. If the transaction terminates before its sub transactions terminate, the conditions on the development objects checked out to the transaction that were agreed upon when the transaction was initiated, will in general not have been met. In that case the conditions that have not been met will have to be modified and the responsibilities divided among and turned over to the sub transactions. This is in fact equivalent to terminating the old transaction together with its sub transactions, and the creation of a new set of transactions together with a new set of conditions to fulfil the original commitments of the original transaction. If this does not happen, the transaction would have failed. Thus, it makes sense to say that a sub transaction cannot live longer than its superior.

A sub transaction will not be allowed to operate on, i.e. modify, any development objects that were outside the scope of the superior transaction. However, objects other than those checked out by the superior may be checked out to the sub transaction provided that they are not going to be modified. If the sub transactions were allowed to modify objects that were not within the scope of the superior transaction this would be inconsistent with the conditions agreed upon when the superior was initiated. This is clearly undesirable. Thus, it makes sense to say that a sub transaction may only modify objects that may be modified by its superior.

3.2. Check-out and check-in

The development transaction is implemented by the check-out and the check-in operations. Check-out creates a private repository (or workspace) of the development objects that the transaction is going to operate on. Check-in returns the development object in the private repository to the shared repository. Modifications made to a development object when it is checked out are considered private and kept separate until check-in time.

There are several issues related to the actual semantics of the check-out and check-in operations that have to be decided on:

Authorisation on checked out development objects

The most frequently used authorisation rights are the *shared* and *exclusive* lock modes used in databases. This is sufficient for the average database transaction, but for long lived development transactions the solution is too restrictive. The following four authorisation rights, may prove more appropriate [22]: *Read only*, *access*, *modify*, *delete*. The authorisation right characterise the relationship between a development object and a developer.

- Authorisation *read only* implies that development objects can be read, but not changed or referenced. Associations to the object cannot be added or deleted.
- Authorisation *access* implies that development objects cannot be deleted or changed. Associations with the object can be added and deleted.
- Authorisation *modify* implies that objects can be changed but not deleted. Associations with the object can be added and deleted if the deletion does not imply deletion of the object.
- Authorisation *delete* implies that development objects can be deleted. If the object is used by other objects it may be necessary to delete references to the object before deleting it.

Figure 2 depicts the compatibility matrix for these authorisation rights. E.g. if a developer has been granted *delete* authorisation to a development object, then other developers may have at most *read only* authorisation to this development object.

Max. authorisation granted	Highest authorisation other developers may have
Delete	Read only
Modify	Access
Access	Modify
Read only	Delete

Figure 2. Authorisation rights compatibility matrix

Relaxed authorisation rights

We propose to relax the authorisation rights such that several developers may check out a development object with the intention of modifying it, i.e. check-out with authorisation *modify* or *delete*. At check-in time the potential candidates for the next version of the development object, candidate versions, will be checked for overlap. Where overlap is detected a cooperative session among the involved developers is initiated. The purpose of the cooperative session is to negotiate a new version of the development object. The negotiations are based on the conflicting candidate versions. The negotiation session may be synchronous or asynchronous.

Propagation of authorisation rights in the development object hierarchy.

Authorisation rights will be automatically propagated through the development object hierarchy. It is possible to override the propagated authorisation rights in the following way: The developer may be granted the same or more restrictive authorisation rights to subordinate development objects. I.e., if a developer has *delete* authorisation to a development object, he may have either *delete*, *modify*, *access*, or *read only* authorisation to its subordinates. To grant a developer less restrictive authorisation rights to subordinate development objects, one must make sure that conflicts with other developers accessing the same development object does not arise. I.e., if a developer has *read only* authorisation to a development object, he can only be granted *access*, *modify*, or *delete* authorisation to its subordinates provided that this is not in conflict with authorisation rights being held by other developers on the same development objects. To grant a developer an authorisation right that is in conflict with the compatibility matrix in figure 2, one must first change the authorisation rights of other developers.

Single or multi repository check-out.

Multi repository check-out means that one is allowed to check-out development objects from several shared repositories into a private sub-repository. Single repository check-out means that one is obliged to have a one-to-one relationship between a sub-repository and a shared repository.

The single repository check-out solution is the simpler. There is no need to keep track of where different development objects in the private repository belong, because they all belong to the same repository. However, the solution limits the possibility to share development objects among several repositories. It seems artificial to introduce this limitation. The added cost of allowing multi repository check-out is to keep information on where the development objects belong. This is a reasonable price for added flexibility.

Individual or total check-in of development objects.

Individual check-in of objects means that the development objects may be checked back into the shared repository on individual basis. Total check-in of objects means that development objects that were checked-out together at the beginning of the transaction, are checked back into the repository together. This usually happens as an integral part of the termination of the development transaction.

A transaction is an assembly of work that logically belong together. The transaction is started at one point in time, and it should be terminated at one point in time. At that time all development objects manipulated by the transaction should be checked back into the shared repository.

3.3. Development teams

Development of complex information systems necessarily involves several systems developers working in a team. The development team may be geographically distributed. The team members collaborate in developing a new version of a development object. Team work implies that large tasks can be undertaken, at the cost of increased communication and coordination overhead.

In developing a new version of a development object several developers may be involved, submitting different contributions which need to be considered when assembling the new version. We propose a scheme that will allow the individual developers involved in the process of merging the different contributions to browse each others proposals. A developer may thus view the work of other developers while working on their own contribution.

To support this team process we need to take administrative measures to avoid chaos when the version is checked back in. A consequence of allowing several developers to work in parallel based on the same development object version, is the need to merge the different contributions made by the developers. The result of merging different contributions constitutes the next version of the development object.

Synchronising transactions

Although a system is described as a hierarchy of system components, dependencies between components that are not directly related in the hierarchy will exist. During a development transaction there may be a need to synchronise, or coordinate, the work taking place within a transaction, with on-going development work on development objects checked out to other transactions. Work taking place in one transaction may depend on the results of other transactions. Synchronising transactions may be needed both when there is overlap among the development objects checked out to the different transactions and when no overlap exists.

The synchronisation of transactions is done through the use of *check-out contracts* and *transaction logs*.

- The transaction log is a record of the development state of a transaction and its related development objects. A transaction log is associated with a transaction. It contains information on the development objects currently checked out by the transaction, dependencies on other transactions, in addition to a record of the development history within the transaction. The transaction log is established at check-out time.
- The check-out contract is a record of the development state of a development object. A check-out contract is associated with a version of a development object. It contains information on responsible developer, development status, dependencies on other objects, and the development transactions that currently has checked out the object. The check-out contract is established when the placeholder for the version of the development object is created.

Dependencies between a specific transaction and other transactions that currently have checked out development objects that overlap or are dependent on development objects currently checked out by the specific transaction will be recorded in the transaction log. When checking out a development object the check-out contract is inspected and the transaction log is updated together with notification of the developer, of any other developers having checked out the same object and any dependencies between this object and any other objects.

The check-out contract is updated with information on dependencies, if any, between this object and any other objects currently checked out. This information is supplied by the developer responsible for the transaction.

At check-in time the transaction is checked for consistency against the existing contract and contracts on related transactions. Provisions are made for merging different proposals.

We introduce the possibility for transactions to *publish* local revisions of the development objects it has checked out, and for transactions to *subscribe* to local revisions of development objects of other transactions. A subscription is negotiated and established as part of updating the transaction log and the check-out contract when checking out an object. When a transaction publish a local revision of a development object, any transaction having subscribed to this development object will automatically be informed of, and have access to, the new release of an intermediary version.

3.4. The consensus

At check-in time a development transaction will possibly check several development objects back into the specification repository with the purpose of updating the repository with new versions of the development objects. In the general case there will be several candidates provided by several transactions, for the new version of these development objects.

Merging of candidate versions

A strategy for merging these candidate versions is necessary to be able to support teams in systems development. The efficiency of the merging strategy is heavily dependent on the quality of the conflict resolution mechanism that is applied when overlap between candidate versions have been detected.

There are several policies for handling the situation where several candidate versions of a development object exists:

Priority Let the first, last, or some other candidate with priority win. This may waste weeks of work, and is clearly not acceptable.

Rollback Where conflicting overlap exists, roll back the transaction. This may waste weeks of work, and is clearly not acceptable.

Locking Going down one level in granularity together with an adequate set of authorisation rights, may remove the problem.

Merging Generalised merging of several candidate versions. May be semi automatic or entirely manual.

The reasonable solution is to provide merging of candidate versions. Some observations on merging of candidate versions:

- A human developer exists as the intelligent agent behind the development transaction.
- Coarse grained version control may lead to flagging of update conflicts which by deeper semantic analysis are found to be non-existent.

The support of the merging process is very much an administrative problem. The bottom line conflict resolution mechanism when merging, is detection and notification of potential conflict, and the request for manual intervention. As deeper knowledge of the models involved is gained, and experimentation with alternative solutions can be carried out, a better and more informed strategy for merging can be provided.

A strategy for supporting the merging of candidate versions, is as follows: When a transaction is initiated and a set of development objects are checked out for further development, *placeholders* for new versions of the development objects are created. The *placeholders* serve the purpose of defining whether the new version is revision related or variant related to the version that has been checked out. A transaction log is established for this transaction, and a check-out contract for the object (the placeholder) is created. The check-out contract will require that the developer points out dependencies between development objects that have been checked out by this transaction, and development objects that have been checked out by other transactions. The dependencies may exist both when the development objects overlap and when they do not overlap. During a transaction the developer may create a chain of revisions of the development objects that have been checked out. When the chain of development revisions necessary to do the modification is completed, the developer may terminate the transaction by checking the new version of the development objects back into the shared repository, thus attempting to fill the placeholder. If transactions that have checked out an overlapping set of development objects exist, we potentially have a conflict. A potential conflict triggers the conflict resolution mechanism.

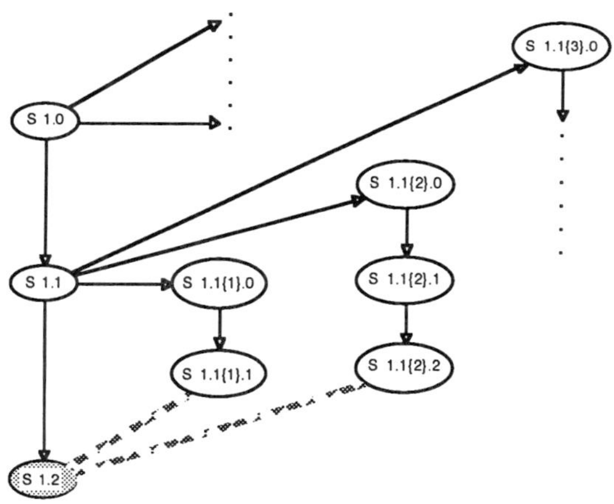

Figure 3. Multi transaction check-out and check-in

The chains of intermediary revisions created during the development transaction can be handled as intermediary structures on the version graphs [2]. The intermediary structures may be discarded after successful check-in of the new version. The check-out contract associated with the placeholder may also be discarded. However, if it is desirable to keep the full development history then the intermediary structures and the check-out contract must be stored.

Figure 3 depicts a version graph where *S 1.1* have been checked out by three transactions. Each transaction have developed intermediary revisions of the development object local to the transaction. The checked out development object is identified by the name *S 1.1{τ}.λ*, where *{τ}* indicates that it belongs to transaction τ, and λ is the revision number local to the transaction. When either of the transactions attempt to check-in the development object, merging is attempted. The placeholder for the new version of *S*, *S 1.2*, is grey in the graphical representation in figure 3. When the placeholder is filled, it will be changed to white.

Conflict resolution

When several candidates for a new version of a development object exist, merging of the candidates must be performed. All developers having checked out the said version are notified, and a suitable time for attempted merging is negotiated. The time to merge is determined by the developer responsible for the development object. Responsibility for development objects is determined by the allocation of manpower in the project organisation. Some developer may need an extra day or an extra week before he is ready to merge with the others. This will have to be negotiated among all developers involved, and sanctioned by the developer responsible for the development object. The responsible developer will still have priority in determining the time of merging, so that the work will not be unnecessarily delayed.

Merging of the candidate versions is attempted. When a conflict has been detected a cooperative session among the developers of the candidate versions is initiated. The purpose of the cooperative session is to negotiate a new version of the development object. I.e. the goal of the negotiations is to achieve consensus on a new version of the development object. The negotiations are based on the conflicting candidates. The negotiation session may be synchronous or asynchronous [5]. Tool support may be provided through the integration of multi user editing capabilities [19][8][16][6][15]. Added functionality to the negotiation support may be obtained by integrating synchronous video conferencing [10] and multi media annotation [7].

Synchronous negotiations

In the synchronous case all candidate versions are available to all involved developers during the negotiation session. The candidate versions are available through a shared workspace for comments and comparisons. A developer may comment on any proposal. Comparisons may be based on the textual or diagrammatic specifications, i.e. a non-executable basis, as well as by simulation or execution of “executable” components. The synchronous shared workspace supports several modes of working [10]:

- The *public screen* and *public desktop* allow all developers involved in the negotiation to view one single developer’s screen or desktop.

This mode implements multicasting of one developer's screen or desktop to all the other members of the negotiation. While the screen or desktop may only be manipulated by its owner this mode may be used when a developer is explaining a diagram or arguing a point to the other developers involved in the negotiation. To support the spoken explanation or arguments the developer may simultaneously be drawing sketches or extending the diagrams on the desktop or screen and pointing to objects in a sketch or diagram.

- *Desktop on screen* and *desktop on desktop* allow developers to draw sketches and comment the contents of other developer's screens or desktops.

  This mode implements translucent overlay of live video images of individual screens or desktops. It offers an efficient possibility of interactively commenting the contents of another developer's screen or desktop. Images of desktops may overlay screens or images of other desktops. A screen or desktop image that is overlaid by an image of a desktop may already have images of other desktops overlaid. Experimental evidence indicates that users easily differentiate up to three overlays [10]. When there are more than three overlays differentiating between them may be alleviated by introducing colour coding of the different layers.

- The *shared tool* mode allows all developers involved in the negotiation to simultaneously view and manipulate (edit) one or several development object candidates using the appropriate tool on their private workstations.

  This mode offers joint editing functionality on a development object. A telepointer is available for global pointing. There is no special floor control policy. One relies on the informal social protocol agreed by the developers through synchronous voice or video communication. The tool to be used is dependent on what tool was used to develop the development object candidates that are the subject of the negotiation process.

The usefulness of these modes are dependent on the presence of two additional factors; the addition of synchronised sound or video and the possibility of flexible switching between modes.

Firstly, all three modes must be used together with synchronised sound, e.g. using speakerphones. It would be impossible to e.g. conduct interactive joint editing without possibilities of synchronising actions through speech. Better still would be to use synchronised video to capture facial cast and body language as well as speech. This will enable synchronised negotiation sessions to take place in geographically distributed environments. It is possible for the developers to stay in their respective offices and still have a meeting with the feeling of eye contact. In addition to the obvious benefits of not having to move from your office where you have your work context, e.g. your papers, files, workstation etc., distributed meetings offer the added flexibility of allowing the participants to enter and leave the meeting at different times during the meeting without too much disturbance to the rest of the participants. The alternative to distributed meetings is either to have the participants meet in one room or conduct an asynchronous negotiation session.

Secondly, it is necessary that switching between modes is flexible. For example, a developer may operate in *public screen* mode to explain some issues in his development object candidate. When somebody wants to comment on the object currently in the public screen, one may switch to *desktop on screen* mode to be able to make a sketch and do some pointing to explain the comment. Other developers may chain on to the comments so far to give their comments. This may be done by simply overlaying their own desktops on top of the ones that are already present. In the end an agreed position will be reached, and a consolidated proposal will be developed. The consolidated proposal may typically be in the form of sketches and comments overlaid on some developer's screen or desktop. It is then possible to enter into the *shared tool* mode to jointly perform the necessary modifications to the original development object candidate as indicated by the sketches in the overlaid desktops.

There are some projected negative aspects of the proposed synchronous modes of operation:

- The *public screen* and *public desktop* mode offers a plain "one way" communication with much the same features as traditional lectures. The only possible feedback is through spoken comments. However, this may be improved when necessary by switching to an overlay mode where additional input may be given by those who wish to add comments.
- The *desktop on screen* or *desktop on desktop* mode offers indirect drawing an pointing on an overlaid desktop by hand. This needs time and effort to get used to. This is similar to the learning process required for learning to use indirect pointing devices, e.g. a mouse.
- The *desktop on screen* or *desktop on desktop* mode offers the use of many overlays. This may cause confusion. This may be remedied by using colour coding of layers, dimming of layers, or conceptually removing layers from the picture.
- The *desktop on screen* or *desktop on desktop* mode offers the results of the negotiations as a many layered object. The consensus is not directly recorded in the "primary object". Individual contributions are overlaid to make the complete picture and they are physically stored in different places and on different media. One will therefore have to perform the modifications that were agreed upon on the primary object in a separate editing session.
- The *shared tool* mode implements an informal social floor control. This may cause confusion when several developers input data at the same time. We wish to have a flexible *shared tool* mode, consequently we do not wish to implement a more rigorous floor control policy which restricts concurrent input, e.g. a token based approach.

Asynchronous negotiations

In the asynchronous case one has to rely on written communication in the form of comments and cut-and-paste versions, and multi media annotations to the candidate development objects to convey opinions among the developers that are involved in the negotiation process.

The multi media messages passed between the developers are based on the candidate versions. The messages will contain annotations to one or several candidate versions in the form of synchronised pointing, drawing, writing, and speaking [7]. To annotate a local version of a development object, e.g. in the form of a Data Flow diagram, one would add a transparent annotation layer to the object. The annotation layer allows the developer to point, write, draw sketches, and add voice comments to the diagram by using a voice handset, a tablet, and a "pencil" stylus. The keyboard may be used for lengthy input of text.

The multi media annotations may be played back in synchronous mode. This will play back the voice comments, the stylus cursor's movement, as well as the hand drawn and typed messages. For instance, when reviewing a Data Flow diagram one may point to a specific process and say, "This process consumes data from our *Order History* files. This seems to have been omitted in this candidate version."

People are accustomed to annotating paper documents. The combination of written and spoken annotation, commonly used only in meetings, will increase the information content and precision in asynchronous communication. Comments may be added as the multi media annotated development object pass from one developer to the next. The object holds the accumulated signatures and comments of several developers involved in the negotiation on the candidate objects. One will observe a conversation unfolding over time as the objects are passed back and forth among developers for continued annotations.

There are some projected negative aspects of the proposed asynchronous annotation scheme:

- The result of the asynchronous annotation session is a many layered multi media document. Navigating among a high number of layers may be confusing. The navigation and playback of the recorded annotations may be alleviated by disciplined, focused, and too the point annotations.
- The result of the asynchronous annotation session is an annotated multi media document. The modifications proposed are not implemented in the primary object. The modifications that have been agreed upon must therefore be implemented in a separate editing session. This may be done either as a synchronous group task through a joint editing session, or by the developer responsible for the primary object.

Many layered objects

During a negotiation session, synchronous or asynchronous, the development object that is the "object of" the negotiation will be a many-layered object, as depicted in figure 4. The primary layer will consist of the local development object itself. There will be a number of transparent secondary layers containing overlaid desktops or screens and multi media annotations. The different overlays may have been added in synchronous or asynchronous mode. The developers may dim or conceptually remove any layer to make it easier to interpret the possibly complex picture that may arise from the existence of many layers. Colour coding of different layers will also improve the readability of the many layered object.

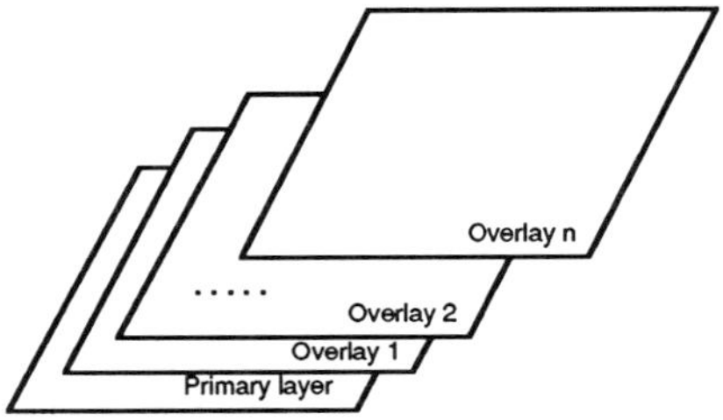

Figure 4. Many layered object during negotiations

A successful negotiation session results in an agreement on a reconciled version of the development object. This reconciled version will be the next version of the development object and update the repository. This concludes the merging operation, and the development transactions that are involved may terminate.

4. FUTURE WORK

A successful implementation of the proposed functionality for conflict management depends on two issues: (1) Integration with a shared repository where the public specifications may be kept. This repository must offer a versioned interface to the system specifications. (2) Integration with a suitable CASE tool.

The specification repository

The specification repository collects all relevant development project data to be shared by all interested parties. It contains data to serve the needs of system analysts, system designers, programmers, and the project managers.

To be able to satisfy these requirements, the repository must encompass concepts from four different domains [23]: The *subject domain*, the *implementation domain*, the *development object administration domain*, and the *development project domain*.

The schema for such a repository would consist of four partly overlapping sub-schemata, i.e., four interrelated sub-models are considered, as illustrated in figure 5.

The concepts in the *subject domain* sub-schema are concerned with the subject domain, and with building a model of the real world that caters for behavioural, performance, and environment interaction aspects. It is important that the model lends itself to transformation into system specifications.

The concepts in the *implementation domain* sub-schema are concerned with system specifications on various levels of abstraction. The system specifications are related to both the subject domain model and the development object administration model.

The concepts in the *development object administration domain* sub-schema are concerned with system and system component management. Concepts such as versions and configurations of systems and system components are related to the system specifications on one hand, and the development project organisation on the other.

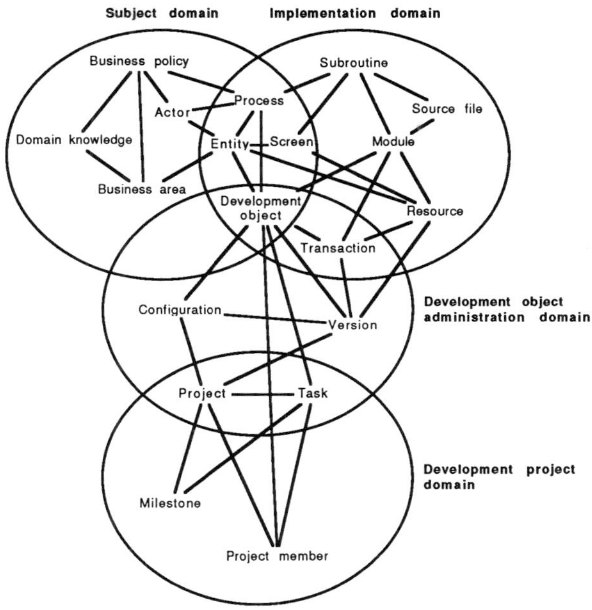

Figure 5. Concepts in systems development

Version and configuration management keep track of versions of system components developed by several developers working in a geographically distributed development environment. A version of a system is an immutable, identifiable edition of a system. A system is composed of a number of components. A component may either be composed of a number of components, e.g. a Data Flow diagram, or be a flat structure, e.g. an Entity Relationship diagram. A version of a system is a composition of versions of system components. Each version is potentially developed by one of a number of different developers. Some versions are developed only to be discarded, some versions are merged in a negotiating session, while some versions directly update the repository.

The concepts in the *development project domain* sub-schema are concerned with the development project organisation, monitoring, and management of project resources.

A prototype implementation of a repository that meets these requirements has been developed by Kimmel [11]. The prototype has been developed on Sun workstations with the Techra database system [12].

Integration with a CASE tool

A CASE tool will record and maintain data belonging to the *subject domain* sub-schema and the *implementation domain* sub-schema. The conflict management presented in chapter 3 integrated with adequate version and configuration management will manipulate the concepts in the *development object administration domain* sub-schema. The functionality necessary to manipulate concepts in the *development project domain* sub-schema may be added. This will only work properly if

As suggested by the initial sketch of the repository schema, the repository will contain interrelated sets of concepts partly maintained by the CASE tool, partly by conflict management functionality, partly by version and configuration control, and partly by project administration software. Precisely which concepts and what the relationships between them are, are determined by the meta models of the CASE tool, and the software for conflict management, version and configuration control, and project administration respectively.

REFERENCES

[1] R. Andersen, "Management of Teamwork in Information Systems Development", PhD Thesis - forthcoming, The Norwegian Institute of Technology, University of Trondheim, 1993.

[2] R. Andersen, E. Hodneland jr. and R. Knarbakk, "KOKO - Konfigurasjonskontroll i TINA", Master Thesis (in Norwegian), University of Trondheim, The Norwegian Institute of Technology, 1985.

[3] R. Conradi and C. C. Malm, "Cooperating Transactions against the EPOS Database", in"*3rd International Workshop on Software Configuration Management",* Ed. P. H. Feiler, pp. 98-101, Trondheim, Norway, ACM Press, 1991.

[4] B. I. Danielsen, "Method: Myths and Reality in AD/Cycle", in"*Focus on AD/Cycle",* Oslo, The Norwegian Information Processing Society, 1991.

[5] C. A. Ellis, S. J. Gibbs and G. L. Rein, "Groupware: Some Issues and Experiences", *Communications of the ACM*, vol. 34, no. 1, pp. 1991.

[6] R. S. Fish, R. E. Kraut, M. D. P. Leland and M. Cohen, "Quilt: A collaborative tool for cooperative writing", in"*Conference on Office Information Systems",* Palo Alto, ACM, 1988.

[7] E. Francik, S. E. Rudman, D. Cooper and S. Levine, "Putting Innovation to Work: Adoption Strategies for Multimedia Communication Systems", *Communications of the ACM*, vol. 34, no. 12, pp. 52-63, 1991.

[8] I. Greif, R. Seliger and W. Weihl, "Atomic data abstractions in a distributed collaborative editing system", in"*The 13th Annual Symposium on Principles of Programming Languages",* St. Petersburg, ACM, 1986.

[9] IBM, "Repository Manager/MVS - General Information", IBM Corporation, 1989.

[10] H. Ishii and N. Miyake, "Toward an Oper Shared Workspace: Computer and Video Fusion Approach of Teamworkstation", *Communications of the ACM*, vol. 34, no. 12, pp. 36-50, 1991.

[11] G. Kimmel, "Design and Implementation of a Multi User Version Control System for Decentralized Systems Engineering", The Norwegian Institute of Technology & Universität Karlsruhe, 1992.

[12] KVATRO, "Techra - Concepts and Facilities", KVATRO T-008, KVATRO, 1992.

[13] M. Lacroix, D. Roelants and J. E. Waroquier, "Flexible Support for Cooperation in Software Development", in"*3rd International Workshop on Software Configuration Management",* Ed. P. H. Feiler, pp. 102-108, Trondheim, Norway, ACM Press, 1991.

[14] B. Langefors, "Theoretical Analysis of Information Systems", Studentlitteratur, Lund, 1966.

[15] M. D. P. Leland, R. S. Fish and R. E. Kraut, "Collaborative document production using Quilt", in"*Conference on Computer-Supported Cooperative Work",* Portland, ACM, 1988.

[16] B. T. Lewis and J. D. Hodges, "Shared Books: Collaborative publication management for an office information system", in"*Conference on Office Information Systems",* Palo Alto, ACM, 1988.

[17] A. Lie, "Versioning in Software Engineering Databases", PhD Thesis, The Norwegian Institute of Technology, University of Trondheim, 1990.

[18] K. J. MacCallum and I. M. Carter, "Opportunistic software architecture for support for design coordination", *Butterworth-Heinemann Ltd., Knowledge-Based Systems*, vol. 5, no. 1, pp. 55-65, 1992.

[19] S. Opper, "A groupware toolbox", *Byte*, December 1988.

[20] A. Sølvberg and C. Kung, "Information Systems Engineering", Springer Verlag, Heidelberg, forthcoming, 1993.

[21] Texas Instruments, "IEF Technology Overview", Texas Instruments Inc., 1989.

[22] Texas Instruments, "Information Engineering Facility - Central Encyclopedia Guide", Texas Instruments Inc., 1989.

[23] T. Winograd, "Beyond Programming Languages", *Communications of the ACM*, vol. 22, no. July, pp. 391-401, 1979.

7.

PROCESS/PRODUCT MODELING II

Information System Development Process (A-30)
N. Prakash, C. Rolland and B. Pernici (Editors)
Elsevier Science Publishers B.V. (North-Holland)

© 1993 IFIP. All rights reserved.

Product Modeling for Requirements Engineering Process Modeling [£]

Jean-Roch SCHMITT

- Centre de Recherche en Informatique ; Université de Paris 1 Panthéon-Sorbonne
  17, rue de Tolbiac ; 75013 PARIS ; FRANCE
- GSI-Tecsi ; 176 Av. Charles de Gaulle ; 92200 NEUILLY SUR SEINE ; FRANCE
  e-mail : JRSchmitt@masi.ibp.fr

Abstract : *Current Information Systems (IS) development methodologies only sketch the definition of their development process, resulting in a low level of support to the developers.*

This paper first stresses the need to define new process models to underlie better the specifications development process. Second, it provides an overview of the solution proposed in the esprit project NATURE project, in the context of the Requirements Engineering phase.

Then, the emphasis is put on the need to precisely model the IS development product in order to support process modeling. A product model is thus detailed, argued and illustrated on examples.

Keywords Codes : D.2.1; D.2.6; D.2.10
Keywords : Software Engineering, Requirements/Specification; Programming Environments; Design

1. INTRODUCTION

Today's Information Systems (IS) developments suffer from the unbalanced description of (1) their modeling formalisms and (2) the way developers must follow to obtain the expected computerised system as it is prescribed by methodologies used in these developments [Rolland & Cauvet 1992].

The modeling formalisms provided by the methodologies define sets of concepts that allow the description of the system. They let designers reason about the system and validate its representation according to users' requirements.

The way-of-working of a methodology prescribes what kind of activities can be performed in the development and when they can be performed.

Up to now, a large amount of research effort has been dedicated to the modeling of Information Systems. This research has resulted in the development of a great number of sophisticated modeling formalisms adapted to the particularities of the system to be built and to the development environment.

Furthermore, Information Systems meta-models of have been developed that abstract from specific models and define generic concepts suitable to describe models. Such meta-models allow the comparison of several models and the adaptation of models according to the particular needs of an IS development.

£ This work was supported by ESPRIT project Basic Research Action 6353 (NATURE) which is concerned with Novel Approaches to Theories Underlying Requirements Engineering.

Contrarily, current methodologies hardly define the way-of-working designers can or must follow to proceed in the development : most of the process semantics is missing. This weakness can be explained by the little amount of research work that has been devoted to the modeling of the development process, relatively to the IS modeling effort.

This imbalance between models and way-of-working definition has also notable consequences on the CASE tools that more and more often support IS developments. The current CASE tools are efficient in recording, retrieving and manipulating the schemes representing the system undergoing development. But they are almost unable to actually provide assistance to the developers in deciding and performing the activities transforming these schemes.

We consider that this weakness in the prescription of methodologies ways-of-working stems from the inadequacy of the currently available process modeling approaches that support their description. We think that, in order to be suitable, new approaches should allow the ways-of-working description at various granularity levels and with a deeper semantic representation capability.

This need to model the IS development process motivates the "Process Theory" stream of the "NATURE" Esprit project. NATURE aims at investigating three complementary aspects of the Requirements Engineering (RE) phase of IS development : (1) knowledge representation, (2) domain knowledge definition and usage and (3) RE process modeling.
The objective of this last "Process Theory" stream is to propose an approach for the modeling of the development process adapted to the RE phase. This will allow detailed descriptions of methodologies ways-of-working and their integration in CASE tools.

The contribution of this paper is twofold. It first stresses that the particular process modeling approach proposed in NATURE requires the RE product to be precisely modeled. Secondly, it presents and exemplifies a product model that meets the requirements.

After a short presentation of the main arguments supporting the development of a new way of modeling the RE process, **section 2** gives an overview of the approach adopted in NATURE. In **section 3**, we stress why this process modeling approach requires a parallel modeling of the product and detail the model we propose. Finally, in the **section 4**, we shall show how this product modeling is used in the modeling of the process through the notion of "Situation" whose modeling will be sketched and illustrated through examples.

2. THE NATURE PROCESS MODELING APPROACH

2.1. Motivations for a new approach in development process modeling

As mentioned in the introduction, current IS development methodologies offer a great number of IS modeling formalisms but hardly detail the way-of-working developers must follow in order to deliver the computerised system starting from the initial users' requirements.
Indeed, most of the existing methodologies give only few insights concerning the way developers can make the system description evolve. Developers are most of the time provided with the definition of big phases and with constraints stating that a given phase cannot be undertaken before the previous one has been completed. These phases most often correspond to the various schemes to be developed. The developers are thus required to produce these

schemes at predetermined milestones, but they are not guided in the actual production of these schemes.

Moreover, although some methodologies recognise the need of iteration in design by allowing it among phases, they rarely prescribe the iteration conditions, resulting in an overall poor level of prescription.

This limited ability to specify the way-of-working developers must follow is still more hindering in the context of RE which is particularly characterised by :

- its highly creative, non-deterministic, interactive and cooperative nature,
- the alternative techniques that can be applied to proceed, at any stage : domain analysis, reverse engineering, reuse, etc....
- its major importance over all the development life-cycle : the solutions adopted during the RE have consequences on all the succeeding phases,
- and its mixing of modeling formalisms, with various levels of formality.

To be more efficiently usable, a RE methodology should specify what kind of activities can be performed, what they modify, when and by whom they can be performed ; and this should be specified for any stage of the process. In other words, the developers would much more precisely know how to proceed during RE.

Furthermore, such a detailed knowledge could be introduced in CASE tools that would then be able to guide developers in their decision making process and in the resulting IS schemes transformations.

The prescription capability of a way-of-working specification highly depends on its underlying process modeling approach. According to [Dowson 1987], the existing process models, on which methodologies ways-of-working specifications are based, can be classified in three categories:

- activity-oriented models,
- product-oriented models,
- decision-oriented models.

Activity-oriented models come from an analogy with problem solving, i.e. finding and executing a plan of actions leading to the solution. They are sequential in nature and provide a frame for manual management of projects developed in a linear fashion. Such a linear view of the design process is inadequate for methodologies which support backtracking, reuse of previous designs and have to support parallel engineering activities. The first widely used model, the Waterfall model [Royce 1970], falls into this category, along with the Spiral model [Boehm 1988] and the Fountain model [Henderson-Sellers & Edwards 1990] which try to eliminate the well recognised lack of flexibility of the Waterfall model. Limitations and drawbacks of activity-centred development approaches come from their representation of development processes like programs which do not integrate at all the interactive aspects of IS development.

The product-oriented process models represent the development process through the evolution of the product. They promote a view of development processes which is still centred around the notion of development activity but present the advantage to link development activities to their output : the product. The ViewPoints model [Finkelstein & al. 1990] belongs to this category as well as the development process model proposed in the European Software Factory (ESF) project [Peugeot and Franckson 1991].

A more recent class of process models follows a *decision-oriented paradigm.* The successive transformations of the product are looked upon as consequences of decisions. The process model of the DAIDA project [Jarke & al. 1990; Rose & al. 1991] and of [Potts 1989] fall into this category. Such models are semantically more powerful than the previous ones because they explain not only how the process proceeds but also why transformations happen.

They provide a more complete knowledge about the process which is particularly useful for reuse of developed products, or of design decisions, and for backtracking purposes when a modification in requirements has to be considered either during the design process itself or during the maintenance of the IS.

2.2. Overview of the NATURE process modeling approach

Considering the characteristics of the RE mentioned above, it appears that only the decision-oriented approach, with its transformation justification capability, is partially appropriate to the NATURE process modeling goals.

In this context, a *decision* is a choice the requirements engineer makes and it induces a transformation of the product.

However, the decision-oriented approach offers only limited knowledge about when and how to decide on what.

To solve this limitation, we enhance the decision-oriented approach by introducing the notion of *context*. This enhancement stems from the recognition that analysts react *contextually* according to the domain knowledge they acquire and react by analogy with previous situations they have encountered.

A *context* is defined as the association of a decision with some the parts of the IS being developed, called a *situation*, on which the decision is made.

Based on this intimate grouping of a decision with the situation on which it is made, called "context", the NATURE process modeling approach allows a better representation of RE processes. These processes are thus considered not only as collection of transformation activities but explicitly as ordered sets of decisions made on situations, recognised in the IS specification.

This approach is an extension of the one presented in [Grosz & Rolland 1990] and implemented in the "OICSI" prototype CASE tool [Rolland & Cauvet 1991].

The NATURE process meta-model, whose main concepts are the ones of situation, decision, context, action and argument is very simply overviewed in the figure 1 :

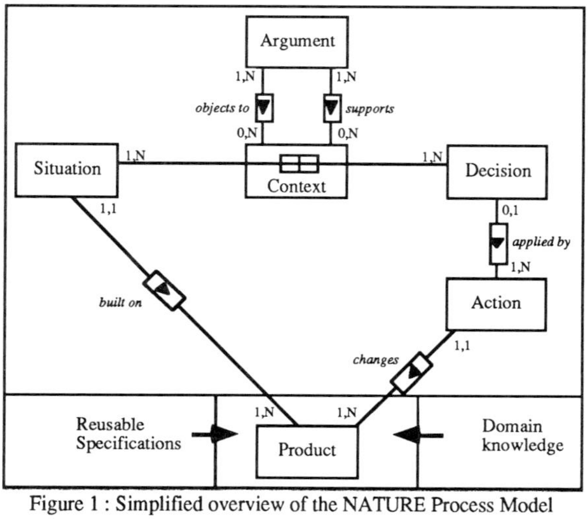

Figure 1 : Simplified overview of the NATURE Process Model

In this figure, an ER-like notation is adopted to highlight the main concepts (rectangles) and their inter-relationships (boxed arrows). "context" is both the situation-decision association and a concept. The bottom of the figure illustrates the integration, in the "product" concept, of previously developed reusable specifications and of domain knowledge.

Note that this figure also highlights the basic loop of the process modeling approach : situations motivate decisions that are applied by actions that modify the product in which situations are recognised.

A *situation* is most often a part of the product it makes sense to make a decision on. It represents the context of a decision. It can be a statement about the application domain or a requirement. It can also be an historical knowledge about previous developments or about generic domains.

A *decision* reflects a choice that a requirements engineer makes at a given point in time of the RE process. A decision can be looked upon as the intention of product transformations.

A *context* is the association of a situation and a decision made on it.

An *action* performs a transformation on the IS description. It is a materialisation of the decision. Performing an action changes the description and may generate new situations, subjects to new decisions.

Arguments are statements supporting or objecting to decisions made in a given situation, i.e. support or object to contexts.

[Rolland 1993] details the NATURE process meta-model and the reader is invited to refer to it for a complete presentation of these concepts.

With such a process model, the description of a way-of-working is made by specifying what kinds of decisions can be made in what kinds of situations and what kinds of actions have to be performed to apply the decisions.

The figure 1 also illustrates the link existing between the RE product development process and the product itself : the product is the source of the situations recognition and is modified by the performance of actions.

The main consequence of this intimate relationship is that a detailed process model cannot be obtained without a parallel *product model.*

In the remaining of this paper, we present the product model and illustrate its use in the building of situations; the relationship between the process model and the product model, through the action, will not be presented here.

Let first make clear the abstraction level we focus on.

One of the requirements of the NATURE process modeling approach is that it must be defined independently from any specific methodology. The result of the work must then be a model (an abstraction), of process models : a process meta-model.

Like any meta-model, this process meta-model is a set of generic concepts suitable to represent the process model of any given RE methodology.

In NATURE, the Telos [Mylopoulos et al. 1990] knowledge representation language allows a formal expression of process models and of the process meta-model.

3. PRODUCT MODELING

The purpose of this section is to present the RE "product" modeling we propose in NATURE to fit the needs discussed above. In this section, we successively give an intuitive definition of the concept of "product" and detail its modeling, illustrated on examples.

3.1. Intuitive definition of the concept of product

Let's first define the RE "product" as the IS undergoing development during the Requirements Engineering phase.

Traditional IS development methodologies define their product like they define their process : they decompose it into sub-products as they decompose broad phases into sub-phases. Each sub-phase of the development process being defined relatively to its output : a sub-product.

These methodologies often decompose the product into conceptual, logical and physical sub-products. The conceptual sub-product is for example decomposed into structural and functional schemes.

The very nature of IS the development product is however much more complex, particularly in the context of Requirements Engineering. The RE product has some important characteristics that must be taken into account for its precise modeling.

Firstly, let's now define the "Product" as all the knowledge the different stakeholders of the RE phase have about the system to be built. At the beginning of the RE phase, the product may be a collection of users' requirements, whatever their expression media : natural language sentences, forms, drawings, etc.... This initial understanding of the system is usually controversial, opaque and informal [NATURE 1992]. At the end of the RE phase, the product must contain the conceptual specification of the system.

In between these two stages, the product is actually a mix of initial requirements, intermediate schemes and partial conceptual schemes. Moreover, each product component may be characterised by its own specification, agreement and formality levels, according to the framework proposed in [NATURE 1992].

Secondly, the schemes that compose the product are sets of instances of modeling formalisms concepts, such as the E/R or data-flow concepts. But the use of a given formalism is not unique. For example, let's consider two methodologies using the data-flow formalism to describe the functional perspective of a system. The first one may define "flat" data-flow schemes as being composed of processes, flows, stores, etc.... . The second methodology may define data-flow schemes as being composed of data-flow diagrams, themselves composed of processes, flows, etc. , i.e. it introduces an hierarchical building of data-flow-schemes. This example shows that the product is built from views of modeling formalisms that is relative to the methodology.

Thirdly, the product may also carry knowledge concerning the state of the process. For example, a data-flow schema may be in a "verified" state. The RE process then making these sub-products evolve from states to states. Such a piece of information is of course not defined by the data-flow formalism and is thus relative to the methodology.

The last two points motivate the clear distinction we make between the modeling formalisms used by a methodology and the product model defined by the methodology.

Section 2 has introduced the intimate relationship existing between the modelings of the *process* and the *product* as proposed in NATURE. The previous discussion has shown that the modeling of the product is based on the *modeling formalisms* provided by development methodologies. Figure 2 illustrates the relationships between these three kinds of models.

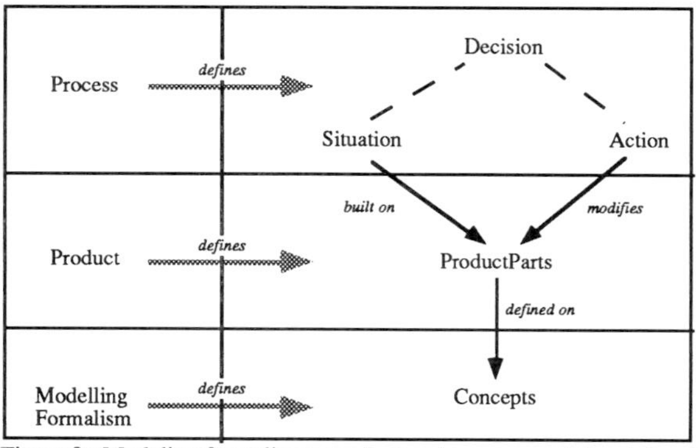

Figure 2 : Modeling formalisms, product and process models relationships.

Finally, IS developments more and more often tend to reuse knowledge acquired during previous developments. This existing knowledge can be made, for examples, of conceptual specifications whose elements can be integrated in the new specification or of DB-programs code which can be reverse-engineered. It can also be made of generic domain knowledge pieces that can be specialised and adapted to the system undergoing development.

As the activities of reusing this existing knowledge are actual activities of the RE process, the corresponding decisions are made on situations built both on parts of the product undergoing development and on parts of existing products. This brings the need to extend the notion of product with existing knowledge. The complete RE product is then made of two parts : the existing products and the product under development.

To summarise this discussion, we recognise the following characteristics of the definition of the product of IS development methodologies :

- its building :
  * from which models, of which formality level
  * by which decomposition hierarchy
- the allowed advancement states of its parts
- the kind of existing products that can be reused to build it

3.2. Product model

According to section 2, the product model we present here is in fact a product meta-model, i.e. the definition of generic concepts allowing the description of the types of products defined by RE methodologies. However, for the sake of clarity, we will describe this meta-model using terms belonging to the process abstraction level instead of the process model level. For example, instead of saying that instances of the "ProductElement" concept of the meta-model are ProductElement-types whose instances are elements of the schemes composing the product, we will say that instances of the "ProductElement" concept are elements of the schemes composing the product.

Figure 3 presents, using a E/R-like notation, the product model centred around the notion of "Product Component". In the sequel, we present each of the concepts of this model in turn.

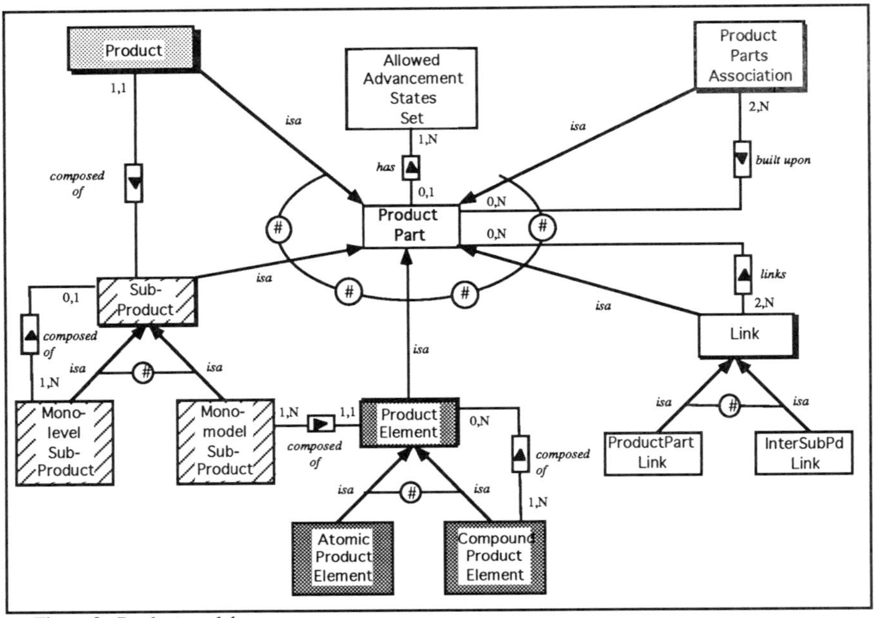

Figure 3 : Product model

The following RE-product example, depicted in figure 4, is a partial instanciation of the product model (figure 3) and will be used throughout this section to illustrate its concepts :

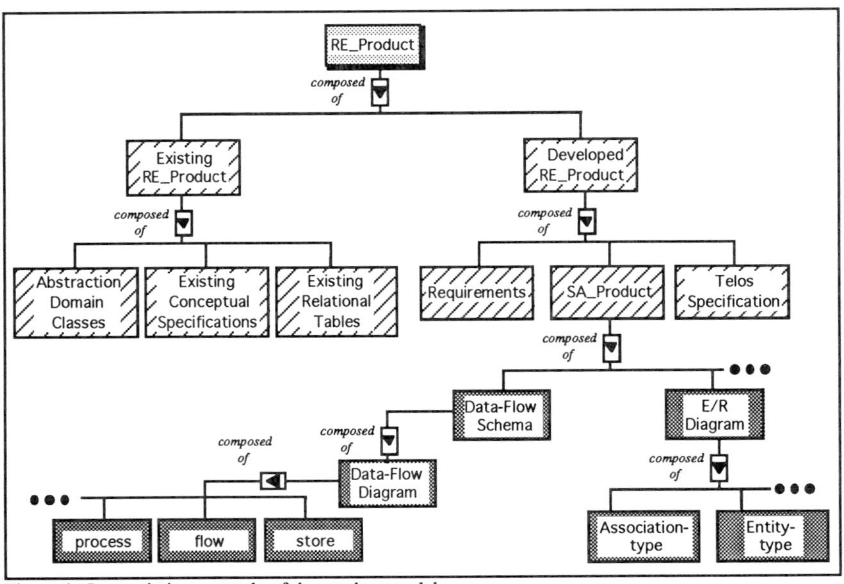

Figure 4 : Instanciation example of the product model

The central concept of the product model is the "ProductPart". It represents any set of elements carrying knowledge about the product, be it the developed product or the existing product. These sets of product elements can be either the product itself, sub-products, instances of modeling formalisms concepts, links or product parts associations. The "ProductPart" concept is thus specialised in the concepts "Product", "SubProduct", "ProductElement", "Link" and "ProductPartsAssociation".

In the sequel, we detail each of those product model parts in turn.

IS development methodologies - ways-of-working - are usually divided into phases, such as the "conceptual modeling phase" or the "formalisation phase". Such phases yield in parts of the product, referred to as "SubProducts" in figure 3. These phases may themselves be sub-divided into sub-phases, resulting in an hierarchical composition of sub-products. As each phase of a methodology results in a partial specification of the system at a given level of abstraction, each sub-product belongs to only one abstraction level.

Furthermore, a sub-product may either use one or several of the modeling formalisms provided by the methodology. In figure 3, this distinction is represented by the "MonoLevelSubProduct" and "MonoModelSubProduct" subtypes of "SubProduct". "Mono-ModelSubProduct" represents the sub-products that are made of concepts of a same modeling formalism (i.e. what is traditionally called "schema"). "MonoLevelSubProduct" represents sub-products that are composed of sub-products and belong to the same abstraction level.

In the example (figure 4), the RE-product is made of, on one side, an existing product composed of conceptual specifications, relational tables and domain abstraction classes [NATURE 1992]. Elements of the conceptual specifications may be reused if satisfactory similarities are found with elements of the system to be developed. Relational tables may be reverse-engineered into reusable conceptual specifications. Domain abstraction classes may be matched against elements of the developed product and then be adapted.

The developed product, on the other side, is composed of a set of requirements, a Structured-Analysis-oriented modeling and a formal Telos specification. These sub-products are the "conceptual" level and are respectively "informal", "semi-formal" and "formal".

The "SA_Product" is composed of the sub-products "ER-diagram" and "Data-Flow-schema", to cite only two of them. Each of these component sub-products uses one formalism, they are thus instances of the "MonoModelSubProduct" concept. Since its different components do not use the same formalism, the "SA_Product" is contrarily an instance of the "MonoLevelSubProduct" concept.

The dark grey boxes shown on figure 3 represent the building of schemes from the concepts provided by the modeling formalisms. We are now going to detail this part of the product model.

According to [Rolland & Souveyet 1990], any modeling formalism provided by IS development methods defines a set of concepts and constraints suitable to represent information systems. For example, extended E/R formalisms define the concepts "entity-type" and "association-type" and the disjunction constraint between two sub-types of an entity-type.

These concepts and constraints serve as a basis for the definition of the product elements that compose the schemes representing an IS.

We saw that a methodology defines its product as a decomposition into sub-products. Complementarily, it also specifies the decomposition hierarchy of these sub-products into product elements based on the concepts and constraints of the formalisms.

The concept "ProductElement" (figure 3) represents the components of a "MonoFormalismSubProduct". For examples, an E/R diagram is composed of entity-types and association-types, a data-flow schema may be composed of data-flow diagrams, themselves composed of processes, flows, stores, etc. . These two examples illustrate that there are two kinds of product elements : atomic and compound. Instances of the "AtomicProductElement" concept cannot be decomposed into other product elements and are directly defined on the concepts and constraints of their formalism. Instances of the "CompoundProductElement" concept, in contrary, are composed of other product elements.

Up to now, we have seen how the product model allows the specification of the hierarchical decomposition of the product into sub-products which are themselves decomposed until undecomposable product elements are reached. These "leaves" product elements are then defined on the concepts and constraints defined by the modeling formalisms provided by the method.

It is important to remember that given a common set of modeling formalisms, two different methodologies may specify two different decomposition hierarchies, thus defining two different products.

Let's now consider the "Link" sub-type of the "ProductPart" concept in figure 3.

This concept represents the knowledge the developers have about the relationships existing between parts of the product. A link relates two parts of the product, be them sub-products, product elements, product parts association or even links.

For example, it may be necessary to record in the product that an entity-type of an E/R diagram corresponds to a relational table of the existing product. It may also be necessary to record the similarity value [NATURE 1992] existing between two data-flows diagrams, or to record that a given store in a data-flow diagram corresponds to a given entity-type.

We recognise three sub-types of the "Link" concept, according to the semantics of the link. The first type of links is the *"MappingLink"* type which represents the links that relates an association of product parts to the one it has been mapped into. Note that the two product parts associations must then be at different abstraction levels. The previous example concerning the relational table / entity-type link falls in this category. The example of the store / entity-type link is of the second type of link : the *"CrossRefLink"* which represents correspondence links within a given level of abstraction. These two types of links are represented by the "InterSubPdLink" concept that generally handles the modeling of the links defined between modeling formalisms. The last type of links, the *"SpecificLink"* concept, is the one of the links which do not fall in the two previous categories and that depend on methodologies. Similarity links for example fall in this category. This category is represented in figure 3 by the "ProductPartLink" concept.

Finally, the last kind of product part that can carry knowledge about the system is a grouping of product parts, represented by the concept "ProductPartsAssociation". An instance of this concept is a set of product parts, whatever their type is, except the product itself : sub-products, product elements, links or even product parts associations.

Actually, this concept is necessary to represent any group of product elements carrying knowledge about the system that is neither a node of the product decomposition hierarchy nor a link.

For example, the following figure shows two product parts associations between which a similarity link has been established by a developer. :

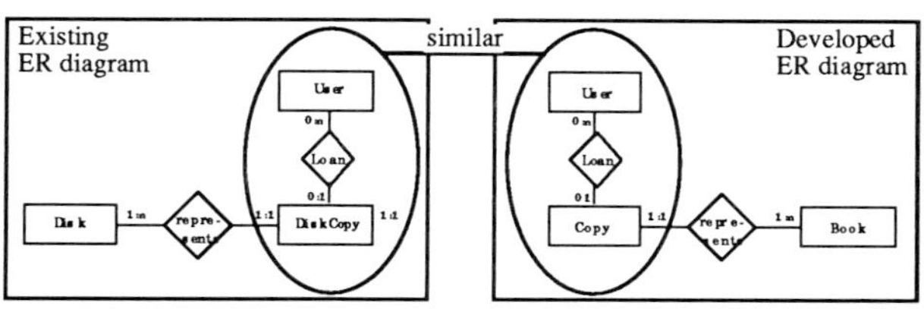

Figure 5 : Example of product parts associations

According to section 3.1, the definition of a methodology's product must contain the definition of the possible states of advancement of each part of the product and must specify the allowed transitions between states.

IS development methodologies often define states for the product parts, states that correspond to the achievement of sub-phases. The OPML model [Peugeot and Franckson 1991], for example, allows detailed representations of object-states graphs. Here, such graphs are referred to as "evolution graphs".

Furthermore, [NATURE 1992] introduces a three dimensional framework in which the RE product can be located, at any stage of the RE. The three axis represent the specification (degree of understanding) , representation (formality level) and agreement (stakeholders' view) dimensions. The specification and agreement dimensions are good extensions of the classical definition of the state of product parts while the formality level is defined as a characteristic of the modeling formalism and does not need to be modeled in the product model. The "AllowedAdvancementStatesSet" concept (figure 3) is introduced in the model to handle the representation of this kind of information.

4. SITUATION BUILDING UPON THE PRODUCT

The purpose of this section is to show how the concepts of the product model presented in the previous section can serve as basic building blocks of the situations developers may make decisions on.

As it is beyond the scope of this paper to detail the whole process model of NATURE, we only sketch the modeling of situations and we shall give examples of situations building and decisions that may be made on them.

4.1. Definition of the notion of situation

According to the presentation of the process model proposed in NATURE as described in section 2, the concept of "Situation" is a key notion in the contextual approach. Requirements engineers react to situations recognised in the product by making decisions on them. Those decisions which are in turn applied by actions performed on the product.

As a first definition of the notion of situation, let's define it as the minimal set of product parts a given decision can be associated to, e.g. on which it makes sense to make this decision on. This definition says firstly that the existence of a situation is motivated by the existence of a decision. Secondly, the definition states that two situations associated to a same decision should not have an inclusion relationship between them (minimality).

It is important to note that although situations are built from products parts similarly to the building of compound product parts from smaller ones, the two building semantics are different.

On the one hand, product parts are defined because they carry knowledge about the system undergoing development.

On the other hand, situations are defined and built from product parts because they represent products parts sets it makes sense to make decisions on.

4.2. Situation modeling

Before presenting the modeling of situations, let's discuss its requirements. First, we need to give a means for representing all the combinations of product parts on which the decisions of a methodology can be made. Secondly, conditions may constraint product parts sets in order to be acceptable situations.

For example, the way-of-working of a given methodology may specify that the decision to verify an E/R diagram cannot be made if the diagram is not in the "frozen" state. Similarly, it may be specified that the decision to create a disjunction constraint between two subtypes of an entity-type should not be made if the constraint already exists.

Thus, the modeling of situations must allow the representation of the building of situations upon the product parts and the expression of conditions constraining this building.
This modeling is illustrated by the figure 6.

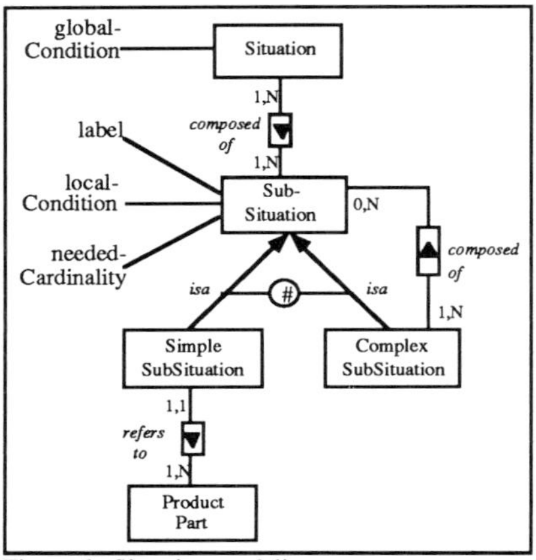

Figure 6 : Situation modeling

This modeling of situations is centred around the concept "SubSituation" which represents sets of product parts of the same type and satisfying the same condition. A situation is composed of a set of sub-situations.

The attributes of "SubSituation" are its needed cardinality, a local condition to be satisfied by product parts to belong to this sub-situation and a label allowing to reference its elements in the expression of the conditions. The needed cardinality may be exactly known or not ; if it is exactly known, it may be any integer - including "0" - , if it is not exactly known, it may be either "some" or "all". A value of "0" means that no corresponding product part satisfying the local condition should be in the situation. An integer value other than "0" means that the situation contains exactly this number of product parts of this type and satisfying the local condition. The values "some" and "all" respectively mean that some or all of the product parts, of the given type, can be in the situation, if they satisfy the local condition.

Sub-typing sub-situations into simple and complex one allows a hierarchical building of situations. A complex sub-situation is composed of sub-situations. A simple sub-situation refers to the type of product parts is defined on.

A global condition is also defined to represent the conditions constraining the situation and that are not related to its elements, or to represent the conditions existing between elements of the situation. For example, the User-Loan-Copy situation in figure 5 may be constrained by a condition stating that the ER diagram should be in a given state for the decision to be made : this condition does not bear on elements of this situation.

4.3. Situation examples

In order to illustrate the use of this situation modeling, we are now presenting some examples of situations, together with the decision that justify their definition. Remember that the association situation-decision partly represents the conditions under which a decision can be made.

Assume that the methodology at hand only specifies its way-of-working by defining phases and by stating conditions constraining the succession of these phases. This can be represented by defining a decision for each phase, by defining the product parts corresponding to the phases and by defining states for these products parts. These states are then used in the definition of the situations in which the decisions can be made.

For example, the decision "MakeDesign" is associated to the situation made of the "AnalysisSubProduct" which is constrained by the "state is 'analysis completed' " condition (mark 1 in figure 7). The definition of the corresponding situation is the following :

```
Decision : MakeDesign
Situation :
        globalCondition = none
        SubSituation1 :
                label = none
                ReferredProductPart = "AnalysisSubProduct"        (1)
                localCondition = "State is 'AnalysisCompleted' "
                NeededCardinality = 1
```

Figure 7 : Coarse grained situation example

If the methodology would provide a much finer level of granularity, it may specify that whenever two entity-types are sub-types of a same entity-type a decision may be made that creates a disjunction constraint between the sub-types, if this constraint does not already exists (mark 1 in figure 8). The corresponding situation is defined as follows :

```
Decision : CreateDisjuctionConstraint
Situation :
globalCondition =   "superType = IsA.x.target"
                            "constraint.left = IsA.1" & "constraint.right = IsA.2"
        SubSituation1 :
                label = "superType"
                ReferredProductPart = "EntityType"
                localCondition = none
                NeededCardinality = 1
        SubSituation2 :
                label = "subTypesGroup"
                NeededCardinality = 2
                localCondition "IsA_link.source = 'subType.x' "
                SubSituation2.1
                        label = "subType.x"
                        NeededCardinality =1
                        localCondition = none
                        ReferredProductPart = "EntityType"
                SubSituation2.2
                        label = "IsA.x"
                        NeededCardinality =1
                        localCondition = none
                        ReferredProductPart = "IsA_link"
        SubSituation3 :
                label = "constraint"
                NeededCardinality = 0                (1)
                localCondition = none
                ReferredProductPart = "DisjunctionConstraint"
```

Figure 8 : Fine grained situation example

These examples of situation, although quite simple, illustrate how the situation-decision association of the notions of allows the representation of the prescriptions of a methodology, at any level of granularity : a very broad one as in the first example and a very fine one in the second.

5. CONCLUSION

In this paper, we proposed a model of the Requirements Engineering (RE) product.
We first argued that the low level of detail provided in the specification of their way-of-working by the classical IS development methodologies is a real handicap, particularly for the RE phase and in the context of CASE tools supported development environments.
We then showed how the RE process modeling approach proposed in the NATURE project can solve this limitation.
Thereafter, we explained that the particular NATURE process model requires the RE product to be modelled in details,
The main part of the paper was then a presentation of our product model.

Although it was not discussed in the paper, we want to pinpoint here that our RE product model can be easily extended to allow the representation of IS development products over all the life-cycle, from RE to maintenance.

In order to operationally prove the validity of the product model by developing the NATURE RE CASE tool prototype, we are currently undertaking its formal description in the Telos language.

Acknowledgement
The author thanks the NATURE project partners for their feedback and is particularly grateful to Georges Grosz and Carine Souveyet for their fruitful advice.

REFERENCES

[Boehm 1988] Boehm B.W.: A spiral model of software development and enhancement; IEEE Computer 21.

[Dowson 1987] Dowson M.: Iteration in the software process. Proc. 9th Intl Conf Software Engineering, Monterey, Ca.

[Finkelstein et al. 1990] : Finkelstein A., Kramer J., Goedicke M.; "ViewPoint Oriented Software Development"; Proc. Conf "Le Génie Logiciel et ses Applications", Toulouse, p 337-351, 1990.

[Grosz & Rolland 1990]: G. Grosz, C. Rolland; Using artificial intelligence techniques to formalize the information system design process; Proc. Intl. Conf. Databases and Expert Systems Applications, 374-380.

[Henderson-Sellers and Edwards 1990] : Henderson-Sellers B., Edwards J.M.; "The Object-oriented Systems Life-Cycle"; Comm. ACM, 09/1990.

[Jarke et al. 1992] : Jarke M., Mylopoulos J., Schmidt J.W., Vassiliou Y.; “DAIDA - An Environment for Evolving Information Systems”; ACM Transcactions on Information Systems, Vol. 10, No. 1, 1992.

[Mylopoulos et al. 1990] Mylopoulos J., Borgida A., Jarke M. and Koubarakis M.: Telos:Representing Knowledge About Information Systems. ACM Trans. Information Systems 8, 4, 325-362.

[NATURE 1992] : Jarke M., Sutcliffe A., Vassiliou Y., Rolland C., Bubenko J.; NATURE Esprit III project n° 6353, Deliverable NATURE.D-I, 12/1992.

[Peugeot and Franckson 1991] : Peugeot C., Franckson M.; "Specification of the Object and Process Modeling Language", ESF Report n° D122-OPML-1.0, 1991.

[Potts 1989] : Potts C.; “A Generic Model for Representing Design Methods”; Proceed. 11th International Conference on Software Engineering, 1989.

[Rolland & Cauvet 1991] : Rolland, C., Cauvet, C. : An Expert System for Requirements Engineering, in "Advanced Information Systems Engineering"; R. Andersen, J.A. Bubenko, A. Solvberg (Eds), Springer Verlag 1991.

[Rolland & Souveyet 1990] : C. Rolland, C. Souveyet;" An Object Oriented Framework for Information Systems"; Proc of the Intern. Conf. on Management of Data (COMAD'90), New Delhi, India, 12-14 déc. 1990, pp 280-303.

[Rolland & Cauvet 1992] : Rolland C., Cauvet C.; "Trends and Perspectives in Conceptual Modeling"; in "Conceptual Modeling, Databases, and CASE, An integrated View of Information Systems Development", Loucopoulos P. & Zicari R. Eds, WILEY, 1992, pp 27-48.

[Rolland 1993] : Rolland C. ; "Modeling the Requirements Engineering Process" ; 3rd European-Japanese Seminar on Information Modeling and Knowledge Bases, Budapest, Hungary, 1993, to be published.

[Rose et al. 1991] Rose T., Jarke M., Gocek M., Maltzahn C., Nissen H.: A decision-based configuration process environment. Software Engineering Journal 6, 5.

[Royce1970] : Royce W.W.; "Managing the development of large Software Systems"; Proc. IEEE WESCON 08/1970.

Information System Development Process (A-30)
N. Prakash, C. Rolland and B. Pernici (Editors)
Elsevier Science Publishers B.V. (North–Holland)
1993 IFIP.

A Development Model: Application to Z Specifications

R. Darimont[(1)] and J. Souquières[(2)]

[(1)]Université Catholique de Louvain-La-Neuve, Place sainte-Barbe, 2, B-1348 Louvain-La-Neuve, Belgique

[(2)]CRIN-CNRS & INRIA-LORRAINE, BP. 239, F-54506 Vandœuvre-lès-Nancy Cedex, France

Abstract

This paper describes a model for supporting the process of specification construction. The model encompasses planification of development activities, incremental construction of specifications and development operators. The operators are independant of the specification language. An operator instantiated to Z is presented and the approach is illustrated on the development of a Z specification.

Keyword Codes: D.2.1, D.2.2, D.2.6
Keywords: Software Engineering, Requirements/Specifications; Tools and Techniques; Programming Environments.

1 Introduction

Facing up to the need for production of high-quality software, the software community has been very prolix in developing frameworks for acquiring requirements and specifying systems. But little attention has been paid to *development processes* themselves. Development processes are worth being studied to extract the similarities of different methods and to provide guidance to developers in the application of methods. In particular for specifications, although the use of different notations leads to different specifications, the underlying derivation processes present strong similarities [9]. This paper aims at proposing a model for supporting the incremental construction of a specification and the development process behind the construction, including the record of specification decisions and their rationales.

The need for formalizing software development independently of a specification language has already been claimed by several authors [15], [8], [16]. Feather and Johnson [10], propose a fairly large library of evolution transformations to elaborate specifications with a derivation model based on parallel development [5]. They suggest that documenting evolution steps allows one to undo, replay, and combine derivation histories.

Modelling a software development process requires both a general framework and eliciting strategies or development operators from practical experiments. The idea of using development operators as a standardizing, unifying tool in specification development has been stressed by several authors. Wile [21] describes the Popart-Paddle framework for experimenting with program development strategies expressed through goal structures. The approach followed by Carbonell, [2], strongly based on AI techniques, emphasizes the construction of the workplan. Potts [14] proposes a generic model for representing design methods based on the entity-relationship model, augmented with generalization and specialization. Conklin and Begeman [3] use a hypertext system to record and retrieve design rationales. The workplan is a key to these two last studies. The idea guiding the next step of the development does not seem to be addressed.

The proposed model is composed of a workplan, a product, and links between them [17]. The workplan describes the organization of the work already done and of the work still to be accomplished. The product is the target specification under construction. The workplan and the product evolve incrementally by the application of development operators [18]. The availability of these operators is a critical point of the approach.

The paper is organized as follows. Section 2 describes the proposed process model and gives an example operator. Section 3 shows excerpts from the development process followed specifying a *Phone Network* in Z.

2 A Model for Developing Specifications

The proposed model belongs to the class of state-transition systems. The elaboration of a specification is viewed as a sequence of development steps [17]; each step is defined by an application of a development operator. A development state is represented by a *workplan* and a *product*, which are connected by *links*. Both are structured and may contain different versions of their components.

2.1 Workplan

A workplan describes the organization of the work already done and of the work still to be accomplished: it is a collection of tasks. A *task* denotes a work to be done in order to produce a piece of specification, called the goal. Tasks are generally subdivided into subtasks. The subtasks of a task T are expected to achieve, all together, the goal assigned to T. A *reduction* links a task with its possibly empty set of subtasks. There are often several ways to decompose a task into subtasks. A reduction represents one choice among alternative decompositions. A task may therefore have several reductions.

As in the classical top-down reduction approach to problem solving [13], a workplan is represented by an *and/or*–graph with two kinds of nodes: task nodes and reduction nodes. This graph has a unique root node which is a task. *And*–nodes represent the decomposition of tasks into subtasks whereas *or*–nodes represent alternative decompositions.

Figure 1 represents a workplan. The root task, *" Specify Phone Network System"*, must produce a formal specification expressing the behaviour of a Phone Network System. This task has one reduction introducing three subtasks, *"Identify Phone Network Intermediates"*, *"Specify Phone Network Intermediates"* and *"Specify Phone Network knowing intermediates"*.

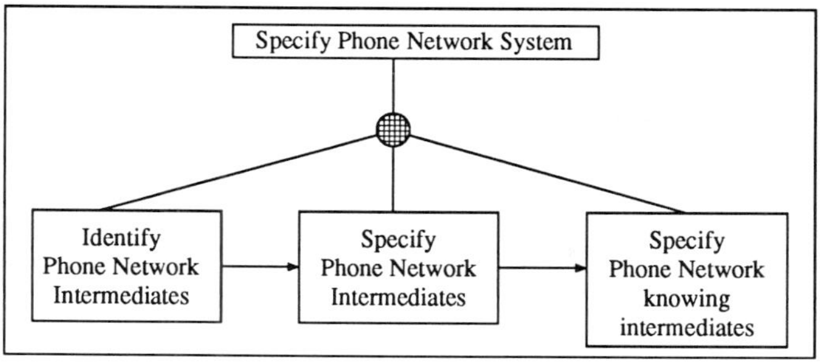

Figure 1: Workplan and workplan symbols

Developing a workplan consists in identifying new reductions and new tasks. Supplying at once all needed subtasks to solve a given task is often too restrictive. A specifier should be allowed, for instance, to decompose a task into its main subtasks first and then to complete the reduction later, when the work would have progressed enough. This desirable behaviour is expressed by means of reduction *states* as shown in Figure 1:

- A reduction is *partial* if the list of its subtasks may be further extended with other subtasks.
- A reduction is *complete* otherwise.
- A reduction is a *dead-end* if the decomposition cannot yield progress towards the objective associated with the parent task. This failure is recorded to facilitate understanding and replaying the development.

As explained above, a task T can have alternative reductions, which can be interpreted as different ways of solving T. One of these reductions is called *current*, corresponding to the way of solving T which is currently retained. From time to time (e.g. in case of a dead-end), the specifier may wish to backtrack on an alternative reduction, which becomes current.

- The *current workplan* of a workplan W is an *and*–tree consisting of the root task of W, all current reductions in W and their associated tasks.

The reduction is not the only interesting relation on tasks. A developer might wish to express the fact that reducing some task requires some others to be reduced first. This point motivates the introduction of *precedence relations*: a *precedence relation* is a strict partial order on sister tasks. Two kinds of precedence relations are introduced, which are denoted in the workplan as shown in Figure 1. Let *T1* and *T2* be subtasks of the same reduction instance of a task T in a workplan W.

- *Strong-precedence.* The pair $\langle T1, T2 \rangle$ is a member of the strong-precedence relation on W iff the task *T2* cannot be reduced while *T1* has a current *nonterminated* reduction.

  A reduction is *terminated* if its associated product is finished.

Imposing a strong precedence between two tasks may often be too restrictive in practice.

- *Weak-precedence.* The pair $\langle T1, T2 \rangle$ is a member of the weak-precedence relation on W iff the reduction of task *T2* may start as soon as the reduction of *T1* has made *sufficient progress.* Knowing whether sufficient progress has been made, can often be decided by the specifier only.

2.2 Product and Workplan-Product links

$$PhoneState \mathrel{\widehat{=}} idle \mid dialTone \mid waiting \mid seized \mid ringTone \mid ringing \mid busyTone \mid blockedTone \mid notAttributeTone$$

Phone

$State : PhoneState$

...

...

Figure 2: A Product State

Not only the final specification but also intermediate specifications are needed to facilitate specification development, documentation and replay. For example, specifiers should be allowed letting some parts unfinished and completing them later.

A product refers to versions of the developed specification. It can be described as an *and/or*–abstract syntax graph [4] representing a particular production. Nodes may contain pieces of specification, informal text or nonterminal nodes. Nonterminal nodes are labeled with type expressions, which determine the type of the specification component to be developed. A typical development consists in manipulating such graphs, for example, expanding them by refining nodes top-down, merging them bottom-up or fixing leaf information. The product state is structured similarly to the workplan state : versions correspond to alternative reductions. Figure 2 presents an unfinished product in the Z language in which nonterminal product components are denoted by "...".

Links are defined as a relation over tasks and product items. They associate product items with the tasks that produce them or with the tasks that need them to achieve their objectives.

2.3 Development Operators

The availability of development operators is a crucial point of the specification development model. They perform some part of the work planned in the current workplan and make the development evolve by their simultaneous action on the state of the workplan, the product and the links, as follows:

Task	Precedence	Candidate Operators
T2	1	Map-structure
T3	2	Iterate
T4	3	Define-Structure

Figure 3: Application of the Agenda to the Previous Workplan State

- the workplan is updated either by the addition to a new reduction to a given task or by the modification of an existing one,
- new links can be defined,
- the product can be completed or modified.

Operators observe or modify a development state. Observation operators give access to information that can be derived from a development state. An example of application of the *Agenda* operator is shown Figure 3. To each task of the current workplan not yet reduced, it gives an order of possible resolution (*T2* has to be reduced first, then *T3* then *T4*) and a list of candidate operators able to solve the associated task.

A modification operator applies to a whole development and extends it by producing a new development state. Its application is subjected to preconditions. For instance, a task can only be reduced if the semantics of the precedence relations is respected and if it has no current reduction.

An Example of Development Operator

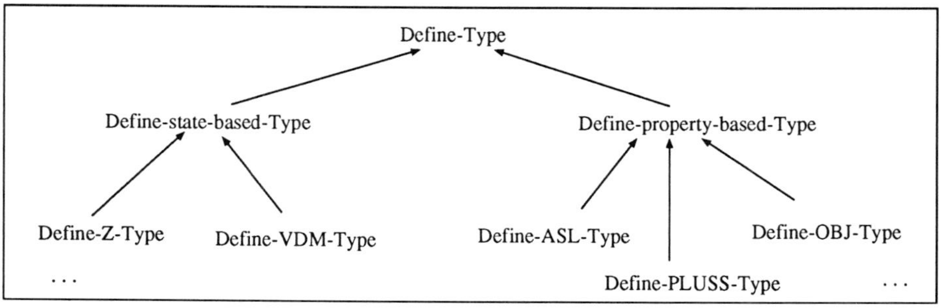

Figure 4: Hierarchy of *Define-Type* operators

A type definition depends on the specification style and the selected language. Two main classes of approaches are generally followed when defining a type, one called *model-oriented* or *state-based* approach, the other *property-oriented* approach. The model-oriented approach aims at constructing an abstract model of the system being specified reusing predefined data

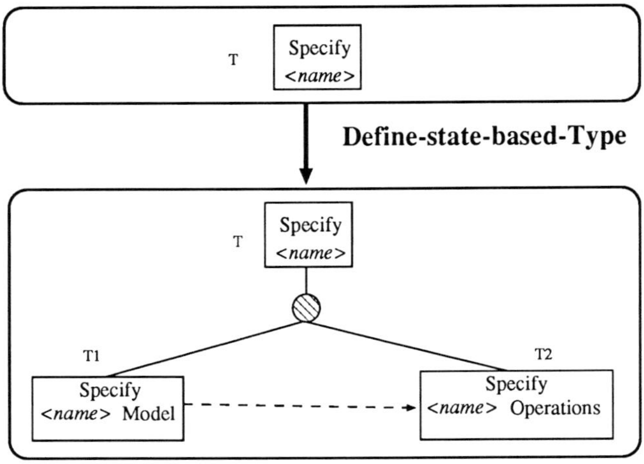

Figure 5: The *Define-state-based-type* operator

structures. This approach can be followed when writing Z [20] or VDM [11] specifications. The aim of the property-oriented approach is to describe a system in terms of its desired properties without constructing an explicit model. It can be followed when writing algebraic specifications, using for example ASL [1], OBJ [6], or PLUSS [7]. Some specializations of the *Define-Type* operator are presented in Figure 4.

Figure 5 shows how the *Define-state-based-Type* applied to a type specification task refines the workplan. A (state-based) type specification requires the definition of a model (state) (task *T1*) and of operations working on it (task *T2*). The reduction of *T* is partial in order to let the way open to type extensions. The weak precedence link between *T1* and *T2* means that the model does not need to be completely fixed for specifying some operations: an operation generally affects only a part of the state.

The choice of a target specification language allows refining the *Define-state-based-Type* operator. Figure 6 presents the *Define-Z-Type* operator as a *specialization* of the *Define-state-based-Type* operator. The higher the level of a task in the hierarchy of tasks, the more the task is general and common to all definitions of types. Leaves of the workplan define tasks that are typically Z-oriented. For instance the task *Investigate Preconditions* is a typical activity in Z, while the correctness of a schema is for instance differently checked in VDM where preconditions are explicited [9].

Applying *Define-Z-Type* allows generating the skeleton of a Z specification (see Figure 7). The "..." notation indicates placeholders which must be completed by resolving tasks. Links between tasks and products are represented directly in the product by referencing there the tasks responsible for its production. For example, task *T6* aims at precising the definition of operation initialisation. A formalization of the model in terms of graph grammars and type systems [19] allows to precisely define this operator.

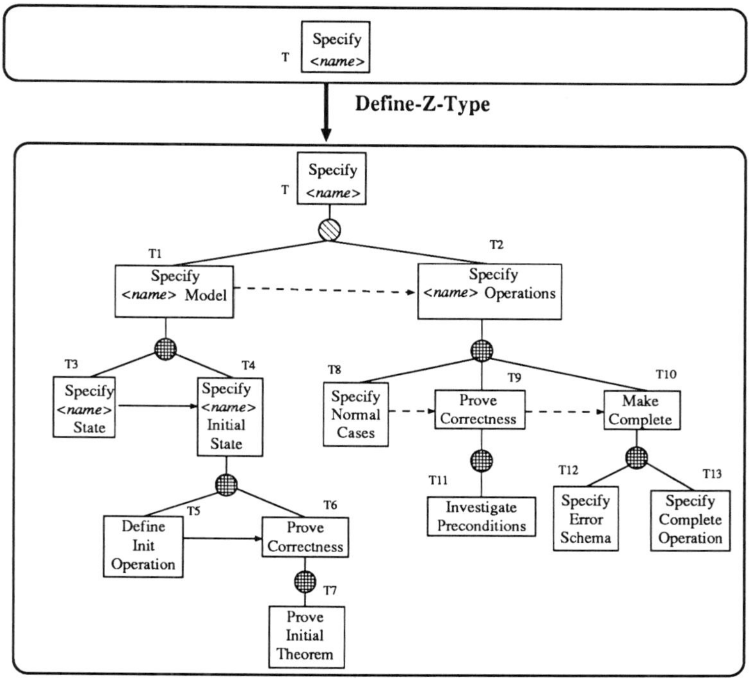

Figure 6: The *Define-Z-Type* operator

3 Phone Network Case Study

This section aims at illustrating the use of development operators on an example. Because studying, recording and documenting a development process is a very long task, only the most significant excerpts of the development will be shown. In the sequel, the case study is first presented informally in few words – assuming that the reader is acquainted with the use of phones. Next an intermediate state is presented and then a few steps of the development is shown. A phone network is composed of phones. Phones allow pairs of users to communicate.

3.1 Informal Requirements

To communicate with user B, user A picks up his phone and, after having been prompted by the exchange, dials B's address. After some delay, user A hears a tone, the meaning of which depends on whether (i) the callee B is free, (ii) the callee is busy, (iii) the network is blocked, (iv) the dialled number is not attributed. If (i) holds, the callee phone begins to ring. Caller A and callee B are connected as soon as B picks up his ringing phone. A picked up phone can be hung up at any time. A call request is cancelled by the caller who hangs up. A communication

State . . .

$\langle name \rangle$

... ($T3$)

... ($T3$)

Operations

$\langle name \rangle Init$

$\langle name \rangle'$

... ($T6$)

...

... ($T6$)

... ($T6$)

$\vdash \exists < name >' \bullet \langle name \rangle Init$

Proof

. . . (T8)

Figure 7: Z-type product introduced by *Define-Z-type*

ends as soon as one of the communicating users hangs up. The other one is then immediately prompted by the exchange to issue a new call. If user A is unable to compose the first digit of the callee number within 30 seconds after having been prompted by the exchange, the line is seized.

3.2 Preliminary Specification Choices

A brief analysis shows that phones can be described as **state** machines. The requirements address mainly transitions between phone states. Therefore, a **state-based** specification style seems appropriate for specifying the phone network. Among the possible choices, the Z language ([Spiv89]) has been selected.

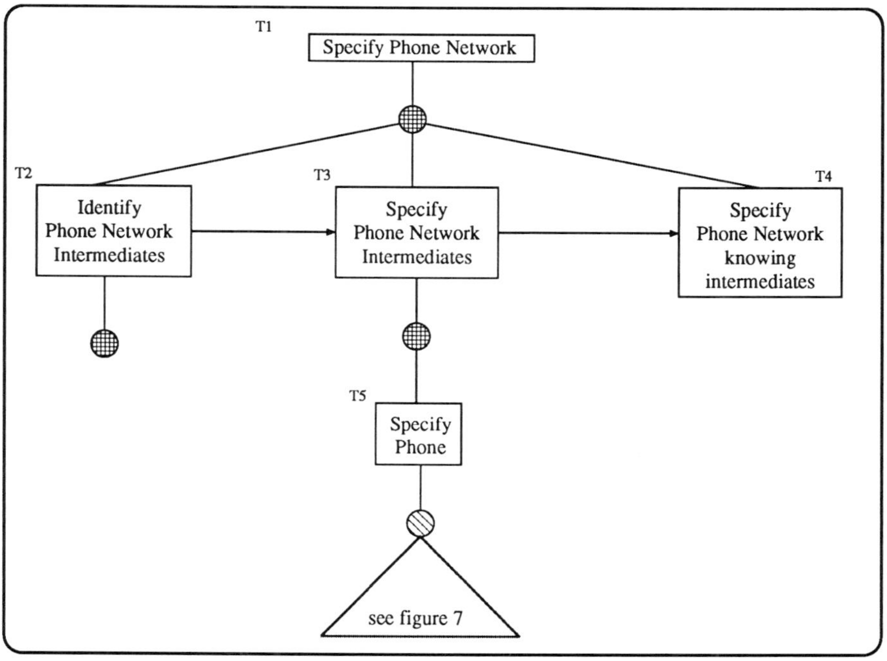

Figure 8: Workplan after the *Phone* specification

3.3 First Steps: orchestrating the development and specifying *Phone*

A phone network is a collection of interacting phones, the behaviours of which are restricted by the requirements. A Z specification should therefore address (i) the specification of a phone; (ii) the specification of a phone network as a collection of phones. Let us suppose having decomposed the specification of a phone network in subtasks (see figure 1), having identified and specified the *Phone* intermediate by instantiating the *Define-Z-Type* operator depicted in figure 6 to *Phone*. Figure 8 sketches out the top of the current workplan state and the associated product is listed below. The specification mainly describes phone states and some transitions between these states 10.

3.4 Specifying Phone Network

The remaining task to achieve is *Specifying PhoneNetwork knowing intermediates* (T4); as a phone network is composed of phones, the *Define-Z-Type* operator is used to reduce T4. This development operator has many specializations depending on the selected kind of structure. Hereafter we have chosen to model the phone network as a **set** of phones. Using *Define-Z-Set* refines the workplan as shown in figure 9. For simplicity, figure 9 shows only the part of the workplan rooted at T4.

Define-Z-Set is a **specialization** of *Define-Z-Type*; figure 9 distinghuishes the part of the workplan relevant to *Define-Z-Type* (recall figure 6) from the part refined by *Define-Z-Set*. A *Set* is indeed a type with a state and a list of operations. But here (i) the state of the *PhoneNetwork* is known (T48): it is the states of all the objects composing it; (ii) some operations (T56) like insertion, deletion are known but may need refinements (additional constraints on the objects that can be inserted, deleted, ...) while other operations are completely determined (e.g. membership); (iii) equality of members should be studied carefully (T55); (iv) promotion of phone operations at the *Phone Network* level should be provided (T64).

Step 48	**Selected Task**: T4 **Selected Operator**: Define-Z-Set **Rationale**: a phone network is a structure of phones **Workplan**: figure 9

Agenda 48:

Task	Precedence	Candidate Operators
T55	1	Define-Key
T62	2	Constrain-Assertion
T63	2	Constrain-Assertion
T66	2	Top-Down
T67	2	Top-Down
T69	2	Select-in-List
T70	2	Constrain-Assertion
T58	3	Iterate
T59	3	Iterate
T60	3	Iterate

Tasks *Define Equality of Members* (T55), *Constrain Container Operations* (T56) and *Promote Operations* (T64) are worth being studied and are detailed hereafter.

3.4.1 Equality of Phones

Equality of objects is needed when objects belong to structures (sets, lits, ...): one has frequently to check whether an object belongs to the structure or not. Task T55 aims at capturing this typical activity. Two types of equality can be considered: the **weak** and the **strong** equality.

- Two objects *a* and *b* are **weakly equal** (denoted $Same(a, b)$) iff $key(a) = key(b)$ where *key* is a function on the object states.
- In particular, if *key* is the identity function, both objects *a* and *b* are **strongly equal**, i.e. their states are equal (denoted $a = b$).

Many Z operations require weak equality as will be seen later. Looking at the current phone specification, one can observe they are described only by their states (idle, ringTone, connected, ...). Hence in the current specification, there are as many different phones as there are different states, i.e. nine! The definition of a phone must clearly be extended by providing a unique phone

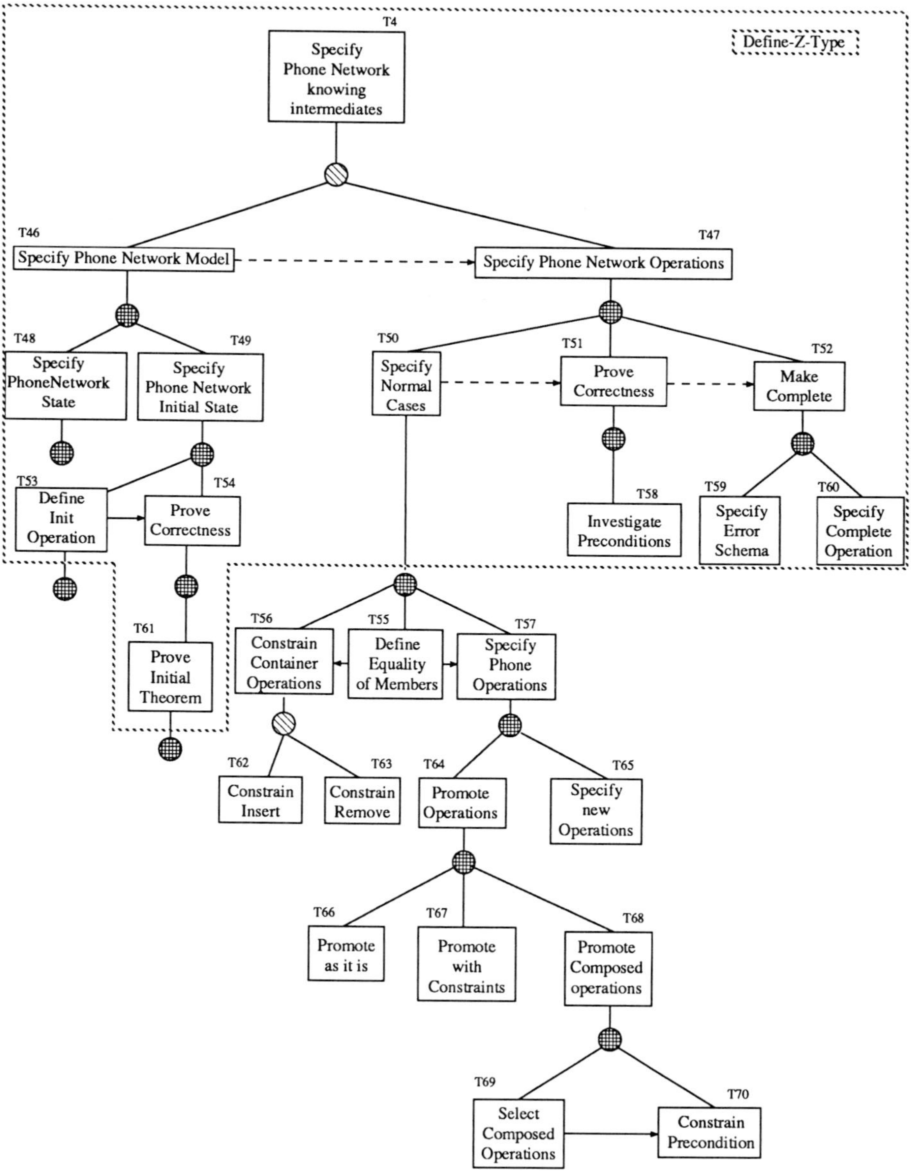

Figure 9: Partial workplan after application of Define-Z-Set operator

$$PhoneState \mathrel{\widehat=} idle \mid dialTone \mid waiting \mid seized \mid ringTone \mid ringing \mid busyTone \mid blockedTone \mid notAttributedTone$$

Phone

$State : PhoneState$

$$PhoneInitState \mathrel{\widehat=} idle$$

PhoneInit

$Phone'$

$state' \in PhoneInitState$

Initial Theorem

⊢ ∃ Phone' • PhoneInit

Proof

⊢ ∃ State': PhoneState • State' ∈ PhoneInitState
⊢ ∃ State': PhoneState • State' = idle
⊢ idle ∈ PhoneState
⊢ true

$PickUpFromIdle \mathrel{\widehat=} [\Delta Phone \mid State = idle \land State' = dialTone]$
$ConnectCaller \mathrel{\widehat=} [\Delta Phone \mid State = ringTone \land State' = connected]$
$ConnectCallee \mathrel{\widehat=} [\Delta Phone \mid State = ringing \land State' = connected]$
$HangUp1 \mathrel{\widehat=} [\Delta Phone \mid (State = dialTone \lor State = seized) \land State' = idle]$
$HangUp2 \mathrel{\widehat=} [\Delta Phone \mid (State = busyTone \mid blockedTone \mid notAttributeTone) \land State' = idle]$
$HangUp3 \mathrel{\widehat=} [\Delta Phone \mid State = ringTone \land State' = idle]$
$HangUp4 \mathrel{\widehat=} [\Delta Phone \mid State = ringing \land State' = idle]$
$HangUp5 \mathrel{\widehat=} [\Delta Phone \mid State = connected \land State' = idle]$
...

Figure 10: Product state

identification: the **phone number**. This identification will serve as the key for the weak equality. For these reasons, the *Define-Key* operator proposed by agenda 48 fails by lack of information. This failure triggers the operator *Extend-Type* on *Phone*, which allows the specifier to (i) extend the *Phone* state by defining the *PhoneNumber* feature; (ii) define a predicate *Same* that compares two phones and returns true if and only if both phones have the same *PhoneNumber* key; (iii) automatically provide an observer *GetPhoneNumber* returning a phone number and a modifier *UpdatePhoneNumber* that, given a phone number in input, replaces the old phone number with the new one; (iv) constrain existing *Phone* operations (*PickUpFromIdle, ...*) by specifying their effects on the *PhoneNumber* feature:

1. in case of a schema in which a ΞPhone clause appears, the operation schema is unaffected;
2. in case of a schema in which a ΔPhone clause appears, the default assertion $PhoneNumber' = PhoneNumber$ is proposed;
3. in case of a schema *OpSchema* in which a Phone' clause appears, the schema is updated by default as follows:

```
┌─ OpSchema ──────────────────────────────
│ Phone'
│ pn? : PhoneNumberType
│ ...
├──────────────
│ PhoneNumber' = pn?
│ ...
└─────────────────────────────────────────
```

The definition of the weak-equality for phones allows solving task T55 and generating the following *Phone Network* operations:

```
┌─ PhoneNetwork ──────────────────────────
│ Stock : ℙ Phone
├──────────────
│ ∀ p1, p2 ∈ Stock • ¬ Same(p1, p2)
└─────────────────────────────────────────
```

```
┌─ PhoneNetworkInit ──────────────────────
│ PhoneNetwork'
├──────────────
│ Stock' = ∅
└─────────────────────────────────────────
```

```
┌─ IsIn ──────────────────────────────────
│ ΞPhoneNetwork
│ p? : Phone
│ answer! : Boolean
├──────────────
│ answer! = (∃ q ∈ Stock • Same(p?, q))
└─────────────────────────────────────────
```

$$
\begin{array}{|l}
\multicolumn{1}{l}{\in} \\
\Xi PhoneNetwork \\
p? : Phone \\
answer! : Boolean \\
\hline
answer! = p? \in Stock \\
\hline
\end{array}
$$

IsIn uses the weak equality while ∈ uses the strong one.

3.4.2 Constrain Container Operations

The *Insert* and *Remove* operations proposed as standard operations on sets by the *Define-Z-Set* operator may need some refinement. In case of phones, a phone may not be inserted or removed in any state. The *Constrain-Assertion* operator applied to T62 and T63 allows the specifier to indicate that phones must be idle before insertion and deletion.

$$
\begin{array}{|l}
\multicolumn{1}{l}{Insert} \\
\Delta PhoneNetwork \\
p? : Phone \\
\hline
\neg\ \exists\, q \in Stock \bullet Same(p?, q) \\
p?.State = idle \\
Stock' = Stock \cup \{p?\} \\
\hline
\end{array}
$$

$$
\begin{array}{|l}
\multicolumn{1}{l}{Remove} \\
\Delta PhoneNetwork \\
p? : Phone \\
\hline
\exists\, q \in Stock \bullet Same(p?, q) \\
q.State = idle \\
Stock' = Stock \setminus \{q\} \\
\hline
\end{array}
$$

The weak equality is used for *Insert* and *Remove* because if the strong equality was used, we could have a phone network with two phones having the same phone number and differing from each other only by their states.

3.4.3 Promote Operations

Phone operations have been specified so far independently of their membership to a network. Operation promotions from *Phone* to *PhoneNetwork* mean to specify *Phone* operations as *PhoneNetwork* operations. This promotion can be direct, require additional constraints and/or composition of *Phone* operations. Here follows an example of a direct promotion.

$$\begin{array}{l}
\textit{NPickUp1} \\
\hline
\Delta \textit{PhoneNetwork} \\
\textit{PickUpFromIdle} \\
\hline
\theta \textit{Phone} \in \textit{Stock} \\
\textit{Stock}' = \textit{Stock} \setminus \{\theta \textit{Phone}\} \cup \{\theta \textit{Phone}'\}
\end{array}$$

In the following example, the promotion is constrained and two simultaneous *Phone* operations are composed: when a callee picks up his ringing phone, a call request must exist for him (constraint) and both the caller and the callee must be connected at the same time (composition):

$$\begin{array}{l}
\textit{NPickUpFromRinging} \\
\hline
\Delta \textit{PhoneNetwork} \\
\textit{ConnectCaller}[\textit{Phone1}/\textit{Phone}] \\
\textit{ConnectCaller}[\textit{Phone2}/\textit{Phone}] \\
\hline
\{\theta \textit{Phone1}, \theta \textit{Phone2}\} \subseteq \textit{Stock} \\
\textit{Stock}' = \textit{Stock} \setminus \{\theta \textit{Phone1}, \theta \textit{Phone2}\} \cup \{\theta \textit{Phone1}', \theta \textit{Phone2}'\} \\
(\theta \textit{Phone1} \mapsto \theta \textit{Phone2}) \in \textit{CallRequest}
\end{array}$$

The notation $S\ [Q/P]$ renames any occurrence of P in schema S with Q. The *CallRequest* relation referred in the schema requires a type extension similar to the type extension made on *Phone* for the introduction of the *PhoneNumber*, but this time, the extension is performed on the *PhoneNetwork*:

$$\begin{array}{l}
\textit{PhoneNetwork} \\
\hline
\textit{Stock} : \mathbb{P}\ \textit{Phone} \\
\textit{CallRequest} : \textit{Phone} \twoheadrightarrow\!\!\!\!\leftarrow \textit{Phone}
\end{array}$$

$$\begin{array}{l}
\textit{PhoneNetworkInit} \\
\hline
\textit{PhoneNetwork}' \\
\hline
\textit{Stock}' = \varnothing \\
\textit{CallRequest} = \varnothing
\end{array}$$

$$\begin{array}{l}
\textit{Insert} \\
\hline
\Delta \textit{PhoneNetwork} \\
p? : \textit{Phone} \\
\hline
\neg\ \exists\, q \in \textit{Stock} \bullet \textit{Same}(p?, q) \\
p?.\textit{State} = \textit{idle} \\
\textit{Stock}' = \textit{Stock} \cup \{p?\} \\
\textit{CallRequest}' = \textit{CallRequest}
\end{array}$$

$$\begin{array}{|l}
\multicolumn{1}{l}{\textit{Remove}} \\
\Delta PhoneNetwork \\
p? : Phone \\
\hline
\exists\, q \in Stock \bullet Same(p?, q) \\
p?.State = idle \\
Stock' = Stock \setminus \{p?\} \\
CallRequest' = CallRequest \\
\hline
\end{array}$$

$$\begin{array}{|l}
\multicolumn{1}{l}{\textit{CheckCallRequest}} \\
\Xi PhoneNetwork \\
p1?, p2? : Phone \\
ok! : Boolean \\
\hline
ok! = (p1? \mapsto p2?) \in CallRequest \\
\hline
\end{array}$$

$$\begin{array}{|l}
\multicolumn{1}{l}{\textit{InsertCallRequest}} \\
\Delta PhoneNetwork \\
p1?, p2? : Phone \\
\hline
p1?, p2? \in Stock \\
CallRequest' = CallRequest \oplus \{p1? \mapsto p2?\} \\
\hline
\end{array}$$

$$\begin{array}{|l}
\multicolumn{1}{l}{\textit{RemoveCallRequest}} \\
\Delta PhoneNetwork \\
p? : Phone \\
\hline
p? \in Stock \\
p? \in \mathrm{dom}\ CallRequest \\
CallRequest' = \{p?\} \lhd CallRequest \\
\hline
\end{array}$$

4 Conclusion

This paper has proposed a generic development process model and has described its instantiation to the development of Z specifications. The main benefits of the approach are:

- the use of workplans which enable the specifier to know what must be done next at any time of the development;
- the availibility of a library of generic operators which can be instantiated to specific languages; Z has been used in this paper but some of the operators have been instantiated to GLIDER [12] and PLUSS [18];
- the possibility of replaying a development, since each single step —even a dead end— is recorded with its decisions and rationale.

Developing specifications with the proposed approach requires an environment to manage the workplan, the current specification, and the links between them. A prototype of this environment has been developed. Operators arechosen via menus dynamically defined according to the current task type. Their application is interactive with information being gathered from the current development state and visualized.

Acknowledgment This work was partially supported by the ESPRIT2 Project ICARUS, number 2537. We are indebded to our colleagues of the project and in particular to A. Van Lamsweerde, P. Du Bois and E. Dubois for many discussions on the subject. Many thanks to J.-P. Finance, J.-P. Jacquot, N. Lévy and S. Vorobyov with whom this work is carried out. Thanks to P.-Y. Schobbens for his judicious comments on a preliminary version of the paper.

References

[1] E. Astesiano and M. Wirsing. An introduction to ASL. In *Proc. of the IFIP WG 2.1 Conf. on Program Specifications and Transformations*, 1986.

[2] J.-C. Carbonell. *DERIVATIONAL ANALOGY: A Theory of Reconstructive Problem Solving and Expertise Acquisition*, volume 2. Machine Learning, An Artificial Intelligence Approach, 1986. Chap. 14.

[3] J. Conklin and M. Begeman. Gibis : A hypertext tool for exploratory policy discussion. *ACM Transaction on Office Information System*, 6(4):303–331, October 1988.

[4] V. Donzeau-Gouge, B. Lang, and Mélèse B. Practical applications of a syntax directed program manipulation environment. In I.E.E.E., editor, *7 th ICSE*, pages 346–354, Orlando, 1984.

[5] M.S. Feather. Constructing specification by combining parallel elaborations. In *Transactions on Software Engineering*, pages 198–208. I.E.E.E., 1989. 15(2).

[6] K. Futatsugi, JA. Goguen, JP. Jouannaud, and J. Meseguer. Principles of OBJ2. In *Proceedings of the 12th ACM Symposium on Principles Of Programmingg Languages*, pages 51–60, 1987.

[7] M.-C. Gaudel. Structuring and modularizing algebraic specifications: the PLUSS specification language, evolutions and perspectives. In *Proc. 9th Annual Symp. on Theoretical Aspects of Computer Science (STACS'92)*, pages 3–18. LNCS 557, 1992.

[8] Anna Gram. *Raisonner pour Programmer*. Dunod, 1986.

[9] I. Hayes. VDM and Z: A comparative case study. *Formal Aspects of Computing*, 4:76–99, 1992.

[10] W.L. Johnson and MS. Feather. Building an evolution transformation library. In *Proc. 12th ICSE*, pages 238–248, Nice, France, 1990.

[11] C.B. Jones. *Systematic Software Development using VDM*. Prentice Hall, 1986.

[12] N. Levy. Definition of Add_a_Component, a specification construction process operator. Technical Report ForSem-005-R, ICARUS, 1990.

[13] N.-J. Nilsson. *Problem Solving Methods in Artificial Intelligence.* Computer Sciences Series. Mac Graw-Hill, 1971.

[14] C. Potts. A generic model for representing design models. In *Proc. ICSE 11*. I.E.E.E., 1989.

[15] W. Scherlis and D. Scott. First steps toward inferential programming. In *IFIP Congress Proc.*, 1983.

[16] M. Sintzoff. Software engineering formalization. In *3rd conference on software Engineering*, pages 33–39, Versailles, AFCET, 1986.

[17] J. Souquières. Aides au développement de spécifications. Thèse d'ètat, CRIN, Janvier 1993. Université de Nancy 1.

[18] J. Souquières and N. Lévy. Description of the specification development. In *Proc. of RE'93, January 1993*, San Diego(CA), 1993.

[19] J. Souquières and S. Vorobyov. A Generic Specification Development Model. Rapport technique du CRIN 92-R-165, Centre de Recherche en Informatique de Nancy, October 1992.

[20] J.-M. Spivey. *The Z Notation.* Prentice Hall, 1989.

[21] D.S. Wile. Program developments : Formal explanation of implementations. *Communication of the ACM*, 26(11):902–911, 1983.

8.

REUSE II

Information System Development Process (A-30)
N. Prakash, C. Rolland and B. Pernici (Editors)
Elsevier Science Publishers B.V. (North–Holland)

© 1993 IFIP. All rights reserved.

Reusing Process Specifications

S. Castano V. De Antonellis

Politecnico di Milano
Dipartimento di Elettronica e Informazione
Piazza Leonardo da Vinci 32 - 20133 Milano
Email: {castano, deantone}@ipmel2.elet.polimi.it
Fax: +39-2-23993411
Tel.: +39-2-23993651

ABSTRACT

A methodological approach to the reuse of process behavior specifications is presented, from a design-for-reuse perspective. More precisely, we present modeling and methodological tools for preparing reusable behavioral components to be exploited for designing dynamic specifications of applications not from scratch, but tailoring and adapting existing components. Reusable behavioral components are defined as generic process classes with associated meta-process classes providing guidelines for reuse in a given application.

1. INTRODUCTION

Object-oriented models provide the application designers with a uniform conceptual framework for defining the knowledge of interest, with the possibility of incapsulating directly in the specification, the allowed operations, without the traditional separation of concern between modeling static and dynamic aspects [4, 8, 25, 9]. The main difficulty with using an object-oriented approach for conceptual modeling is the complexity of specifying in a uniform and integrated way the single object behavior, the coordinated behavior of different objects cooperating in a common process, and the related behavioral constraints and rules. To overcome this difficulty, novel approaches have been proposed for extending object-oriented conceptual models by introducing conceptual abstractions to specify the object behavior and the rules for communication and cooperation in common processes [11, 12, 13, 18].

In this paper we address the problem of reusing conceptual object behavior specifications. Reusability of conceptual specifications can facilitate both effective development of good quality applications by exploiting existing validated components, and easy re-development of applications by stressing and promoting a modular design approach [3,1,24,2]. In fact, it. Reusability can be considered from two different perspectives. According to a *design-by-reuse* perspective, an application can be obtained by tailoring existing components extracted from an available repository. According to a *design-for-reuse* perspective, a repository must be populated with reusable components, properly defined to be exploitable for designing new applications not from scratch. Integrated environments have been developed to support the design-by-reuse approach, where a set of tools assist the application developer during both the selection of the reusable components that best match the needs of the application at hand, and the tailoring and the adaptation of the selected components [15, 20, 14, 21]. Models and methods to support the development of reusable components, according to a *design-for-reuse* strategy, have been defined for both software components [16, 19, Maid92] and conceptual specifications [5, 6, 7]. Specifically, in this area, we have proposed methods and techniques for reusing static specifications of an application, that is, objects and their structural properties, providing the application designers with a set of generic classes that can be personalized and adapted for being reused in different contexts and applications. But, in order to gain true reusability of object-oriented specifications, reusable components abstracting not only the static features of an application, but also the dynamic ones, are needed. To this purpose, in the present paper, we extend our approach with the definition of reusable behavioral components that can be exploited for designing new dynamic specifications not from scratch. Reusable behavioral components are defined as *generic process classes* and associated *meta-process classes*, providing guidelines for reuse in a given application. A generic process class is extracted from a set of similar application-dependent process specifications, factoring out their common behavior. A meta-process class is defined to guide the reuse of a generic process class, suggesting how to specialize and adapt its behavior in a given application.

The paper is organized in the following way. In Sect. 2 the main issues related to conceptual modeling according to the object-oriented paradigm are discussed and a model for representing cooperation and communication behavior is presented. Sect. 3 illustrates the methodological approach to reuse object-oriented specifications. In Sect. 4 our concluding remarks are given.

2. CONCEPTUAL MODELING

The conceptual design phase of the development lifecycle is concerned with the formal description of the requirements of the application to be modeled, using a formal, well suited conceptual model [4]. In this paper we consider the F-ORM (Functionality in Objects with Roles Model) object-oriented model [11, 12, 13].

The conceptual elementary unit in F-ORM is the class. A class describes the characteristics common to the set of objects defined as its instances. A class is defined by specifying its name and a set of role types. Role types are used to partition different behaviors of an object during its lifetime. An object can play different roles at different times and may also play more than one role at the same time. Every class has a base role type, which describes properties common to all the role types and rules regulating the transitions from one role to another according to the object lifecycle.

To ease the task of describing the dynamic aspects of an application, two distinct classes are predefined: *resource class* and *process class*. Resource classes define characteristics of agents and information; the concept of role is used to model the different behaviors which an object can have in its life-cycle according to the execution of procedures. Process classes are defined to describe interactions between different resources in common procedures. Here, the concept of role is used to model the communication/cooperation patterns and rules for the involved resources.

As an example of resource class, in Fig.1, a skeleton structure of a conference class is given, describing its properties and lifecycle. Lifecycle evolution is driven by the processes the resource takes part to and is described by the rules defined in the base-role. For example, when an instance of conference is created, it can be involved in the process of conference definition, and only when this process is completed the conference can be publicized. With respect to each process, a resource exhibits a defined behavior determined by the set of messages that it can receive/send in that process.

In a process class, the role types are used to precisely describe, in terms of message exchange modalities and constraints, the behavior of the resources involved in the accomplishment of a procedure. As an example, let us consider the Conference-Publicity process class, which is composed of several roles corresponding to the involved resources, for example, ProgramCommitteeChair, ProgramCommitteeMember, Secretary, Conference, and Call-for-paper. In Fig.2 a skeleton sample of the process class is shown. For the Secretary role, rules are defined in which, to each possible message for the Secretary in this process, a state transition is associated, regulating the behavior of the secretary. The state transitions specify how the secretary behaves in publicizing the conference.

To provide a graphical representation of process classes pointing out the involved resources and their communication patterns, Communication Diagrams have been defined. A Communication Diagram (CD) is a bipartite graph <R,C;M>, where R is the set of the involved resources (graphically represented by ovals), C is the set of communication channels between the resources (graphically represented by semicircles), and M is a correspondence between R and C to represent the set of exchanged messages (graphically represented by edges). Edges are labeled, directed lines between nodes, representing messages and their direction. To each message m, sent by a resource (channel) node to a channel (resource) node, a signature s is associated:

$$s = < mn, (<mp_1, d_1>,..., <mp_n, d_n>) >$$

where mn is the name of the message, and $(<mp_1, d_1>,..., <mp_n, d_n>)$ is the list of the parameters associated to the message, with the corresponding domains, d_k, k=1..n. Parameters represent sent or received values between nodes.

```
resource class (
    CONFERENCE,
    <base-role,
            properties={  (title, string),
                          (date, date),
                          (place, string),
                          (topics, {string}),
                          (sponsors, string),
                          },
               rules={ */precedence relations among the possible roles, that is, lifecycle definition/*
                          msg(->create-object)
                           ⇒ msg (<-allow-role(conference-definition)),
                          msg(-> conference-definition completed)
                           ⇒ msg (<-allow-role(conference-publicity)),
                          ...
                          }
    >,
    <conference-definition,
            messages={  */possible messages within the specified process/*
            <define-conference(c)>, ...
                          },
    >,
    <conference-publicity,
            messages= { < call_for_paper-ready>, <send-call-for-papers(c)>, ...
                          },
    >,      ...
                 )
```

Fig.1 Resource class CONFERENCE

```
process class (
    Conference-Publicity,
    <base-role,
            properties= {  ...
                          },
               rules={  */precedence relations between the possible roles, that is,
                             global rules on the cooperation between resources and on the
                             communication sequence/*
                          }
    >,
    <secretary,
               rules={  */precedence relations between the possible messages for
                          the secretary in this process/*
                          msg(call_for_paper-ready(cfp:Call-for-paper)),
                              state (starting) ⇒ state (cfp-received),
                          msg(send-call-for-paper(cfp:Call-for-paper)),
                              state (cfp-received) ⇒ state (call_for_paper-sent)
                          msg(publicized(cfp:Call-for-paper)),
                              state (call_for_paper-sent) ⇒ state (terminated)
               }
    >,
    ...
    )
```

Fig.2 The process class Conference-Publicity

Communication channels have been introduced for modeling the following cases:

- Multiple senders of a message. In this case, all the senders must synchronize themselves for sending the message. As many edges as the total number of objects senders are incoming into the communication channel, for expressing the synchronization. Let $c \in C$ be a communication channel, and $M_c=\{m_1, ..., m_t\}$ the set of incoming messages from the senders. All the incoming messages of c have the same signature, that is,

$$\forall\ m_i, m_k \in M_c,\ s_i = s_k \quad i \neq k$$

An example is the communication channel between the ProgramCommitteeChair and the ProgramCommitteeMember of the Conference-Publicity process (see Fig.3 of the Appendix), as they have to synchronize themselves for preparing the call for paper of the conference.

- Multiple receivers of a message. In this case, the same message has to be sent to multiple receivers, and as many edges as the total number of receivers are outgoing from the communication channel. Let $c \in C$ be a communication channel, and $\underline{M}_c=\{m_1, ..., m_q\}$ the set of outgoing messages to the receivers. All the outgoing messages of c have the same signature, that is,

$$\forall\ m_j, m_l \in \underline{M}_c,\ s_j = s_l \quad j \neq l$$

For a communication channel c, the incoming messages and the outgoing messages can have the same signature. The complete CDs for the Conference-Publicity is shown in Fig. 3.

3. REUSE OF CONCEPTUAL SPECIFICATIONS

In this section, we present a methodology for defining reusable *application-independent* specifications starting from existing *application-dependent* specifications. The design of reusable specifications is based on the following methodological phases:

- classification of existing conceptual schemas;
- design of reusable resources;
- design of reusable processes.

3.1. Classification of conceptual schemas

Reusable components are defined by abstracting common properties and behavior from different existing conceptual specifications. To facilitate the definition of reusable components, we propose the definition of a Library (or repository) of conceptual schemas, where schemas belonging to one or more applications, in one or several domains are properly classified and arranged in similarity cluster hierarchies, according to the domain they belong to [5, 6]. The classification model is based on indexing criteria and clustering techniques, derived from the Information Retrieval area [22]. Schemas are indexed by means of a set of Schema Descriptors, selected among the names associated to the objects of the schema, for their capability of describing the schema subject [10].

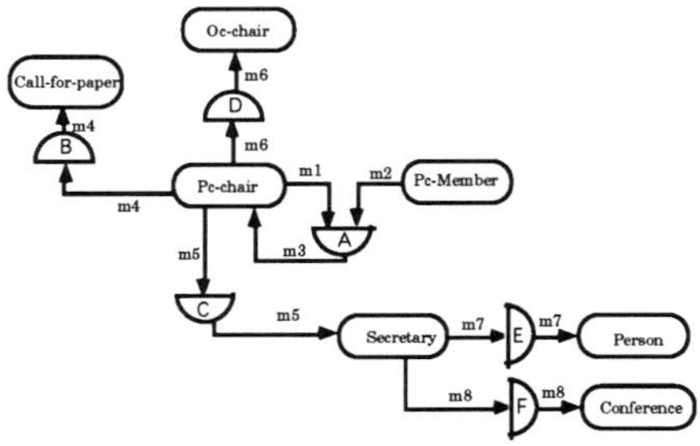

Legend
m1=m2=m3= prepare-call_for_paper(cfp:Call-for-paper)
m4= create-object
m5=call_for_paper-ready(cfp:Call-for-paper)
m6=send-letter(l:letter)
m7= send-call_for_paper(cfp:Call-for-paper)
m8= publicized(cfp:Call-for-paper)

Coordination constraints
c1. B AFTER A
c2. C AFTER B
c3. D AFTER B
c4. E AFTER C
c5. F AFTER E

Fig.3 Communication Diagram for the Conference-Publicity process class

The procedure for the extraction of the Schema Descriptors is illustrated in [7]. In brief, it is based on the assignment of a weight to the schema objects, on the basis of a combined criterion, that takes into account the constructs of the model used for defining the conceptual schema (e.g., object properties, is-a hierarchies, relationships). Weighted objects that exceed an established threshold become Schema Descriptors. Similarity between a pair of schemas is computed on the basis of the number of Schema Descriptors they share, with the help of a dictionary of synonyms. Schemas of a given domain whose similarity exceeds a predefined threshold are arranged inside the same cluster in the Library, using the single link clustering technique [22]. A detailed description of the classification process can be found in [5, 6, 7].

The clustering of similar schemas facilitates the identification of reusable components, in that in each cluster we find similar schemas and we can easily recognize and extract common properties and behavior.

3.2. Definition of reusable resources

Reusable resources are defined as *generic resource classes* and associated *meta-resource classes*, providing guidelines for their reuse. Generic resources are extracted by analyzing the resource classes corresponding to the Schema Descriptors of schemas belonging to a given cluster of the Library. Extraction is based on pairwise comparisons between the identified resource classes, and on the computation of the level of semantic affinity between them.

Semantic affinity is defined in terms of a set of affinity coefficients, that take into account common properties of the objects (Structural Affinity), and common context (i.e., is-a hierarchies and relationships) in which the objects are placed in their respective schemas (Hierarchy Affinity and Adjacency Affinity). The affinity coefficients are computed using the Dice's coefficient [19]:

$$\frac{2D}{A+B}$$

where D is the number of common elements (i.e., properties, ascendants and descendants objects, related objects) of a pair of objects having a number A and B of elements, respectively. Each coefficient can assume values between 0 and 1. The value 0 represents a situation of absence of affinity (no commonalities exist between the considered objects for that coefficient), while the value 1 represents a situation of identity (considered objects are equally defined in both schemas, with respect to the coefficient). Intermediate values describe situations of more or less affinity, corresponding to more or less commonalities (i.e., equal structural features) between the objects in their respective schemas.

Given two classes C_1, C_2, for them all the computed values are summarized to determine the Global Affinity, $GA(C_1,C_2)$, of C_1, C_2, that is,

$$GA(C_1,C_2) = SA(C_1,C_2) + HA(C_1,C_2) + AA(C_1,C_2)$$

where the summed terms indicates the Structural Affinity, the Hierarchy Affinity and the Adjacency Affinity coefficients of C_1, C_2, respectively.

A threshold value is defined for a given cluster, and only the class pairs whose Global Affinity exceeds the threshold are classified and grouped into what we call *affinity sets*, using the complete-link clustering technique [22]. In general, several disjoint *affinity sets* are automatically generated, partitioning the selected class pairs according to their level of semantic affinity. More formally, an affinity set AS includes the most tightly linked classes among those selected, according to their global affinity coefficients, that is,

$$AS = \{ C_i, C_j \in Cl \mid GA(C_i,C_j) \geq t \}$$

where t indicates the established threshold, and Cl the examined cluster.

The affinity sets generated for a cluster of the Library are then proposed to the application engineer who evaluates the opportunity of defining the corresponding generic classes, analyzing the meaning and the role of each object included in the affinity set [17]. For each affinity set AS_i that has passed the semantic analysis, the corresponding generic resource class is defined, factoring out the properties common to all the objects C_j belonging to AS_i.

3.2.1. Abstraction of generic resource classes

In the following, the process of abstraction of the common properties into the corresponding generic class is defined.

According to the object-oriented paradigm, objects can be complex, i.e., their properties can refer to other objects, or can have a complex domain, defined as a set/list of simple domains. Let C and C' two classes belonging to the same affinity set AS. They can have the following properties:

Class C		**Class C'**	
properties	p_1, d_1	**properties**	p'_1, d'_1
	....		....
	p_n, d_n		p'_m, d'_m

where $m \neq n$.

The domain of C and C', d_C and $d_{C'}$ respectively, are defined as the cartesian product of the domains of their properties, that is:

$$d_C = d_1 \times ... \times d_n$$

$$d_{C'} = d'_1 \times ... \times d'_m$$

The abstraction mapping of two domains (d, d') is a function ϕ defined as follows:

$$\varphi\,(d, d') =_{def} \textbf{if}\ d, d' \text{ predefined scalar domains } \textbf{then}\ d \cap d' \\ \textbf{else}\ \ \textbf{if}\ d \in AS_i \wedge d' \in AS_i\ \textbf{then}\ \underline{d} \\ \textbf{else}\ \bot$$

where $\underline{d}$ is the name associated to $d \in AS_i$, and the symbol $\bot$ stands, from now on, for 'undefined'.

Let be Syn a relation, $Syn \subseteq Names \times Names$, where Syn(n, n') holds iff n and n' are synonyms. Let $P = \{pn'' \mid Syn(pn, pn'') \wedge Syn(pn', pn'')\}$. The abstraction mapping of two property names is a function ϕ defined as follows:

$$\varphi\,(pn, pn') =_{def} \textbf{if}\ Syn(pn, pn')\ \textbf{then}\ pn \\ \textbf{else}\ \ \textbf{if}\ P \neq \varnothing\ \textbf{then}\ pn'' \\ \textbf{else}\ \bot$$

where pn" is any element belonging to P. The choice of pn" is lead to the application engineer, who can make use of a set of naming suggestions, as described in [5].

The abstraction mapping of two properties (p, p') of C and C', respectively, with p=(pn, d) and p'=(pn', d') is a function ϕ defined as follows:

$$\varphi\,(p, p') =_{def} \textbf{if}\ (\ \underline{d} = \varphi\,(d, d') \wedge \underline{pn} = \varphi\,(pn, pn')\ )\ \textbf{then}\ (\underline{pn}, \underline{d})\ \textbf{else}\ \bot$$

Let $p_{ij} = (pn_{ij}, d_{ij})$ be a property of a resource class C_j belonging to the affinity set AS_i. The generic class, GC_i, abstraction of all the classes C_j belonging to the affinity set AS_i, is composed of all the properties which can be abstracted from all the classes of the affinity set, that is:

$$GC_i = \{ \underline{p} = (\underline{pn}, \underline{d}) \mid \forall C_j, C_k \in AS_i, \exists pn_{ij}, pn'_{ik}, \underline{pn} = \varphi(pn_{ij}, pn'_{ik}) \wedge \exists d_{ij}, d'_{ik}, \underline{d} = \varphi(d_{ij}, d'_{ik}) \}$$

and its domain, d_{GC_i}, is defined as the cartesian product:

$$d_{GC_i} = \underline{d}_1 \times \ldots \times \underline{d}_l$$

of the domains $\underline{d}_1, \ldots, \underline{d}_l$ corresponding to the properties of GC_i.

The abstraction mapping of two classes C and C' is a function ϕ defined as follows:

$$\varphi(C, C') =_{def} \textbf{if } (C \in AS_i \wedge C' \in AS_i) \textbf{ then } GC_i \textbf{ else } \perp$$

Suppose to analyze in the Education domain, the conceptual specifications for the organization of a conference and the preparation of a seminar. From the computed affinity sets:

AS1={Call-for-Paper, Brochure}, AS2= {Pc-chair, Organizer}, AS3= {Conference, Seminar}

we could obtain the following abstractions:

ϕ(Call-for-Paper, Brochure) = Meeting-Document

ϕ(Pc-chair, Organizer) = Meeting-Organizer

ϕ(Conference, Seminar) = Meeting

Generic resource classes have associated meta-resource classes describing how the generic resource can be reused and tailored. Reuse suggestions are given in form of properties in the meta-resource class. A "meta-of" link connects the meta-resource class with the corresponding generic resource class. Reuse suggestions incorporate information concerning the most common design choices, according to the design history information of the clustered schemas [23].

3.3. Definition of reusable processes

As for the resources, reusable processes are defined as generic process classes and associated meta-process classes, providing guidelines for their reuse. A generic process class is defined abstracting the behavior commonalities from a set of behavior-equivalent processes. Behavioral equivalence (defined in the following) exists between processes in different schemas if they behave in the same or similar way. Behavioral equivalence between processes in different schemas is computed taking into consideration also the semantic affinity of the involved resources.

Starting from the set of generic resource classes extracted from a given cluster, the application engineer identifies a *key resource*, that, together with its associated affinity set, is used as a reference point for initiating the design of the reusable processes for that cluster. The identification can be based on criteria concerning, for example, the importance and the representativeness of the resource inside the cluster, the number of resources entering in the abstraction and constituting the affinity set, the number of schemas in which such a resource can be reused. For each resource class belonging to the affinity set of the key resource, the processes where they are involved are listed in the corresponding class specification, as role names. Such processes become candidates for extracting the reusable processes for that domain.

According to this approach, for a given domain, a set of key generic resources and their related generic processes are defined. The same generic processes could be defined starting from generic resources different from the key resource. A key resource is selected only for avoiding repeated comparisons of the same processes involving several resources and possible duplications of generic processes.

3.3.1. Generic process classes and meta-process classes

The abstraction of generic process classes and the definition of the associated meta-process classes providing guidelines for their reuse are described.

A generic process is defined abstracting the commonalities of a set of candidate processes that are proved to be equivalent with respect to their behavior. To determine process behavioral equivalence, we are interested in evidencing how the processes evolve with respect to the message exchanges among the involved resources. To this purpose, a set of *coordination constraints* on the message exchanges are defined for a process, expressing the correct order of the communications among the involved resources, and, consequently, the process behavior. Equivalence of different processes is then studied on the basis of the involved resources, exchanged messages and message constraints. In the following, the steps for defining generic process classes are illustrated.

Coordination constraint definition.

Coordination constraints are defined for a process to specify the correct order of the message exchanges among the involved resources. Using the Communication Diagrams for representing process classes, coordination constraints are associated to the communication channels. They can be easily derived from the process class specification. In fact, with the F-ORM model, the base-role of the process class gives information about the precedence relations among roles, and contains global rules on the cooperation between resources and on the communication sequence. The coordination constraints for the Conference-Publicity process class are shown in Fig.3.

In general, coordination constraints are defined for specifying precedence and synchronization relationships between messages sent by different resources. More precisely, the precedence constraint has the form:

$$< c_1 \text{ AFTER } c_2 >$$

where c_1 and c_2 are communication channels, and specifies that the

communication taking place in c_1 must precede the communication taking place in c_2, i.e., the incoming message in c_2 is sent after the outgoing message from c_1 has been received. An example is the constraint B AFTER A, specifying that the creation of the call-for-paper (message m4) can happen only after the its contents have been decided by the program committee (message m3).
The synchronization constraint has the form:

<c_1 AND c_2>

and expresses the fact that both the communications in c_1 and c_2 must be occurred before other communications can take place.
If no constraints are specified, the communications are assumed to be concurrent.
Information about cooperation of multiple agents are already captured by means of the communication channels, and are expressed in the extended signature of a message (by specifying multiple senders for that message).
Constraints can be combined to express more complex requirement. For example, the constraint s4 of the Seminar-Publicity process class, shown in Fig.4, states that the secretary notifies the completion of the publicity procedure to the seminar class, after the mailing of both the brochure, and the speaker letter (it combines precedence and synchronization constraints).

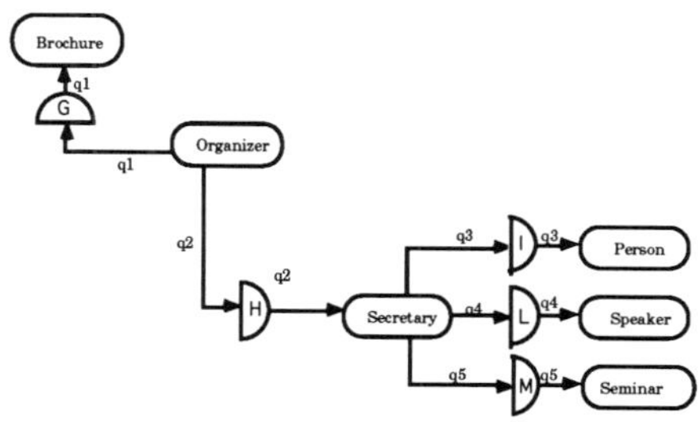

Legend
q1= create-object
q2= brochure-ready(b:Brochure)
q3= send-brochure(b:Brochure)
q4= send-notification(l:letter)
q5= publicized(b:Brochure)

Coordination constraints
```
s1. H AFTER G
s2. I AFTER H
s3. L AFTER H
s4. M AFTER (I AND L)
```

Fig.4 Communication Diagram for the Seminar-Publicity process class

Generic message definition.

In order to define generic processes, we are interested in distinguish the messages inside a process, with respect to the sender, the receiver, and the parameter list they have. An *extended signature* of the message is associated to each message, with the following format:

$$es = < mn, <s, (<mp_1, d_1>,..., <mp_n, d_n>), r >$$

where, in addition, the sender(s) and the receiver(s) of the message are specified. In case of multiple senders (receivers), the corresponding fields of the extended signature contain a list of elements. Using extended signatures, it is possible to identify messages of different processes that are compatible, and use them for the generic message definition. More precisely, given two extended signatures related to the messages m and m', es =(mn, <s, mp, r>) and es'= (mn', <s', mp', r'>), the corresponding messages are *compatible* if the following conditions are satisfied:

1. $\exists\ GC_k \mid \varphi\ (s_i, s_j') = GC_k\ ,\ s_i \in s,\ s_j' \in s'$
   Two messages are compatible with respect to their senders if a generic class has been defined for them. In case of multiple senders, it is sufficient that a generic class exists for at least one of them in each message.

2. $\exists\ GC_k \mid \varphi\ (r_i, r_j') = GC_k,\ r_i \in r,\ r_j' \in r'$
   Two messages are compatible with respect to their receivers if a generic class has been defined for them. In case of multiple receivers, it is sufficient that a generic class exists for at least one of them in each message.

3. $\forall\ mp_i \in mp,\ \forall\ mp_j' \in mp',\ \exists\ GC_k \mid GC_k = \varphi\ (d_i, d_j')$
   Two messages are compatible with respect to their parameters, if they have, in general, the same number of parameters and if they are defined on domains for which a generic class is defined.

For instance, with reference to the CDs in Figg.3 and 4, let us consider the messages m4 and q1. They extended signatures are:
es_{m4}= (create-object, <Pc-chair, ø, Call-for-Paper>) and es_{q1}= (create-object, <Organizer, ø, Brochure>)
where the symbol ø is used in case of absence of parameters for a message. According to the mapping ϕ defined in the previous section, they are compatible, since:

ϕ(Call-for-paper, Brochure) = Meeting-Document

ϕ(Pc-chair, Organizer) = Meeting-Organizer

Pairs of compatible messages can be automatically identified, and proposed to the application engineer. Interactive approach is preferable, as particular situations can be managed in a more flexible way. For example, it can happen that a message in a process can be compatible with more than one message in the other process. In this case, the application engineer can select the most significant pair, with respect to the overall semantics of the

processes, and propose such a pair for the definition of the corresponding generic message. It other cases, the application engineer can force the compatibility of two messages, though they do not have the same number of parameters.
Given a pair of compatible messages, the corresponding generic message is obtained by considering the extended signature of one message of the pairs, and by replacing the fields using the following rules:

- <u>name</u>: the name is selected by the application engineer, with respect to the names of the compatible messages, and according to their semantics and role in the respective processes. Suggestions about the naming of generic components are given in [7].
- <u>sender</u> (<u>receiver</u>): the sender (receiver) is the generic class of the senders (receivers). In case of multiple senders (receivers), this field contains the generic classes of the senders (receivers) for which the function ϕ is defined;
- <u>parameter(s)</u>: it is (they are) defined on the generic domain. Considerations described for message names hold for parameter names too.

With reference to the messages m4 and q1, the corresponding generic message is defined as follows:

p1= create-object (Meeting-Organizer, ø, Meeting-Document)

In the same way, the generic messages:

p2=meeting_document-ready(Meeting-Organizer, md:Meeting-Document, Secretary)
p3= send-meeting_document(Secretary, md:Meeting-Document, Person)
p4= publicized(Secretary, md:Meeting-Document, Meeting)

are defined for the pairs (m5, q2), (m7, q3), (m8, q5), respectively. The remaining message pairs are not compatible, and no generic message is defined.

Generic process class definition.

Once the generic messages are defined, the resource classes for the generic process class are to be identified. Starting from the resource classes of the considered process classes, only the resource classes for which the function ϕ is defined are included in the corresponding generic process class. More precisely, let be R={C_1, ..., C_m} and R'={C'_1, ..., C'_n} the set of resource classes of the considered process classes P and P', respectively. The corresponding generic process class <u>P</u> is defined with the resource class set <u>R</u>={GC_1, ..., GC_q}, where:

$$\forall\, GC_i \in \underline{R},\ \exists\, C_i \in R, C_j \in R' \mid GC_i = \phi\,(C_i, C_j)$$

With reference to the Conference-Publicity and Seminar-Publicity process classes, and to the mapping ϕ on the resource classes, the Meeting-Publicity generic process class is defined with Meeting, Meeting-Organizer, Meeting-document, Secretary and Person resource classes.
Once the generic resource classes are defined too, we are interested in identifying also the coordination constraints that continue to hold, if any, in the generic process class. In general, two coordination constraints in

different processes are considered compatible if:
i) they involve compatible messages, i.e., if all the specified the communication channels involve compatible messages, and
ii) if they are of the same type (e.g., after, and).
With reference to the Conference-Publicity and Seminar-Publicity process classes, the pairs of constraints that result compatible are the following:

(c2, s1)

(c4, s2)

They can be abstracted also in the corresponding generic process class, meaning that, in publicizing a meeting, in general, a meeting organizer notifies the availability of the meeting document to the secretary after its creation, and that the secretary can mail the meeting document to the interested people after the reception of the meeting organizer notification. Remaining constraints are not considered compatible. For example, the constraints c5 and s4, while involving some compatible messages, are not considered compatible, since they have different types, and some other non compatible messages.
The CD for the resulting Meeting-Publicity generic process class is shown in Fig.5.
More in general, we can distinguish between the following types of equivalence between process classes:

- *Weak equivalence*
  In this case, only the communication messages among resource classes are specified, but no coordination constraints are given. This means that, starting from the compared processes, no common order on message exchanges can be identified, and the order is left open in the corresponding generic process class.

- *Strong equivalence*
  In this case, coordination constraints specifying common sequences are identified in the compared process classes, and they are abstracted in the corresponding generic process class. In this case more information is given to the application designer.

To each generic process class a meta-process class has to be finally associated, containing the guidelines for specializing and completing generic processes, according to particular needs of the application at hand. In particular, a meta-process class provides:
- suggestions about composition of the generic process with other processes, defining specific causal dependencies;
- suggestions about the ways of either enriching/completing the set of generic coordination constraints, with constraints typical of the application at hand;
- suggestions about possible specializations of the generic resources, according to the target application context.

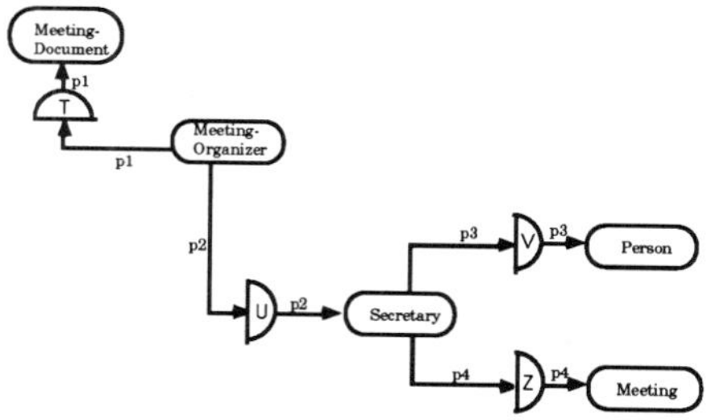

Legenda
p1= create-object
p2=meeting_document-ready(md:Meeting-Document)
p3= send-meeting_document(md:Meeting-Document)
p4= publicized(md:Meeting-Document)

Coordination constraints
```
m1. U AFTER T
m2. V AFTER U
```

Fig.5 Communication Diagram for the Meeting-Publicity generic process class

4. CONCLUDING REMARKS

In this paper the main issues concerning reuse of process specifications have been described and a methodological approach has been presented. Reuse of specifications is considered a fruitful technique to reduce the complexity and difficulty of application development. The advantage of the proposed approach is that the structure and the behavior of an application can be considered in an integrated way and reusable components can be exploited in the design process.

The proposed approach supports the application engineer in the analysis of existing conceptual schemas and in the extraction of reusable components. Major contributions of the approach consist in the definition of techniques for the automatic indexing of schemas and their clustering according to similarity levels, and in the development of models and methods for the extraction and definition of reusable structural and behavioral components. Further research work is needed to complete the approach for the aspects related to provide automatic support in classifying generic classes and meta-classes in the Library, as already done for application schemas.

Acknowledgements

Part of this work has been supported by the F^3 Esprit Project N.6612, by the Italian National Research Council Project "Sistemi Informatici e Calcolo Parallelo", L.R.C. INFOKIT, and by MURST 40%.

REFERENCES

[1] ACM Issue on Object-Oriented Design, September 1990

[2] V.R. Basili, G. Caldiera, G. Cantone, "A Reference Architecture for the Component Factory", ACM TOSEM, Vol.1, N.1, January 1992, pp. 53-80

[3] T.J. Biggerstaff, A.J. Perlins (eds.), *Software Reusability- Concepts and Models*, vol.I, ACM Press, Addison-Wesley, 1990

[4] G. Booch, *Object-Oriented Design*, Benjamin Cummings, 1991

[5] S.Castano, V. DeAntonellis, B. Zonta, "Classifying and Reusing Conceptual Schemas", *in Proc. of the Int. Conf. on the Entity-Relationship Approach*, Karlsruhe, LNCS n.645, Springer Verlag, October 1992, pp.121-138

[6] S.Castano, V.DeAntonellis, "Reuse of Conceptual Requirement Specifications", *in Proc. of RE '93, ACM/IEEE Int. Conf. on Requirements Engineering*, San Diego, CA, January 1993, pp.121-124

[7] S.Castano, V. DeAntonellis, "A Constructive Approach to Reuse of Conceptual Components", *in Proc. of 2nd ACM/IEEE Int. Workshop on Software Reusability*, Lucca, Italy, March 1993, pp.19-28

[8] P. Coad, E. Yourdon, *Object-Oriented Design*, Yourdon Press Computing Series, 1991

[9] D. Coleman, F.Hayes, S. Bear, "Introducing Objectcharts or How to Use Statecharts in Object-Oriented Design", IEEE TSE, Vol.18, No.1, January 1992, pp.9-18

[10] V. DeAntonellis, B. Zonta, "A disciplined Approach to Office Analysis", IEEE TSE, Vol. 16, No. 8, 1990, pp. 822-828

[11] V. DeAntonellis, B. Pernici, P. Samarati, "Object orientation in the analysis of work organization and agent cooperation ", *2nd Int. Conf. on Dynamic Aspects on Information Systems, Washington*, DC, July 1991

[12] V. DeAntonellis, B. Pernici, P. Samarati, "F-ORM METHOD: A F-ORM Methodology for Reusing Specifications", in Proc. of *IFIP WG 8.4 Working Conf. on Object Oriented Aspects in Information Systems*, Quebec, October 1991

[13] V. DeAntonellis, S. Castano, B. Pernici, A. Piovesana, "The ITHACA Object Oriented Methodology: Application Developer Manual", ITHACA Report, ITHACA.POLIMI-UDUNIV, 1992

[14] W.B. Frakes, P.B. Gandel, "Classification, storage and retrieval of reusable components", *in Proc. of SIGIR'89 (Cambridge, MA)*, N.J. Belkin and C.J. van Rijsbergen, Eds., June 1989, pp. 251-254

[15] M.G. Fugini, O. Nierstrasz, B. Pernici, "Application Development through Reuse: the Ithaca Tools Environment", ACM SIGOIS Bulletin, August 1992

[16] J.W. Hooper, R. O. Chester, *Software Reuse: Guidelines and Methods*, Plenum Press, Division of Plenum Publishing Corporation, New York, 1991

[17] J. Leite, P.A. Freeman, "Requirements validation through viewpoint resolution", IEEE TSE, Vol.17, N.12, December 1991

[18] L. Liu, R. Meersman, "Activity Model: A Declarative Approach for Capturing Communication Behavior in Object-Oriented Databases", *in Proc. VLDB '92, Int. Conf. on Very Large DataBases*, Vancouver, Canada, August 1992, pp. 481-493

[19] Y.S. Maarek, D.M. Berry, G.E. Kaiser, "An Information Retrieval Approach For Automatically Constructing Software Libraries", IEEE TSE, Vol.17, No.8, August 1991, pp.800-813

[20] E. Ostertag, J. Hendler, R. Prieto-Diaz, C. Braun, "Computing Similarity in a Reuse Library System: An AI-Based Approach", ACM TOSEM, Proc. of COMPSAC '87, 1987, pp.23-2

[21] R. Prieto-Diaz, "Implementing Faceted Classification for Software Reuse", Communications of the ACM, Vol.34 N.5, May 1991

[22] G. Salton, C. Buckley, "Term Weighting Approaches in Automatic Text Retrieval", Information Processing and Management, Vol. 24 N.5, 1989, pp.513-523

[23] J. Souquières, N. Lévy, “Description of a Specification Development Model”, *in Proc. of RE'93, Int. IEEE/ACM Conf. on Requirements Engineering*, San Diego, CA, January 1993

[24] W. Tracz ed., *Software Reuse: Emerging Technology*, Computer Society Press, Washington D.C., 1988

[25] R. Wirfs-Brock, B. Wilkerson, L. Wiener, *Designing Object-Oriented Software*, Englewood Cliffs, NJ: Prentice Hall, 1990

Information System Development Process (A-30)
N. Prakash, C. Rolland and B. Pernici (Editors)
Elsevier Science Publishers B.V. (North-Holland)
1993 IFIP.

Repositories for Software Reuse: The Software Information Base

Panos Constantopoulos, Martin Doerr and Yannis Vassiliou

Institute of Computer Science
Foundation of Research and Technology - Hellas
Heraklion, Crete, Greece
e-mail: {panos|martin|yannis}@ics.forth.gr

Abstract
Repositories play a pivotal role in an integrated reuse- based application development environment. Reusing software components implies their persistent storage and maintenance, and the ability to efficiently find them. Repositories built with reuse in mind can be considered as special-purpose information systems, required to support powerful semantic modelling, flexible retrieval of varied software descriptions of multimedia nature, and efficiency optimization directed towards a large variety of classes rather than large populations per class. The Software Information Base (SIB), described in this paper, is an illustrative case where issues of organisation, multi-paradigm access and challenging implementation choices are set forth.

Keyword Codes: D.2.2; D.2.9; H.3.3
Keywords: Software Engineering, Tools and Techniques; Management; Information Storage and Retrieval, Information Search and Retrieval

1. INTRODUCTION

Software reuse [Bigg87, Bigg89, Meye87] is being touted as a very promising approach to deal with the software crisis constituents (late deliveries, unreliable software, prohibitive development and maintenance costs, etc.) It is commonly agreed that software reuse does not only concern code; reuse of a software object implies the concurrent (re)use of objects associated with it, plus information about the objects. Thus, designs requirements specifications, development processes, and decision experiences are also candidates for reuse.

Software artifacts are stored in a repository which supports their efficient selection. Comprehending their functionality and usage before adaptation and subsequent use in the composition of a new application, is also recognised as essential in the reuse process.

Adopting the reuse-based development cycle of Figure 1.1, one can immediately detect the important role played by a reuse-targeted repository, together with its associated functions/tools. Such special-purpose repositories are often lightly mentioned or assumed while discussing reuse issues (e.g., designing-for-reuse), without the proper consideration of the idiosyncrasies, research challenges, and implementation difficulties they present. This paper reports the experiences in building a repository system (the *Software Information Base - SIB*) targeted to support the component-based development of very large software systems within the ITHACA project (Esprit No.2705) [Ader90]. The SIB can be seen as a complex functionality information system (like a large DBMS) providing for persistent storing, sharing, accessing, managing and controlling data. What mostly distinguishes it from a traditional DBMS is its support for conceptual modelling which

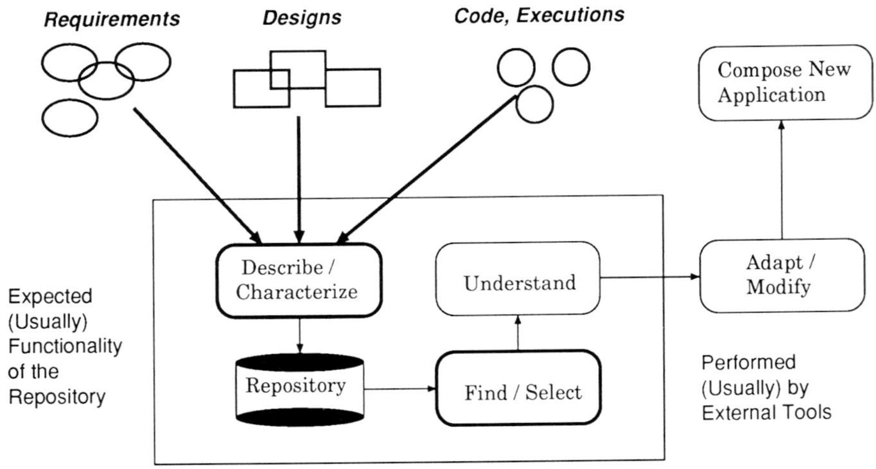

Figure 1.1: The Reuse Process

features, in addition to the usual constructs, a capacity for uniform treatment of schemata and data allowing schema definition at runtime and a uniform treatment of entities and relations. Other distinguishing characteristics are its capacity for flexible retrieval and browsing of multimedia data; and the optimization of efficiency for network structures consisting of a large variety of classes rather than relatively few classes with large populations per class (typical in a DBMS).

As can be seen in Figure 1.2, which applies the reuse process in our setting, the TELOS conceptual modelling language is used for the uniform description and organisation of software artifacts. TELOS is a specialised knowledge representation language for the development of information systems [Mylo90]. A corresponding graphical visualisation for each artifact description is readily available. The software components are located and retrieved via a selection mechanism comprising querying and browsing modes. Finally, the semantic nature of TELOS descriptions assists in understanding the functionality, usage and behaviour of the software components described. The latter is assisted by associated multimedia annotations.

Software reuse via repositories is not a new concept; there have been several approaches, not necessarily resembling the framework presented in our work, which can be characterised on two orthogonal dimensions. The first dimension concerns the methodologies for organising the reusable components in the repository, while the second concerns the methodologies for selecting the appropriate object(s) for reuse.

Library cataloguing (e.g., mathematical libraries - [Hopk88]) has been a prevalent way to organise code. In recent years we have seen shifts from simple *hierarchical classification* schemes to *faceted* ones (e.g., [Prie91]). *Hypertext* software organisation forms [Conk87] have also been applied for instance at HP's Kiosk, while semantic organisations range from simple object-oriented libraries (Eiffel [Meye90], Objective-C) to ER models (e.g., IBM's Repository [Low88]), to richer semantic models (LaSSIE at AT&T [Deva91]). *Hybrid* organisations (combining principles from the above) appear

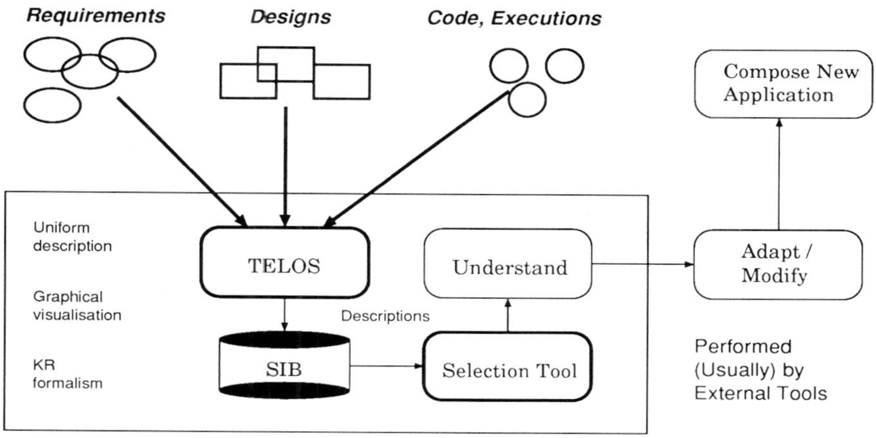

Figure 1.2: The Reuse Process with the SIB

promising [Cons93].

In terms of selection/retrieval methodologies, one can distinguish between *formal specifications* (e.g., VDM, ESF-Rose), to *database retrieval* (Cactis of Arcadia [Tayl88], PCTE [Boud88]), to *Knowledge-based* forms of reasoning (Practitioner, LaSSIE) , to *hypertext style* browsing (e.g., DIF [GaSc87]), to *Information Retrieval* (e.g., Catalog, Proteus), finally to *Wide-Spectrum* approaches like the one followed in ISHYS [GaSc89].

Our conjecture and the motivation behind this work is that the software repository necessary to support reuse should be seen as a special-purpose information system providing a complete and effective functionality. Its development necessitates the harmonious coexistence and co-use of methodologies and techniques from a variety of areas, including (object-oriented) *databases, knowledge representation, hypermedia* and *information retrieval.*

Section 2 summarises the structure of the SIB, while Section 3 presents the functionality and the architectural principles of the system. An example illustrates the usage of the SIB in Section 4, followed by the implementation decisions and principles in Section 5. Our concluding remarks are made in Section 6. The interested reader can find more information about the SIB in [Vass90, Cons91, Cons93].

2. DESCRIPTION OF SOFTWARE

The SIB is structured as an attributed directed graph the nodes and links of which represent descriptions of software objects and semantic relations respectively. There are three kinds of descriptions

(1) requirements descriptions (RD);
(2) design descriptions (DD); and
(3) implementation descriptions (ID).

These descriptions provide three corresponding views of a software object:
(1) an application view, according to a requirements specification model (e.g., SADT);

(2) a system view, according to a design specification model (e.g., ER or DFD); and
(3) an implementation view, according to an implementation model (e.g., set of C++ classes together with documentation).

Descriptions can be simple or composite, consisting of other descriptions. The term *descriptions* reflects the fact that these entities only describe software objects. The objects themselves reside outside the SIB. Descriptions are related to each other through a number of semantic relations listed below. In addition to the usual isA, instanceOf and attribute relations supported by object-oriented data models and knowledge representation schemes, several special attribute categories have been defined for the purposes of the SIB. The SIB is defined, as mentioned, in terms of the Telos knowledge representation language which supports creating an infinite instantiation hierarchy and treats attributes as objects in their own right (which, therefore, can also have attributes). These features of Telos are fully exploited in structuring the SIB.

The modelling constructs used in the SIB can be distinguished into four categories:

(I) *General structural/semantic relationships*, including attribution, classification and generalisation. These are the basic modelling mechanisms offered by the knowledge representation language.

(II) *Special structural/semantic relationships*, including aggregation, correspondence, similarity and genericity. These have been defined as a minimal set of system-supplied special descriptors for the purpose of software description.

(III) *User-defined and informal links*, including versioning, hypertext, etc. The attribute definition facility supported by TELOS can be used to form this set of links.

(IV) *Associations*. These are sets of descriptors along with private symbol tables, which allow for the construction of materialised views (through queries) and of contexts (or workspaces).

In what follows we present the above constructs in a sequence that facilitates the exposition, rather than dealing with each of the three groups in turn. The link representation referring to each relation is the one appearing on the user interface of the Graphical Browser of the SIB (see Figure 4.1).

(1) *Attribution*, represented by *attribute* links. This is a general, rather unconstrained representation of semantic relations, whereby the attributes of a description are defined to be instances of other descriptions. An attribute can have zero or more values.

Example:
```
Description SoftwareObject with
     attributes
          author: Person
          version: VersionNumber
```

`SoftwareObject` has attributes `author` and `version` whose values are instances of `Person` and `VersionNumber` respectively.

(2) *Aggregation*, represented by *hasPart* links. This relates an object to its components.

Example:
```
Description SoftwareObject with
  ...
```

```
    hasPart
         components: SoftwareObject
```

The components of an object have a distinct role in the function of the object and any possible changes to them affect the aggregate object as well (e.g., new version).

(3) *Classification* (opposite *instantiation*), represented by *instanceOf* links. Objects sharing common properties can be grouped into classes. An object can belong to more than one classes. Classes themselves are treated as generic objects, which their members are instances of, and which, in turn, can be instances of other, more generic objects. In fact, every SIB object has to be declared as an instance of at least one class. Effectively, an infinite classification hierarchy is established starting with objects that have no instances of their own, called tokens. Multiple instantiation is allowed. Instantiation of a class involves instantiating all the associated semantic relations. Thus relations are treated as objects themselves.

Example:

```
Description BankIS instanceOf SoftwareObject with
     author
          : Panos
     version
          : 0.1
     components
          : CustomerAccounts, Credit, Investments
```

The `attribute` and `hasPart` links of `BankIS` are instances of the corresponding `attribute` and `components` links of `SoftwareObject`.

Classification is perhaps the most important modelling mechanism in the SIB ([Veze91, PeVe91] give a detailed account of the construction of models and descriptions in the SIB).

(4) *Generalisation* (opposite *specialisation*), represented by *isA* links. This allows multiple, strict inheritance of properties between classes leading to the creation of multiple generalisation hierarchies. A class inherits all the attributes of its superclasses (possibly more than one - multiple inheritance), however inherited properties can only be constrained, not overridden (strict inheritance).

(5) *Correspondence*, represented by *correspondsTo* links. A software object can have zero or more associated requirements, design and implementation descriptions. Correspondence relations concern the identity of an object described by different descriptions and can have as parts other correspondence relations between parts of the corresponding descriptions. Correspondence links actually indicate that the descriptions they link describe the same object at different levels of abstraction. The correspondences of the parts need not be one-to-one. For instance, a requirements specification may correspond to more than one designs and a design may have more than one alternative implementations. Similarly, a single implementation could correspond to more than one design entities.

An important type of controlled correspondence in the SIB is the *Application Frame (AF)*. Application frames represent complete systems or families of systems and comprise (*hasPart*) at least one implementation and optional design and requirements descriptions. AFs are further distinguished into specific and generic (SAFs and GAFs) while the RDs, DDs and IDs of an AF should properly be considered as groupings of such descriptions (i.e., other associations.)

A SAF describes a complete system (be it a linear programming package, a text processor or an airline reservation system) and includes exactly one ID. A GAF is an abstraction of a collection of applications pertinent to a particular application domain and includes one RD, one or more DDs and one or more IDs for each DD. For an extensive presentation of the concepts and structure of the SIB, as well as the role of Application Frames in the Ithaca application development methodology, the interested reader is referred to [Vass90, Cons91, deAn92].
.sp (6) *Similarity*, represented by *similarTo* links. The similarity relation is defined between objects of the same kind (i.e., RD, DD, ID, or AF) and has two attributes: a similarity criterion and a similarity measure. Two objects are said to be similar with respect to some criterion if they can substitute one another with regard to this criterion. The similarity criterion can be endogenous defined in terms of relations already stored in the SIB, or exogenous, provided by the user who specifies a particular similarity link. Accordingly, similarity links can be computed or user-defined. The similarity measure expresses the degree to which the substitution of two similar objects, in either direction, is satisfactory and is a number in the range [0,1]. The similarity criterion is a mandatory attribute while the measure is optional.

(7) *Genericity*, represented by *specialCaseOf* links. This relation is defined only between application frames (see below) to denote that one application frame is less parameterized than another. E.g., a bank accounting and a hotel accounting application frame could both be derived from a more general, parametric accounting application frame.

(8) *Informal and user-defined links*. When users have foreseeable needs for other types of links they can define them using the attribute definition facility of TELOS. For instance, versioning can be modelled by special correspondence links labeled *derivedFrom*. Furthermore, random needs for representation and reference can be served by informal links, such as hypertext links which allow the attachment of multimedia annotations to SIB objects.

(9) *Association* is an encapsulation mechanism intended to allow the grouping of descriptions that play together a functional role [Brod84]. For example, we may define as an association the descriptions that constitute a design specification for a hotel information system, or all the classes that define an implementation of that same system. The contents of an association can only be accessed through the entry points defined in a private symbol table. Thus, an association is, actually, a tuple:

Association = (setOfDescriptions, symbolTable)

The SIB itself is a global association containing all objects included in any association. Its symbol table contains all the external names of every object. Name conflicts can be resolved by a precedence rule.

Associations can be derived from other associations through queries or set operations. Furthermore, associations can be considered as materialised views. Non-materialised views, or simply *views*, differ from associations in that they cannot be updated directly, but rather, through updates of the associations which they are derived from.

3. FUNCTIONALITY AND ARCHITECTURE OF THE SIB

The SIB system offers a number of maintenance, selection and workspace management functions. Maintenance functions include insertion, deletion and update of information in the SIB and are supported by appropriate access language and interactive form based data entry tools. The latter adapt themselves to the type of object to be edited by reading out schema information from the database itself. There is no distinction between schema and data, giving the possibility to deal with a continuously growing number of classes and special cases, and to refine existing descriptions to more and more detail in a formal way. Selection functions include querying and browsing the SIB for purposes of selecting reusable artifacts and understanding their structure and functionality. Workspace management involves the dynamic definition and modification of workspaces to provide easier and more efficient interaction with the SIB.

Maintenance and selection operations are performed on *workspaces* which are application-specific and/or user-specific subsets of the SIB represented as associations. Between several workspaces, the notion of identity of shared objects is kept by reference to the identifiers in the global workspace. Classification and generalization links are also shared between the workspaces, being an integral part of the object's identity. Using workspaces carries several benefits, such as focusing attention to selected parts of the SIB by hiding irrelevant information; creating convenient views of the same objects either by renaming them or by hiding particular parts of their descriptions; improving search performance by effectively restricting the search space; and supporting privacy. In terms of the structure introduced in the previous section, workspaces are special cases of associations. The default workspace is the entire SIB (global workspace).

Queries to the SIB can be classified from a user's point of view as *explicit* or *implicit*. An *explicit* query involves an arbitrary predicate explicitly formulated in a query language or through an appropriate form interface. An *implicit* query, on the other hand, is one generated as a result of navigational commands in the browsing mode, or one of particular significance and frequent occurence, "pre-canned" for ease of use and offered as a button or menu option. Browsing commands and explicit queries can also be issued through appropriate interfaces from external tools such as the Visual Scripting Tool of ITHACA [deMe91].

The selection of software descriptions from the SIB is accomplished through the *Selection Tool* (ST) by an iterative process comprising alternate stages of explicit queries (retrieval) and browsing. Browsing usually is the final and often the only stage of the process. The functional difference between the retrieval and the browsing mode is that the former supports the retrieval of an arbitrary subset of the SIB based on some user's knowledge about the SIB contents, while the latter supports local exploratory searches withing a given subset of the SIB without need of previous knowlegde. Operationally, both selection modes address queries to the SIB.

We now present the basic functions of the SIB in the manner of defining the operations on an abstract data type:

Maintenance functions:
Insert: Descriptions X Associations -> Associations
Delete: Identifiers X Associations -> Associations
Update: Descriptions X Associations -> Associations
NewVersion: Descriptions X Associations -> Associations

The insert function takes as input a description and an association and inserts that description to the association as well as the global association (SIB). If the description is that of an association, insertion includes materialisation of the association. The delete function takes the name of a description and an association and deletes the description from the association. Update modifies a particular version of a description, while NewVersion turns the updated description into a new version.

Selection functions:
Retrieve: Query X Associations -> SetOf (Descriptions X Weights)
Browse: Identifier X Links X Associations -> Views

The *Retrieve* function takes as input an association and a (compound) non-Boolean query and returns a subset of the association with weights attached indicating the degree to which the descriptions in the answer set match the query. In the current implementation only Boolean queries are supported, yet the extension to non-Boolean is currently undertaken.

Browsing is a special retrieval operation. It starts at a specified SIB description which is the focus of attention and is called *current object* and produces a view of a neighbourhood of interest of the current object within a given association. Since the SIB has a network structure, the neighbourhood of the current object (node) is defined in terms of the links of interest adjacent to it. As we shall later see, the size of the neighbourhood can also be controlled. Thus, the *Browse* function takes as input the identifier (name) of the current object, a list of names of link classes of interest and an association, and determines a local view centred around the current object. This local view can be extended to the transitive closure of one or more relations (link classes), e.g. hasPart. By calling *Browse* again with the identifier argument equal to the name of one of the objects contained in the browser's view, that object is made current and the view is updated. Effectively, the *Browse* function provides a moving window with controllable filters and size, which allows navigational search over subsets of the SIB network. The default association is the entire SIB.

The multimedia nature of SIB descriptions calls for the development of a hypermedia annotation mechanism that would gracefully complement the SIB semantic network. This is accomplished by establishing referential links between descriptions, treated as a special category of attribute links, thus completely integrated in the SIB network model. Hypermedia annotations include text, graphics, raster images and algorithm animations.

The SIB system consists of the following major parts (Figure 3.1):

(1) The *SIB Interactive User Interface* generates and coordinates the other parts, including the interface tools of the Data Entry Forms and the Selection Tool, except for the Graphical Browser. It is implemented using the OSF/Motif toolkit.

(2) The *Graphical Browser* presents parts of the SIB network graphically and allows the user to browse through it by sending messages to the SIB Interactive User Interface in response to user actions. The Graphical Browser is a LABY graphical editor with only the working area present. LABY is a general purpose graphical editor developed in part within the ITHACA project at the Institute of Computer Science, FORTH [Kate90].

(3) The *Display Forms* are used to provide information about the current node or another selected node in a form layout. They are designed to support multimedia information (text, graphics, images, animation, etc.).

(4) A special *Data Entry Form* provides for entering data into the SIB through a form interface.

(5) The *Query Interface* handles queries about SIB objects, issued to it by the various components of the ST or by the Data Entry Form. As a result of processing a query it constructs a file suitable for display by the Graphical Browser or the Data Entry Form. In the current implementation a separate query interface (based on the client-server model) is used for programmatic queries. However, the two query interfaces will be integrated in the future.

The ST user interface consists of the following windows (Figure 4.1):

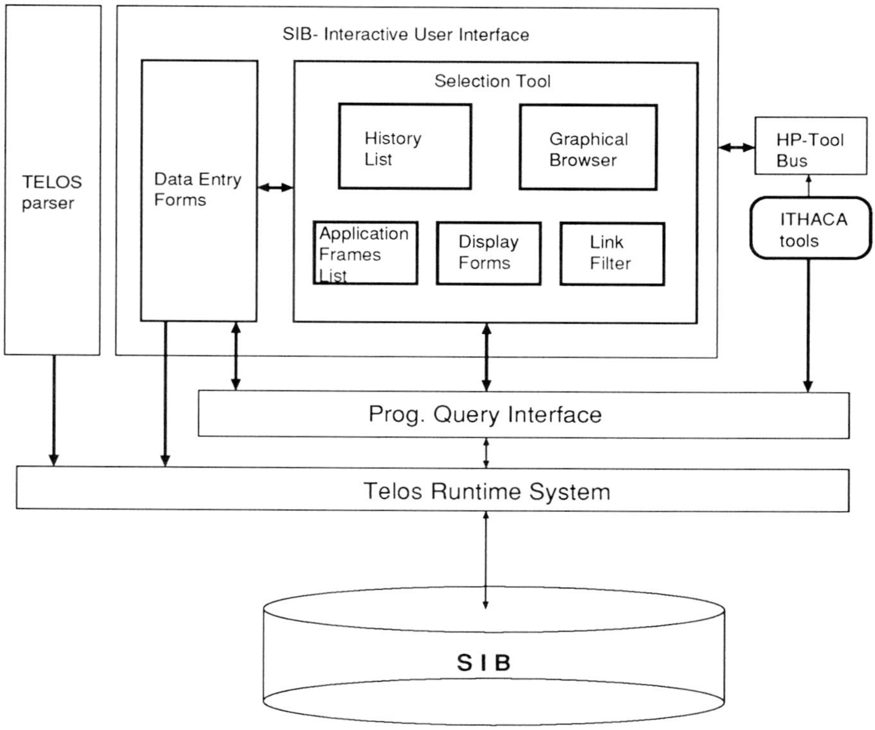

Figure 3.1. SIB architecture

(1) *Graphical Browser*:
The Graphical Browser, built using the LABY graphical editor,
displays a part of the SIB network around a selected object (*current object*). The structures currently displayed have the form of a star whose central node is the current object. The window of the Graphical Browser is semantically divided in two parts. From each node appearing in the lower part emanates at least one link pointing to the current node. Similarly, there is at least one link emanating from the current node and pointing to each node appearing in the upper part. The types of links are denoted by a colour code. For example the isA relation is shown with red links while the instanceOf relation with green links. The colour code is shown in the Link Filter. Nodes appearing in the graph of the browser are selectable with the mouse. When selected, a node becomes current, it is placed in the middle of the display and a move in the SIB network results. The links displayed include direct links from the current object to other objects and computed isA and instanceOf links.

The population of the display is controlled by means of the *Link Filter* (see below) and the *Instance Box*. The Instance Box appears in the display of the Graphical Browser when the instances of a certain active link class (i.e. selected by the Link Filter) adjacent to the current object are too many to be shown on the display. On selecting the Instance

Box of a link class with the mouse, a list of objects related to the current one by that type of links appears (Figure 4.2). The objects on this list are selectable just as those displayed graphically.

(2) *Link Filter*:
The Link Filter provides buttons corresponding to link classes and is used for activating/deactivating links thus controlling the information displayed in the Graphical Browser. Each button acts as a filter on a certain relation. If the button is selected (on), the corresponding relation is displayed and vice versa. The isA and instanceOf buttons further offer the option of displaying computed in addition to direct isA and instanceOf links. All buttons show the colour code of the link classes and have a help facility. When moving from node to node in the Graphical Browser, the state of the Link Filter does not change unless the user does so explicitly.

(3) *History List*:
The History List is a navigation aid intended to prevent users from getting lost, a common problem in hypertext systems [Conk87]. The History List is scrollable and contains the names of the objects selected as current during a session in chronological order, the most recent one shown at the bottom (as in the history command of Unix). All entries of the list are selectable. A selection made on the History List is functionally equivalent to one made on the Graphical Browser.

(4) *Application Frames List*:
The Application Frames List contains the names of the application frames, reflecting the overall structure and contents of the SIB. The purpose of the Application Frames List is to compensate for the limited scope of the Graphical Browser, which is a shortcoming if an extended area of interest is sought by navigation rather than by explicit querying. The application frames are displayed in an indented list representing the existing hierarchical structure. Each item on the list is selectable, which effectively allows big steps over the SIB network in the browsing mode. Moreover, the Application Frames List serves as the initial entry point to the ST.

(5) *Main Form*:
The Main Form is the top right-most window of the ST and invariably displays information about the current object. It shows the abstracted definition of the object in a form layout. The information presented is generated by unparsing the SIB. The form can also contain multimedia annotations to the object, each one displayed in a separate window. At present, this annotation is textual and graphical (Figure 4.3), but can be of any other type with no additional effort, provided that appropriate tools exist in the working environment.

(6) *Auxiliary Form*:
To get information about a displayed object, other than the current one, without changing the actual view in the Graphical Browser, the user can select the name of the desired object on the Main Form in a hypertext-like fashion (see Figure 4.1). An Auxiliary Form will appear at the bottom right of the ST and display information about the selected object in the manner of the Main Form. To prevent user distraction, only one auxiliary form can be open at a time; also objects are not selectable on auxiliary forms. The auxiliary form is actually a preview mechanism and is offered as an orientation aid.

(7) *Button Panel*:
Through the Button Panel, several other windows for performing various useful functions can appear on demand. Currently these functions are:

GotoObject: Allows direct access to invisible objects by name.

EnterData: A Data Entry Form is offered for entering data into the SIB (Figure 4.4). The Query Form, currently under construction, will have a similar appearance.
KeepObject: Keeps a retrieved object in a local workspace.
Iconify and *Quit*: Closes and iconifies a window; and quits the ST respectively.

4. USAGE EXAMPLE

Suppose we would like to include in the SIB an application dealing with processing of letters, which will assist secretaries, managers, and others to write professional letters, check them, and, after final approval, mail them through post or electronic mail. Looking at the Application Frames List, we observe that there is already an Office Information System called `WooRKS`. The basic concepts in `WooRKS` are actors, roles and procedures.

Our starting point will be `WooRKS`, which we select through the Application Frames List. As we can read in the natural language comment attached to the corresponding Main Form, `WooRKS` is a work flow system for offices, which handles a variety of activities (see Figure 4.1). So this might be one of the candidate places to search for a letter processing application. `WooRKS` has three attributes which are further explained in its Main Form. One of them, *reqDescr*, deals with `WooRKS` requirements descriptions and it will probably provide us with more information about what the `WooRKS` system actually does. Before making it current, we preview its contents on the Auxiliary Form, by selecting `WooRKS1_RD_FORM` from the Main Form, and we decide to visit it.

In Figure 4.2 `WooRKS1_RD_FORM` is current in the Graphical Browser window. Among the *classes* of activities that it handles, `OrderProcessing` appears to be the closest such as checking and archiving. We decide to visit `Order Processing` to see if it includes what is needed for letter processing in general. After we conclude that this is not true. We backtrack to `WooRKS1_RD_FORM` through the History List and decide to preview `WarehouseProcessing` and `AccountProcessing` to see if there is anything relevant there. By previewing these nodes we realise that none of them fullfils our needs. We further notice that they are all instances of `FormProcessClass`.

We take a closer look on `FormProcessClass` by moving to it through the GotoObject facility (Figure 4.3). As `FormProcessClass` is a subclass of `FormClass`, it inherits its attributes. By previewing `FormClass`, we find out that it has two attributes, *roles* and *baseRole* (see Figure 4.3) and decide to create a new instance of `FormProcessClass`, called `LetterProcessing`, whose *roles* will correspond to the initial requirements imposed on our letter processing application. In particular, the *baseRole* of `LetterProcessing` will be `sp_base_role`, and the *roles* will be `sp_letterCompose`, `LP_letterCheck`, `sp_letterApprove`, `LP_letterSend`, `LP_letterReceive`, and `sp_letterArchive`.

We have chosen this convention for naming the *roles* by analogy to the existing *roles* of the other activities. To see these names we first made `FormRole` current using the GotoObject facility (see Figure 4.4). Since `FormRole` has too many instances to be displayed on the Graphical Browser, an Instance Box appears by clicking on the "MANY INSTANCES" box of the Browser.

At this point we start creating the *roles* and *baseRole* of `LetterProcessing`. Before creating `sp_letterArchive`, we visit `OP_orderArchive` by selecting it from the Instance Box (Figure 4.4). This act is worthwhile because we find a *correspondsTo* link from `OP_orderArchive` to `ArchiveAct`, which is an instance of `ADMActivity` (see the Main Form in Figure 4.5). Knowing that `ADMActivity`

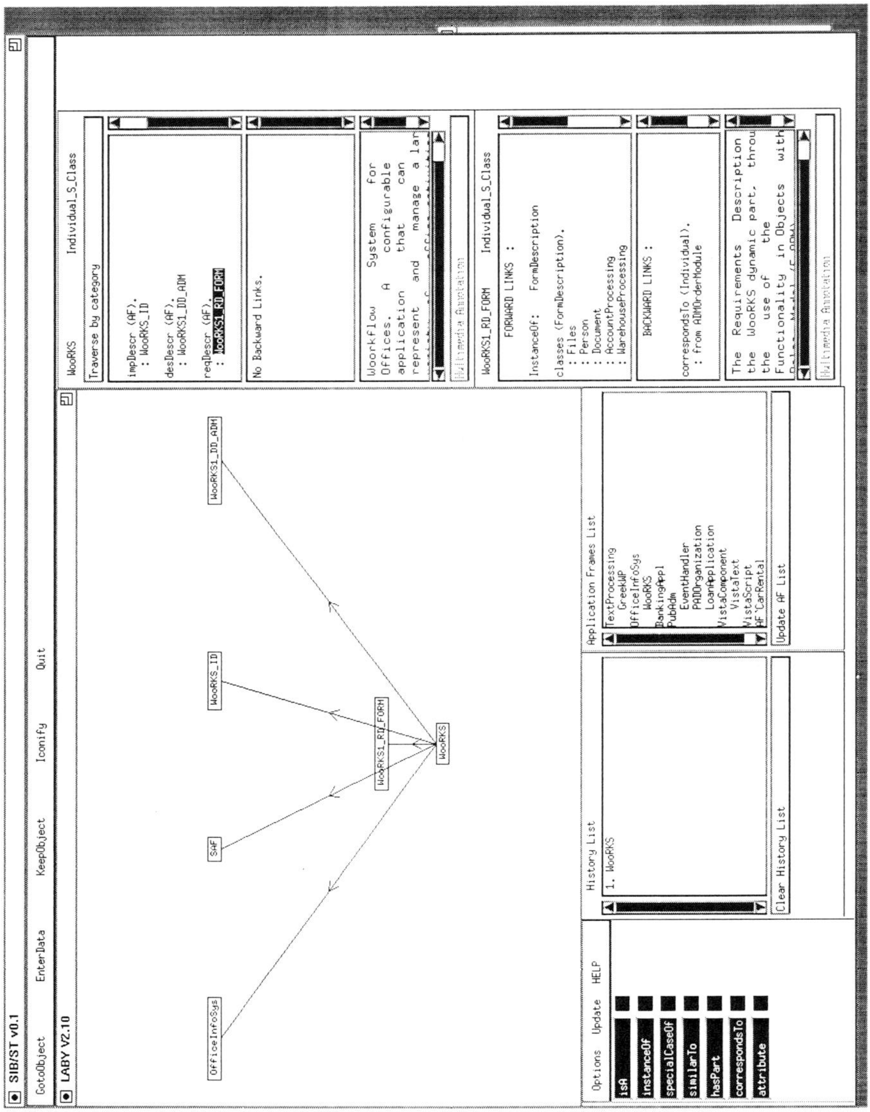

Figure 4.1. : The Selection Tool of the Software Information Base. Current in the Graphical Browser is WooRKS, the starting point of the usage example.

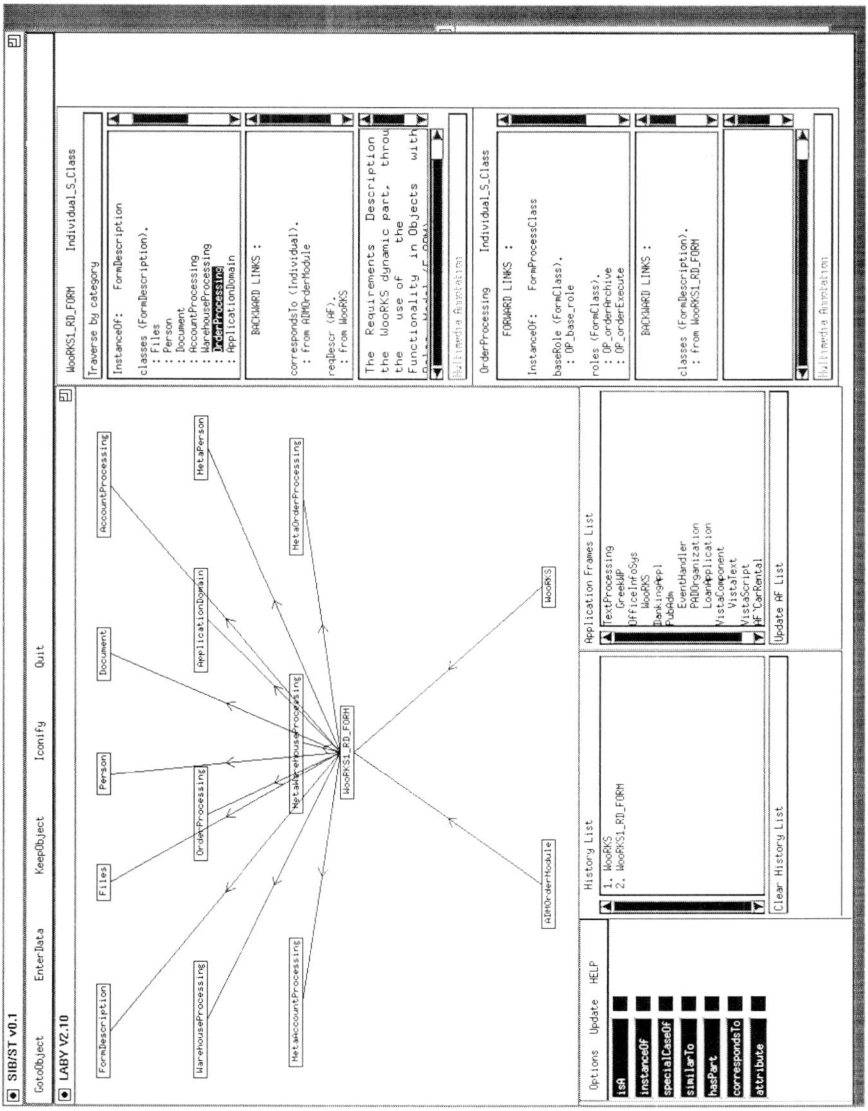

Figure 4.2. : Inspecting the requirements of WooRKS and previewing OrderProcessing.

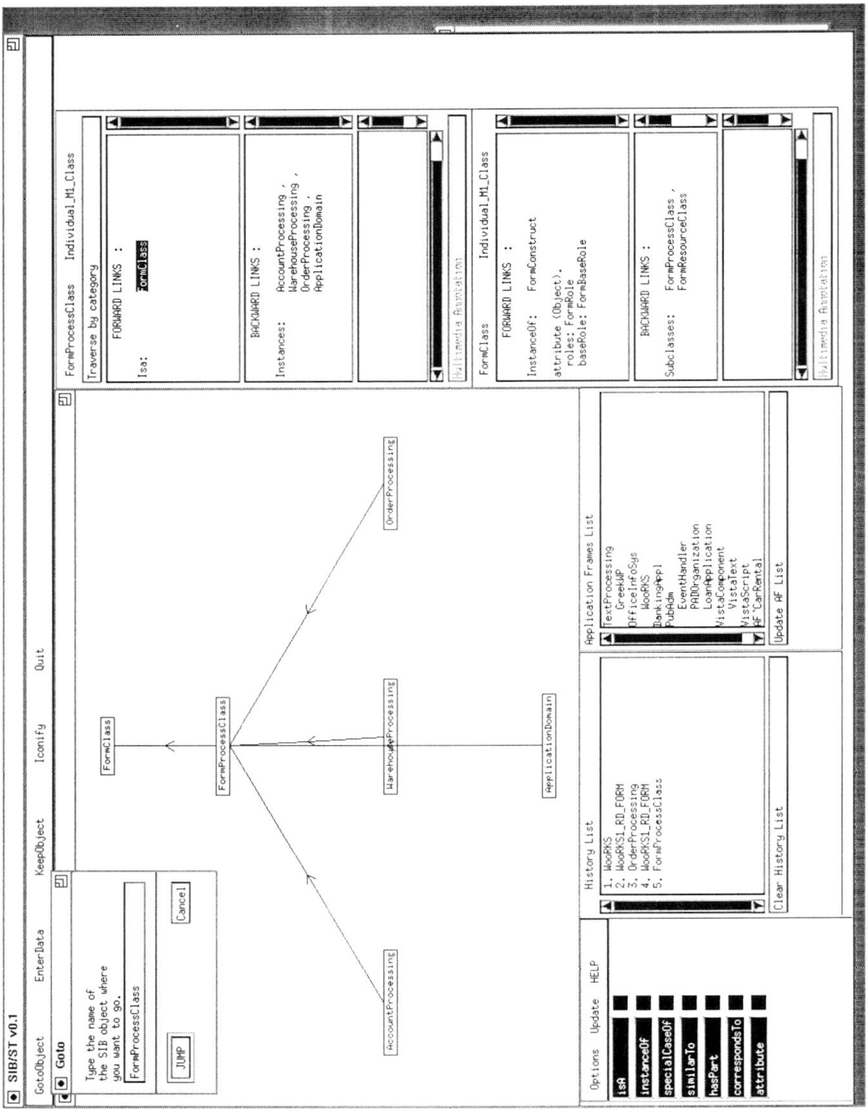

Figure 4.3. : Visiting FormProcessClass and previewing its superclass, FormClass.

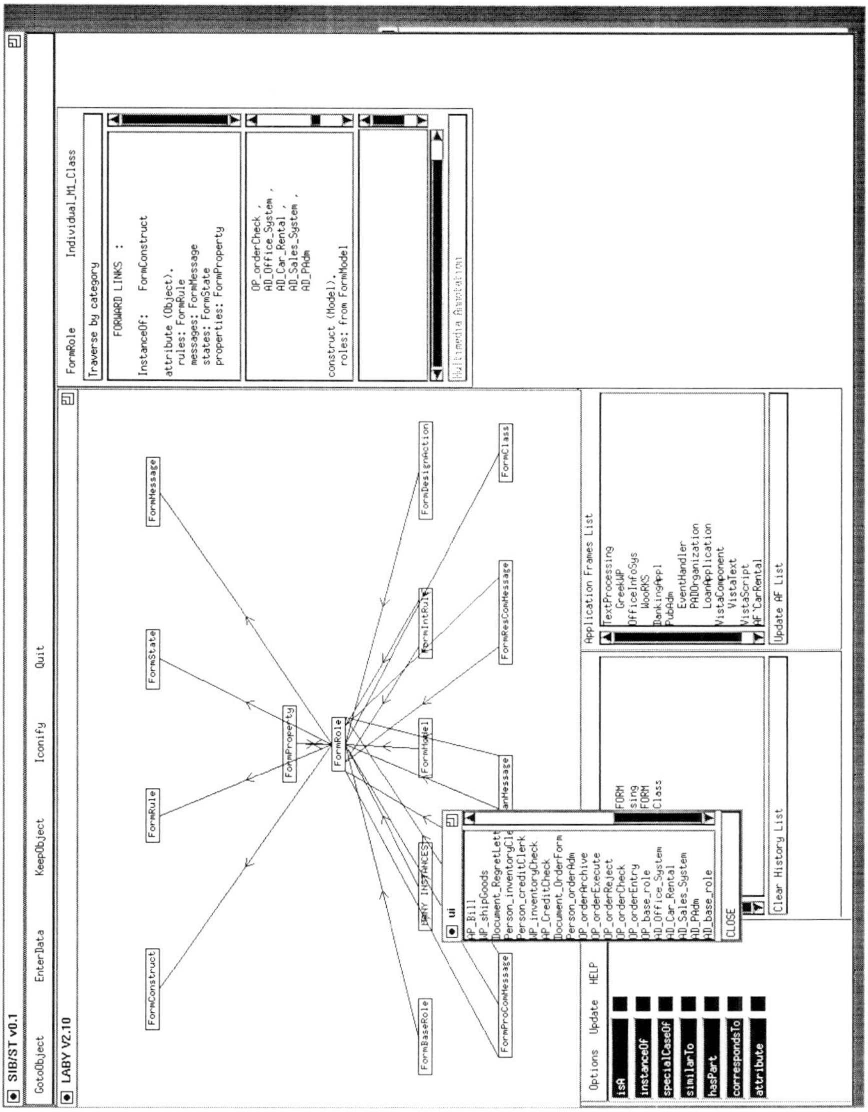

Figure 4.4. : The Instance Box handles the instances of FormRole.

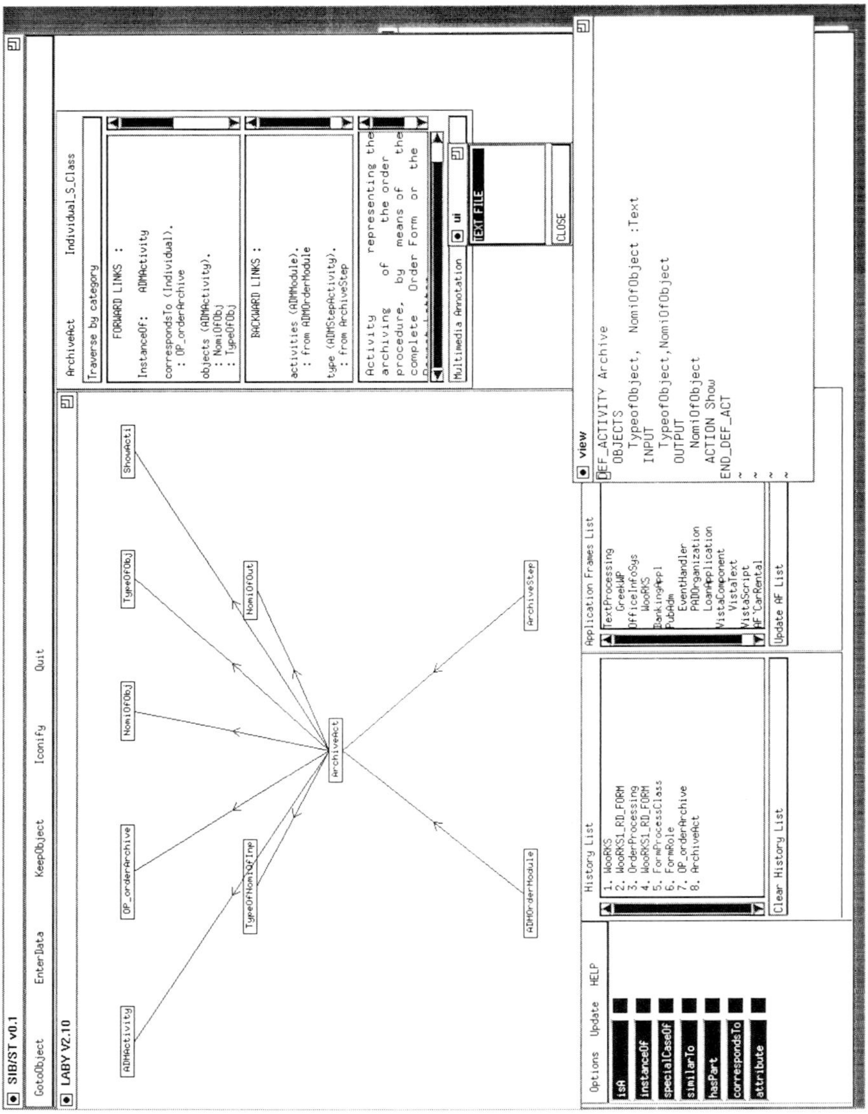

Figure 4.5. : An annotation attached to ArchiveAct.

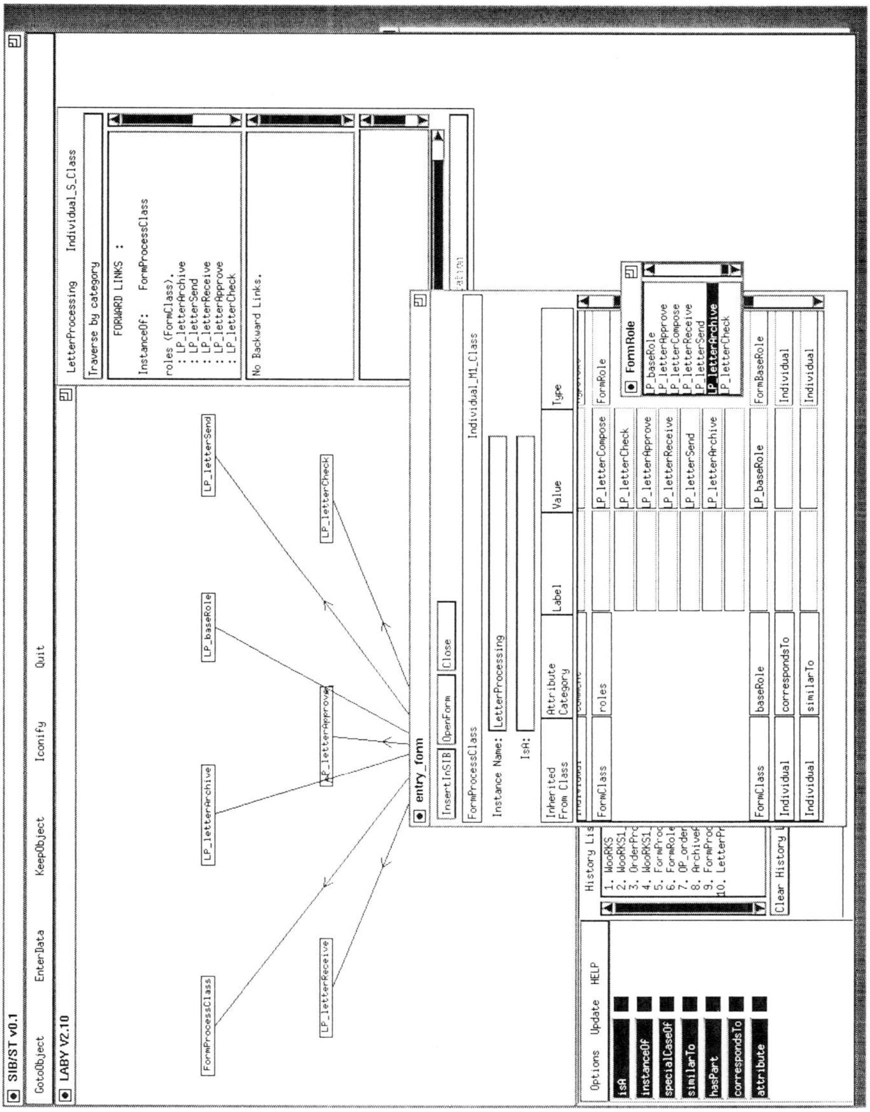

Figure 4.6. : The EnterData facility used to insert LetterProcessing in the SIB.

handles the design descriptions, we can further proceed by defining the ADMActivity corresponding to the new sp_letterArchive in a similar way, or even use the ArchiveAct as the ADMActivity of sp_letterArchive. Similarly, we may use CompileRefAct and/or EvaluationOrderAct which *correspondTo* OP_orderCheck as the ADMActivity of sp_letterCheck, etc.

Finally, we are in a position to define the new LetterProcessing node. We move to FormProcessClass using the GotoObject option and use the EnterData facility, which will make our task easy, even if we have no knowledge of the syntax of Telos. The Data Entry Form for LetterProcessing is shown in Figure 4.6. In the same figure you can see the results of entering the information.

5. IMPLEMENTATION

The SIB is an essential component of a complete application development environment, interfaced cleanly with several tools and the object store as shown in Figure 5.1. A zoom at the runtime system is made in Figure 5.2

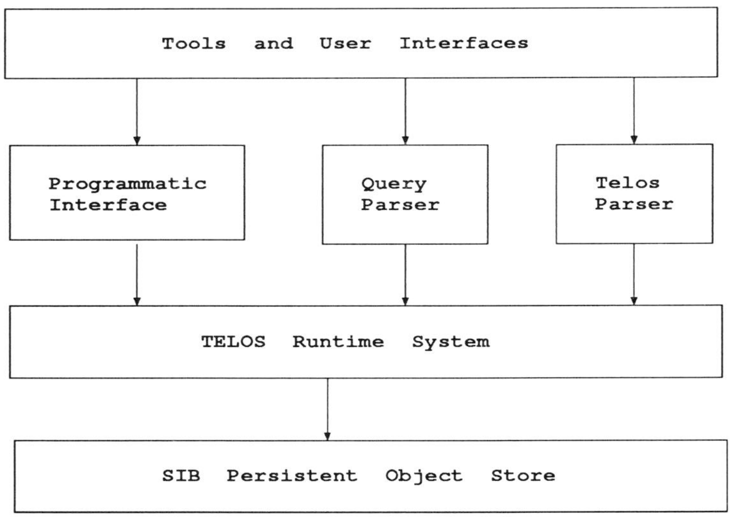

Figure 5.1: Interfaces of the TELOS Runtime with Tools and the Object Store

The TELOS data model and system without its time reasoning mechanism and its assertional language was used for the construction of the SIB. TELOS was chosen for its powerful representation and modelling facilities, as well as for superior flexibility and efficiency over other database systems (relational or object-oriented), as indicated by early experimentation. The current implementation of TELOS, all using C++ as opposed to the earlier Prolog implementation, specifically attends to the needs of the SIB.

Architecturally, the system contains all main components of a typical object-oriented DBMS implementation (see Figure 5.2), but low-level optimizations and data structures are rather different. All data fields are set-valued. Stress is laid on efficient handling of network-like structures and fast retrieval of transitive closures with respect to certain link

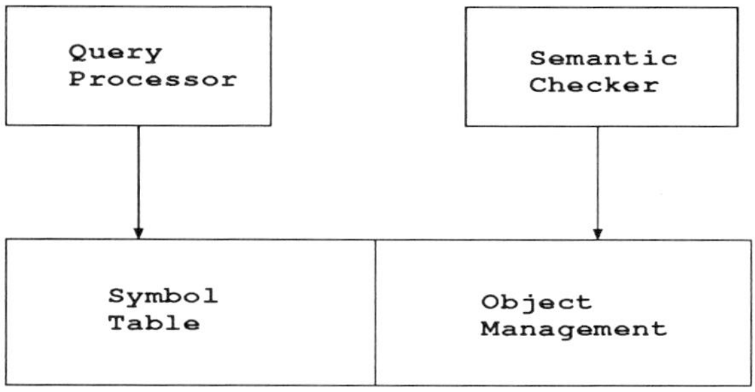

Figure 5.2: Structure of the TELOS Runtime system

types. No optimization is done for range queries on primitive values (integers, floats etc.). The schema is completely kept at data-level, which allows fast schema extensions at run-time. The data of an information system are in general rather static, with infrequent and bulk changes, which leads to a strong preference of query optimization against update optimization.

TELOS objects identify themselves to the user by logical names, which are the links to the real world objects they describe. Internally they carry a unique system identifier [KhCo86, KiKi89] which is invisible to the outside. The TELOS logical names are kept in symbol tables, one for each association, which establish mappings between system identifiers and logical names. The symbol tables may map arbitrary subsets of the database, with the only restriction that the database must be semantically consistent within each association, and on system identifier level as a whole [WiAl88]. There are no restrictions on the logical names one system identifier is mapped to in different symbol tables, but the user will be enabled to check under which name an object within one association will appear in another.

Five C++ classes are used for representing the TELOS objects. The contents of the five classes are sets of system identifiers for the *instanceOf*, *isA*, *attribute* and *trigger* relations. All these relations are kept in both directions to allow very fast query processing.

Triggers are either built-in or user-supplied, in which case they must be linked to the runtime system. They allow access even to data outside the database, thus providing a very powerful interface mechanism.

The TELOS objects are kept persistent on disk and copied to memory in a cache-like way. We implement demand loading in the first step, which will later be replaced by a prefetch mechanism [Low88]. During one transaction, all modifications done on existing objects and newly created objects are kept in memory only. They become persistent at the end of the transaction. Queries may be allowed on these objects before end of transaction under certain restrictions. All dynamic memory allocations are done on a fixed granularity base, first to reduce allocation time and, still more important, to avoid cluttering the virtual address space after longer execution times. Similar issues have been discussed in [KhFr88, MeLa87, SkZd86] too.

The association of system identifiers with object locations in persistent store and/or in memory is done by the system catalogue. The system identifiers are kept dense, in the sense that the numerically lowest free identifier is allocated first. As system identifiers are only internal, there are no identity conflicts as with other database identifiers. Density allows a virtual memory - like indexing of the system catalogue with use of page tables. Requiring an additional indirection step after a growth of the database by a factor of 1000, this design leads to nearly size-independent performance.

Symbol tables translate from logical names to system identifiers and vice-versa. The symbol table tuples are organized as the system catalogue, giving the same high performance for system identifier to logical name translation. The translation from logical names to system identifiers is supported by B-Trees, which are the only element introducing some degradation of performance with growing database size. Fortunately, the frequency of the translation from logical names to system identifiers is roughly an order of magnitude lower than that of the inverse. The reason is that query answer sets are usually larger than the respective argument sets, and all internal query processing is done on the basis of system identifiers. Symbol tables as well as the system catalogue are cached.

Concurrency control in network-like structures poses particular problems, as database parts to be locked are hard to determine. Under the assumption that the frequency of updates is low, only read and write locks for the whole database are provided. This implies that locks may be held only for short time intervals. Interactive data entry forms must check consistency when the data are actually to be committed to the database. Cache invalidation is done at lock grant on demand of each server instance, which prevent degradation of performance as the number of clients increases. The lock mechanism works reliably on local area networks.

Emphasis in the implementation is placed on *portability* of the platform across all UNIX systems and a variety of hardware settings, including PC-based ones. The system currently runs on Sun3, Sun4 series, SparcStations and 386 machines under UNIX. Porting to IBM Risc machines is currently undertaken. The X window system is required, preferably with a colour monitor. The system, based on a client-server architecture, may run in a local area network. Query processing, using caches of controllable size, is mainly done on the server side. Usage of shared caches for read-only access is currently under investigation. Concurrent access is foreseen for about eight to ten users (members of a software development team) at a time. *Scalability* and *size-independent performance* have been the main principles of the implementation. This is strengthened from the fact that for an information base, the more items it contains - the more useful it becomes.

6. CONCLUSION

We presented the Software Information Base, a reuse-targeted repository system, and first experiences from the development of a high-performance prototype. While this is a continuing effort, some conclusions can be drawn.

Pivotal role in being able to locate software components is played by the rich organisation facilities offered by a proper (meta-)modelling system (e.g., several extensible semantic/structural/referential links which are bi-directional and machine-supported). This should be coupled by graphical and others aids for the user interaction and component comprehension. In terms of implementation, no single technology is sufficient; a harmonious co-use of techniques from several areas is being found effective. Prime role among those is played by the technologies of databases, knowledge representation, hypermedia and information retrieval.

This paper concentrated on presenting functionality and implementation aspects of the SIB system. An empirical evaluation of the SIB model and system in the context of a specific methodology developed in the project ITHACA is reported in [Cons93]. Moreover, we have started evaluating the model with other object-oriented analysis and design methodologies (e.g., the Booch design methodology).

REFERENCES

[Ader90] M. Ader, O. Nierstrasz, S. McMahon, G. Mueller, A-K. Proefrock, The ITHACA Technology: A Landscape for Object-Oriented Application Development, *Proc. ESPRIT'90 Conf.*, Kluwer Academic Publishers, November 1990.

[Bigg87] Biggerstaff, T. et al., "Information Management Challenges in the Software Design Process", *IEEE Database Engineering*, Vol 10, March 1987.

[Bigg89] T. J. Biggerstaff, A. J. Perlis, *Software Reusability, Volume 1: Concepts and Models, Volume 2: Applications and Experience*, Addison-Wesley, Reading, Massachusetts, 1989.

[Boud88] Boudier, G., et al., "An overview of PCTE and PCTE+", Proc. ACM SIGSOFT/SIGPLAN Software Engineering Symposium on Practical Software Development Environments, ACM Software Engineering Notes, Vol. 13, No. 5, pp. 248-257, November 1988.

[Brod84] Brodie, M. and Ridjanovic, D., "On the Design and Specification of Database Transactions", in: Brodie, M., Mylopoulos, J. and Schmidt, J. (eds.), *On Conceptual Modelling: Perspectives from Artificial Intelligence, Databases and Programming Languages*, Springer-Verlag, 1984.

[Conk87] Conklin J., "Hypertext: An Introduction and Survey", *IEEE Computer*, Sept. 1987.

[Cons91] Constantopoulos, P., et al., The Software Information Base - Selection Tool Integrated Prototype, ITHACA.FORTH.91.E2.#3, Institute of Computer Science, Foundation of Research and Technology - Hellas, January 1991.

[Cons93] Constantopoulos, P., Jarke, M., Mylopoulos, J., and Vassiliou, Y., The Software Information Base: A Server for Reuse, Technical Report, Institute of Computer Science, Foundation of Research and Technology - Hellas, Heraklion, Crete, March 1993 (submitted for publication).

[deAn92] De Antonellis, et al, Ithaca Object-Oriented Methodology Manual, ITHACA. POLIMI-UDUNIV.E.8.6, Politecnico di Milano, 1992.

[deMe91] de Mey, V. et al., "The Implementation of VISTA - a Visual Scripting Tool", in: Tsichritzis, D. (ed.), *Object Composition*, Centre Universitaire d'Informatique, Universite de Geneve, 1991, pp. 31-56.

[Deva91] Devanbu, P., et al., "LaSSIE: A Knowledge-Based Software Information System", *Communications of the ACM*, May 1991.

[GaSc87] P. Garg, W. Scacchi, "On Designing Intelligent Hypertext Systems for Information Management in Software Engineering, DIF", Proceedings of Hypertext 87, pp. 409-431, November 1987

[GaSc89] P. Garg, W. Scacchi, "ISHYS: Designing an Intelligent Software Hypertext System", IEEE Expert, pp.52-62, 1989

[Hopk88] T. Hopking, C. Phillips, *Numerical methods in practice: using the NAG library*, Addison Wesley, New York, 1988.

[Kate90] Katevenis, M., et al., LABY User's Manual, Version 2.10, ITHACA.FORTH.90.E.3.3.#7, Institute of Computer Science, Foundation of research and Technology - Hellas, 1990.

[KhCo86] Khosafian S., Copeland G.P., "Object Identity", *ACM OOPSLA '86*.

[KhFr88] Khosafian S., Frank D., "Implementation Techniques for Object Oriented Databases", *Proc. AOODS*, Springer 1988.

[KiKi89] Kim, W., Kim, K.C., and Dale, A., "Indexing Techniques for Object Oriented Databases", in: *Object-Oriented Concepts, Databases, and Applications*, ACM Press New York 1989.

[Low88] Low C., "A Shared, Persistent Object Store", *Proc. ECOOP'88*,1988.

[MeLa87] Merrow T., Laursen J., "A Pragmatic System for Shared Persistent Objects", Proc. *OOPSLA'87*, 1987.

[Meye87] B.Meyer, Reusability: The Case for Object-Oriented Design, *IEEE Software*, March 1987.

[Meye90] B. Meyer, *Eiffel: the libraries*, Prentice-Hall, New York 1990.

[Mylo90] J. Mylopoulos, A. Borgida, M. Jarke, M. Koubarakis, Telos: Representing Knowledge About Information Systems, *ACM Transactions on Information Systems*, p.p. 325-362, October 1990.

[PeVe91] Petra, E., and Vezerides, C., SIB Contents' Manual, ITHACA.FORTH.91.E.2.#4, Institute of Computer Science, Foundation of Research and Technology - Hellas, January 1991.

[Prie91] Prieto-Diaz, R., "Implementing Faceted Classification for Software Reuse", *Communications of the ACM*, May 1991.

[SkZd86] Skarra A.H., Zdonik S.B., "The Management of Changing Types in an Object-Oriented Database", *Proc. OOPSLA'86*, 1986.

[Tayl88] Taylor et al, "Foundations for the Arcadia Environment Architecture", Proceedings of the ACM SIGSOFT/SIGPLAN Software Engin. Symposium on Practical Software Development Environments, ACM Software Engineering Notes, vol.13, no.5, pp.1-13, November 1988.

[Veze92] Vezerides, C., The organization of a Software Information Base for software reuse by a community of programmers, Master's Thesis, Department of Computer Science,

University of Crete, May 1992.

[WiAl88] Wile D.S., Allard D.G., Worlds: Aggregates for Object Bases, USC/Information Sciences Institute, Marina del Rey,CA 90292, 1988.

[Vass90] Vassiliou, Y., et al., Technical Description of the SIB, Technical Report, Institute of Computer Science, Foundation of Research and Technology - Hellas, Heraklion, Crete, January 1990.

9.

INFORMATION SYSTEM ENGINEERING

Information System Development Process (A-30)
N. Prakash, C. Rolland and B. Pernici (Editors)
Elsevier Science Publishers B.V. (North–Holland)

© 1993 IFIP. All rights reserved.

Concurrent engineering of information systems

A. T. Berztiss

Department of Computer Science, University of Pittsburgh, Pittsburgh, PA 15260, USA
(e-mail: alpha@cs.pitt.edu; fax: +412-624-8854)

and

SYSLAB, University of Stockholm

A generic software process model based on prototyping is introduced, and some observations have been collected that are to assist in transformation of the generic model into a concurrent software process for the development of information systems. Concurrency relates to both product and process: early modularization partitions the software product into manageable components that can be developed in parallel, and overlap of the phases of the software process allows for parallelism in the process. We use the executable specification language SF for the specification of software processes.

Keyword Codes: K.6.3, H.0, D.2.0

Keywords: Software Management; Information Systems, General; Software Engineering, General

1. INTRODUCTION

Concurrent engineering in manufacturing removes the walls between design office, toolshop, and factory floor. Instead of designers handing complete detailed designs to toolmakers, toolmakers defining the complete tool support for the manufacturing process, and installation crews only then doing the tooling-up, an interdisciplinary team carries a design through to installation of the manufacturing process while the design is still being completed. The primary objective is to reduce the time it takes to get a product to market, but this approach has the added advantages of improved utilization of human resources by reducing waiting time, improved product quality by making quality a concern of all participants in the concurrent engineering process, and ongoing concern with improvement of the process itself. For more detailed discussion of concurrent engineering see [1].

The replacement of the waterfall model of the software process by an integrated development model [2] was a step toward concurrent software engineering – it actually predates concurrency in the more traditional engineering disciplines. Our task here is to develop the concurrent software engineering process paradigm further. To do so we shall consider the introduction of concurrency along two dimensions: a horizontal partitioning of a software project into subprojects, and a vertical integration of the different phases of software development.

Section 2 defines a generic software development process based on prototyping. In Sections 3 and 4 we introduce concurrency based on early modularization, and on overlapping of phases of the process, respectively. In Section 5 we give examples of how the specification language SF is used to define the software process and introduce changes into the process. In Section 6 we present conclusions and recommendations.

2. A GENERIC SOFTWARE PROCESS

In this section we have collected some observations that are particularly relevant to the form that a generic software process for information systems (ISs) is to take.

OBSERVATION 1. Some important characteristics of the domain in which the software development process operates are volatile requirements that are adjusted iteratively, the need to record requirement changes and design decisions, and early creation of user documentation.

OBSERVATION 2. Different module interaction mechanisms have different effectiveness in different application settings. The three most common mechanisms are call-return, pipelining, and message passing. The loosest coupling between modules is achieved with message passing, which is particularly effective for ISs.

OBSERVATION 3. A conceptual model based on data types as the structuring mechanism for the data of an application allows an easy partition of a software project into subprojects. Data types that consist of sets and functions associated with the sets are the natural objects on which to base modularization. If communication between the data types is by message passing, we have then an object-oriented conceptual model.

OBSERVATION 4. The software process is to make use of knowledge-based assistance. The effectiveness of such assistance depends greatly on the way it is introduced into the software process. Although many knowledge-based "apprentices" have been proposed, little has been done on defining how software developers are to interact with the "apprentices" in a large-scale software development project. No attention seems to have been given to the cost-effectiveness of "apprentices". For a survey see [3]; further reading on "apprentices" for specific tasks in the software process is provided by [4-9].

OBSERVATION 5. An adaptable software process depends for its effectiveness on a well-developed infrastructure consisting of tool sets and communication links. Introduction of concurrent engineering in traditional engineering domains has required very large investments in infrastructure. Failure to invest heavily in software engineering environments is false economy in any case [10]; failure to do so for concurrent software engineering can make the concurrent approach counterproductive.

Figure 1 shows an integrated software development model based on a prototype that is used to validate requirements, and is later transformed into an operational system. This is a generic model of the software process that has to be refined into a detailed model of the development of ISs. In the refinement note is to be taken of the observations made above. The refinement will not be carried out here – the purpose of this paper is to introduce concurrent software engineering of ISs without going into detail.

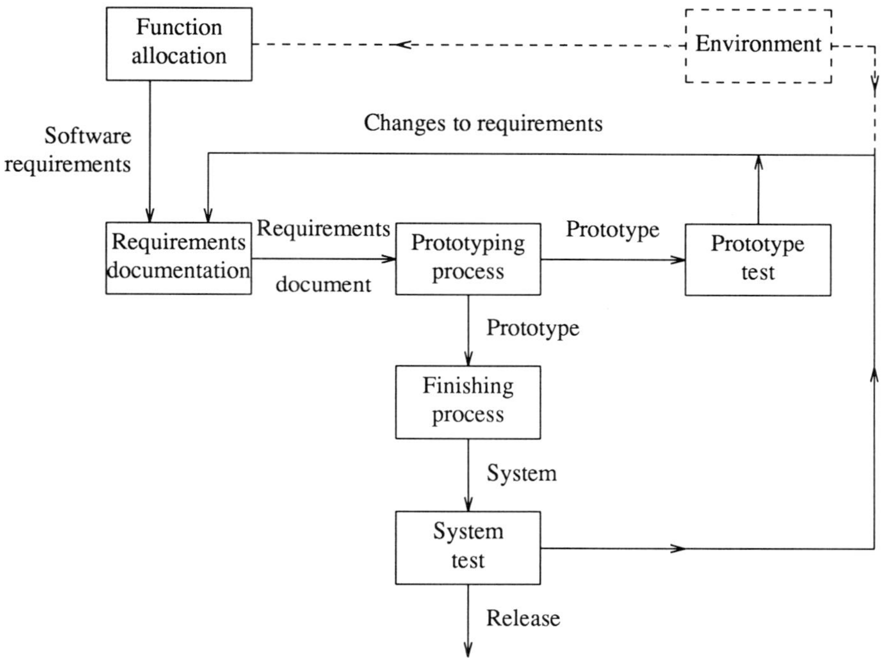

Figure 1. Prototyping-based evolutionary software process

In Figure 1 the "Function allocation" box represents the assignment of system functions to people, software, and hardware. One result of the allocation is an informal software requirements statement that is formalized and structured in the "Requirements documentation" box. ISs have a strong dependence on the environment. In Figure 1 this effect is represented by the box "Environment".

Our recommendation is that the requirements document be structured in the form of system modules – for ISs the modules are data types. Then reliable cost, risk, and performance estimates can be obtained early. If an estimate is unacceptable, the software project can be cancelled while expenditures are still moderate. Also, the requirements document needs to be given structure, and a modular structure is appropriate for this. It is understood that a technical review of the requirements document is an integral part of requirements documentation. To quote Philip Crosby, quality is conformance to requirements [11]. The requirements documentation process is therefore the most important component of the software process.

The requirements document is submitted to a prototyping process, a prototype emerges from this process, and the prototype is tested. There can be great variability in what the "Prototyping process" and the "Prototype test" boxes contain, and how the two processes are related. For example, the "Requirements document" may contain an executable specification, in which case there is no need for a separate prototyping process. In some software processes the prototype test would be prototype execution with user participation. Under Cleanroom [12], the prototype would be validated by means of semi-formal proofs. The "Requirements documentation" – "Prototyping process" – "Prototype test" loop is iterated until the prototype passes an acceptance review, which we regard to be a part of "Prototyping process". The prototype test assumes particular importance for ISs – such systems are based on conceptual models of their domains, and the models cannot be validated without participation of domain experts and ultimate users of the system. The "Changes to requirements", which originate in the two test boxes or in the environment are change *requests*. Each request is reviewed as part of the requirements documentation process, and only approved changes are incorporated in the requirements document.

The accepted prototype moves through the "Finishing process" box in which prototype is turned into deliverable system. This may mean the integration of prototypes of several subsystems into a composite system, and addition of ancillary features, such as a help system. Again we assume that a technical review is part of this process. The composite system is then put through a system test.

3. PARTITIONING OF AN INFORMATION SYSTEM

Our first example is a toy information system that relates students, courses, and instructors. Figure 2 shows an entity-relationship (ER) diagram for this system in the OMT notation [13]. Each box in the diagram represents an entity class. The boxes list also attributes of the entities. Relationships between entities are indicated by labels on lines joining boxes. The multiplicity of a relation is indicated graphically: thus, a many-one relation is represented by a bullet at the "many" end and no bullet at the "one" end. Attributes of relationships are indicated by a special symbol: the "student takes course" relationship has attribute *grade* – there is a grade associated with every <student, course> pair. The triangle indicates an "is a" relationship. Here it shows that the class *Person* has subclasses *Instructor* and *Student*.

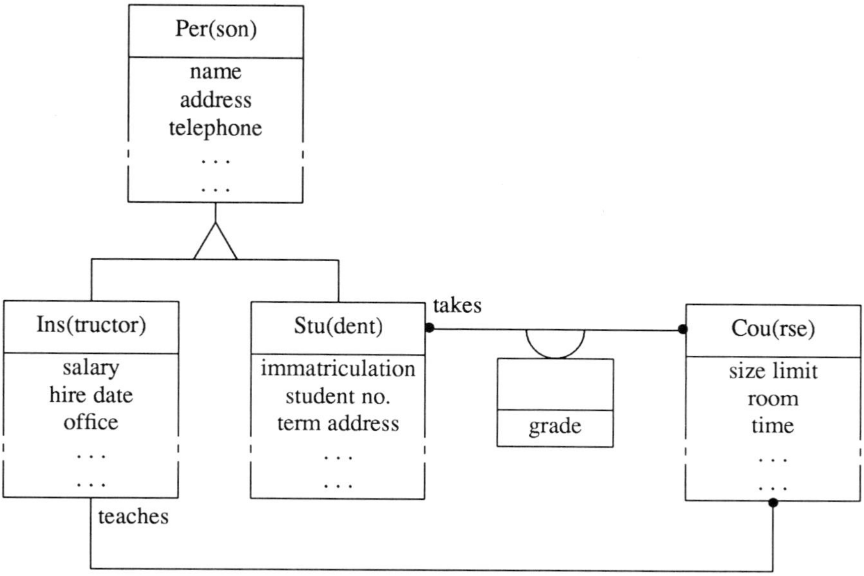

Figure 2. ER diagram for a toy example

The next task is to convert the ER diagram into a data type diagram. Our convention is that all functions belonging to a type map from the set of this type or some subset of this set. Attributes already agree with the convention. However, each relation and attribute of a relation has to be converted into a function mapping from a set, and it then becomes part of the data type of this set. The rules for one-one and one-many relations are simple: for a one-one relation spanning sets X and Y it does not matter whether the relation becomes a function from X to Y or from Y to X; a one-many relation becomes a function that maps from the "many" set, e.g., our "teaches" relation becomes the function

$$TaughtBy: \quad Cou \longrightarrow Ins.$$

In the transformation of a many-many relation we cannot avoid ending up with a set-valued function: the value of *Takes*(s) is the set of courses taken by student s; the value of *Taken*(c) is the set of students taking course c. In the prototyping stage it makes little difference which function is chosen – as a rule of thumb, choose the mapping under which the average size of the value sets is smaller, but do so in the realization that during the finishing process concerns such as storage economy, access rights, and performance may cause a reconsideration. We expect smaller function values under *Takes* than under *Taken*, and of all functions that could represent the *grade* attribute, we expect smallest function values under

$$StuGra: \quad Stu \longrightarrow (Cou \times Grade)\text{-set}.$$

Hence, the result of the transformations is as shown in the type diagram Figure 3.

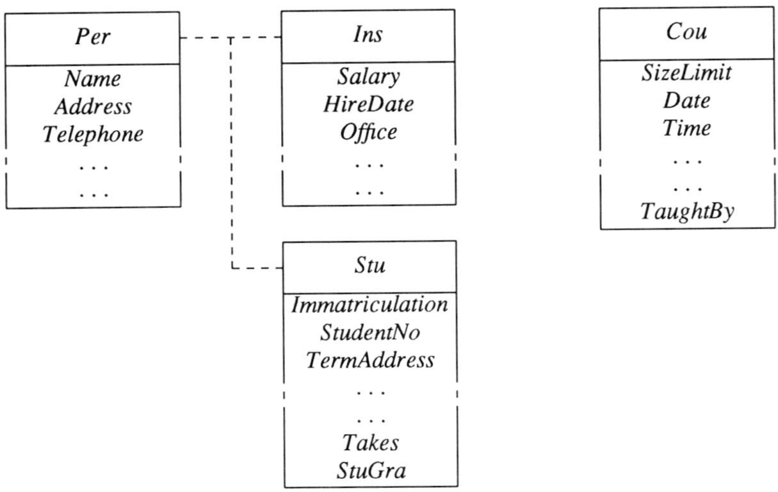

Figure 3. Type diagram corresponding to ER diagram of Figure 2

4. CONCURRENCY IN THE SOFTWARE PROCESS

Our next task is to see how the different phases of Figure 1 could be overlapped. The software process has to address quality issues by means of five types of tests:

- Reliability – functionality tests
- Robustness – exceptional condition tests
- Performance – simulation and timing tests
- Usability – user (external) interface tests
- Understandability – documentation tests

Let us look at how each attribute relates to the others. Reliability (as regards functional correctness) is unrelated to any other attribute except, perhaps, robustness. If a system has enhanced robustness, then the adverse effect of faults in the system is reduced. Now, robustness can be improved each time the system developer thinks of another exceptional condition. These exceptional conditions would affect interface and documentation – the user has to be made aware of the exceptional condition, and the nature of the exceptional condition has to be explained to the user by means of documentation.

The purpose of detection of exceptional conditions is to prevent the exceptional condition from leading to a system failure. One of the tasks of a system developer is to imagine exceptional conditions. Another is to make sure that the system meets performance requirements. However, exceptions rarely affect performance in a significant way [14]. This means that these two tasks can proceed in parallel. Performance has little effect on usability, but the actual performance characteristics of a system must be clearly documented, and usability is closely related to documentation.

To ensure effective concurrency in the software process, software development will have to become a collaborative effort of experts in various specialities. But, for collaboration to be effective, there has to be a common reference point – this is a detailed model of the process. We need a representation of the model, means of implementing changes in the model, means of communicating information relating to the changes, and means of implementing partial or total automation of the change process as our understanding increases. In our work we are using the SF specification language as the representation language. We shall take this up in the next section.

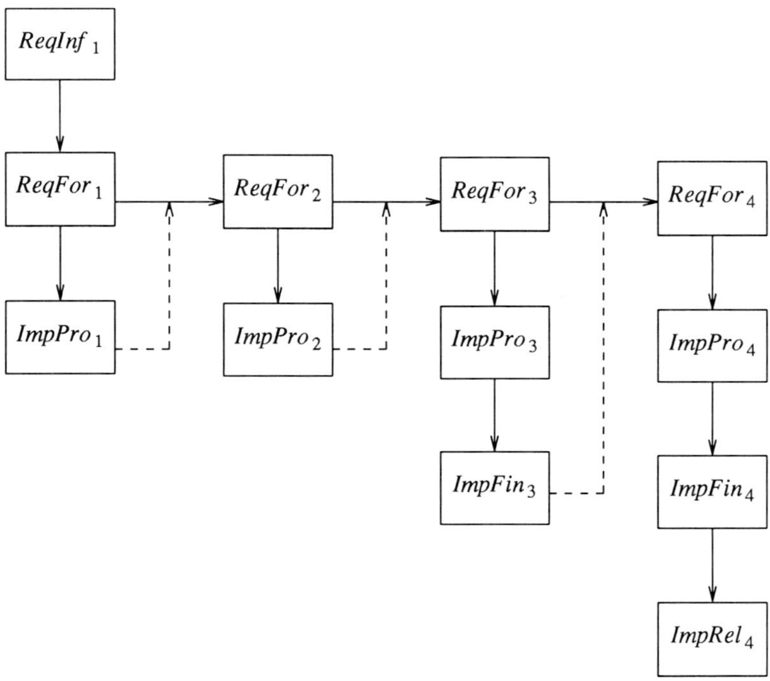

Figure 4. Versions of a module

Our concern is with modules, system developers, user representatives, and the environment, with emphasis on modules. In keeping with Section 3, we assume that we are dealing with a set of modules from the very start, and that each module exists as a chain of representations: as a collection of informal requirements (*ReqInf*), as a formal requirements definition (*ReqFor*), as a prototype implementation (*ImpPro*), as a "finished" implementation (*ImpFin*), and as a component of a software release (*ImpRel*). For each module there is just one *ReqInf* and just one *ImpRel*, but multiple versions can exist of intermediate members of the chain, as shown in Figure 4 – prototype test causes two changes to *ReqFor*, and system test causes a third change. Although the changes are made to *ReqFor*, the causes for the changes originate elsewhere – in Figure 4 this dependence is indicated by the broken lines.

At the beginning of this section we discussed what effect changes that aim at improving one particular software quality attribute have on other attributes. The discussion, when related to Figure 4, suggests two principles that are to be applied in detailed development of the software process. First, because documentation is affected by most changes, automation of documentation is to receive top priority. Documentation puts the requirements document *ReqFor* into a readable form, so automation here is essentially the paraphrasing of *ReqFor*. Automation will not only speed up the development process, but will also guarantee that the documentation accompanying the released system is consistent with the final version of *ReqFor*.

Second, it is most important to reduce the time spent in the prototyping loop. Everything can be automated, at least in principle, except input from users participating in the prototype test. Joint Application Development (JAD) – see, e.g., [15] – can greatly reduce prototyping time. Under one version of JAD, developers and user representatives meet in a workshop lasting several days in which an initial prototype (the $ImpPro_1$ of Figure 4) is transformed into a system ready for the finishing process ($ImpPro_3$). Of course, the changes brought about by testing $ImpFin_3$ can still be extensive, but user participation is no longer needed, so that there is full potential for automation of the processing chain that turns $ReqFor_4$ into $ImpRel_4$.

5. SF SPECIFICATION OF A CONCURRENT SOFTWARE PROCESS

Space limitations force us to assume that the reader has some familiarity with SF. If the assumption is wrong, refer to [16-19]. We shall define three SF data types. Type *Module* captures the history of changes to a module as illustrated by Figure 4. Type *Instance* is to hold data relating to a particular version of a module. Type *ModuleChange* relates to requests for changes to the requirements.

There are five functions in type *Module*, corresponding to the five classes of versions associated with a module. The value of *ReqInf*(*m*) is an ordered pair consisting of the time the informal requirements of *m* were created, and the identifier of this version of *m*. The value of *ImpRel*(*m*) is an ordered triple consisting of the time of creation of the released version of *m*, the identifier of this version, and the identifier of the version from which the released version derives. As regards formal requirements definition, prototype implementation, and "finished" implementation, several versions may exist in each case. Hence the value of the corresponding function for a given m is set-valued, where each set consists of triples analogous in form to the triple *ImpRel*(m).

TYPE *Module*;

SET M;

FUNCTIONS $ReqInf: \; M \longrightarrow Timestamp \times Instance;$

$ReqFor: \; M \longrightarrow (Timestamp \times Instance \times Instance)\text{–set};$

$ImpPro: \; M \longrightarrow (Timestamp \times Instance \times Instance)\text{–set};$

$ImpFin: \; M \longrightarrow (Timestamp \times Instance \times Instance)\text{–set};$

$ImpRel: \; M \longrightarrow Timestamp \times Instance \times Instance;$

ENDTYPE;

Type *Instance* is based on set *VER*, which is partitioned into five subsets, one for each of our five classes of versions. This type can contain any number of functions – we list only a few in our schema definition. Function *ModId* associates a given member of set *VER* with the module to which it relates, and the value of *VerText*(v) is the text of version v. Function *ReqSource* is defined for informal requirements alone – it identifies the source from which the informal requirements were obtained.

TYPE *Instance*;

SET VER (SUBSETS: RI, RF, IP, IF, IR);

FUNCTIONS $ModId: \; VER \longrightarrow Module;$

$VerText: \; VER \longrightarrow Text;$

$ReqSource: \; RI \longrightarrow Id;$

... ...

... ...

ENDTYPE;

Information regarding change requests and their disposition is collected as type *ChangeRequest*. The set of this type is C, and it is partitioned into subsets *EV* and *NOTEV*, corresponding to change requests that have or have not been evaluated. Evaluated change requests are further partitioned into sets *ACC*(epted) and *REJ*(ected). Each change request cr relates to some instance that is identified by *VerId*(cr), and its text is the value of *ChReqText*(cr). The originator of the change request is identified by *ChReqSource*(cr), the date on which the request was received by *ChReqReceived*(cr), and the date on which it was reviewed by *ChReqReviewed*(cr). Function *ChReqReviewed* is defined for change requests in set *EV* alone.

TYPE $ChangeRequest$;

SET C (SUBSETS: $NOTEV$, EV (SUBSETS: ACC, REJ));

FUNCTIONS $VerId: C \longrightarrow Instance$;

$ChReqText: C \longrightarrow Text$;

$ChReqSource: C \longrightarrow Id$;

$ChReqReceived: C \longrightarrow Timestamp$;

$ChReqReviewed: EV \longrightarrow Timestamp$;

ENDTYPE;

The three types serve as a data base on which to superimpose a software process defined in terms of events and transactions. We shall discuss only two events and one transaction, hopefully enough to convey a flavor of the approach. Suppose a request *cr* for a module change has been received. This request is made part of the data base by event *EnterChRequest*, with arguments that define the module instance to which *cr* relates, the text of the changes, and the identifier of the originator of the request. This information is enough to update four of the functions listed in the schema for *ChangeRequest*. Change request *cr* is made part of *NOTEV*. The event also issues the signal *EvaluateCR*. The signal is picked up by a transaction that prompts the software developers to review request *cr* and supply the result of the review as an argument to event *DecisionOnCR*. The argument is of type Boolean – true if the request is approved; false otherwise.

EVENT *EnterChRequest*(*cr*: *ChangeRequest*, *m*: *Instance*, *ctext*: *Text*, *orig*: *Id*);

DATACONDITIONS $NOTEV' = NOTEV \cup \{cr\}$;

$VerId'(cr) = m$;

$ChReqText'(cr) = ctext$;

$ChReqSource'(cr) = orig$;

$ChReqReceived'(cr) = Time.Now$;

SIGCONDITIONS (*EvaluateCR* (*cr*))ON;

ENDEVENT;

TRANSACTION *PromptForEvaluationOfCR*;

@( ): ON(*EvaluateCR* (*cr*))OFF: PROMPT(*DecisionOnCR* (*cr*, _));

ENDTRANSACTION;

EVENT *DecisionOnCR*(*cr*: *ChangeRequest*, *decision*: *Boolean*);

DATACONDITIONS $NOTEV' = NOTEV - \{cr\}$;

$decision \longrightarrow ACC' = ACC \cup \{cr\}$;

not($decision$) $\longrightarrow REJ' = REJ \cup \{cr\}$;

$ChReqReviewed'(cr) = Time.\ Now$;

SIGCONDITIONS (*SModifyReqFor* (*cr*))ON;

ENDEVENT;

Event *DecisionOnCR* has raised signal *SModifyReqFor*, which is to be picked up by transaction *TModifyReqFor* (not defined here), which in turn is to issue a prompt regarding event *ModifyReqFor* (also not defined). The purpose of *ModifyReqFor* is to adjust the functions of type *Instance*.

Consider now a change to the process. We do not contemplate a major paradigm shift – our process is still as shown in Figure 1, and a module goes through a sequence of versions in the manner illustrated by Figure 4. This means that we are limited to changes that improve the process by increased automation within an essentially stable process model. Let us consider processes in SF. An event, by raising a signal, invokes a transaction, the transaction initiates an event or causes an event to be initiated, this event invokes another transaction, and so forth. Thus transactions can link events into complex processes. The process structure is interpreted as having Petri net semantics, with events corresponding to places, transactions to transitions, and tokens to signals. More precisely, because a transaction is sometimes specified by two times that define an interval within which the transaction is to take place, SF processes obey the semantics of time Petri nets (see, e.g., [20]). The Petri net displays opportunities for concurrency, and it may be analyzed for properties such as liveness. The aim is to design into the Petri net as much parallelism as possible, and to increase the number of events initiated by the system, thus increasing automation of the software process.

Of particular interest for this are transactions that issue prompts. A prompt is issued when the system has determined that an event is to be initiated, but the system cannot initiate the event on its own. We find a prompt in transaction *PromptForEvaluationOfCR*, which is reached after a change request has been submitted. The request is to be evaluated, and there are three options: (i) a change manager makes the evaluation without any support by the system; (ii) the system helps the change manager by supplying information that the system deems relevant, and we have a rudimentary DSS (Decision Support System); (iii) an ES (Expert System) is developed to do the evaluation, i.e., the function of the change manager is now fully automated. Under the first two options the transaction continues to issue a prompt; under the third the system is made to initiate the change evaluation event on its own. Note the distinction we make between a DSS and an ES – an ES makes a decision totally on its own, although it may request input of additional data; a DSS merely supports a human decision maker. In an SF model of an enterprise the transactions that issue prompts represent all opportunities for introducing a DSS or an ES, the cost-effectiveness of each prospective DSS or ES can be worked out, and these systems can be introduced incrementally, one DSS or ES at a time, according to the availability of resources. In our example a DSS would be used to begin with. However, with growing understanding of the principles underlying the evaluation of change requests, more and more of the decision making can be taken over by the DSS, until finally the DSS has become an ES.

6. CONCLUSIONS AND RECOMMENDATIONS

We ourselves consider the emphasis on early modularization the most important aspect of this paper. We recommend that the formal requirements document be structured in the form of system modules – concurrent engineering of an information-control system has to be based on modular structure of the system. Moreover, a well-designed modular structure is crucial for integration that extends beyond a single enterprise. As more and more enterprises merge, or enter into partnerships with their customers and suppliers, integration with external systems becomes essential for effective executive information systems [21]. Modularization based on data types fosters such integration. Both the modularization process and the conversion of requirements into a released system are to be guided by the observations of Section 2. In particular we want to emphasize again the need for a well-developed infrastructure (Observation 5).

In [22] we give an operational definition of engineering in general, and indicate how the definition relates to software engineering. The concerns of engineering are listed as process definition, resolution of conflicts in requirements, use of standards, anticipation of change, provision for the unexpected, transfer of theory into practice, scaling up of models into systems, quality control, tool selection, cooperation in teams of experts, management, and technological adventure. In an SF specification of the concurrent software process, which is being elaborated by a group of students at the University of Pittsburgh, these engineering principles are being built into the software process.

The software process needs to be continually updated and upgraded. Concurrent engineering is part of such updating. We are recommending that the process be receptive to all proven innovations, and that it become a testbed for innovations that are still to be proven. In this context we have emphasized technical reviews, Cleanroom techniques, and JAD. A mature discipline is characterized by codification of cause-effect relationships that are ultimately expressed as laws. Our task is to uncover the cause-effect relationships for the software process as it relates to information systems. A rigorously specified model of the software process will help us in this task.

REFERENCES

1. Yeh, R.T., Notes on concurrent engineering. *IEEE Trans. Knowledge and Data Eng.* **4** (1992), 407-414.
2. Balzer, R., Cheatham, T.E., and Green C., Software technology in the 1990's: using a new paradigm. *Computer* **16**, 11 (Nov.1983), 39-45.
3. Rich, C., and Waters, R.C., *The Programmer's Apprentice*. Addison-Wesley, Reading, MA, 1990.
4. Cauvet, C., Proix, C., and Rolland, C., ALECI: an expert system for requirements engineering. In *Advanced Information Systems Engineering* (LNCS No.498), B.Andersen, J.A.Bubenko, and A.Solvberg, (Eds.), Springer-Verlag, Berlin, 1991, pp.31-49.
5. Johnson, W.L., Deriving specifications from requirements. *Proc. 10th Internat. Conf. Software Eng.*, Computer Society Press, Washington, DC, 1988, 428-438.
6. Lubars, M.D., and Harandi, M.T., Intelligent support for software specification and design. *IEEE Expert* **1**, 4 (Winter 1986), 33-41.
7. Karimi, J., and Konsynski, B.R., An automated software design assistant. *IEEE Trans. Software Eng.* **14** (1988), 194-210.
8. Lor, K.-W.E., and Berry, D.M., Automatic synthesis of SARA design models from system requirements. *IEEE Trans. Software Eng.* **17** (1991), 1229-1240.
9. Luqi, Knowledge-based support for rapid software prototyping. *IEEE Expert* **3**, 4 (Winter 1988), 9-18.
10. Yourdon, E., *The Decline and Fall of the American Programmer.* Yourdon Press, Englewood Cliffs, NJ, 1992.
11. Crosby, P.B., *Quality Without Tears – The Art of Hassle-Free Management.* McGraw-Hill, New York, 1984.
12. Dyer, M., *The Cleanroom Approach to Quality Software Development.* Wiley, New York, 1992.
13. Rumbaugh, J., Blaha, M., Premerlani, W., Eddy, F., and Lorensen, W., *Object-Oriented Modeling and Design.* Prentice-Hall, Englewood Cliffs, NJ, 1991.
14. Smith, C.U., *Performance Engineering of Software Systems.* Addison-Wesley, Reading, MA, 1990.
15. August, J.H., *Joint Application Design: The Group Session Approach to System Design.* Yourdon Press, Englewood Cliffs, NJ, 1991.
16. Berztiss, A.T., Data abstraction in the specification of information systems. *Proc. IFIP World Congress 86*, pp.83-90.
17. Berztiss, A., The set-function approach to conceptual modeling. In *Information System Design Methodologies: Improving the Practice*, T.W.Olle, H.G.Sol, and A.A.Verrijn-Stuart (Eds.), North-Holland, Amsterdam, 1986, pp.107-144.

18. Berztiss, A., Formal specification methods and visualization. In *Principles of Visual Programming Systems*, S.-K.Chang (Ed.), Prentice-Hall, Englewood Cliffs, NJ, 1990, pp.231-290.
19. Berztiss, A.T., The specification and prototyping language SF. SYSLAB Report 78, University of Stockholm, 1990.
20. Berthomieu, B., and Diaz, M., Modeling and verification of time dependent systems using time Petri nets. *IEEE Trans. Software Eng.* **17** (1991), 259-273.
21. Smith, P., *Client/Server Computing*. SAMS Publishing, Carmel, IN, 1992.
22. Berztiss, A.T., Engineering principles and software engineering. In *Software Engineering Education* (LNCS No.640), C.Sledge (Ed.), Springer-Verlag, Berlin, 1992, pp.437-451.

Information System Development Process (A-30)
N. Prakash, C. Rolland and B. Pernici (Editors)
Elsevier Science Publishers B.V. (North–Holland)
1993 IFIP.

Business Process Redesign and Information Systems Design: A Happy Couple?

Han Gerrits

Vrije Universiteit, Faculty of Economic Sciences, Business Administration and Econometrics
Department of Information Management and Information Technology
De Boelelaan 1105, 1081 HV Amsterdam, The Netherlands
e-mail: hgerrits@econ.vu.nl

ABSTRACT

This article focusses on organizations that deliver products consisting of information. These organizations have gained fewer benefits from the introduction of information technology then manufacturing companies. An explanation for this finding is that current information system design methodologies do not provide the appropriate tools. They are directed at analyzing and designing information systems for control and do not make a distinction between information handling processes that are part of the control system of an organization and information processes that are part of the production system.

The business process redesign approach that gets more and more attention offers a way of thinking and designing to overcome these shortcomings. Comparing business process redesign with information systems design makes the strong points of both visible. We propose an integration of business process redesign in the system design process as a solution.

Keyword Codes: H.1.0, H.4.0, H.4.2
Keywords: Information Systems, Models and Principles, General; Information Systems Applications, General & Types of Systems

SETTING THE SCOPE

The introduction of information technology in organizations does not automatically lead to performance improvements. To realize the possible benefits of information technology it is necessary to redesign[1] business processes (Thurow, 1991, Davenport & Short, 1990). Redesigning business processes means that information technology should not be just another means (e.g., a replacement for forms, card-trays, calculators and the internal post system) to execute the same old business processes, but should be used as an enabler for new process designs. Hammer (1990) points at this as follows: "They (organizations, HG) leave the existing processes intact and use computers simply to speed them up". Norton (1989) indicates that this kind of application of information technology does not really enhance the performance of organizations by writing: "New world technology plus old world management equals old world results!".[2]

As research shows (Davenport & Short, 1990, Hammer, 1990, Fortune, 1991), the introduction of information technology led to a greater performance improvement in manufacturing companies than in offices. The cause for this difference is that manufacturing companies, unlike offices, do indeed redesign their business processes when introducing information technology. In this article we elaborate this point some more. We will discuss why this difference in performance exists and, looking at offices, what business process redesign and information systems design methodologies can yield.

While business process redesign is a quite new area, a general accepted terminology is yet missing. Therefore we introduce definitions for the concepts used in this article in table 1. Besides this, we would like to broaden the notion of offices and manufacturing companies by defining information production and material production. Products delivered by organizations can be material, like cars or airplanes, or consist of information[3], like insurance or mortgages. Production of the first kind we call *material production* and production of the last kind we entitle *information production*. The information products in most cases do have some kind of physical appearance of course, but the very added value lies in the information that is the output of the primary process. Material production organizations have business processes that transform materials while information production organizations have business processes that process information.

WHY REDESIGN BUSINESS PROCESSES?

To gain benefits from investments in new technology, either information technology or any other kind of technology, the performance of the business processes should be improved. This performance gain is either a higher productivity (efficiency) or a better effectiveness of the organization (Drucker, 1974). Looking at efficiency, research (Fortune, 1991) shows that productivity in information production is at best equal to the productivity of a decade ago, while in the same period material production achieved about 30% productivity gain. Other writers (Davenport & Short, 1990, Hammer, 1990) also point at this difference, but do not give measurements.

DEFINITIONS

- ***Activity***: *A solitary kind of operation, using inputs and delivering outputs. An activity proceeds with no interruption. Executing an activity adds value to the inputs (cf. Porter, 1985).*
- ***Process***: *A sequence of activities, delivering a product or service*[4] *to an internal or external customer. The process starts with after the occurence of an event, for example a request for a product and ends with the delivery of the product to the customer.*
- ***Business process***: *a process delivering the products to customers of the organization. A business process will in most cases be cross-functional, i.e., pass through more organization units. Business processes can be material processing as well as information processing.*
- ***Information process***: *A process that processes information for management purposes. In comparison with a business process that produces information, an information process has an internal customer.*
- ***Information systems***: *The means to execute information processing.*
- ***Information technology***: *All information handling and processing technology used for building information systems.*
- ***Business strategy***: *The strategy the business pursues (cf. Porter, 1980).*

Table 1

Considering effectiveness, the figures also indicate a difference between material production and information production. In the same interval as described in the former paragraph, material production succeeded for example in shortening the delivery times (the time elapsed between an order for a product from a customer and the final delivery of the product to the customer) while at the same time increasing flexibility making possible client-specific products. Japanese electronics and car companies provide some good examples of this.
In information production effectiveness improvements have barely been achieved. It looks as if the introduction of information technology did not deliver added value to information production companies but only has led to higher costs.

For an explanation of this we take a better look at the idea of added value. Porter (1985) writes: "In competitive terms, value is the amount buyers are willing to pay for what a firm provides them.". In other words: only if customers are aware of the introduction of new technology in the organization, this new technology provides added value; for if the introduction of new technology remains unaware to the customers, they won't be willing to pay more. This implies that introducing new technology will only give added value if the business processes that deliver the products are changed in such a way that the customers can be served better, or are charged lower costs. If the business processes stay exactly the same, the customers are not able to appreciate the investments the company has made.

An example to elucidate this point: a car manufacturer is working with day batches: every day the half-products are brought to the next station. There are 5 stations, leading to a production time of 5 days. The painting station is the station with the longest batch time, thereby defining the minimum batch time: this station takes 4 hours to die all the products and 4 hours to clean. If this company buys a new painting machine that only takes 2 hours to paint and 1 hour to clean, but leaves the business processes intact, the production time stays the same, the clients will never know of the new machine, so no added value is created and the investment will not pay off. What the company should do, is redesign the production process, for example to make it possible to have half day batches, resulting in a production time of 2 and a half day. That would be an improvement that customers appreciate (they receive their custom-made car earlier) and therefore creates added value.

WHY BUSINESS PROCESSES IN INFORMATION PRODUCTION ARE NOT REDESIGNED

The fact is that material production companies do redesign their business processes when they introduce new technology, whether it is production machines or information technology. Information production companies are among the companies that invested a lot in information technology. However, in most of the cases it didn't pay off. It did bring some benefits of course. For example, it wouldn't have been possible handle the increasing amount of transactions without automation of the back office of banks, but the value added has been minimal. Financial transactions still take tenfold of the time that's really worked on a product because the business processes are still the same as in the days of paper and calculator. In those days it was not possible to execute these processes faster, but now we have new technology at our disposal that can speed things up. Also, in contrast to material production, most financial institutions until now only offer standard products that clients can choose of and are not able to deliver client specific products.

Information system design methodologies do not make a difference between information processes (processes delivering information for management purposes) and business processes that produce information. This distinction should be made because the demands for the design of these processes are different. When designing business processes that deliver information products we would like to look at these processes as production processes and talk about them in production terms. Examples of aspects of business processes that we are interested in are production time, stock levels, delivery time and work in progress. Current information system design methodologies do not take these aspects into account. The (implicit) paradigm is that the information system is supplying information for managerial decision making (cf. Blumenthal, 1969).

Looking at material production one sees a large body of knowledge that supports the design of business processes. Operations management, logistics and materials management literature are examples of this. We use information system design methodologies to design information systems in material production. In material production these information systems are literally management information systems: systems to be used to control the business processes.

However in information production we do not have methods to design information systems that are actually production systems executing business processes. We use information systems design methodologies for designing management information systems as well as for designing information processes that actually execute the production of the organization. In our view this is the main reason for the problems we face now in information production.
This leads to the conclusion that current information systems design methodologies are based on another philosophy than what's needed for business process redesign. The methodologies do have their merits for designing and building information systems, but should be supplemented. Let's explore the differences between these methodologies and business process redesign some more, to get more insight in the possibilities for improvements.

Business Process Redesign versus Information System Design

It will be clear that we are in need of methodologies that support the (re)design of business processes in information production. As we indicated before, current information system design methodologies are not suited for this. The view on business process redesign as presented here is based on different sources (Davenport & Short, 1990; Hammer, 1990; Harrington, 1991; Keen, 1991; Scott Morton, 1991; Tapscott & Caston, 1993). We have extracted the main points of business process redesign as discussed in these sources. The characteristics of information systems design stem from diverse sources too (Arthur Young & Company, 1987; DeMarco, 1979; Gane & Sarson, 1979; Martin, 1989; Olle, 1992; Orr, 1981; Yourdon, 1982). Along with these paper sources, case studies in both fields support the views. In the following paragraphs we do not make explicit references to the literature sources[5].

Comparing business process redesign with the current information system design methodologies reveals the following differences (table 2).

	information systems design	***business process redesign***
1 area of interest	information processes	business processes
2 process concept	function / activity	cross functional process
3 process view	circular	linear
4 role of information system	management control	user support
5 role of designer	expert	participation

Table 2

1. Area of Interest

Building information systems and redesigning business processes involves analysis and design of different problem areas. To depict the difference we distinguish four areas of interest in which analysis is needed to design business processes and information systems. The areas are connected since a demand in one area asks for a solution in another area. The areas are depicted in figure 1, indicating the demand-support relations between the areas: demands in an area need solutions in the level(s) beneath.

The areas of interest are defined as follows (figure 1):

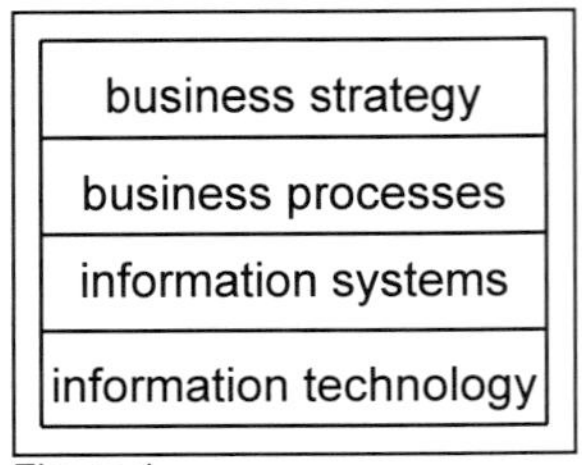

Figure 1

- Business strategy: the definition of an explicit strategy is necessary to be able to redesign the business processes. The strategy is the basis for making design choices. Without an explicit statement considering the strategy of the organization, design choices can not be made. An example we ran across in one of our research projects is the simultaneous execution of activities as part of the same business process. Information technology makes this simultaneity possible. It will be clear that the extra coordination needed to synchronize the activities will higher the total costs of the business process. In addition in some situations extra costs occur because of the unnecessary work that's done because the two parallel activities are always executed both, also in cases the sequential activities would stop after the execution of the first activity.

  If the strategy is to have a short production time, every possibility to execute processes in parallel should be used to shorten the production time. If, on the other hand the company follows a low cost strategy, it could be better to execute the processes in sequence because of the lower costs.

- Business processes: defined in table 1. Be aware that these business processes can be material as well as information production. We are talking here about the processes bringing forth the products of the organization, the processes that add value by transforming raw materials into products and delivering the products to the customers.

- Information systems: the means to execute information processing. In material production these will be information systems to manage the business processes, in information production, these systems will also be the production system of the organization.

- Information technology: the technology used for building the information system. All technology that processes information one way or another is meant.

Business process redesign methodologies do hardly support the design of information systems but cover the upper two levels. The results of business process redesign will be (global) specifications for the information system.
Present information system design methodologies are focused on the analysis and design of information processes. Some methodologies point to the fact that business processes can be changed when introducing new information technology, but don't give tools for structured analysis and design thereof.
So we can conclude that concerning the areas of interest, the methods are complementary. Business process redesign focusses at the business processes and assumes the necessary information systems can be provided and information systems design covers this area.

2. Process Concept

Both business process redesign and information system design are looking at processes. The concept of a process in business process redesign is mostly referred to as cross-functional process. With the help of our definitions we state that a process in business process redesign is a series of activities providing a product to a customer, whereby the different activities may be executed by different organizational units. These units are in most organizations functionally organized, explaining the term cross-functional.

In information system design a quite different concept of process is used. It is oriented towards a singular information processing function, performed by a single organizational unit. Every singular function or task is analyzed and designed as if it is a complete, self-contained unit. This does indeed reflect the way of thinking that has been dominating industrial engineering since the introduction of scientific management by Taylor (Davenport and Short, 1990). However, this view completely goes by the fact that the demands on organizations and that capabilities of IT have changed drastically. Working with a scope of a single function leads to optimization of the single functions, but this does not automatically mean that the process as a whole will be optimized. Working this way leads to sub-optimization of business process performance. There was a purpose in the earlier days to work this way: coupling of tasks leads to a greater need for coordination and communication that could not be supplied then. However, the advances in information technology have brought means to facilitate communication and coordination and therefore the need to restrict analysis to singular activities or functions is diminished.

To succeed in redesigning business processes, it is absolutely necessary to have a complete overview of the business processes, from product development to financial administration, so we can conclude that current information system design methodologies are not suited for designing business processes handling information.

3. Process view

Process modelling tools of current information systems methodologies give instruments to make models of the process within the area of the study. Well-known examples of these modelling languages are flow charts and data flow diagrams. Notwithstanding the usefulness of these process models for information systems design, the models are not suited for business process redesign. This stems from the fact that the models have another view of processes than what's needed for business process redesign. Most of the models have possibilities for circular processes, arising from the need to discover similar processing.
This means that there can be activities whose output goes back into an upstream activity as depicted in figure 2 (a very simple example).

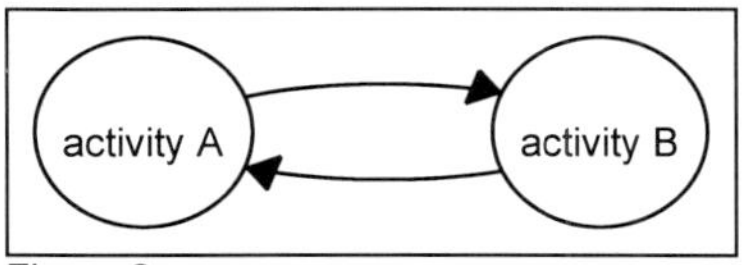

Figure 2

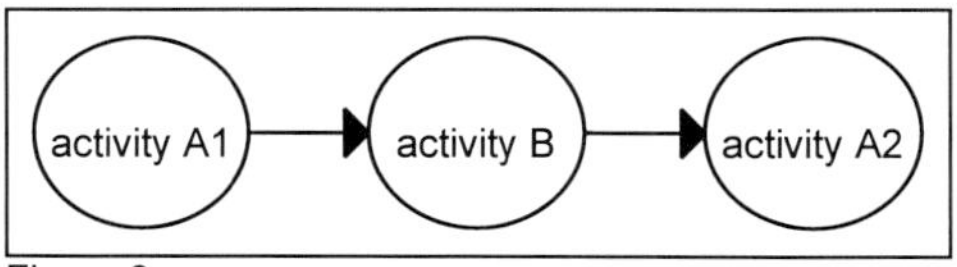

Figure 3

This view is inappropriate for business process redesign because it does not make clear how for example the total time of the process to be executed is build up of the times of the different activities and how the different activities are coupled. For business process redesign a linear view of the process is most appropriate: a view that starts with an event that takes place in the environment of the organization and ends with the completion of the handling of the event being the delivery of the product. This means that for business process redesign instead of the model depicted in figure 2 the model of figure 3 would be more useful. This model depicts the stream of activities in order, giving the necessary cross-functional process overview.

Another important shortcoming of currently used process models is that they leave out physical details like the location where an activity is executed to get a "logical" or conceptual view. Also the means used to execute the activities are important to model when redesigning business processes. Current process models do not provide solutions to these needs. Experience with models geared towards these needs (Gerrits, 1993), shows that not only the business analyst gets a better picture of the business process, but that also the employees working in the process get a better view of their process. This enhances the validity of the models and paves the way for users to get involved.

4. Role of information system

Most current information system design methodologies and as a result also most information systems, are based on the view of an information system that is used to control processes. Information processes make models of the business processes so that control can be executed. In this way, information systems are a means to obtain indirect control, as opposed to direct control, i.e., a manager that supervises processes by visual inspection. Since the industrial revolution, companies have grown too large to be controlled by visual inspection, so information systems are needed to support the management. Essentially, information systems used in this management control way, make it possible to distinguish between the place and time of occurrence of facts concerning the business processes and the place and time that the responsible managers use these facts to control the business processes. One could say that the main user of the information system was the management, and that the other users were expected to fill the system with data to get controlled.

Business process redesign leads to a revaluation of the user of the information system. No longer the management control that is needed is the leading design principle, but the user of the system. This user, in information production most of the times an expert, a knowledge worker, needs to be supported as good as possible in doing his job. That's the leading principle in business process redesign when designing the business processes and information systems. The reason will be clear: only when the workers in the business processes will perform better than before, the added value will increase and only then the investments will pay back.

Attendant effect is that more exact information is supplied for management control. Research shows that information systems that are set up to control business processes and employees are susceptible for incorrect use. Users will feed the system with information that reflects what they think their boss expects. The input into the system not necessarily has to reflect the facts in reality, because it makes no sense to supply that information when the only effect will be to have problems with the boss. On the other hand, information systems that are set up to support users, have data that does reflect reality, because the users need that data to do their own jobs. They are not putting in data for their boss, but for themselves and hence the quality of the data is better.

5 Role of designer

In information system design the designer tends to have an expert role. The designer is the person that has got the knowledge to transform the demands of the users of the information system to be, also the less structured demands, into a specification that can be used to build the needed information system. Most users can not make specifications themselves nor factually validate the specifications made by the analyst. This makes the analyst / designer having the expert role. It will be clear that the possibilities for redesigning processes are limited in that situation, because the people that have the knowledge of the business processes can not really participate in the design.

For business process redesign to be effective, this knowledge of the employees working in the business processes should be mobilized. Only then, new ways of executing the processes can be found. The best way to do this is to set up workshops consisting of employees working in the business process and covering the whole process. The role of the business process designer is to stimulate the workshop to bring up ideas concerning possible improvements and to point at new capabilities of IT that can be used. The users redesign the processes themselves and the designer just facilitates the design process.

Coupling Business Process Redesign and Information System Design

We pointed at the fact that business process redesign is needed in information production to ensure beneficial application of information technology. We discussed the shortcomings of current information system design methodologies to support business process redesign, and described the merits of business process redesign and information system design. Both have their strong points and both are needed to implement redesigned business processes in information production. Therefore coupling business process redesign and information system design seems to be profitable.

Information system design is mostly started with some form of information planning. The business strategy is used to plan the information systems design projects. The business strategy as described in the information plan forms the basis for prioritizing business areas that need information systems development. Doing so, strategy is used to point at the most important, areas of the business. See for example Critical Success Factors (Rockart, 1988), Business Systems Planning (IBM, 1981) or (Olle, 1992). For business process redesign this approach has a pro and a contra. The pro is the definition of the business strategy, that absolutely is needed to execute business process redesign. The contra is that this approach does not guarantee the identification of the most important business processes because it is functionally oriented, and business processes are mostly cross-functional. We conclude that information planning might be adjusted to come to meet the demands of business process redesign, but leave it now as a topic of further research[6].

As information planning is most of the time followed by information systems design, there's no explicit focus on business process redesign. One could say that after the areas to be analyzed are defined in information planning the project team jumps to the information processes leaving the business processes as they are. Introducing a business process redesign phase as a front end to the information system design process, would overcome this shortcoming (depicted in figure 4).

The products of the information planning phase are (cf. Olle, 1992):

- strategy formulation
- business areas
- information technology plan
- project plan
- resources plan

These products provide valuable input to business process redesign, except the definition of business areas as we indicated before. Assuming this shortcoming is solved, step 1 and 2 of the 5-stages business process redesign approach of Davenport and Short (Davenport & Short, 1990) have been executed. Improvements in the transfer from information planning to business process redesign can be made by using the same business process modelling language in information planning as will be used in business process redesign.

After indicating that business process redesign should follow information planning, a possibility would be to extend the analysis phase of system design with business process redesign. A separate business process redesign phase seems most appropriate because of the following reasons.

- Business process redesign needs another team of participants than system analysis. For business process redesign to succeed, it is necessary to have a project team that reflects the complete business process. This means that in the project team for the redesign phase, employees of all functional areas the process crosses would be present. For information systems design this group may be split up for the design of subsystems.
- The working methods of business process redesign are different. To redesign the processes discussed, participating design in a workshop approach works best. The big difference with regular process design is that an overview of the *complete* process is available and that it is possible to get direct feedback on ideas for improvement that go beyond the borders of the individual activities. The interview approach that most information systems design methodologies propose, is not an appropriate tool for this.
- The design process is a creative one that can be frustrated by the mostly rigid methods used in information systems design. The formal structured models of information system design methodologies confront employees with

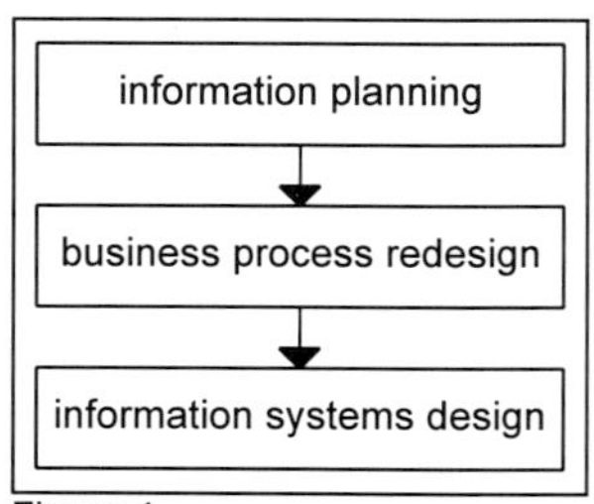

Figure 4

models they not always fathom because they don't depict the business processes but the information processes, thus disabling them to actively participate.

- The expertise needed to guide the redesign process needs other specialists like business analysts instead of technical experts.

Therefore we prefer a separate business process redesign phase, situated between information planning and information system design. In figure 5 the inputs and output of the proposed business process redesign phase are depicted. In business process redesign the business process will be analyzed in more detail. The global description of the information planning phase will be refined, to be able to validate the models of the current situation and to design new processes.

The business strategy will be translated in design criteria to be used in business process redesign. This should lead to measurable criteria regarding different aspects. Examples are financial criteria and logistical criteria, as for example the cost should be down 50 % and the production time should be less then 1 day.

Explicit attention should be paid to new capabilities of information technology. In information production, e.g., imaging and work flow management software might provide the means to implement redesigned business processes.

The outcome of business process redesign will consist of various designs. The new process and activities of course but also a new organization structure and management structure and new activity and task definitions and eventually new employee demand. The most important part for information system design is the demands for the information system. These will serve as input for system design. Depending on the specific situation, this description of the demands will more or less ease system design because a part of the analysis will already be done. The information system project will take these demands to design and build the needed information systems.

CONCLUSION

It was argued that on one hand business process redesign is needed to increase the benefits of the application of IT in information production. On the other hand, current system design methodologies are not suited to support this. An integration of business process redesign and information systems design is proposed. This integrated approach discovers all the areas that are needed to analyze: business strategy, business processes, information system and information technology. Business process redesign is positioned as a separate phase between information planning and system design. For being successful and efficient, it is absolutely necessary to adjust information planning, business process redesign and information system design to each other.

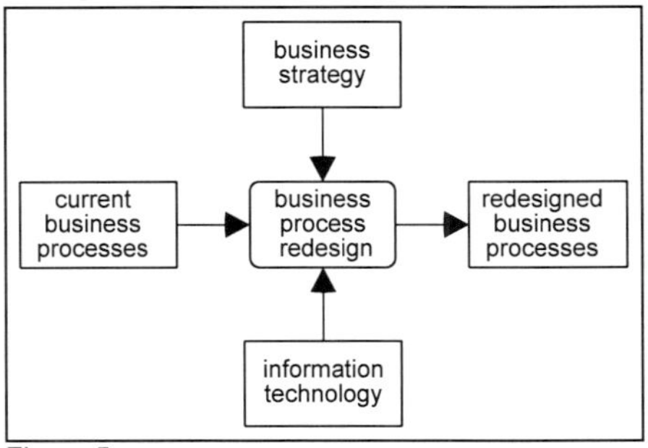

Figure 5

References

Arthur Young & Company (1987), *The Arthur Young Practical Guide to Information Engineering*, John Wiley & Sons, New York

Blumenthal, S.C. (1969), *Management Information Systems*: A Framework for Planning and Development, Prentice Hall, Englewood Cliffs

Davenport, Thomas H. & James E. Short (1990), "The New Industrial Engineering: Information Technology and Business Process Redesign", *Sloan Management Review*, Summer

DeMarco, T. (1979), *Structured Analysis and System Specification*, Prentice-Hall, Englewood Cliffs

Drucker, Peter F. (1974), *Management: Tasks, Responsibilities, Practices*, Heinemann, London

Fortune (1991) "The Service 500", *Fortune*, June 3

Gane C. & T. Sarson (1979), *Structured Systems Analysis: Tools and Techniques*, Prentice-Hall, Englewood Cliffs

Gerrits, Han (1992), "Redesigning Information Production Processes for Controlled Production Time", *Proceedings of the 12th IFIP World Computer Congress,* Madrid, 7-11 sept 1992

Gerrits, Han (1993), *A Business Model for Information Production*, Working Paper Vrije Universiteit, to be published

Hammer, M. (1990), "Re engineering Work: Don't Automate, Obliterate", *Harvard Business Review*, July-August

IBM (1984), *BSP-Business Systems Planning, Information Systems Planning Guide*, IBM-manual

Keen, Peter. G.W. (1991), "Shaping the Future: Business Design through Information Technology," Harvard Business School Press, Boston

Martin, J. (1984), *Information Engineering* (3 volumes), Prentice-Hall, Englewood Cliffs

Norton, David P. (1989), "Strategic Integrated Systems: The Next Frontier", *Stage by Stage*, Vol. 8, Number 6

Olle, T. William, et al. (1992), *Information Systems Methodologies: A Framework for Understanding*, 2 ed., Wokingham, Addison Wesley

Orr, Ken (1981), *Structured Requirements Definition*, Ken Orr and Associates, Topeka

Porter, Michael E. (1985), *Competitive Advantage*, Free Press, New York

Porter, Michael E. (1980), *Competitive Strategy*, Free Press, New York

Rockart, J.F. (1979), "Chief Executives Define Their Own Data Needs", *Harvard Business Review*, March-April

Thurow, Lester, (1991), "Foreword", *The Corporation of the 1990s: Information Technology and Organizational Change*, Michael S. Scott Morton, editor, Oxford University Press, New York.

Yourdon, E. (1982), *Managing the System Life Cycle*, Yourdon Press, New York

---

[1]Various writers use different terminology to denote the same concept. Examples are business process re-engineering and business process improvement. For sake of clearity we only use the term business process redesign in this article.

[2]Though one could argue that organizations need to learn how to utilize new technologies, and that the learning process implies simple applications of technology in the earlier phases.

[3]We will not make a difference between information and data in this article because that is not really needed for our discussion.

[4]In the rest of the article only the word product is used for both concepts.

[5]Because we try to give general viewpoints of business process redesign and information system design, certain statements may not be valid for specific methodologies.

[6]A detailed investigation of the goal of the definition of business areas should be one of the research objectives. Different interpretations exist, one being the definition of business areas an instrument for alignment of business strategy and information strategy, the other one perceiving this definition merely as an means to decompose the problem area.

AUTHOR INDEX

IFIP

The INTERNATIONAL FEDERATION FOR INFORMATION PROCESSING is a multinational federation of professional and technical organisations (or national groupings of such organisations) concerned with information processing. From any one country, only one such organisation – which must be representative of the national activities in the field of information processing – can be admitted as a Full Member. In addition a regional group of developing countries can be admitted as a Full Member. On 1 October 1992, 45 organisations were Full Members of the Federation, representing 62 countries.

The aims of IFIP are to promote information science and technology by:

- fostering international co-operation in the field of information processing;
- stimulating research, development and the application of information processing in science and human activity;
- furthering the dissemination and exchange of information about the subject;
- encouraging education in information processing.

IFIP is dedicated to improving worldwide communication and increased understanding among practitioners of all nations about the role information processing can play in all walks of life.

Information technology is a potent instrument in today's world, affecting people in everything from their education and work to their leisure and in their homes. It is a powerful tool in science and engineering, in commerce and industry, in education and adminstration. It is truly international in its scope and offers a significant opportunity for developing countries. IFIP helps to bring together workers at the leading edge of the technology to share their knowledge and experience, and acts as a catalyst to advance the state of the art.

IFIP came into official existence in January, 1960. It was established to meet a need identified at the first International Conference on Information Processing which was held in Paris in June, 1959, under the sponsorship of UNESCO.

Organisational Structure

The Federation is governed by a GENERAL ASSEMBLY, which meets once every year and consists of one representative from each Member organisation. The General Assembly decides on all important matters, such as general policy, the programme of activities, admissions, elections and budget.

IFIP ORGANISATION CHART

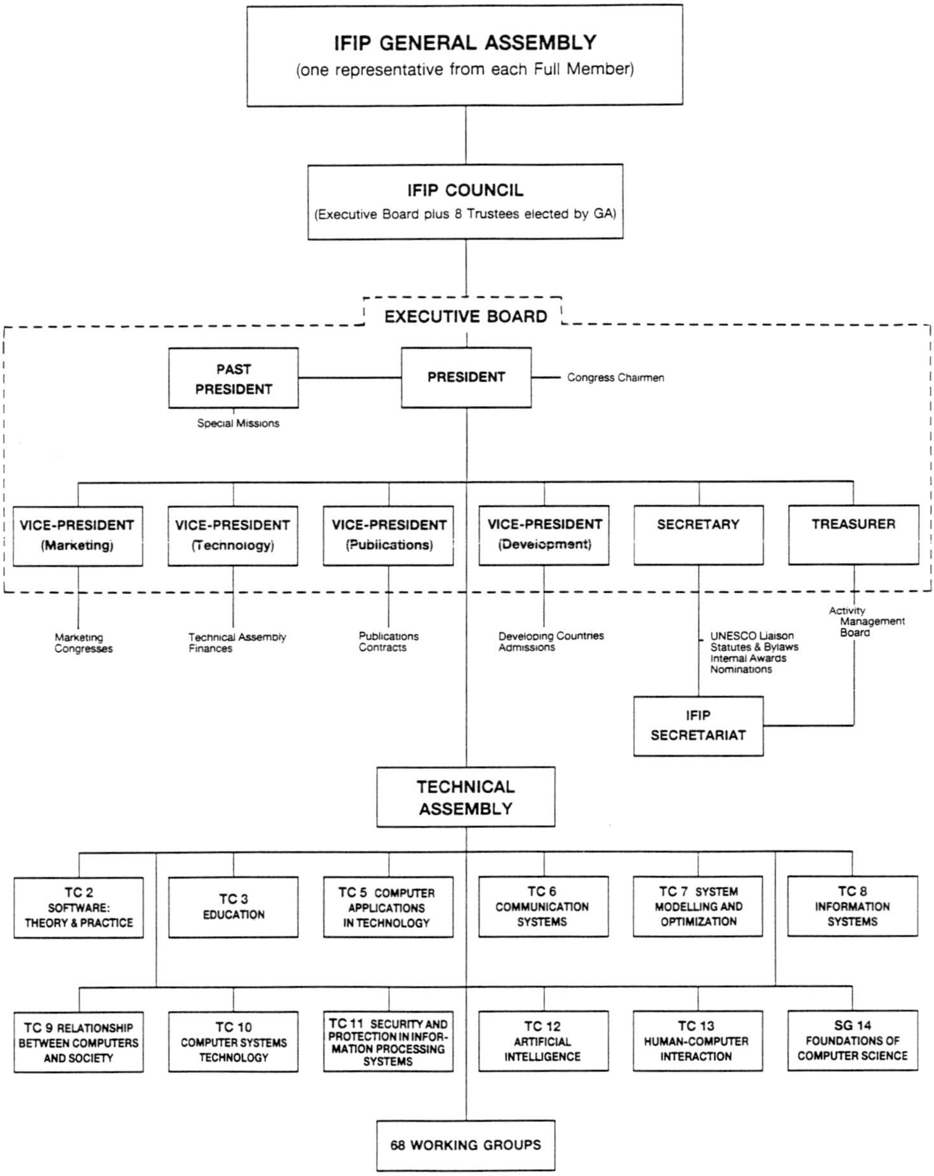

September 1992

The day-to-day work of IFIP is directed by its Officers: the President, Vice-Presidents, Secretary and Treasurer, who are elected by the General Assembly and together constitute the EXECUTIVE BOARD.

The COUNCIL, consisting of the Officers and up to eight Trustees elected from the General Assembly, meets twice a year and takes decisions which become necessary between General Assembly meetings.

The headquarters of the Federation are in Geneva, Switzerland where the IFIP Secretariat administers its affairs.

For further information please contact:

IFIP Secretariat
attn. Mme. GWYNETH ROBERTS
16 Place Longemalle
CH-1204 Geneva, Switzerland
telephone: 41 (22) 28 26 49
facsimile: 41 (22) 781 23 22
Bitnet: ifip@cgeuge51

IFIP's MISSION STATEMENT

IFIP's mission is to be the leading, truly international, apolitical organisation which encourages and assists in the development, exploitation and application of Information Technology for the benefit of all people.

Principal Elements

1. To stimulate, encourage and participate in research, development and application of Information Technology (IT) and to foster international co-operation in these activities.
2. To provide a meeting place where national IT Societies can discuss and plan courses of action on issues in our field which are of international significance and thereby to forge increasingly strong links between them and with IFIP.
3. To promote international co-operation directly and through national IT Societies in a free environment between individuals, national and international governmental bodies and kindred scientific and professional organisations.
4. To pay special attention to the needs of developing countries and to assist them in appropriate ways to secure the optimum benefit from the application of IT.
5. To promote professionalism, incorporating high standards of ethics and conduct, among all IT practitioners.
6. To provide a forum for assessing the social consequences of IT applications; to campaign for the safe and beneficial development and use of IT and the protection of people from abuse through its improper application.

7. To foster and facilitate co-operation between academics, the IT industry and governmental bodies and to seek to represent the interest of users.
8. To provide a vehicle for work on the international aspects of IT development and application including the necessary preparatory work for the generation of international standards.
9. To contribute to the formulation of the education and training needed by IT practitioners, users and the public at large.

Note to Conference Organizers

Organizers of upcoming IFIP Working Conferences are urged to contact the Publisher. Please send full details of the Conference to:

Mrs. STEPHANIE SMIT
Administrative Editor – IFIP Publications
ELSEVIER SCIENCE PUBLISHERS
P.O. Box 103, 1000 AC Amsterdam
The Netherlands
telephone: 31 (20) 5862481
facsimile: 31 (20) 5862616
email: s.smit@elsevier.nl

IFIP TRANSACTIONS

IFIP TRANSACTIONS is a serial consisting of 15,000 pages of valuable scientific information from leading researchers, published in 35 volumes per year. The serial includes contributed volumes, proceedings of the IFIP World Conferences, and conferences at Technical Committee and Working Group level. Mainstream areas in the IFIP TRANSACTIONS can be found in Computer Science and Technology, Computer Applications in Technology, and Communication Systems.

From 1993 onwards the IFIP TRANSACTIONS are only available as a full set.

IFIP TRANSACTIONS A:
Computer Science and Technology
1992: Volumes A1–A19
1993: Volumes A20–A40
ISSN 0926-5473

IFIP Technical Committees that are involved in IFIP TRANSACTIONS A

Software: Theory and Practice (TC2)
Education (TC3)
System Modelling and Optimization (TC7)
Information Systems (TC8)
Relationship Between Computers and Society (TC9)

Computer Systems Technology (TC10)
Security and Protection in Information Processing Systems (TC11)
Artificial Intelligence (TC12)
Human-Computer Interaction (TC13)
Foundations of Computer Science (SG14)

IFIP TRANSACTIONS B:
Applications in Technology
1992: Volumes B1–B8
1993: Volumes B9–B14
ISSN 0926-5481

IFIP Technical Committee that is involved in IFIP TRANSACTIONS B
Computer Applications in Technology (TC5)

IFIP TRANSACTIONS C:
Communication Systems
1992: Volumes C1–C8
1993: Volumes C9–C16
ISSN 0926-549X

IFIP Technical Committee that is involved in IFIP TRANSACTIONS C
Communication Systems (TC6)

IFIP TRANSACTIONS FULL SET: A, B & C
1992: 35 Volumes. US $ 1892.00/Dfl. 3500.00
1993: 35 Volumes. US $ 2340.00/Dfl. 3885.00
The Dutch Guilder prices (Dfl.) are definitive. The US $ prices mentioned above are for your guidance only and are subject to exchange rate fluctuations. Prices include postage and handling charges.

The volumes are also available separately in book form.

Please address all orders and correspondence to:

ELSEVIER SCIENCE PUBLISHERS
attn. PETRA VAN DER MEER
P.O. Box 103, 1000 AC Amsterdam
The Netherlands
telephone: 31 (20) 5862602
facsimile: 31 (20) 5862616
email: m.haccou@elsevier.nl